D1498820

MOVIES ON MY MIND

DEDICATION

*To my mother, Barbara Allen Gardner, and my father, Anthony "Sonny" Frinzi,
both of whom always encouraged me in my creative pursuits.*

Copyright © 2013 by Joe R. Frinzi

All rights reserved. No part of this book may be
reproduced or utilized in any form or by any means,
electronic or mechanical, or by any information storage
or retrieval system, without written permission from the
author and publisher. Direct all inquiries to the author
online through SanctumPress@gmail.com

MOVIES
ON MY MIND

**My First Dozen Years as a Film Critic
for the Easton Irregular 1998 - 2010**

Joe R. Frinzi

Tom,
Thanks for all your support
and friendship. Best wishes,

Joe R. Frinzi

SANCTUM PRESS

Sanctum Press – Easton, PA

INTRODUCTION

It was an offer any writer with a passion for film dreamed about. I was given carte blanche to write a monthly film column about whatever I wanted. And I got paid for it, too! It was early February 1998 and, up until that time, I had been vaguely aware of *The Easton Irregular*, the local arts newspaper that had been circulating around for a number of years. Though, at that time, I was not a consistent reader of the free publication, I had picked it up on several occasions and enjoyed it. I specifically remember an article about the old Boyd Theatre which had been egregiously torn down in the 1970s that had caught my eye; having grown up in the 1960s before the era of anonymous multiplexes, I had fond memories of going to the Boyd on my own and with my friends. The article, written by local movie theatre historian Ken Klabunde, told the story of this remarkable movie house (known as an "atmospheric," I learned from the article) and its heartbreaking demolition to make way for a parking lot. It was that article which made me realize that this was a worthwhile publication, one perhaps I might even write for someday.

I began my own literary career in 1980 with an article on creating a spacesuit costume, which I wrote for a small, national special effects magazine called *Illusions*. I found I had a real knack for writing, especially about film (which was a major passion of mine, having made some artsy Super 8 shorts after I'd graduated from high school in 1973). Throughout the eighties and nineties I continued to churn out articles—film related and otherwise—for various publications, and even did some scriptwriting, but nothing of a steady nature until the offer came along from Carole Heffley at *The Easton Irregular*. It turned out to be a fortuitous encounter for both of us.

Since I was new to writing an ongoing column, I was basically feeling my way through the process. For those first two years I did all my research from books and magazines, writing my pieces first in longhand and then typing up the results on an electric typewriter. I didn't get a computer until 2000 and only became familiar with the Internet many years later. But somehow I managed to meet my deadlines and satisfy Carole and her partner-in-crime, Jim Hicks, both of whom became my good friends. A dozen-plus years later, the paper is being shepherded by others, but I'm still writing my column and I still count Jim and Carole as friends.

The genesis for this book came about as a bridge between my work as a columnist and my interest in pursuing the dream of writing movie books. I spent the better part of a decade working on a definitive account about my favorite film of all time, *2001: A Space Odyssey*. The finished book, titled "Open the Pod Bay Doors Hal. Unlocking the Secrets Behind Kubrick's Epic Motion Picture *2001: A Space Odyssey*," has been in the hands of several agents and publishers over the years, but has yet to be realized in print. With the rise and acceptance of self-publishing over the last several years, it made sense for me to consider doing a book of my columns in that way (given its highly localized appeal), which might then serve as a useful, if expensive, calling card to a legitimate publisher for my far more expansive book project. Based on the success others have had in self-publishing, I am now looking to do my *2001* book this way, as well, until I can find a publisher to release it in a more traditional manner.

Putting my collected columns into book form allowed me to go back and clean them up a bit, correcting typos and mistakes that have a way of creeping into work that is beholden to deadlines and the vagaries of others. Much of this may be forgivable in a disposable medium like a newspaper, but it has no real place in a more permanent record, such as a book. And given that my dozen-plus years of writing for *The Irregular* have been more or less scattered to the four winds as far as most of the public is concerned, it obviously falls upon me to be the documentarian and archivist of my work. To that end, I've added some commentary to the text of several of the original articles to better put them into perspective. For those of you who may have some interest in revisiting the cinematic ramblings from my first twelve years as a writer for *The Irregular*, it is my pleasure and honor to share them with you again. For those who come to this collection anew, I hope that a little bit of my passion for movies and for "the art of cinema" comes across, and that you find some measure of enjoyment through the encounter.

Joe R. Frinzi
November 2013

TITANIC ENDEAVORS
(March 1998)

This was the very first article I wrote for the Irregular. My friend, Isadore LaDuca, who had started a month earlier with an Arts column, told me that Carole Heffley, the founder and editor of the paper, was looking for someone to do a film column. Naturally, he thought of me and suggested my name to her. Even before I met Carole at an Art show opening, I began to think about what to write. I decided that a piece on the new Titanic film would be good, perhaps comparing it to other Titanic movies. Five minutes after Carole and I met she agreed to hire me. She didn't even want to see examples of my writing. When I asked her when she'd like the piece (figuring I'd have at least a week to do it), she said, "Oh, maybe in two days?" I gulped and said I'd do my best. That night I began writing the piece (on my typewriter) and three days later I turned it in.

Conceptually, I decided that my column would not be negative or nasty, and would never put down or trash films I didn't like. Instead, I would exalt the positive aspects of cinema, promoting movies I deemed worthy of attention. I also decided the column would never be about me. It would never be about "the knowledgeable columnist" bestowing his wisdom on "the masses." It would always only be about the movies themselves. I wanted a name for my column that would reflect the arts and also be recognizable from issue to issue, so I chose "THE ART OF CINEMA." For the article itself, I came up with "TITANIC ENDEAVORS." The double meaning of the title was an example of the kind of wordplay that I enjoy using in my writing and is an identifiable part of my style.

I dropped off the finished article at the Irregular office where I got to meet Jim Hicks, the publisher of the paper (and the other half of the "Irregular Team"). At that time Jim also wrote an ongoing humor column about Easton called "PARKZILLA" which poked fun at a variety of local institutions and people. Both Carole and Jim were extremely happy with the article, the quality of the writing and the level of information I included. They said it went way beyond their expectations which was very gratifying to me. From that point on I was given free rein to write about whatever I wanted and thus began my career as a columnist.

With a price tag in excess of $200 million and a running time clocking in at 3 hours and 15 minutes, James Cameron's *Titanic* certainly fills the bill as an epic production. However, unlike many other elephantine, big budget films (*Speed 2; Batman & Robin*), *Titanic* is not an amalgam of explosions, special effects and third-rate scriptwriting. Instead, for all its decadent expenditure, *Titanic* is a thoughtful, well-balanced and original take on a subject that was thought to be, more or less, done to death. It's an old fashioned love story dressed up with mammoth sets and state-of-the-art special effects.

Titanic's cinematic antecedents hold a mixed pedigree regarding accuracy and artistry. Shortly after the disaster there were several filmed dramas, at least one of which starred an actual survivor. These tended to be crude, sensationalistic and slap dash, lacking any pretense of truth or sincerity. They were akin to the instant books and telefilms that crop up today in the wake of catastrophes and unseemly news stories.

By 1950, many of the facts about the Titanic had been forgotten by the public at large. However in 1953, 41 years after the actual event, Hollywood decided that the Titanic name alone would be enough to support a story about a fictional family on board the ill-fated vessel. Titled simply *Titanic*, it starred Clifton Webb, Barbara Stanwyck and a very young Robert Wagner. Though entertaining on its own terms, it is replete with inaccuracies. No attempt was made to faithfully replicate the decor of the ship, its staterooms, crew areas, etc. Even the elaborate model of the ship contains the glaring flub of having "Southampton" inscribed below the ship's name on the stern, instead of the correct "Liverpool." The sinking of the ship serves mainly as a backdrop for the fictitious family story. The true account of the Titanic would not return to public awareness until the publication in 1955 of Walter Lord's exhaustively researched book, "A Night to Remember."

Walter Lord's book was an immediate success and it caught the eye of British film producer William MacQuitty, who had actually seen the launch of the Titanic when he was all of three years old. Obsessed with the ship, MacQuitty wanted to do the definitive film version of the Titanic tale. Shot in docu-drama style in crisp black and white, the film shows the crisis through the rigid class distinctions in place at the time, and how both passengers and crew dealt with these inequities.

At the center of the story is second officer Charles Lightoller, played with great strength and sympathy by Kenneth More. (Cameron's film would take a decidedly different view of the man.) Nearly all the characters are based on real people who were aboard the ship, giving the film even greater authenticity. Painstaking attention was paid to set design, costumes and shipboard events, all of which made *A Night to Remember* the most accurate film depiction of the disaster for its time, a distinction it would retain for nearly 40 years until 1997 and the release of James Cameron's *Titanic*.

"If you're not breaking new ground, what's the point?" Jim Cameron said these words as a way of explanation for his decision to enter into Titanic territory and his desire to create a truly definitive account of this mythic story. By combining the fictitious character element from the 1953 film with the documentary realism and accuracy of the 1958 version, and then overlaying that with the advances in special effects and information gleaned from a decade of study of the actual wreck, the new Titanic movie is indeed a marvel to behold. While it doesn't diminish the pleasure of the previous films, it sets new standards for accuracy, realism and visceral dynamics to which all future historical films must now live up.

It is refreshing in this era when most super big-budget films tend to be as dumb as a bag of rocks, to see such excess lavished in the service of an intelligent, emotionally-satisfying and artistically triumphant production. Rather than focusing on the cost of the movie, I believe the true legacy of James Cameron's *Titanic* will be for the story it told and how it affected those who saw it, much like the great ship itself.

BEYOND THE THREE-ACT PLAY
(April 1998)

> For my second column, I strove to do a much more ambitious (and longer) piece about experimentation in story structure that goes beyond the conventional. This allowed me the chance to indulge my passion for *2001: A Space Odyssey* (my favorite film of all time), along with several other films that shared a similar degree of innovation. It gave me the opportunity to synopsize the plot of *2001*, which was not only fun, but also a bit of a challenge. For examples of unconventional films to write about, I initially came up with a list of about two dozen titles which I then whittled down to a more manageable nine (three categories with three films in each). The article ended up being far longer than I'd anticipated (about 2200 words, over three times the length of the previous one), but to Carole's credit, she ran the whole thing. I made sure never to write such a lengthy piece again.

This month marks the 30th anniversary of a cinematic milestone—*2001: A Space Odyssey*. Beyond its revolution in special effects, realistic hardware and set design, and its intellectual art house storyline (virtually unheard of in science fiction films at the time), *2001* boasted a radical departure from traditional plot structure, narrative advancement and character importance. Previously, other films had dabbled in these experimental realms (*Citizen Kane, Rashomon* and *Wild Strawberries* to name but a few), but *2001*, with its bold, anthology-like framework of telling several seemingly unrelated stories set in different time frames, coupled with its many other innovations, became a true phenomenon.

For those who've never seen this masterpiece, *2001* recounts mankind's contact with an alien intelligence over a span of four million years. In the first section, titled "The Dawn of Man," an alien artifact in the form of a black, rectangular monolith appears before a tribe of man-apes fighting for survival in drought-stricken prehistoric Africa. It somehow imbues them with the knowledge to overcome their hardships and eventually evolve. The next section begins, after a brilliant jump-cut from a hurled bone to an orbiting spacecraft, in the year 2001 where another monolith has been found on the moon by American astronauts. A group of officials goes to the site to examine the enigmatic object, during which it lets out a piercing radio signal when it is struck by the rays of the rising sun. Part three begins with a title card reading "Jupiter Mission—18 Months Later" as we find ourselves aboard a huge spaceship. Five astronauts (three of whom are in "hibernation") and a talking, almost sentient, computer named Hal, make up the crew compliment. During a repair mission outside the ship one astronaut dies and hurtles off into space while his colleague attempts to rescue him. On board the ship the computer malfunctions and kills the three hibernating crewmen. The fifth astronaut manages to re-enter the ship and disconnects the computer. Only then does he (and the audience) learn that the radio signal from the monolith on the moon was aimed at Jupiter. In the final segment, portentously titled "Jupiter and Beyond the Infinite," the loan astronaut, Dave Bowman, sees another monolith floating among the many Jovian moons. Taking out a one-man space pod to explore the object, Bowman is swept into a time/space vortex created by the monolith. He is taken on a kaleidoscopic voyage through endless corridors of light, past cosmic dust clouds and newly forming suns, and over wildly-colored alien landscapes. Finally the pod comes to rest in a surreal, weirdly-lit hotel suite where the aliens, never seen, manipulate their human subject, first aging him, letting him die and then having him reborn as a cosmic fetus, a star-child, the next step in human evolution. This haunting creature is last seen floating in space near Earth and turning its gaze directly on the audience as the screen fades to black.

Unfortunately, this straightforward account of 2001's plot does little to convey its enormous visual and aural impact on the viewer. As one of the most influential and successful films of the 1960s, it paved the way for other filmmakers to try new ways of telling stories. By blending form and content so completely, 2001 fathered a whole generation of fresh and exciting films that were both artistically satisfying and, on occasion, financially successful. While most films still retain the convention of the three-act play, many of the techniques pioneered by 2001 and its brethren have found their way into the language of mainstream filmmaking. Whether it is the use of a jarring edit from one scene to another, or a wordless musical interlude used to advance the story, or simply some extended visual sequence intended to blow you away, they can all be traced back to 2001.

Following is an examination of several post-2001 movies that have gone that extra step and abandoned the standard three-act structure to tell their story. I have broken them down into three categories: non-linear chronology, parallel chronology and montage. If you have never seen these movies, I urge you to seek them out at your local video store. And if you have seen them, I hope my reflections will offer you new insights into their artistry and originality in the medium of film.

*   *   *

NON-LINEAR CHRONOLOGY (story told out of order)
ANNIE HALL (1977)—Starring Woody Allen and Diane Keaton. Directed by Woody Allen. This is considered by most critics to be Allen's first mature work as a filmmaker, as well as one of his most successful. It won Academy Awards for best picture, director, actress and original screenplay. Ironically, prior to its completion, it was a chaotic collection of scenes that would not cut together.

Originally titled "Anhedonia," which means the inability to experience pleasure, the film was meant to be a much darker story in which the love relationship between Allen and Keaton was not so central. At that point the film had no usable ending and Woody was shooting new material to remedy the problem. Eventually it was realized that the relationship was the spine of the story, and with the help of Woody's longtime editor, Ralph Rosenblum, the film finally began to take on its familiar form. Whole sequences were pared down or removed entirely, replaced with flashbacks, time shifts, fantasy scenes and even animation, all held together by Woody's signature narration. Instead of a meandering, depressing saga about being unhappy, it became a wistful, almost bittersweet tale about the rise and fall of a relationship. "Anhedonia" became *Annie Hall*, a film that, if not saved in the editing room was, at the very least, created there.

*BETRAYAL (1983)—Starring Jeremy Irons, Patricia Hodge and Ben Kingsley. Directed by David Jones. Based on the play by Harold Pinter, this film's unique claim to fame is that the story about a love affair is told in reverse, beginning with the couple's breakup and moving back to the moment they first meet. This concept allows one to see the nature of cause and effect in a way that is not available in normal chronology. The fact that the viewer is aware of events in the plot prior to the characters actually experiencing them inverts the normal process of revelation inherent in most storytelling. Recently *Seinfeld* used this reverse structure in an episode with excellent results.

*PULP FICTION (1994)—Starring John Travolta, Samuel L. Jackson, Uma Thurman and Bruce Willis. Directed by Quentin Tarantino. Here we have three connected stories that are told out of sequence and that overlap one another creating a non-linear narrative. So cleverly is this done that it isn't until the third segment begins that you even realize the chronology is being altered. Still, I was amazed to learn that some people did not pick up on this and were confused by a character apparently being killed in the middle of the film and then showing up alive and well later on. It's a shame since this skewed format allows one to reflect at the end, when one character decides to leave the business and then he and the other head off to their separate destinies, one promising and the other, doomed.

*   *   *

PARALLEL CHRONOLOGY (shifting between two or more storylines)
*THE FRENCH LIEUTENANT'S WOMAN (1981)—Starring Meryl Streep and Jeremy Irons. Directed by Karel Reisz. Adapted by Harold Pinter from the novel by John Fowles about a Victorian love affair and its social ramifications, the filmmakers had the intriguing idea of telling two parallel stories. In the novel Fowles uses footnotes to comment contemporarily on the Victorian era; in the film the Victorian tale is paralleled with a contemporary story involving a twist—

a film within the film: Streep and Irons play fictional actors engaged in an affair who are making a film version of Fowles' book. The contemporary couple is, thus, played against the Victorian couple in much the same way as the footnotes comment on the novel. And like the book, which has two endings, one happy and one sad, the movie is able to have it both ways as well, each couple given their appropriate due.

BRAZIL (1985)—Starring Jonathan Pryce, Robert DeNiro, Katherine Helmond and Michael Palin. Directed by Terry Gilliam. In a sort of "George Orwell meets Monty Python," this humorous riff on "1984" concerns a meek government clerk named Sam Lowry trying to cope with a totalitarian bureaucracy gone mad. His salvation is a rich fantasy life in which he is a winged, armored warrior fighting the forces of evil to save the woman of his dreams. This film has imagination to spare and is a real treat visually, comedicly and intellectually. The balance between the real and fantasy worlds is nicely maintained, with the latter providing symbolic verity to Sam's actions in the former. Gilliam's work, as always, is deeply textured and laced with anarchy, both of which are represented to their fullest in this film.

MISHIMA: A LIFE IN FOUR CHAPTERS (1985)—Starring Ken Ogata. Narrated by Roy Scheider. Directed by Paul Schrader. This is one of the most remarkable films I have ever seen in both subject matter and style. Ostensibly, this is about the life of famed Japanese writer Yukio Mishima who committed ritual suicide in 1970 after seizing the headquarters of Japan's Eastern Army. The film is divided into four parts (beauty, art, action and the harmony of pen and sword), each containing three strikingly different strands woven together. The strands include a documentary-style account of Mishima's last day, black and white flashbacks of his earlier years and highly stylized dramatizations from three of his novels that illuminate his beliefs. Never before has a film so captured the essence of artistic drive and how it is bound up in the artist's quirks, flaws and forbidden passions. This film may be hard to find at video stores but it is definitely worth seeking out. Special mention must be made of Eiko Ishioka's beautifully stylized set designs for the novel dramatizations, and the terrific Philip Glass score. In Japanese with subtitles.

*   *   *

MONTAGE (anthology and fragmented non-narrative)

KOYAANISQATSI (1983)—Directed by Godfrey Reggio. No dialogue, no actors, no storyline to speak of, so what exactly is it? The title comes from the Hopi Indian word meaning "life out of balance." Pristine landscapes with frenetically moving clouds and shadows give way to urban centers with hyper-fast traffic and pedestrians, looking for all the world like the speeded-up life cycles of amoebae under a microscope. This "God's eye" view of life on our planet allows us to see the patterns of our everyday existence, both good and bad, like never before. Since the release of this stunning movie many of its visual flourishes have been co-opted by commercials and mainstream films, taking some of the edge off of it. Still, this is a highly original and personal work of great artistry and deep spiritualism. The wall-to-wall music by Philip Glass perfectly complements the images. After seeing this movie you will definitely view the world, and perhaps your own life, differently.

AKIRA KUROSAWA'S DREAMS (1990)—Starring Akira Terao and Martin Scorsese. Directed by Akira Kurosawa. The arc from birth to death is explored in eight luminous fables. Kurosawa says "man is a genius when he is dreaming" and he goes on to prove it by bringing forth his own dreams in astonishing visual splendor. Ranging from a blizzard of peach blossoms to an army of phantom soldiers emerging from a dark tunnel to an art student wandering through the paintings of Van Gogh to the cataclysmic destruction of Mount Fugi, Kurosawa creates indelible images that will stay with you forever. Incredibly, he was 80 years old and half blind when he made this jewel, which just goes to show you what the spirit can still accomplish even when the flesh is no longer quite as willing. In Japanese with subtitles.

THIRTY-TWO SHORT FILMS ABOUT GLENN GOULD (1993)—Starring Colm Feore. Directed by Francios Girard. A most unusual documentary about eccentric composer/pianist Glenn Gould, this movie is literally 32 vignettes that, in various ways, illustrate and illuminate what made this odd character tick. Colm Feore gives a riveting portrayal as Gould, conveying all the subtle nuances and complexities of this troubled genius. In addition to the dramatized biographical segments, the film also includes interviews with people who knew Gould and experimental, purely visual, pieces set against recordings of Gould's performances, which connect the viewer directly to the sheer pleasure of music.

* * *

Though these nine films, along with *2001*, represent a nice sampling of unconventional structure in cinema, there are many others I would like to have talked about as well. These include *Baraka; Cries & Whispers; DreamChild; Equus; Heavenly Creatures; JFK; The Joy Luck Club; Lost Highway; Mystery Train; Night On Earth; The Pillow Book; Shine* and *Twelve Monkeys*. While these films are all very different, the one thing they have in common is that they allow you to view the art of cinema in a whole new light. All, I believe, are worth your time.

THE MOVIE EXPERIENCE
(May 1998)

For my third venture, I decided to tackle the debate over widescreen videos. This was the pre-DVD era when videotapes were still the norm and 12" laserdiscs were only a niche market. Most tapes presented movies full screen (top to bottom) which meant nearly all films were cropped right and left to fit a conventional TV (widescreen sets were still quite rare). Having worked in a video store for a number of years, I'd seen, first hand, how most people were predisposed against the widescreen video format (with the black bars at the top and bottom of the screen), so it became a challenge for me to find a way to introduce the benefits to the reader before their prejudice had a chance to kick in. It was vital that I made them feel a sense of loss, and the scenario I concocted was a clever way to illustrate the point of just how much picture information is lost when you watch a tape that isn't "letterboxed." As a strong advocate for widescreen videos, the column provided me a powerful forum to disseminate my message that wasn't preachy. I'd had a lot of practice at my video store job at the mall explaining the benefits of letterboxed movies to customers, persuading them to consider it before making a purchase, so I felt sure I could write a convincing argument for the widescreen format. The lists of letterboxed titles that accompanied the article also helped make the point that there were a lot of widescreen choices out there. Now, of course, literally everything is available in its original aspect ratio.

Most people love going to the movies. Even though the seats may not always be comfortable and the floors can be a bit sticky, the movie-going experience is still, by and large, a pleasurable event. Let's imagine, then, that you are going to the local multiplex to see the latest flick. You've been waiting to see this film for weeks, you've seen the ads for it, heard it was great, saw the stars interviewed on TV, etc., etc., etc. You are excited. So, you plunk down your cash, give the usher your ticket, buy yourself a popcorn and drink, enter the auditorium and take your seat. The theatre begins filling up, the audience buzzing with anticipation. You are really psyched for this movie. Finally, the lights dim, the intermission music cuts out and you gaze up at the large, rectangular screen primed for a cinematic experience.

Then, suddenly, two swaths of black drapery unfurl vertically down either side of the screen, obliterating over a third of the picture, reducing the beautiful rectangle nearly into a square. Where, once, three actors had been on the screen, now there are only two. As scene after scene reels by, you try to enjoy the film but you can't; all you can do is wonder what you're not seeing on the sides of the screen, the sections that are obscured by the black drapes.

If the preceding scenario sounds farfetched, get ready for a shock—until recently, every time you rented a videotape, purchased a videotape or watched a movie on HBO, that very same situation occurred. That's right! Depending on the aspect ratio of the movie, anywhere from 23% to 48% of the rectangular picture was routinely sacrificed to make it square for the picture tube. This means actors are missing from scenes, compositions are arbitrarily destroyed and in some cases the video is "panned and scanned" to follow the action of the larger screen image through the smaller square of the television. This creates false camera moves that the director never intended and can be very distracting. In some instances, where action is occurring simultaneously at opposite ends of the picture, the video might cut back and forth from one side of the screen to the other, giving the impression that they are separate shots, creating edits the director never intended. It's all a matter of simple geometry—TV sets are square, movie screens are rectangular. So, what's a film buff with artistic integrity to do? The answer is widescreen videos.

Widescreen or "letterbox" videos allow you to see the entire theatrical image on your regular TV set. Since you are placing the movie rectangle on your square TV, there will be empty space above and below the picture. While some people find these black spaces annoying, to my mind they are infinitely preferable to the emasculation committed to films by standard pan and scan videos. If this all seems a trifle picayune, remember, film is primarily a visual medium, and composition and editing (montage) are the heart of its creativity. Tamper with the form and you are tampering with the content. Cut out part of the picture and you are cutting out story. Just as you wouldn't want to listen to music with some of the notes missing, or read a book with pages torn out, seeing a cropped version of a movie can be an equally diminished experience.

The aspect ratio of movies can vary widely, but generally it falls into four main sizes. 1:33 to 1 (also called Academy standard since it uses the full frame of 35mm film) is the most square format and is the same dimension as a regular TV set. Movies made prior to 1950 are usually in this category therefore no picture information is lost when shown on TV. The next size, 1:66 to 1, was the first real attempt by the studios to break away from the square format. In some cases the 1:33 film stock was simply matted into this wider shape when projected. Many films from the 1950s and 1960s are in this ratio and it is still in use today. The third size, 1:85 to 1, has become the standard since most films made today are shot this way. It presents a pleasingly artistic rectangle without the complex compositional challenges inherent in the fourth size, 2:35 to 1. This last encompasses the epic formats known as Cinerama, Super Panavision, Cinemascope, Vista Vision and others with similar monikers, all designed in the 1950s and 1960s to compete with the growing phenomenon of television which was keeping people at home. By offering an extremely wide canvas on which to paint cinematic epics, the movie industry made a valiant effort to lure the masses away from their free entertainment. Nowadays, this format is especially popular with sci-fi, action and special effects extravaganzas.

Since the loss of picture information is most notable in the latter two formats, following is a list of titles available on tape in widescreen. Beyond these, there are hundreds of others so go out and explore this new way to look at movies on tape. It brings the movie experience right into your home. Compared to the regular versions, you will be amazed at how much you've been missing.

1:85 to 1—*Schindler's List; Fargo; Men in Black; Jurassic Park; Liar, Liar; Dead Man Walking; E.T.; Silence of the Lambs; Shine; The Terminator; Vertigo; The English Patient; Get Shorty; The Crow; The Color Purple; Sense and Sensibility; Bram Stoker's Dracula; The Piano; From Dusk Till Dawn; Natural Born Killers; Raising Arizona*

2:35 to 1—*Lawrence of Arabia; Pulp Fiction; Independence Day; Dune; Casino; 2001: A Space Odyssey; Evita; The Usual Suspects; Kalifornia; Ben Hur; Twister; Scream; The Abyss; Seven; The Bible; Contact; It's a Mad, Mad, Mad, Mad World; Apollo 13; The Ten Commandments; Air Force One; Lost Highway; The Star Wars Trilogy; The Alien Films; Sleeping Beauty; Blade Runner; Dr. Zhivago; Fierce Creatures; Mars Attacks; Last of the Mohicans; Close Encounters of the Third Kind; Unforgiven; Jesus Christ Superstar; Last Year at Marienbad; Woodstock*

SUMMER MOVIES OR "THE INVASION OF THE GREAT HYPE MACHINE"

(June 1998)

> I lightened up a bit for my fourth piece, as the title clearly indicates. Since there was no Irregular published in July or August, I realized this article would have to carry me through the whole summer. It therefore seemed fitting to cover the entire slate of summer films. I decided to pick, for each month, one high profile film and two or three obscure titles. This required a lot of research on my part, since none of the films I would be talking about had been released yet and I had no access to the Internet. For the obscure films, there weren't even trailers to look at. I was truly flying blind. My final choices weren't always on target either. I really missed the mark with *The Avengers* which initially looked to be a great film. I still hedged my bets with my wrap-up of that title, since I was finally learning how to protect myself from fully endorsing anything I hadn't actually seen.

What an appropriate metaphor it is that the closing of school heralds the arrival of the summer movie season. It has long been a given that summertime and mindless entertainment go hand-in-hand. "Step right up., check your brain at the door, enjoy the show." Furthering the amusement analogy, many big dumb action flicks are often referred to in reviews and press releases as "rollercoaster rides" while also employing such overworked descriptives as "high octane" and "pure dynamite." And, what had once been only a three-month assault on our collective systems has now expanded an extra month with the co-opting of much of May (*Deep Impact, Godzilla*).

However, as with many metaphors, one can also find exceptions to the rules. Amid the hype, designed to separate you from your entertainment dollars, there are real gems, big and small, hoping you'll notice their distinctive glints. So, while I will the big high-concept flicks, several of which look to be quite good, I also want to shine a light on the smaller, more thoughtful movies that are scrambling to find a handhold on the sheer rock face that is the summer movie blitz. Whether they find an audience or fall into oblivion is up to each and every one of us.

HIGH CONCEPT

The studios are banking megabucks that you'll want to see these high profile films. They're spending millions on TV commercials and full-page print ads in many national magazines. Sometimes this works (*Independence Day, Jurassic Park*) and sometimes it fails (*Speed 2, Batman & Robin*) and sometimes it really, really works (*Titanic*). It's therefore fitting that the first big out of the gate this June is being touted as a "near masterpiece" and "the film of the decade." I am referring to *The Truman Show*. While most will think of it as a "Jim Carrey film," I prefer to look at it as a "Peter Weir movie." The Australian director has fashioned a modern fable about our relationship with television and, with Carrey in the lead, stands a chance (like Titanic) of having an art house blockbuster. With a little luck it will be the film we remember at summer's end. Also in June: *6 Days, 7 Nights* with Harrison Ford and Anne Heche, directed by Ivan Reitman; *A Perfect Murder* with Michael Douglas and Gwyneth Paltrow, directed by Andrew Davis; *The X-Files* with David Duchovny and Gillian Anderson, directed by Rob Bowman; Disney's animated feature *Mulan*; *Doctor Doolittle* with Eddie Murphy, directed by Betty Thomas; and *Out of Sight* with George Clooney and Jennifer Lopez, directed by Steven Soderbergh.

The saving grace in July may be Steven Spielberg's *Saving Private Ryan*, which stars Tom Hanks and Tom Sizemore. For once, Spielberg uses the summer for serious fare, rather than another *Jurassic Park* epic. *Ryan* has its share of action though, including storming the beaches of Normandy on D-Day, complete with thousands of extras. It remains to be seen whether *Ryan* is another *Schindler* or not. Also in July: *Armageddon* with Bruce Willis and Billy Bob Thornton, directed by Michael Bay; *Lethal Weapon 4* with Mel Gibson and Danny Glover, directed by Richard Donner; *Small Soldiers* with Kirsten Dunst and Phil Hartman, directed by Joe Dante; *The Mask of Zorro* with Antonio Banderas and Anthony Hopkins, directed by Martin Campbell; and *Baseketball* with Trey Parker and Matt Stone, directed by David Zucker.

August is a study in extremes; it is a dumping ground for films expected to do poorly in the summer, and a launching pad for movies that may have legs for the fall. I think the most interesting film in this bunch may be the remake of *The Avengers*, starring Uma Thurman and Ralph Fiennes, plus a wicked villain turn by none other than Sean Connery. The movie, directed by Jeremiah Chechik, promises to keep the quirky, off-kilter nature and dry wit of the original show, while upping the ante on production design. Uma's leather jumpsuit will be a surefire draw for males, while bowler-hatted Fiennes should prove irresistible to the ladies. If this film fails to hit the mark, no one will be more disappointed than I. Also in August: *Snake Eyes* with Nicolas Cage and Gary Sinise, directed by Brian DePalma; *Ever After* with Drew Barrymore and Angelica Huston, directed by Andy Tennant; *Virus* with Jamie Lee Curtis and Donald Sutherland, directed by John Bruno; and *54* with Mike Myers and Salma Hayek, directed by Mark Christopher.

SHINING A LIGHT

And then there are the others, the smaller films, some of which will get lost in the klieg light glare generated by the ultra-hyped big films. Several of these little flicks began life as entries in the Sundance Film Festival, which showcases independent productions that are looking for distributors. The fact that these films have found distribution and are being released at this time is a credit to the studios' confidence in their potential.

JUNE: Former brat packer Ally Sheedy makes her comeback try as a lesbian, heroin-addicted photographer in writer/director Lisa Cholodenko's film *High Art*. Irish director Paddy Breathnach's *I Went Down* was a hit on his home turf and he expects it to succeed here as well. The comedic thriller is said to evoke the flavor of *Trainspotting* and *Pulp Fiction*, so you have been duly warned. *Smoke Signals* is a modern Native American tale about two young men and the death of the one's estranged father. *Buffalo 66* is decidedly not about Indians, but an ex-con psycho (Vincent Gallo, who also directed) who kidnaps Christina Ricci to pose as his wife and fake out his football-loving parents (they're Bills fans, hence the title). This dark comedy will need good word-of-mouth to succeed, but with the presence of the very talented Ricci, it stands a chance.

JULY: *Pi* was the big hit at Sundance. Shot in black & white and made for a paltry $60,000, this sci-fi art house oddity mixes Jewish mysticism with stock market savvy. A lone computer nerd tinkering in his equipment-filled apartment thinks he may have found the key to the universe. The real key is how these disparate elements come together. Based on the buzz this film received, it obviously works. *The Negotiator* stars Samuel L. Jackson and Kevin Spacey as a pair of police negotiators pitted against one another in a cat and mouse scenario. With these two fine actors in play, they could have read the phonebook and made it seem great. Fortunately, they have a bit more with which to work. For *the cult fans there is *Full Tilt Boogie*, a documentary on the making of the Quentin Tarantino-scripted, Robert Rodriguez-directed vampire flick *From Dusk Till Dawn*, still George Clooney's best film. Tarantino and Rodriguez are both huge film geeks, so a glimpse inside their working methods is bound to be both informative and fun.

AUGUST: Two very different films comprise my selections here. First, *Disturbing Behavior* blends the hip teen culture of *Heathers* and *Scream* with the smart, shadowy conspiratorial subplots of *The X-Files*. Imagine the Stepford wives having high school kids and you'll get an idea of what's going on here. First time film director David Nutter cut his teeth calling the shots on *X-Files* episodes. And finally, for those with a burning curiosity about the development of electronic music, there is the documentary *Modulation*. The history of electronic music is largely unknown to the general public, but it has evolved almost as much as computers and video games, so this film promises to take the audience on a very special journey. Seek it out if you can.

Believe it or not, I've covered less than half of the films that will be released this summer. Most of these films will not be hits; even the super-hyped, star-powered major films aren't a guaranteed sure thing. The film industry is still largely a crap shoot. Studios don't have a clue what the public wants. Originality is frowned upon because there is no sure way to market it. Star vehicles and tried-and-true formulaic plots are still seen as the best, safest way to a hit. Since this is actually true some of the time, that is the gamble the studios are willing to take. That's why Harrison Ford gets $20 million a picture and why so many movies are either sequels, remakes or derivative of a previous success. And as long as we continue to go and see these films, that is what we will continue to get. So, while I know you're planning to see *Armageddon* and *Lethal Weapon 4*, please don't forget about *I Went Down* and *Pi*. And, what the heck, go and see *The X-Files*, too. That one looks like it might be pretty good, as well. See you in September.

AMERICAN VISIONS

(September 1998)

> This article was originally written at the request of Carole Heffley (the editor), to be included in the "Heritage Day Book" (an off-shoot publication of the Irregular that came out each summer). For that reason I chose an American-oriented subject. Coincidentally, at around this time, the American Film Institute (AFI) came out with their list of the top 100 American films of all time. This seemed like a great opportunity for me to pick my own top favorites in a number of categories. In retrospect, I think this turned out to be one of my weakest columns; there was nothing to it except my own opinion, something I had vowed not to do. Carole ultimately decided not to run the article in the Heritage book, much to my chagrin, but held it for the September issue. She liked it, but felt it wasn't right for the Heritage issue. To add insult to injury, she ended up cutting the article in half for September and running the remainder in October, even though it wasn't designed to be split. All in all, not one of my happier publishing experiences.

When you think about our American heritage, usually what comes to mind is the legacy of our Constitution and the Declaration of Independence, both forged in the fires of the Revolutionary War. The right to life, liberty and the pursuit of happiness, along with our freedom of religious choice, are staples that we, more or less, take for granted. They are part of what makes us intrinsically American.

Every country has its own culture and history. In our 200-plus years as a nation, we've seen our own culture filtered and embellished through songs and folklore, legends and tales. At the dawn of this century we saw the birth of a new medium, the movies. From crude flip cards and nickelodeon peepshows has evolved the most potent form of expression ever known. In our modern society, it is chiefly this medium that carries forth our culture. Film as collective history. Film as western mythology, even. The movie theatre as Temple, the glowing screen replacing the campfire around which our ancestors once gathered to tell their stories. And while every culture has its own unique stylistic contribution, from German Expressionism to French New Wave, the one that has left the most indelible mark, worldwide, is the American Hollywood movie.

Recently, the American Film Institute released its selection of the 100 Greatest American films ever. Out of an estimated 40,000 titles it is impossible to please everyone with such a restricted list. By and large, the selections tended toward a populist slant, which didn't sit well with some critics. And that begs the question, by what criteria should you choose? Technical (the first films to utilize color or sound)? Cinematic technique (first use of close-up, jump cut, fade or dissolve)? Personal tastes and preferences (subject matter, style, black & white, color, cursing, violence, nudity, all of the above, none of your business!)? Let's move on.

If you asked 100 people to name the ten best movies ever, each list would be different, depending on such factors as the age of the person, the events in their lives that molded their character and tastes, and which films they have seen. It's no coincidence that the films people tend to name the most are the ones that have been hyped the most and are widely available to the public. What chance do obscure films have of becoming popular if they are seen only by the few who seek them out? And to be fair, many of them only play in the big cities like New York and Los Angeles. But now, thanks to the proliferation of home video and cable, more of these hidden treasures are coming to light. That, too, is a part of our American heritage—the little guy triumphing over adversity.

So, as a sort of companion to the AFI Top 100, I am offering my own very personal Top Ten, plus an assortment of other lists that I think are just as important to acknowledge. They range from overrated and underrated to the comedic and bizarre. I'm sure I'll ruffle some feathers with my choices and omissions. I've elected to pass on silent films (which is a medium unto itself), since most people are unfamiliar with the truly great ones. Because of my age, 43, my formative and impressionable years were in the 1960s and '70s, and that is reflected in my choices and tastes—very light in the '30s, '40s and '50s. The hardest part about compiling these lists, however, was limiting them to American releases only. I wanted to keep to the same parameters as the AFI and of course pay homage to our American heritage. Let the celebrations begin.

* THE TOP TEN—These are the films that have had the biggest impact on me. My only hard and fast rule was that I'd limit it to one film per director. (Alphabetical by title.)
* *BONNIE & CLYDE* (1967) Arthur Penn
* *CHINATOWN* (1974) Roman Polanski
* *CITIZEN KANE* (1941) Orson Welles
* *THE GODFATHER* (1972) Francis Ford Coppola
* *JFK* (1991) Oliver Stone
* *KOYAANISQATSI* (1983) Godfrey Reggio
* *LAWRENCE OF ARABIA* (1962) David Lean
* *PSYCHO* (1960) Alfred Hitchcock
* *RAGING BULL* (1980) Martin Scorsese
* *2001: A SPACE ODYSSEY* (1968) Stanley Kubrick

* THE NEXT BEST—I needed to add another ten because I was leaving out too many of my favorites. (The same rules apply.)
* *BRAZIL* (1985) Terry Gilliam
* *DAYS OF HEAVEN* (1978) Terrence Malick

* *FANTASIA* (1940) Walt Disney (producer)
* *THE LAST PICTURE SHOW* (1971) Peter Bogdonavich
* *MILLER'S CROSSING* (1990) Joel & Ethan Coen
* *NASHVILLE* (1975) Robert Altman
* *PULP FICTION* (1993) Quentin Tarantino
* *RADIO DAYS* (1987) Woody Allen
* *THE THIRD MAN* (1949) Carol Reed
* *THE WILD BUNCH* (1969) Sam Peckinpah

Those are my choices, like 'em or not. Following are some other lists which I hope you'll find interesting and amusing. They allow me to praise and damn those films for which there was no place in my previous lists.

* UNDERRATED FAVORITES—These films fared moderately to poorly at the box office and/or were dismissed by critics. I consider them all to be innovative and worth recognition.
* *BARRY LYNDON* (1975) Stanley Kubrick
* *DAZED AND CONFUSED* (1993) Richard Linklater
* *DREAMCHILD* (1985) Gavin Miller
* *ED WOOD* (1994) Tim Burton
* *THE HUDSUCKER PROXY* (1994) Joel & Ethan Coen
* *KAFKA* (1991) Steven Soderbergh
* *THE LAST TEMPTATION OF CHRIST* (1988) Martin Scorsese
* *MODERN ROMANCE* (1981) Albert Brooks
* *THE QUICK AND THE DEAD* (1995) Sam Raimi
* *THE ROCKETEER* (1991) Joe Johnston

* MOST OVERRATED—This list, I fear, will cause the biggest uproar, since I slaughter so many sacred cows. It's not that I feel these films are necessarily bad, just that they're not deserving of the status they've garnered.
* *E.T. THE EXTRA-TERRESTRIAL* (1982) Steven Spielberg
* *FORREST GUMP* (1994) Robert Zemeckis
* *GONE WITH THE WIND* (1939) Victor Fleming
* *GREASE* (1978) Randal Kleiser
* *HALLOWEEN* (1978) John Carpenter
* *HOME ALONE* (1990) Chris Columbus
* *ROCKY* (1976) John G. Avildsen
* *THE SOUND OF MUSIC* (1965) Robert Wise
* *STAR WARS* (1977) George Lucas
* *THE TEN COMMANDMENTS* (1956) Cecil B. DeMulle

* GREAT COMEDIES—Comedies rarely win awards or make the top lists which are usually loaded with dramas, mine included. The ability to make people laugh, and do it in an original way, is as much an art as any great drama. These are some of my favorites.
* *ALL OF ME* (1984) Carl Reiner
* *BEETLEJUICE* (1988) Tim Burton
* *DR. STRANGELOVE* (1964) Stanley Kubrick
* *DUCK SOUP (*1933 Leo McCarey
* *FISH CALLED WANDA* (1988) Charles Crichton
* *GROUNDHOG DAY* (1993) Harold Ramis
* *RAISING ARIZONA* (1987) Joel & Ethan Coen
* *RETURN OF THE PINK PANTHER* (1975) Blake Edwards
* *RUTHLESS PEOPLE* (1986) Jim Abrahams, David Zucker, Jerry Zucker
* *UNFAITHFULLY YOURS* (1948) Preston Sturges

* CINEMA OF THE BIZARRE—Film is capable of so much more than conventional storytelling. Here are ten titles that could only have sprung from minds that are not entirely sane.
* *THE ADVENTURES OF BUCKEROO BONZAI* (1984) W.D. Richter
* *BARTON FINK* (1991) Joel & Ethan Coen
* *THE DARK BACKWARD* (1991) Adam Rifkin
* *EDWARD SCISSORHANDS* (1990) Tim Burton
* *ERASERHEAD* (1978) David Lynch
* *EVIL DEAD 2* (1987) Sam Raimi
* *GLEN OR GLENDA* (1953) Ed Wood
* *NAKED LUNCH* (1991) David Cronenberg
* *THE ROCKY HORROR PICTURE SHOW* (1975) Jim Sharman
* *VAMPIRE'S KISS* (1989) Robert Bierman

Finally, I want to leave you with a very personal recommendation. To those of you who love movies and want to learn more about their history, and the secret language they whisper to us, check out *VISIONS OF LIGHT: THE ART OF CINEMATOGRAPHY*. More than just a tour of technical innovations, *VISIONS* is a celebration of film in its purest form. Seeing this documentary will enlarge your appreciation of movies and moviemaking. It includes interviews with twenty-six cinematographers and is illustrated with scenes from over 100 films. If you want to see the collective influence films have had on our American culture, and the visual legacy they've bestowed on our society, this documentary illustrates it more fully than any other. It's another way to think of movies as part of our American heritage.

THE ALTERNATIVE
HALLOWEEN PARTY
(October 1998)

> Even though Carole was running the remainder of my "American Visions" piece for this month, I managed to convince her to also let me do a piece on Halloween movies. Ironically, I decided to take a Halloween article I'd done several years earlier for an independent zine called "Boom" and revamp it for the Irregular. It wasn't as easy as I thought it would be and I ended up having to cut it down and do a complete rewrite. I don't think I cheated anyone by recycling the piece, given all the reworking I did to it. The original was very well researched and nicely written, but with only a circulation of about 300, no one got to see it. At least that was my justification at the time.

If you plan to have a Halloween party you'll need some appropriate videos to set the mood. But, what sort of horror film should you pick? What defines a horror film, anyway? Despite recent trends, it can be more than scenes of twenty-something actors yelling and screaming while drenched in gallons of fake blood, intercut with close-ups of a special effects dummy with an ax, knife or machete buried in its face. Instead, it can be a thought provoking excursion into another realm. A world of mood, uneasy fantasy and unexpected twists. A horror film that's not just a horror film. A film where, after you've seen it, you'll have something more worthwhile to talk about than how cool it looked when the guy's head exploded. And, as the following choices show, movies can be frightening, unnerving and even shocking without resorting to mindless mayhem and explicit gore.

REPULSION (1965)—Catherine Deneuvre. Directed by Roman Polanski. One of the creepiest films you'll ever see. This is Polish director Polanski's first English language film, but it is still fully laced with all his East European neuroses. The beautiful Deneuvre plays a mentally unstable manicurist (shades of Lorena Bobbitt!) who is driven to murder. As her hold on reality crumbles, we are immersed into her nightmare world of hallucination and delusion. Polanski's mastery of the film medium is absolute, creating a psycho-sexual thriller of the first order.

IRONWEED (1987)—Jack Nicholson, Meryl Streep, Tom Waits. Directed by Hector Babenco. It's about baseball and it's about ghosts, but this ain't no Field of Dreams! Based on the Pulitzer Prize novel by William Kennedy, Nicholson portrays Francis Phelan, an alcoholic ex-baseball player on the skids in

Depression-era Albany. As a homeless tramp, his life is mostly a struggle to simply survive, made no easier by the specters from his past that doggedly pursue him. Their shimmering, unearthly presence I a haunting reminder of Phelan's checkered life, and a personification of the deep guilt he carries with him. One of Nicholson's best performances.

PAPERHOUSE (1989)—Charlotte Burke, Ben Cross. Directed by Bernard Rose. A curious and atmospheric little tale, from Catherine Storr's novel "Marianne Dreams," about a young girl whose innocent drawings take on a life of their own. It all begins when she draws a simple house and then finds herself there in her dreams. Each addition she makes to the drawing adds new dimensions (and consequences) to the reality of her dream world. Disturbing and beautiful at the same time, this is a real gem worth seeking out.

In conclusion, I hope this small offering of offbeat and semi-obscure film choices provides your party with a touch of originality and enjoyment. I think that it's long overdue that we replace the adrenaline rush of the gross out flick with the far more satisfying slow burn that you get from a well-crafted psychological thriller. As Poe, Lovecraft and Blackwood did for literature, these films do for cinema. They scare you by making you think.

ALL I WANT FOR CHRISTMAS . . .

(December 1998)

> In November the Irregular put out their Christmas Book (similar to their July Heritage Book). It was decided that I would not contribute a column then, but would resume it for the December Irregular. It seemed fitting and proper to do a piece about Christmas videos. I had a lot of fun making my choices, trying to balance live action and animated, old and new. On the whole, I think I did a pretty good job. Christmas has always been a favorite time of the year for me, so doing an article on Christmas movies was very enjoyable. This article also had a special meaning for me, since it meant I'd completed a year's worth of work for the Irregular. Every time I'd finished a column I felt an incredible rush, a sense of accomplishment, the knowledge that "I did it again!" Finishing a year's worth of material was enormously satisfying. I felt like a real writer. I had deadlines, had to fill those blank pages and was paid for my efforts. Both Jim and Carole were very happy with my work and always made a point of saying how good I was and what positive feedback they received about my work. I was slowly becoming aware that people were reading my column and seemed to like it. Friends, acquaintances and even a few "strangers" all came up to me and commented favorably on my articles. This was an unusual situation in which to find myself, and I did my best to accept it as graciously as I could. Compared to the writing that appeared in many top national publications, I still felt I had a lot to learn. However, based on the reaction I received, I was determined to continue moving forward, improving my craft and maintaining the highest level of writing I could.

With the approach of the holiday season comes many familiar impressions. Along with a nip in the air and some snow on the ground there are the obvious decorative embellishments—wreaths, electric Santas, ornamented trees and, of course, our own Easton Peace Candle. These are the outward manifestations of the Christmas holiday, a yearly ritual of making this time seem special. But, what about how we, as a society, express the spirit of Christmas. In times past, it was through art, storytelling and songs; in modern times, it is all these things, plus our modern mythology of movies and video.

In the retail world Christmas is big business. On home video the studios gear up for a major selling blitz of new releases, hoping to stuff as many stockings as they can while lining their own pockets with more than just Christmas cheer. Along with the new video releases there is now a sizable second industry in the Christmas video perennial—seasonal videos that are reissued each holiday and are snapped up by eager consumers. Some titles, like *It's a Wonderful Life*, can be purchased year round, but others, such as *How the Grinch Stole Christmas*, are generally only in stock during the fall and winter.

that ever had a running character or guest star don a Santa suit has been packaged in red and green box art with the phrase "a very special Christmas episode> emblazoned on it. From *I Love Lucy* to *The Honeymooners*, from *A Charlie Brown Christmas* to *South Park*'s Mr. Hanky, it's beginning to look a lot like holiday hype!

For those of us old enough to remember a time before videotape, many of these programs were shown on TV each year. Part of the reason we purchase them now, I think, is surely as a nostalgic reminder of those simpler times, and a way to reclaim our youth. *Mr. Magoo's Christmas Carol* is one of those things that can make me ten years old all over again.

Following is a selection of Christmas videos—some old, some new—that offer up a variety of pleasures connected with the holidays. Hopefully there's something for everyone's tastes.

* *BEAUTY AND THE BEAST: THE ENCHANTED CHRISTMAS* (1997)—As direct-to-video sequels go, this is one of the better ones. While clearly cashing in on the Christmas video market, Disney has in fact created a lush and beautiful story about the first Christmas that Belle and the Beast spent together. Though not up to the production values of the original, this is still far more lavish than most other animated fare. Most of the original voice talent is back too, plus some new ones, including Tim Curry as a sinister pipe organ rendered by computer animation.

* *A CHRISTMAS CAROL* (1951)—There are many versions of Dickens' classic story floating around, but this is, hands down, the best. Alastair Sim creates the definitive Scrooge, and every other note is right on key, from the sets and costumes to supporting actors and cinematography. If you own only one *Christmas Carol*, make sure it's this one. Also, beware the colorized version and insist on the original black & white only.

* *A CHRISTMAS STORY* (1983)—Who would have thought that the director of the *Porky's* movies could have made such a wonderful family film? Funny and sweet, with just enough mischief to satisfy today's jaded kids, this sleeper hit offers solid entertainment and more laughs than you can imagine. Author Jean Shepherd provides the wry and humorous first person narration to his story. The great cast includes Darren McGavin, Melinda Dillon and Peter Billingsley.

* *LITTLE WOMEN* (1994)—Though the Christmas sequences comprise only a small portion of this movie, their presence is strongly felt. Sad, touching and heartbreaking, but ultimately uplifting, this version of the classic Alcott novel is blessed with a superlative cast that includes Susan Sarandon, Winona Ryder, Gabriel Byrne and, in one of her last performances, the great character actress, Mary Wickes. The film is also complimented with a beautiful score by Thomas Newman.

* *THE MUPPET CHRISTMAS CAROL* (1992)—Remember when I said that the 1951 Alastair Sim version was the best? Well, believe it or not, this is a close second. Michael Caine plays it straight as Scrooge, while surrounded by the antics of his Muppet co-stars. Kermit the frog is perfectly cast (really!) as Bob Cratchit, while Gonzo appears as on-screen narrator Charles Dickens (really!!). Bright, cheerful songs, well-placed humor and terrific Victorian production design complete the picture. Watch this with your little ones and experience the pleasure of a movie that actively encourages children to read.

* *THE YEAR WITHOUT A SANTA CLAUS* (1974)—While the stop-motion animation in this Rankin-Bass TV special is a bit crude by today's standards, this tale of a sickly old Santa who decides to skip Christmas because he feels no one cares, still has loads of charm. The show-stopper is the Snow Miser/Heat Miser song that's sure to take you back to your younger days when this was shown on TV every Christmas. Mickey Rooney and Shirley Booth provide the voices for Santa and Mrs. Claus, and bring their considerable talents to this endearing little confection.

Christmas should be about caring and giving, and spending quality time with your loved ones. This is a notion that is easy to forget in an era of intense commercialization that has, more or less, come to dominate the holidays. In their own secular way, these videos each remind us of the true spirit of the Christmas season. The qualities of loving and sharing, honor and goodwill, compassion and maybe even peace on Earth, are all present. When much of the entertainment industry seems happy to bombard us with so much mindless junk, it is gratifying to know that there are some worthwhile treasures to be found. And the deeply spiritual message they offer us is in no way diminished by their packaging as lighthearted entertainment.

IS HOLLYWOOD BANKRUPT?
(February 1999)

I began my second year doing the column in the same basic manner as the previous year. I had a formula that worked and loved the fact that I could write about anything I wanted. However, I took that responsibility seriously and did my best to come up with interesting subjects to write about. Since there was no January issue (everyone needs a little time off for the holidays!) my first column of the New Year ran in February.

Cinema has reached its hundredth anniversary but, despite this landmark, compared to the other storytelling arts (plays, poems and novels, all of which can be measured in thousands of years), film is still in its infancy. As the "baby" of the family, film has often been clothed in hand-me-downs; that is, film scripts have often been derived from these elder siblings, as well as from earlier films. This was inevitable, and has led to the mindset that it MUST be derivative of these earlier arts. As such, 90% of all films tend to fall within this conventional realm. That, in and of itself, is not bad since many great movies have come from other source material.

While it is not uncommon for Hollywood to redo earlier versions of films because of their name recognition, in recent years this has led, by logical extension, to the remaking of TV shows into feature films. *The Addams Family, The Brady Bunch, The Fugitive, Maverick, The Flintstones* and *Lost in Space* are but a few examples of the film industry's attempt to vouchsafe a hit. However, history has shown that there are no guarantees—*Car 54, Mr. Magoo, Dragnet* and *The Beverly Hillbillies* were all less than successful.

Perhaps most unsettling is the tendency of Hollywood to release, per calendar year, multiple films that deal, implicitly, with the same subject matter. I first noticed this trend in 1984 with the release of three films in what came to be known as the "back to the farm" movies—*Places in the Heart, Country* and *The River*. Antecedents to this go back at least to 1964 with the pairing of nuclear war films *Dr. Strangelove* and *Fail Safe*. In 1992 there were two Columbus movies— *Christopher Columbus: The Discovery* and *1492: Conquest of Paradise*—neither of which did well. Since then, other twin screenings have included *Tombstone/Wyatt Earp, Dante's Peak/Volcano, Seven Years in Tibet/Kundun* and in 1998 alone, *Deep Impact/Armageddon, Antz/A Bug's Life* and *Saving Private Ryan/ The Thin Red Line*. These titles suggest a real inability for Hollywood to engage in original thinking.

As much as I would like film to be a pure art form, the reality is that it is primarily a business. The bottom line is that studios want their films to make money, so the attraction to remakes and sequels is understandable. Back in the early days, the first real wave of remakes came about when movies changed from silent to sound. *Frankenstein, The Phantom of the Opera* and *The Hunchback of Notre Dame* were among the first to make the transition. Others over the years have included *The Ten Commandments, Ben Hur, King of Kings* and *Nosferatu*.

Foreign films were also ripe for remaking into English language versions with American stars. *The Magnificent Seven* owes its origins to *The Seven Samurai, The Birdcage* to *La Cage aux Folles*, and *City of Angels* to *Wings of Desire*. Forgoing a name change were *Diabolique* and *The Vanishing*, the latter's remake even done by the same director. Perhaps the most unique remake was Terry Gilliam's *12 Monkeys*, which found its source material in a haunting short

Then there are the film franchises—a series of films that follow the same character(s). From *Charlie Chan* to *The Thin Man*; from *Blondie* to *Ma and Pa Kettle*, this was nothing new. More recently, *Batman, Superman, Dirty Harry, Rocky* and *Indiana Jones* have all had their run, along with *Halloween, Friday the 13th* and *Nightmare on Elm Street*. *Planet of the Apes, The Pink Panther, Airport, Jaws, Lethal Weapon, Die Hard, Alien* and *Death Wish* have had their time in the spotlight, too. The longest running, and most durable of the franchises, seems to be the James Bond series which has been going strong since *Dr. No* in 1962.

The downside of franchises is the spate of unnecessary sequels. I won't even get into the plethora of really bad horror film sequels. However, did we need *The Godfather 3* or *Speed 2*? I think not. And nobody was very thrilled to see sequels to such classic films as *Gone with the Wind, 2001: A Space Odyssey* or *The Exorcist*. If nothing else, it just proved that continuing the story of a great film was no guarantee of quality or success.

The play's the thing, or so it's been said, and Hollywood has tried its hand at remaking the stage. Ironically, this is one area in which the transition has been almost unanimously successful, at least artistically speaking. And not just with musicals, either. Non-singing/non-dancing examples include *Who's Afraid of Virginia Woolf?, Driving Miss Daisy, Equus, Amadeus, Betrayal, Glengarry Glen Ross, Dangerous Liaisons, Death and the Maiden* and *The Crucible*.

The "Bard of Avon" has also seen his share of success in this venue, usually in several incarnations. *Hamlet, Othello, Twelfth Night, Much Ado About Nothing, Romeo & Juliet, The Taming of the Shrew, Richard III, Henry V, The Tempest* and *A Midsummer Night's Dream* attest to the durability of Shakespeare's work. And such diverse films as *West Side Story, Forbidden Planet, Ran* and *Chimes at Midnight* were each inspired by one or more Shakespearean plays.

Finally, let's compare some good remakes to some bad ones. On the plus side there is the 1951 *A Christmas Carol* with Alistair Sim, which is superior to the 1938 Reginald Owen version. The 1992 *Last of the Mohicans* is clearly better than the previous incarnations of 1920 and 1936. Finding new territory to explore helped remakes of *The Thing, Invasion of the Body Snatchers, Cape Fear* and *Sorcerer* hold their own with their original counterparts. A visual lushness helped propel *1984, A Secret Garden* and *A Little Princess* above their previous namesakes. And a contemporary sensibility gave fresh appeal to the period veneers of *Little Women, Of Mice and Men* and *The Mask of Zorro*.

Now, on the downside, when remakes were bad, they were generally very bad, or at least pompous, stuffy, self-conscious and in most cases, simply unnecessary. *Sabrina, Stagecoach* and *The Getaway* all failed to attract interest. *Unfaithfully Yours*, though funny, couldn't compare to the Sturges original. *Desperate Hours, D.O.A.* and *Meet Joe Black* all flopped. *Flubber* lacked any of the charm of *The Absent Minded Professor*, substituting way too many special effects. And the completely insane idea of doing a shot-for-shot remake of *Psycho* turned out to be enough of a dud that hopefully no one will open that door again.

So, where does all this leave us? Has Hollywood finally run out of ideas? I do not think there is a simple answer. We are living in a time of extremes and this is reflected in the film industry as well. Movies have never been as good or as bad as they are right now. While we had to suffer through the dumbed down inanity of Jerry Springer in *Ringmaster*, there was also the exquisite beauty of *The Sweet Hereafter*. While audiences flocked to see the mindless *Armageddon*, they also flocked to the thoughtful *Titanic*. If it is truly the best of times and the worst of times, so be it. But let's choose to focus only on the good as often as we can.

IN OSCAR'S SHADOW
(March 1999)

The first quarter of each year has come to be known in the media arts as the awards season. One after another at this time we are inundated with Golden Globes, People's Choices, Grammys, et al, culminating with the Grand Poobah of all awards shows, the Oscars. The media, itself, hypes this event so much that it is almost impossible not to get caught up in it. After all, everybody loves movies, and we all have opinions about what we think are the best films, performances, etc. of the year.

Ironically, during the last quarter of each year, it always seems as if that year has been the worst ever for quality films. And every year, at the end, the floodgates are opened and the quality flicks come gushing forth. This is no accident. The studios want their "Oscar pictures" to still be in theatres (or at least ready for a quick re-release) when the nominations are made in February. This allows them to cash in on the Oscar buzz and generate more money. People who would not normally give the time of day to a film will rush eagerly to the multiplexes to see these newly anointed wonders.

Anything that brings people out to see good movies is just fine with me. It's gratifying when small movies like *Gods and Monsters, Elizabeth, Affliction* and *A Simple Plan* get recognition for their quality and are able to be heard above the din of such lumbering and pinheaded behemoths as *Armageddon* and *The Waterboy*.

Be that as it may, once the Oscars are given out, we should not fall into the trap of believing some sort of final word has been passed on the inherent quality of the films for the year. As in any year, great films are overlooked. *Rocky* won the Oscar for best picture of 1976, but hardly anyone today would seriously argue that its four competitors—*All the President's Men, Bound For Glory, Network* and *Taxi Driver*—are inferior. Equally unbelievable, *Oliver* won best picture of 1968 while *2001: A Space Odyssey* wasn't even nominated in that category!

This year has also seen its share of overlooked films. While I am thrilled that such unorthodox movies as *The Thin Red Line* and *Shakespeare in Love* were nominated in multiple categories, there have been some other wonderful films that failed to get any nominations at all. I do not consider these films to be the best of the year or even, for that matter, better than the other nominees. I just feel they are worthy of more recognition than they received. Rent them now and see for yourself.

* *The Big Lebowski*—Jeff Bridges, John Goodman. Written and directed by Joel and Ethan Coen. The Coen brothers are among the most talented and original filmmakers working today. This comedy has much of the cutting edge bravado as

There's Something About Mary had, while playing with the notion of genre conventions. The cowboy narrator, the Busby Berkeley-esque dance sequence, the Euro-trash nihilists, all seem to be from other films, yet add so much texture and complexity to this story of bowling buddies caught up in a mistaken identity caper. When so many movies follow a formulaic routine, it is refreshing to see a film that is so off-the-wall and unpredictable, and yet so clearly the work of skilled professionals.

* *Sliding Doors*—Gwyneth Paltrow, John Hannah. Written and directed by Peter Howitt. While Paltrow is receiving raves for her performance in Shakespeare in Love, this film gives you two Gwyneths for the price of one. In a highly original scenario, Paltrow's character is on her way home from work when the story splits into two realities, one where she catches the train and one where she misses it. In catching the train, however, she also catches her philandering boyfriend, causing her life to veer in a new direction. The two storylines follow their individual paths and we are drawn in, wondering what the fates of the two Gwyneths will be. As the storylines move farther apart, it is humbling to realize that the source of this growing difference was a simple sliding door on a subway train.

* *The Spanish Prisoner*—Campbell Scott, Steve Martin. Written and directed by David Mamet. Principally known for his work as a playwright (he won a Pulitzer in 1984 for his blistering drama Glengarry Glen Ross), Mamet has also carved out a respectable second career as a screenwriter and movie director (House of Games, Homicide and Oleanna). His signature dialogue style, known as "Mamet-speak," where people talk in fits and starts, interrupting one another, repeating themselves, is unmistakable in its uniqueness. For Prisoner, Mamet uses all his linguistic tricks in a tale of deception, mistaken intent, con artist scams and greed, where the creator of a high tech computer program becomes the prey in a corporate espionage ruse. But, who are the real crooks and who is scamming who? Even if you figure it all out before the end, the journey and the revelations are a pleasure unto themselves.

So, the moral to this story is that while Oscar nominated movies are generally very good (and perhaps even great), there is a whole other universe of movies out there that don't get nominated, receive little or no promotion, yet are very much worth looking at. And I don't think it is mere coincidence that the films I've chosen were all released in the early part of the year (all the better to get lost in the Oscar mania of the previous year's films), or that they were each written by their directors. So often, films are arrived at by committee, which means the original idea may become diluted. These three films speak to the power of a singular creative voice. I believe it is a voice worth hearing.

EYES WIDE: A TRIBUTE TO STANLEY KUBRICK

(May 1999)

> The gap here is due to the fact that I ran a feature article (two actually) about a friend who was a local filmmaker. Since those pieces are very different in style and tone from my usual work, I've elected to withhold them from this collection. The passing of my favorite director in March led me to write this tribute, a piece I'm still very proud of.

On March 7, 1999, one of the brightest lights in cinema's firmament quietly vanished. Stanley Kubrick, perhaps the most unique (and eccentric) director of his time, died in his sleep at age 70. And there will probably never be another like him ever again. In his nearly half century career he established a reputation as a maniacal perfectionist who'd spend years working on a single project; a control freak who demanded a hundred takes from his actors for each shot before he was satisfied; a licensed pilot who refused to fly; an expatriate American who spent the last decades of his life in a rambling manor house near London, so loathe to travel that he shot his Vietnam epic, *Full Metal Jacket*, entirely in England, as he had all his films from *Lolita* (shot in 1961) to his most recent production, the eagerly-anticipated Tom Cruise/Nicole Kidman psycho-sexual thriller, *Eyes Wide Shut* (due out in July).

But the man who gave us such startlingly original, provocative and ahead-of-their-time masterpieces as *Dr. Strangelove, 2001: A Space Odyssey* and *A Clockwork Orange* began his film career on a much more humble note. After several years as a photographer for Look magazine (begun while still a teenager), Kubrick, already a master with camera and lenses, concluded that making movies was where he could make his fortune. He tried his hand at a couple documentary shorts, *Day of the Fight* and *Flying Padre* (both in 1951 and financed through friends and relatives), but they barely broke even. His first forays into feature films, *Fear and Desire* in 1953 and *Killer's Kiss* in 1955 (again self-financed) were similarly unsuccessful. However, Kubrick had found his calling. And it was at this time that he hooked up with James B. Harris, an aspiring film producer who helped the fledgling director get his first real films off the ground and thus, launch his career. It is these early films, less well-known to the general public, which I wish to concentrate on here.

* *The Killing* (1956)—Based on the novel, "Clean Break" by Lionel White about a racetrack heist, what could have been a typical "caper flick" of the time, became instead a boldly original film noir classic. The heist itself is shown

several times as the film backtracks to follow the actions of the main participants, the sequences overlapping one another where the characters intersect. This structure is part of the original novel and seems to be the element which attracted Kubrick and Harris in the first place. They then assembled a first-rate cast of B-movie character actors, headed by Sterling Hayden as Johnny Clay, the mastermind behind the heist. Kubrick would work with Hayden again on *Strangelove*. Rounding out the ensemble were Jay C. Flippen, Ted DeCorsia, Mary Windsor, Timothy Carey and Elisha Cook, Jr. While some of the hard-boiled dialogue is dated, and Kubrick's directing of the actors is a bit shaky, his command of the camera, lighting and editing are all top notch. The lasting legacy of *The Killing* is best exemplified by the fact that Quentin Tarantino borrowed liberally from its structure for his own crime caper classic, *Reservoir Dogs*, a film that was hailed by critics for its boldness and originality. It was, but Kubrick had been there first, 36 years earlier.

* *Paths of Glory* (1957)—Some have called this film Kubrick's "graduation piece," meaning that all his powers as a filmmaker came together here to create a complete masterpiece. Billed as an antiwar film, and taken from the Humphrey Cobb novel of the same name, it tells the tale of a botched military assault by a French regiment during World War I. The General responsible for the blunder, in order to save face (and his career), insists that the regiment failed him and orders a court of inquiry in which three innocent men are chosen to be tried and executed for "cowardice in the face of the enemy." Remarkably, and regrettably, the novel is supposedly based on a true incident during the war and, so powerful was the film that for many years it was banned in France. The able cast includes Kirk Douglas as Colonel Dax, the regiment commander who tries to save the three innocent soldiers, Adolf Menjou and George Macready as the conniving Generals, Wayne Morris as a cowardly Lieutenant and, as the three condemned men, Ralph Meeker, Joseph Turkel and Timothy Carey (last seen in *The Killing*). The trench setting of the battlefield is gritty and atmospheric, and the fluid camera work allows the director to indulge his passion for tracking shots (a Kubrick signature). Equally impressive is the actual attack, a three minute barrage of noise, chaos and death that stands alongside anything Spielberg did in *Saving Private Ryan*. There are many other scenes where Kubrick flexes his directorial brilliance—the kangaroo court martial, envisioned as a human-sized chess game; the dichotomy of war and class, which allows officers to dance in the splendor of a chateau while soldiers die in muddy trenches; and a hideously funny, darkly comic moment when one of the condemned men seeing a cockroach says, "You see that cockroach? Tomorrow morning we'll be dead and it'll be alive. It'll have more contact with my wife and child than I will. I'll be nothing and it'll be alive." One of the other condemned casually smashes the bug and quips, "Now you got the edge on him." However, despite all this, Kubrick

refuses to remain cynical. The film ends on a hopeful, uplifting note, one of the few times this director has allowed himself such a luxury. It is both fitting and necessary, and helps raise the film to the level of a genuinely great work of art.

* *Lolita* (1962)—Kubrick's decision to film Vladimir Nabokov's controversial 1955 novel about a middle aged man's infatuation with a 12-year old girl as his next project was just another example of his desire as a filmmaker to remain on the cutting edge. Given the temper of the times, it was nothing short of a miracle that he was able to actually pull it off, though he did have to resort to suggestion, innuendo, misdirection and much cinematic sleight-of-hand to get it by the censors. Kubrick decided to concentrate on the comic possibilities of the novel and updated it from its period setting to contemporary times, choices that were designed to take the onus off the forbidden nature of the story. As was becoming his forte, the director assembled a marvelous cast with James Mason as the obsessed Humbert, Sue Lyon (then 14) as the eponymous object of his desire, Shelly Winters in a brave performance as the pretentious and pathetic mother, Charlotte, and a brilliant turn by Peter Sellers as the twisted and surreal Clare Quilty, the true monster of the story who makes Humbert's life a living hell. Part of Kubrick's genius is his ability as an editor, which he believes is the most creative part of the filmmaking process. And part of being a great editor is in knowing when *not* to cut. All of Kubrick's films contain scenes with long, uninterrupted shots, but this is especially evident in *Lolita*. It was as if he knew the story would succeed or fail mainly on the strength of the performances. As a result, *Lolita* is his least stylistically intrusive film, and one that contains some of the best acting you'll see in any Stanley Kubrick movie. Nabokov, himself, was supposedly happy (at least initially) with the film version of his most famous novel, even if it did bear only a scant resemblance to the screenplay he wrote. For Kubrick, it was a victory of another sort; after years of struggling in the industry, he finally made a film that got noticed and even turned a profit.

With the completion and release of these three films, *The Killing, Paths of Glory* and *Lolita* (plus his hired hand work for Kirk Douglas on *Spartacus*), in little more than half a decade, Kubrick at last established himself as a highly talented new voice in cinema. He now also had the clout to pursue even more innovative and stylish work. At this point Harris left his would afford him the complete artistic control he needed. Now, only in his mid-thirties, he would embark on the most creative and fruitful period in his career, and make the name "Stanley Kubrick" a legend in the industry.

In 1964, Kubrick released *Dr. Strangelove*, a nightmare comedy about nuclear annihilation. Its combination of sexual humor and Swiftian satire was embraced by the critics and public alike. Four years later, in 1968, he unveiled his masterpiece, *2001: A Space Odyssey*, still the greatest science fiction film ever made and one of the truly original "great films" of all time. In 1971 came *A*

Clockwork Orange, a violent and stunning adaptation of Anthony Burgess's novel, with a tour de force performance by Malcolm McDowell. Lurid and shocking, it anticipated the punk movement as well as the state of violence in our society today. Kubrick left the future for the past in his next film, *Barry Lyndon*, released in 1975. Though underappreciated at the time, it set the template for all other historical films to come, regarding sets, costumes and especially cinematography (it was the first film to be shot by candlelight). Next up was *The Shining* in 1980, based on the novel by the then up and coming Stephen King. Here, Kubrick took the popular horror genre and transformed it into a mythological context as he had done with science fiction in 2001. The results were mixed with King purists unhappy, while others succumbed to the films epic visual opulence. Over the years it has grown in stature and is now considered a horror classic. In 1987 Kubrick returned to war with *Full Metal Jacket*, based on Gustav Hasford's savage Vietnam novel, "The Short-Timers." Though most veterans gave the film thumbs up (as did critics), it was partially overshadowed by the previously released *Platoon*. Still, it did reasonably good business.

For the next decade or so it seemed that Kubrick had disappeared from cinema's radar. Every so often there was talk of this or that project—a Holocaust drama which he scuttled when Schindler's List came out, and a sci-fi epic called A.I. (for artificial intelligence) that would've depicted the Earth covered by melted ice caps (shades of Waterworld!). Then came word that his next film would in fact be a sexual thriller called Eyes Wide Shut (loosely based on Arthur Schnitzler's 1926 novel, "A Dream Story") with Tom Cruise and Nicole Kidman as married psychiatrists who have sexual relations with their patients. Made with a secrecy that rivals the development of the Atom bomb at Los Alamos, it consumed a production schedule of over fifteen months, requiring reshoots and even recasting (Sidney Pollack replacing Harvey Keitel in a key role). Its release date kept retreating too, from the summer of '98 to Christmas and finally to July '99.

Then came the news of Kubrick's sudden death from a heart attack. The man who kept us all waiting over a decade for his grand finale won't be making the premiere. Between the last two films in his baker's dozen oeuvre are the entire directorial careers of Oliver Stone, Spike Lee and the Coen brothers, to name just a few of the more modern talents that have come along. Just days before his death, Kubrick said he believed Eyes was his best work yet. If true, given the caliber of his past accomplishments, it will be an awesome crowning achievement to one of cinema's most singularly successful careers.

Kubrick's vision transformed the movies, and how we see them, in ways we are only beginning to appreciate. As time goes by, and his legendary status grows, we can look back fondly and admirably at a man who, like Welles and Hitchcock before him, was as much a star as any actor in his films. And he did it without ever appearing to the public at large. It's ironic that for most of us, the only time we ever got to hear him speak was when his death was announced on the news and they ran a clip of him giving an acceptance speech for the American Film Institute award he received last year. Though the bespectacled, grey-haired old gentleman in the clip seemed a far cry from the mad maverick with the piercing stare responsible for 2001 and A Clockwork Orange, his words are perhaps the best testimonial to his work as an artist: "Anyone who has ever been privileged to direct a film knows that, although it can be like trying to write 'War and Peace' in a bumper car in an amusement park, when you finally get it right, there are not many joys in life that can equal the feeling." Kubrick certainly got it right most of the time and the joy he brought to all of us with his work will last an eternity.

BOOKS ON KUBRICK
* The Cinema of Stanley Kubrick by Norman Kagan—A good general purpose reference of Kubrick's career and films.
*Stanley Kubrick: A Film Odyssey by Gene D. Phillips—A simple, straightforward coverage of Kubrick's work with lots of pictures.
* Stanley Kubrick Directs by Alexander Walker—This first serious study of Kubrick concentrates mainly on Paths of Glory, Dr. Strangelove, 2001 and A Clockwork Orange. Highly recommended.
* Kubrick: Inside a Film Artist's Maze by Thomas Allen Nelson—The most in-depth study of Kubrick's work to date. Essential reading.
* Kubrick by Michel Ciment—Ambitious, large format book which analyzes Kubrick's visual conceits. Includes interviews with Kubrick and several of his associates.
* The Making of Kubrick's 2001 by Jerome Agel—Long out of print study of 2001. Many photos, reviews, fan letters and world reaction. It also includes the complete Playboy interview with Kubrick from 1968.
* 2001: Filming the Future by Piers Bizony—An excellent, informational and pictorial account of Kubrick's greatest film. Simply wonderful.
* Stanley Kubrick: A Biography by Vincent LoBrutto—The first major biography of Kubrick's life beyond his films. Quite interesting and enlightening.

ON A MOVIE BINGE:
A FIFTH OF SUMMER
(June 1999)

Another summer, another hundred films to see. If you're like most people, however, you'll end up going to only a fraction of the movies released this season. But even if you decide to see no movies at all, you probably won't be able to avoid the steady stream of commercials and ads that the marketing mavens have prepared to saturate your consciousness. In fact, it's already begun with The Mummy, Entrapment and the first real release of the summer season, *Star Wars Episode One: The Phantom Menace*, or "The George Lucas Money Machine." After all, Titanic had no action figures or "Happy Meals" tie-ins.

But, getting back to the summer films, I've whittled them down into two groups. The ones that will be getting the most hype (some deserving, some not) I call "The Big Twelve." Following that set are six lesser known (and lesser hyped) movies that I think are genuinely worth your attention, which I call "The Low-Profile Six." Add them all together and it still only accounts for about one-fifth of the movies scheduled for release between Memorial Day and Labor Day. (Note: Because of studio fickleness, some release dates may be subject to change.)

THE BIG TWELVE
* *Star Wars Episode One: The Phantom Menace* (5/19)—What more can I add to this? If you haven't heard about it, you're probably an amoeba. Just go, it's the law!
*Notting Hill (5/28)—Julia Roberts and Hugh Grant in a romantic comedy from the writer of *Four Weddings and a Funeral*. Sounds like a winner.
*Austin Powers: The Spy Who Shagged Me (6/11)—Mike Meyers returns in a career move to dethrone Adam Sandler as the top comic movie draw. Yeah, baby!
*Tarzan (6/18)—Disney doing what it does best, plus songs written and performed by Phil Collins. Totally cool. What more could you want?
*The Wild, Wild West (7/02)—From the director of *Men in Black* comes Will Smith and Kevin Kline in a remake of the classic '60s TV series. Call it "Men in Black Hats."
*Eyes Wide Shut (7/16)—Stanley Kubrick's final film, featuring Tom Cruise and Nicole Kidman steaming up the screen in this sexy thriller. Destined to be a cult classic.
*The Haunting (7/23)—Remake of the 1963 Robert Wise classic. *Twister* director Jan DeBont is trying for a comeback after the *Speed 2* disaster. Boo!

Summer of Sam (7/30)—Director Spike Lee need a hit. He hopes to have one with this story about serial killer "Son of Sam." This may just be Lee's redemption.

Runaway Bride (7/30)—The other Julia Roberts movie this summer. Co-starring Richard Gere and directed by *Pretty Woman's* Garry Marshall. Will lightning strike twice?

Mystery Men (8/06)—A motley group of superheroes led by Ben Stiller. The oddball cast includes Janeane Garafalo, William H. Macy and Paul Reubens. Hey, it can't be any worse than the last Batman flick.

The Muse (8/20)—Writer/director/star Albert Brooks is the smartest comic filmmaker working today. Sharon Stone and Jeff Bridges are the inspired cast.

Dudley Do-Right (8/?)—Brendan Fraser is so hot right now that anything he does will get attention. Hopefully he's kept his standards high doing "The Full Mounty."

THE LOW-PROFILE SIX

Besieged (5/21)—Italian director Bernardo Bertolucci knows how to tell an intimate story, even in such epics as *1900* and *The Last Emperor*. This time he has Thandie Newton (*Beloved*) and David Thewlis (*Naked*) as lustful partners, with the Italian countryside as a backdrop. The two lovers are an interesting study in contrasts—man and woman, white and black, privileged and servile. Originally made for Euro-TV, this film may prove to be one of the most interesting of the year. Do not hesitate to seek it out.

Limbo (6/4)—Another John Sayles gem. The director of *Lone Star*, *Men with Guns* and *Eight Men Out* stays small and low key with this tale of an Alaskan fisherman (Sayles regular David Strathairn) who meets up with singer Mary Elizabeth Mastrantonio. As in most of Sayles' work, there is a sense of foreboding which permeates the story, along with layers of irony, fear and past tragedy. Hopefully this is one film that won't get lost in the chaos of the summer blockbusters.

Buena Vista Social Club (6/4)—Documentaries notoriously do badly in theatrical release. Yet, very often, they are riveting, moving, highly entertaining works of art. Past examples include *The Thin Blue Line, Roger and Me, Crumb,* and *Hoop Dreams*. The most recent entry into this group, *BVSC*, directed by the brilliant German filmmaker Wim Wenders (*Paris, Texas* and *Wings of Desire*) is a charming and warm look at legendary Cuban musicians. The film chronicles a series of concerts in Amsterdam and New York, featuring such outstanding talents as 80 year old pianist Ruben Gonzolez, 95 year old guitarist Compay Segundo, and others of equal vintage, along with footage shot in small Cuban towns where the music was born. Special care was taken in the recording and sound mix of the concert footage to give the movie audience a spectacular aural experience. This is destined to be one of the great movie documentaries.

Twin Falls, Idaho (7/?)—For those in search of the slightly more bizarre, how about this tale of conjoined twins (two arms, three legs) looking for the love of one girl? Despite its *Twin Peaks* weirdness, this is a truly heartfelt drama. Real life twins, Mark and Michael Polish (who are not conjoined), wrote, directed and starred in this, their first movie.

Stiff Upper Lips (7/?)—Whether you love or hate the Merchant/Ivory drawing-room dramas (*A Room with a View, Howards End*), there is sure to be something amusing for everyone in this very British send-up of everything Edwardian.

The Astronaut's Wife (8/?)—As far removed from the world of *Star Wars* as you can get, this suspense thriller stars Johnny Depp and Charlize Theron (*The Devil's Advocate, Mighty Joe Young*) as a married couple separated by one too many space missions. Returning from a space flight in which he was briefly out of contact with mission control, Depp appears to be "different." Did he meet up with aliens? Is he an alien? Or, is he just feeling alienated? Houston, we've got one hell of a problem! Sort of a cross between *Apollo 13* and *The X-Files*, this could be a real sleeper hit for those tired of the mindless fodder that makes up most of our summer movie diet.

With ticket prices soaring, and concession costs on a par with airport restaurants, you'd need to be pretty well off to see even the few films I've covered. For the price of an evening out at the flicks, you could instead buy a movie on videotape or, horror of horrors, purchase a book to read. The fact is there are many options out there vying for your entertainment dollars. Still, movie-going remains one of the more compelling choices we make. And the movies we do see are mostly those that are highly advertised. The squeaky wheel always gets the grease. So, while I know that "The Big Twelve" will do the biggest business this summer, I hope you are able to check out "The Low Profile Six," and maybe even a film or two that you discovered all on your own, without any hype. Sometimes they are the best ones.

A HUNDRED YEARS OF HORROR
(October 1999)

> Another gap. I still wasn't writing for the July/August Heritage edition at this time, plus I'd written a feature piece for September about my sister and her husband going to China to adopt a baby girl, and there was no room for my September column. It got shifted to December since I already had this Halloween-themed piece planned for October.

Since its earliest days, cinema and horror/fantasy have been close companions. In 1902, at the dawn of real cinema, French filmmaker George Melies released his fanciful masterpiece, A Trip to the Moon, which ran a then epic length 21 minutes at a time when movies were under five minutes each. In 1910, the Edison Company made the first known version of Frankenstein, a 16 minute opus featuring a truly hideous monster. From then on the die was cast; the century of cinema to follow would see such cult trends in the horror genre as the German Expressionists of the 1920s, the Universal horror film cycle of the '30s and '40s, the atomic monster craze of the '50s, the Hammer studio series of the '60s, the highbrow horrors of the '70s, the teen slasher flicks of the '80s, and the ultra-hip scare flicks of the '90s. At century's end we find a virtual renaissance of horror films, from the super low-budget indie sleeper *The Blair Witch Project*, to big-budget studio pictures like *The Sixth Sense, Stigmata*, and the Arnold Schwarzenegger vehicle *End of Days*. It certainly looks like horror and cinema came into this century with a bang and will be going out with one.

So, what better way to celebrate the century of horror this Halloween season than by looking back on a few frightening gems that made a difference. However, rather than choosing the classic, big hit blockbusters that we all know about, I'd rather acknowledge some relatively modern (and relatively modest) films that may have escaped your notice.

The Fourth Man (1984)—Before he achieved fame and fortune in America with such hits as *RoboCop, Total Recall* and *Basic Instinct,* Dutch director Paul Verhoeven made his mark in Holland with several intense films. Jeroen Krabbe plays a bisexual writer who becomes ensnared in the web of a sensual, mysterious woman (Renee Soutendijk) who had three previous husbands, all of whom died under unusual circumstances. The religious subtext in the story, though atmospheric and moody, seems a bit forced. Still, the movie on the whole is visually powerful, genuinely frightening, and leaves one with an overwhelming sense of dread and inevitability.

The Hitcher (1986)—A chance encounter between a young driver (C. Thomas Howell) and a mysterious hitch-hiker (Rutger Hauer) sets in motion a series of grisly murders and a devilish game of cat and mouse. But, is the "hitcher" real or merely a passenger of the young man's id? Strange, provocative, and filled with chilling images, this film remains an effective exploration of the themes of good and evil, the difference between active and passive modes of being, and the existential undercurrents inherent in the mythos of the divided self. While all this may sound a bit highbrow, the movie is readily accessible on many levels.

The Vanishing (1988)—How fate and destiny are intertwined with the choices we make in our lives is at the heart of this remarkable film. A brief respite at a vacation rest stop leads to the disappearance of a man's girlfriend. He then spends the next few years obsessed with discovering the truth behind this enigma. Director George Sluizer proves you can make a riveting thriller without a drop of blood, and shows us that the face of evil can appear as inconspicuous and respectable as a loving husband and father. Succumbing to the lure of Hollywood however, Sluizer remade the film in 1993 as an American feature starring Jeff Bridges, Kiefer Sutherland, Nancy Travis and a then-unknown actress named Sandra Bullock. While the new version has its merits (a cleaner plotline and a larger, more active role for the Travis character), it lacks the poetry and subtext of the original French/Dutch production. Since you are more likely to have seen the American version, the chance to see the original one should be quite a surprising treat for you.

What is it about the horror genre that is so pervasive and long lasting in our species? Every culture everywhere has myths and fables relating to horrific events. I'm sure ancient civilizations sat around their communal campfires and told such tales as well. The cinema screen may be our modern campfire where these same stories are now being shared. Certainly they can have a cathartic effect on us as we live vicariously through the imagination of the storyteller. In a deeper sense, they appeal to our need for a moral imperative by which to live; myths, fairytales and religious writings often incorporate horrific elements as allegory. Perhaps it's this connection with our most ancient heritage that has allowed the horror story, in whatever form, to endure for so long.

SWAN SONGS: THE LAST FILMS
OF THREE GREAT DIRECTORS
(December 1999)

The art of filmmaking has changed considerably over the years. It has grown from its crude origins to the most prolific and expensive business on the planet. Historically, cinema will be regarded as the one true new art form of the twentieth century. However, the business of filmmaking has left little room for the truly artistic to flourish during its century-long incarnation. Too much time, money and manpower are needed for any one individual to put a really personal stamp on a movie.

But, there was a time when a few, so very few, had the clout, the perseverance, and the tenacity to make their films their own. Such was the work of Alfred Hitchcock, David Lean and Stanley Kubrick. The recent death of Kubrick, I think, brought down the curtain on this type of auteur. George Lucas, Steven Spielberg and James Cameron may be the most successful directors, but their bodies of work do not carry the singular fingerprint that identified the films of Hitchcock, Lean and Kubrick. As a tribute to these original and artistic visionaries, let's look at the final films they've left us.

Alfred Hitchcock was born in 1899 and died in 1980. He got his start in films by designing title cards for silent movies. Working his way up through this infant industry, he directed his first film, *The Pleasure Garden*, in 1925. Soon, the suspense thriller became his genre of choice. He made the transition to sound films with no problem, but retained the use of the wordless sequence (or "pure cinema," as he called it), which became his trademark. Always innovative, he changed with the times and constantly reinvented himself while holding to a consistent style. Due to the brief cameos he made in his own movies (another trademark), along with the intros he provided on his anthology TV series, *Alfred Hitchcock Presents*, he became a media icon and one of the few directors who was as well-known as the stars who appeared in his films. His reputation spiked in the early Sixties with *Psycho* and *The Birds*, then dipped with the release of several less-than-successful projects. In the Seventies he was again on the upswing with *Frenzy* and his 53rd and final film, *Family Plot*. Ironically, though nominated numerous times for an Academy Award, Hitch never won a competitive Oscar.

Family Plot (1976) starring Karen Black, Bruce Dern, Barbara Harris, William Devane. Though lightweight in comparison to other Hitchcock films, this still holds up quite well. The story contains two plot threads that run parallel for most of the film and finally intersect near the end. In the first strand, a pair of séance con artists tries to find a client's long lost relative who stands to inherit the family fortune. The second strand follows this relative, now a jewel thief and kidnapper, who knows nothing of his family background (he was raised by others). When he realizes people are trying to find him he thinks it's because of his lawless ways. This misunderstanding allows for a lot of interesting and suspenseful interplay as the two story strands move closer and closer. The film contains the usual Hitchcock motifs—wordless sequences, unsavory characters, dark humor and carefully edited set-pieces, most notably an out-of-control car ride on a mountain road. And as a final irony, Hitch's cameo in his last film would be ominous indeed; he appears as a silhouette in a window!

David Lean was born in 1908 and died in 1991. He began his career in films as a runner, or "gopher" (go fer this, go fer that) and eventually worked his way up to editor. His directing break came when he met the playwright Noel Coward who was writing, directing and starring in a film based on a wartime incident of Lord Mountbatten. Halfway through the production Coward tired of directing and turned the reins over to Lean who was cheeky enough to ask for a co-directing credit. He got it! The film, released in 1942, was called *In Which We Serve.* Lean's subsequent films epitomized what it was to be British, both the good and the bad. He railed against the class system, had an absolute love of trains (they appear in most of his films), and whenever he could, set his stories in lush, exotic locales. Though he had successes all through his career, Lean really made his reputation with his last five films—*The Bridge on the River Kwai, Lawrence of Arabia, Doctor Zhivago, Ryan's Daughter,* and *A Passage to India.* These films are like Rolls Royces—elegant, hand-crafted, and meticulous in every way, from sets and costumes to locations and the breadth of their stories. Nominated seven times for an Academy Award in directing, Lean won twice (for *Bridge* and *Lawrence*). In his forty-two year career as a director, he completed only sixteen films.

A Passage to India (1984) starring Judy Davis, Victor Banerjee, Peggy Ashcroft, James Fox and Alec Guinness. This film recounts the tale of two British women (one young, one old), who visit India in the 1920s. The clash of East and West occurs when a young Indian doctor arranges an elaborate trip to some exotic caves with the women. The doctor and younger woman are alone for a short period at one of the caves, when suddenly she is seen running down the hill, hitting rocks and brambles, looking very much like a rape victim. The doctor is immediately arrested and the remainder of the film covers his trial and its outcome. Lean shows the incident in such a way that, what actually happens remains a mystery for much of the film. Interesting, too, the collision of cultures has positive as well as negative repercussions. As a result of the trial, the doctor finds his true Indian voice and discards his sycophantic notions of Westernization (thus, he has his own "passage" to India). Lean was a master at blending the epic with the romantic, both of which are evident here. Returning from a fourteen year absence (after the initial critical drubbing *Ryan's Daughter* received), Lean proved he still had it in him to deliver a great film.

Stanley Kubrick was born in 1928 and died in 1999. He began his film career as an independent, financing his own projects, first documentaries and then features, his first being *Fear and Desire* in 1953. Of his thirteen features, Kubrick hit his stride in the Sixties and Seventies with *Dr. Strangelove* (1964), *2001: A Space Odyssey* (1968) and *A Clockwork Orange* (1971), establishing his penchant for films that were visually stunning, drolly satiric, and unique in their view of the world. He appeared to favor form over content (giving his films a somewhat detached quality), and he was one of the very few filmmakers who had absolute authority over how his films were made and distributed. He was a filmmaker always ahead of his time. (See the May 1999 Irregular for a fuller review of Kubrick's career.)

Eyes Wide Shut (1999) starring Tom Cruise, Nicole Kidman, Sydney Pollack. An upscale Manhattan couple finds their secure marriage is threatened when the wife reveals to her husband that she once contemplated leaving him for a stranger she'd seen only from across the room. This information sends the husband reeling, and leads him on an odyssey of sexual depravity that goes largely unconsummated. As the title suggests, the couple has been existing in a dream state and, only at the end do they finally wake up and become aware of who they are.

So, what is the world to make of Kubrick's final opus? Like most Kubrick films, this one was highly anticipated. When it was released however, it was met with mixed reactions (also like most Kubrick films). A decade from now it will probably be considered a masterpiece that was ahead of its time. (Do I detect a pattern here?) As Kubrick's final work, *Eyes* has many of the filmmaker's signature trademarks—endless tracking shots, mirrors and mirror images, scenes in bathrooms, and surreal sequences located in large, impressive sets. But unlike most Kubrick films, *Eyes'* preoccupation with interpersonal relationships (and their resolution) marks new territory for this filmmaker. Still, Kubrick, ever the cynic, resists becoming too warm and fuzzy in his examination of what it means to understand your significant other. Even as the couple reflect on what is to become of their lives together, the wife utters an expletive as the final word in what would become Kubrick's final film. However, it is that very glibness at the conclusion of *Eyes* that keeps it from becoming maudlin and sentimental, so that instead, it is ultimately a very intriguing and surreal journey into the psyche of sexuality.

Well, are there any other directors out there to carry on the legacy of these brilliant artists who used film as others might use paint, canvas and clay? The answer is . . . maybe. We live in a different world from the one in which these filmmakers were born. They all came of age before television, so their touchstones were of a different era. Still, there are some younger filmmakers who have developed a visual style that is uniquely their own, and who may one day rise to the heights of Hitchcock, Lean and Kubrick. Ascending the mountain now are such artists as Oliver Stone, Terry Gilliam, David Lynch, Tim Burton, Atom Egoyan and Jim Jarmusch. Some have hit hard times recently, commercially speaking, but here's hoping they will all make a comeback. If film is to survive its next hundred years as an art form, we need to encourage this generation of visionaries. And we need to find new ones.

FEMALE DIRECTORS OR: WOMEN WHO RUN WITH THE FILMS
(February 2000)

> I started my third year eager to continue my run of interesting articles. My skills as a writer were improving and I had a pretty good handle on meeting the deadlines for a monthly column. My biggest fear was that I would run out of topics to write about, but so far, at least, that had never occurred. The biggest change up for me was that the movie theatre where I worked had closed down six months earlier, so I no longer had access to free films and inside information. I still had a part time job at a video store, but since I still wasn't Internet savvy yet, it wasn't always easy finding out new information. Fortunately, I had a lot of historical knowledge I could draw upon.

Despite the strides women have made over the years to establish their voice in society, if you ask them they will tell you that to a great extent, it is still largely a man's world. History is still mostly "his story", and women still face the challenge of making their voices heard. The arts and sciences also reflect this, with the great acknowledged talents, be they painters, sculptors, composers or scientists, being men. Only in the last generation or so has this male dominated mindset shown signs of change. As women have established themselves full time in the workforce, they have slowly gained a foothold in the arts as well.

In the arena of filmmaking, the prestige position (and for the longest time, almost entirely male dominated) has been the director. Women have found success and recognition in cinema in the lesser categories of costume design (Edith Head), editing (Dede Allen, Anne V. Coates) and screenwriting (Frances Goodrich), but except for a few isolated cases (Madeline Brandeis' 1918 film *THE STAR PRINCE*, Dorothy Davenport's and Dorothy Arzner's work in the 1920s and '30s, Leni Reifenstahl's propaganda films for Hitler in the '30s, Ida Lupino and Muriel Box in the '50s and '60s), the director's chair had remained securely behind a ceiling of the most unbreakable glass.

With the rise of the women's movement in the late '60s and early '70s, it was only natural that, while making in-roads in all professions, women would strive to make the director's slot an equal opportunity position, too. One of the first to stake her claim was writer/performer Elaine May, best known at the time for her comedy work with her partner, writer/performer/director Mike Nichols. May's first films were *A NEW LEAF* '71 and *THE HEARTBREAK KID* '72, both of which were minor successes. However, May became disenchanted with the "politics" surrounding directing, and chose to spend the next several years as an actress and screenwriter. She returned to the director's chair in 1987 with the spectacularly bad and expensive *ISHTAR*. She hasn't directed a film since then.

Karen Arthur and Gillian Armstrong began their long, ongoing directing careers in the late '70s with *THE CAGE* '78 and *MY BRILLIANT CAREER* '79, respectively. Perhaps the most bizarre entry into this budding sisterhood was Nancy Walker (character actress best known as Rosie the waitress in the Bounty commercials) whose one and only directorial effort was the Village People opus, *CAN'T STOP THE MUSIC* '80. This slice of disco excess was a major flop and ended Walker's directing career. Women were making headway, but mostly, it seemed, to prove that they could make a movie as badly as any man.

The 1980s, however, would turn out to be the real breakthrough decade for women as directors. Their numbers swelled as did their successes. Setting the tone for the first half of the decade was actress Lee Grant's *TELL ME A RIDDLE* '80, Agnieszka Holland's *PROVINCIAL ACTORS* '80, Penelope Spheeris's *THE DECLINE OF WESTERN CIVILIZATION* '81, Amy Heckerling's *FAST TIMES AT RIDGEMONT HIGH* '82, Kathryn Bigelow's *THE LOVELESS* '83, Barbra Streisand's *YENTL* '83, Martha Coolidge's *VALLEY GIRL* '83, Lizzie Borden's *BORN IN FLAMES* '84, and Susan Seidelman's *DESPERATELY SEEKING SUSAN* '85, to name a few. The latter half of the decade would continue this trend with Penny Marshall's *JUMPIN' JACK FLASH* '86, Jane Campion's *TWO FRIENDS* '86, Randa Haines's *CHILDREN OF A LESSER GOD* '86, Diane Keaton's *HEAVEN* '87, Mira Nair's *SALAAM BOMBAY* '88, and Nancy Savoca's *TRUE LOVE* '89.

The arrival of the 1990s saw women fully taking their place alongside men as directors, becoming more than just a novelty. The successes in the '80s led to business as usual in the '90s. Many of the newest names to the roster were women who came up through the ranks from other industry positions. Leading the pack was actress Dyan Cannon's *THE END OF INNOCENCE* '91, actress Jodie Foster's *LITTLE MAN TATE* '91, Radha Bharadwaj's *CLOSET LAND* '91, novelist and screenwriter Nora Ephron's *THIS IS MY LIFE* '92, stuntwoman and actress Betty Thomas's *ONLY YOU* '92, Allison Anders's *GAS, FOOD, LODGING* '92, Sally Potter's *ORLANDO* '92, Jennifer Lynch's (daughter of director David Lynch) *BOXING HELENA* '93, actress Angelica Huston's *BASTARD OUT OF CAROLINA* '96, Mimi Leder's *THE PEACEMAKER* '97, Lisa Cholodenko's *HIGH ART* '98, actress Joan Chen's *XIU XIU THE SENT DOWN GIRL* '99, Brenda Chapman's animated epic *THE PRINCE OF EGYPT* '99, and most recently, Kimberly Pierce's highly acclaimed *BOYS DON'T CRY* '99.

The growing number of women as directors has led to a growing diversity in their films. Though much of their work deals in one way or another with "relationships," by and large their films go beyond the narrow confines of the term "chick flick." What they do share is a desire to show women as strong and independent, and that their problems are just as important as those of the male characters. They often deal frankly with sexuality, as Jane Campion's *THE PIANO* showed, but they can also be testosterone driven as in the films of Kathryn Bigelow (*BLUE STEEL, POINT BREAK*). However, occasionally women still find they have to deal with stereotypical scrutiny; in Barbra Streisand's *THE PRINCE OF TIDES*, many critics commented more about Babs's perfect manicure than her directorial skills. The fight goes on.

But, the bottom line is that women directors have arrived and are here to stay. We will no longer see the world, in films, only through the male eye. And that is a good thing. Women's contributions to the art of cinema have enriched it and expanded it and made it more interesting and exciting for all of us, whatever our gender.

A SISTERHOOD OF FILMMAKERS
(March 2000)

As it turned out, my February column ran a bit long, so Carole was forced to split it in half and we ran the second part (with some minor additions) in March. I wasn't crazy about doing it this way, since I felt the flow of the piece was disrupted, but it was part of the reality of the journalism industry that I had to deal with.

Last month's article covered the history of women directors in cinema, chronicling their rise and acceptance, over the years, in a largely male-dominated profession. They went from being considered a novelty to becoming almost, but not quite, a commonplace occurrence. Perhaps the next century of cinema will see that come to pass. Still, it's been an impressive achievement for women, and to give some sense of scope of the films they have contributed, following is a fairly comprehensive list of women and their films. Hopefully you will be pleasantly surprised by the breadth and variety of titles. Many of them are quite good; a few of them are bad; most are worth checking out.

THE SISTERHOOD AND THEIR WORKS
Stefani Ames: *A GUN, A CAR, A BLONDE 97;* Allison Anders: *GAS, FOOD, LODGING 92, MI VIDA LOCA 94, FOUR ROOMS*-one segment *95, GRACE OF MY HEART 96;* Gillian Armstrong: *MY BRILLIANT CAREER 79, MRS. SOFFEL 84, HIGH TIDE 87, FIRES WITHIN 91, THE LAST DAYS OF CHEZ NOUS 92, LITTLE WOMEN 94, OSCAR AND LUCINDA 97;* Karen Arthur: *THE CAGE 78, MY SISTER, MY LOVE 80, A BUNNY'S TALE 85, LADY BEWARE 87, RETURN TO EDEN 87, BRIDGE TO SILENCE 89, THE DISAPPEARANCE OF CHRISTINA 93, TRUE WOMEN 97;* Dorothy Arzner: *WILD PARTY 29, CHRISTOPHER STRONG 33, CRAIG'S WIFE 36, THE BRIDE WORE RED 37, DANCE GIRL DANCE 40;* Shirley Barret: *LOVE SERENADE 96;* Zelda Barron: *SECRET PLACES 85, SHAG: THE MOVIE 89, FORBIDDEN SUN 89;* Kathy Bates: *DASH AND LILLY 99;* Radha Bharadwaj: *CLOSET LAND 91, BASIL 98;* Kathryn Bigelow: *THE LOVELESS 83, NEAR DARK 87, BLUE STEEL 90, POINT BREAK 91, STRANGE DAYS 95;* Patricia Birch: *GREASE 2 82;* Lizzie Borden: *BORN IN FLAMES 84, WORKING GIRLS 86, LOVE CRIMES 92, EROTIQUE 94;* Muriel Box: *A NOVEL AFFAIR 57, THE TRUTH ABOUT WOMEN 58;* Madeline Brandeis: *THE STAR PRINCE 18;* Bonnie Burns: *VINCENT 81;* Ellen Cabot: *DEADLY EMBRACE 88, MURDER WEAPON 90, BEACH BABES FROM BEYOND 93, TEST TUBE TEENS FROM THE YEAR 2000 93, PETTICOAT PLANET 95, BIKINI GODDESSES 96;* Jane Campion: *TWO FRIENDS 86, SWEETIE 89, AN ANGEL AT MY TABLE 90, THE PIANO*

93, PORTRAIT OF A LADY 96, HOLY SMOKE 99; Dyan Cannon: *THE END OF INNOCENCE 91;* Kimberly Casey: *DEADLY DANCER 90;* Brenda Chapman: *THE PRINCE OF EGYPT 99;* Joan Chen: *XIU XIU THE SENT DOWN GIRL 99;* Lisa Cholodenko: *HIGH ART 98;* Joyce Chopra: *SMOOTH TALK 85, THE LEMON SISTERS 90, DANGER OF LOVE 95, MY VERY BEST FRIEND 96;* Martha Coolidge: *VALLEY GIRL 83, THE JOY OF SEX 84, REAL GENIUS 85, BARE ESSENTIALS 90, RAMBLING ROSE 91, CRAZY IN LOVE 92, LOST IN YONKERS 93, ANGIE 94, THREE WISHES 95, OUT TO SEA 97;* Dorothy Davenport: *RED KIMONA 25, LINDA 29, SUCKER MONEY 33;* Donna Deitch: *DESERT HEARTS 86, THE WOMEN OF BREWSTER PLACE 89, CRIMINAL PASSION 94;* Doris Dorrie: *STRAIGHT THROUGH THE HEART 83, MEN... 85;* Nora Ephron: *THIS IS MY LIFE 92, SLEEPLESS IN SEATTLE 93, MIXED NUTS 94, MICHAEL 97, YOU'VE GOT MAIL 98;* Jodie Foster: *LITTLE MAN TATE 91, HOME FOR THE HOLIDAYS 95;* Joan Freeman: *STREETWALKIN' 85, SATISFACTION 88;* Lisa Gottlieb: *JUST ONE OF THE GUYS 85, ACROSS THE MOON 94, CADILLAC RANCH 96;* Lee Grant: *TELL ME A RIDDLE 80, DOWN AND OUT IN AMERICA 86, STAYING TOGETHER 89;* Randa Haines: *CHILDREN OF A LESSER GOD 86, THE DOCTOR 91, WRESTLING ERNEST HEMINGWAY 93, DANCE WITH ME 98;* Sarah Harding: *RECKLESS 97;* Amy Heckerling: *FAST TIMES AT RIDGEMONT HIGH 82, JOHNNY DANGEROUSLY 84, NATIONAL LAMPOON'S EUROPEAN VACATION 85, LOOK WHO'S TALKING 89, LOOK WHO'S TALKING, TOO 90, CLUELESS 95;* Agnieszka Holland: *PROVINCIAL ACTORS 80, FEVER 81, A LONELY WOMAN 87, TO KILL A PRIEST 89, EUROPA, EUROPA 91, OLIVIER, OLIVIER 92, THE SECRET GARDEN 93, TOTAL ECLIPSE 95, WASHINGTON SQUARE 97;* Angelica Huston: *BASTARD OUT OF CAROLINA 96;* Diane Keaton: *HEAVEN 87, WILDFLOWER 92, UNSTRUNG HEROES 95;* Barbara Kopple: *WILD MAN BLUES 98;* Mimi Leder: *THE PEACEMAKER 97, DEEP IMPACT 98;* Sondra Locke: *RATBOY 86, IMPULSE 90;* Ida Lupino: *NEVER FEAR 50, THE BIGAMIST 53, THE HITCH HIKER 53, THE TROUBLE WITH ANGELS 66;* Jennifer Lynch: *BOXING HELENA 93;* Penny Marshall: *JUMPIN' JACK FLASH 86, BIG 88, AWAKENINGS 90, A LEAGUE OF THEIR OWN 92, THE PREACHER'S WIFE 96;* Elaine May: *A NEW LEAF 71, THE HEARTBREAK KID 72, ISHTAR 87;* Frieda Lee Mock: *MAYA LIN- A STRONG, CLEAR VISION 94;* Mira Nair: *SALAAM BOMBAY 88, MISSISSIPPI MASALA 92, THE PEREZ FAMILY 95, KAMA SUTRA 96;* Kimberly Pierce: *BOYS DON'T CRY 99;* Sally Potter: *ORLANDO 92, THE TANGO LESSON 97;* Dorothy Ann Puzo: *COLD STEEL 87;* Leni Riefenstahl: *TRIUMPH OF THE WILL 35, OLYMPIA 36;* Nancy Savoca: *TRUE LOVE 89, DOGFIGHT 91, HOUSEHOLD SAINTS 93, 24 HOUR WOMAN 99;* Susan Seidelman: *DESPERATELY SEEKING SUSAN 85, MAKING MR. RIGHT 87, COOKIE 89, SHE-DEVIL 89;*

June Spencer: *LITTLE NOISES 91;* Penelope Spheeris: *THE DECLINE OF WESTERN CIVILIZATION 81, SUBURBIA 83, THE BOYS NEXT STORE 85, WAYNE'S WORLD 92, THE BEVERLY HILLBILLIES 93, THE LITTLE RASCALS 94, BLACK SHEEP 96;* Barbra Streisand: *YENTL 83, THE PRINCE OF TIDES 91, THE MIRROR HAS TWO FACES 96;* Betty Thomas: *ONLY YOU 92, THE BRADY BUNCH MOVIE 95, THE LATE SHIFT 96, PRIVATE PARTS 97, DR. DOLITTLE 98;* Nancy Walker: *CAN'T STOP THE MUSIC 80.* Lina Wertmuller: *THE LIZARDS 63; RITA LA ZANZARRA 66; MIMI THE METALWORKER 72; SWEPT AWAY 74; SEVEN BEAUTIES 76; THE END OF THE WORLD 77; A JOKE OF DESTINY 84; CAMORRA 85; SOTTO...SOTTO 85; SUMMER NIGHT WITH GREEK PROFILE, ALMOND EYES & SCENT OF BASIL 87; CIAO, PROFESSORE! 94*

From this impressive list, I want to single out one film with which you may or may not be familiar. Whatever the case, it exemplifies, perfectly, a vision that could have come only from a woman. Whether or not you like this film, at the very least, after you've seen it, you should be inspired to engage in some lively debate.

* *ORLANDO*—Written and directed by Sally Potter. Based on the novel by Virginia Woolf. This is perhaps the most unique and offbeat "period" film you will ever see. Beginning in 1600, we are introduced to the main character, Orlando, a young, slightly effeminate English nobleman. In this world of privileged men, it is ironic that the first authority figure we encounter is a woman, Queen Elizabeth I. The irony extends to the casting, as well. Orlando is played by actress Tilda Swinton, while Elizabeth is portrayed by gay writer Quentin Crisp! (Even at the very start, Potter is questioning gender barriers.) Orlando gains his identity when the Monarch presents him with home and property. The ailing Queen's only request to Orlando is "Do not fade.". And so he doesn't, for the next 400 years! But he will change. In 1610, Orlando falls for a Russian beauty named Sasha, but despite a mutual attraction, he is ultimately rejected. He is destined to be alone. The years tick by, and the unaging Orlando tries to find some meaning to his life. But, wherever he goes, whatever he does, the world of men holds no satisfaction for him. Men are shown to be vain and shallow, and Orlando's unsuccessful pursuit of happiness as a man leads him to finally reject his very gender. In a deep sleep of many days he makes the ultimate physical (and metaphysical) leap, and upon awakening, finds that he is now a woman! Orlando promptly loses ownership of her property, even as she gains her new identity. As a woman in a man's world of the 1800's, Orlando must now cope with both unwieldy clothing and attitudes. Her enormously cumbersome dresses are a perfect metaphor for the societal struggles and restrictions she now must face. At

this point, Orlando meets Shelmerdine (Billy Zane), an adventurer and self-described "pursuer of liberty". He becomes the embodiment of Orlando's own quest for liberty. Not coincidentally, he is also a virtual doppelganger of the Russian Sasha, perhaps an allusion to timeless love and the pursuit of the "ideal". Orlando's brief interlude with Shelmerdine, however, only reinforces her desire to live outside the shadow of men, to not be defined by them or their goals. As time marches on, Orlando, now pregnant, wanders aimlessly and disinterested, through a World War I battlefield, (another rejection of man's folly). By the end of Orlando's 400 year odyssey, she finds herself as a modern woman, a professional writer and a single parent, her slender androgyny now in vogue. The empowerment first bestowed upon her as a man by Elizabeth has now found fruition for her as a woman. In a final benediction, Orlando and her young daughter are serenaded by a floating angel (a castrato in gold body paint, no less!). For any woman who contemplates the past, and history (his story), Orlando's amazing journey can be seen as very much like their own.

The miracle of *ORLANDO*, the movie, is one of determination. Filmmaker Sally Potter spent a decade seeing this project to its realization, and the finished product shows her passion. The lush, yet austere look of the film belies its low budget origins. A clever use of existing locations, and a priority for costuming, helps elevate the film's production design, which is reminiscent of British filmmaker Peter Greenaway's work, especially *THE DRAUGHTSMAN'S CONTRACT*. This is not surprising since *ORLANDO*'s production designers were Greenaway alums Ben van Os and Jan Roeffs. Even the music score by David Motion and Sally Potter mimics the style of another Greenaway regular, composer Michael Nyman.

In the final analysis, the success of films like *ORLANDO* is important for the film industry in general and women directors in particular. It says that there is more than one way to make a movie, more than one way to depict female characters, more than a single viewpoint on male/female relationships. It also adds another unique thread to the increasingly diverse pattern in the fabric of cinema.

THE ORIGINS OF THE MOTION PICTURE ACADEMY
(April 2000)

When most of us think of the Motion Picture Academy, the first thing that comes to mind is the Academy Awards. Certainly that is the most glamorous and publicized aspect of this organization, and the image of the golden Oscar statuette has become an icon as recognizable as any legendary film star. But the truth is that, at least, originally, the awards were a very minor part of the Academy's intended purpose. Now, however, the awards have come to be seen as the only thing the Academy does, but that is far from the truth. A look into the past may shed some light on the real purpose of this august body.

The idea for a Motion Picture Academy was first conceived in the late 1920's as a way to protect and strengthen collective bargaining among the major talent groups in the industry. It was also seen as judicious for these groups to form an alliance against censorship and attacks from outside groups. On January 11, 1927, thirty-six people became the founders of the Academy of Motion Picture Arts and Sciences (AMPAS), including such industry notables as MGM studio head Louis B. Mayer, and screen legends Mary Pickford and Douglas Fairbanks. Within two months articles of incorporation were presented, and officials elected. On May 4th, a non-profit charter was granted, and a week later an organizational banquet was held at the Biltmore Hotel where more than 200 people joined the Academy.

In addition to labor relations, the Academy pioneered technical research in such fields as cinematography and sound recording, offering training for its members. "Talkies" were just on the horizon, and much of the technique of filmmaking would have to adjust to this latest innovation. University film courses were also established with help from the Academy, along with the publication of various books and technical papers.. Over the years, the Academy has sponsored scholarships and intern programs for young filmmakers, to help promote and nurture new talent. All of these benefits, and many more, can be traced back to the early days of the Academy.

The Awards ceremony, which now overshadows all other aspects of the Academy, began humbly, too. During its creation in 1927, the Academy formed several general committees, including one for "Awards of Merit". Though an awards ceremony was considered, it took a year before the idea caught on. Nominations were initially based on films released from August to July; (five years later, the process was amended to films released during a calendar year). One person from each of the five Academy branches, (Actors, Directors, Producers, Technicians, Writers) sifted through the 1000 nominations, whittling them down to ten choices for each category. Through the years, the number of nominees and categories has changed, as well as who gets to vote. For a while, in the 30's and 40's, voting privileges were extended to industry guilds and unions, as well as the Academy. From 1946-56, the guilds and unions participated only in the nominating process. From 1957 to the present, nominating and voting became exclusive to the Academy members, which currently numbers about 6000. Membership to the Academy is by invitation only, and candidates must be sponsored by two members of the branch they wish to join.

The media circus that the Oscars have now become is due to equal parts of accident and design. Results of the voting were originally revealed immediately, followed by presentation of the awards several months later. By 1940, the results were withheld until the presentations. This remains in effect today, though certain categories (Thalberg, Hersholt, scientific, honorary and technical) are exempt from this policy. The awards ceremony was first televised in 1953 (following a successful run on radio from 1930). For many of these early TV viewers, the awards show was the only chance to see "celebrities" outside of the movies. As the most glamorous and famous element of the organization, it is no wonder the Oscars have become such a phenomenon in our media driven culture. That they are broadcast live only adds to their already inherent excitement, since it means that almost anything can happen.

Perhaps the greatest change in the Academy is the role the award plays in the financial status of the films involved. It is no secret that Oscar gold means more money for the winning films. Studios regularly mount huge multi-million dollar campaigns for films they feel have a chance to win. It's no accident that in our video age, Oscar-calibre films are released mainly at year's end, all the better to still be in theatres come nomination time in February. What the studios choose to support, and what ultimately wins, makes for some intriguing, and sometimes embarrassing, results. Looking back, it's now hard to believe that *CITIZEN KANE* lost to *HOW GREEN WAS MY VALLEY* in 1941; *MOULIN ROUGE* to *AROUND THE WORLD IN 80 DAYS* in 1952; *2001: A SPACE ODYSSEY* (which wasn't even nominated!) to *OLIVER* in 1968; that *ROCKY* beat out four superior contenders (*ALL THE PRESIDENT'S MEN, BOUND FOR GLORY, NETWORK* and *TAXI DRIVER*) in 1976; that the innovative *KOYAANISQATSI* (my dream choice which was never nominated) was bested by the very conventional *TERMS OF ENDEARMENT* in 1983; or that *FORREST GUMP* beat out *PULP FICTION* (where's the outrage?!). Fortunately, there have been times when the Academy did just the right thing: *MUTINY ON THE BOUNTY* 35; *CASABLANCA* 43; *LAWRENCE OF ARABIA* 62; *GODFATHERS 1&2* 72/74; *ANNIE HALL* 77; *THE LAST EMPEROR* 87; and *SILENCE OF THE LAMBS* 91. Such triumphs help us endure the oversights this year of such original works as *FIGHT CLUB* (sound effects editing, big deal); *MAN ON THE MOON; THREE KINGS*; and *EXISTENZ* (these last three, complete shut outs).

As I write this, the awards have yet to be given. No matter what ultimately wins (I'm hoping for *AMERICAN BEAUTY*), in the long run, the films that truly matter will endure, Oscar or no Oscar. The Motion Picture Academy is a wonderful organization that does some real good in the cinema industry. That is its true legacy. Art should never be about getting trophies. As much fun as the Oscars may be, they are, finally, only a small aspect of what the Academy does.

FAMILY FLICKS: MOVIES YOU CAN SHARE WITH YOUR CHILDREN
(May 2000)

With the approach of summer, and the end of school, many parents will be faced with the task of finding something with which to occupy their children's free time. While it is desirable for parents to encourage their kids to explore a variety of non-television pastimes, from reading, to physical recreation, to creative expression, videotape movies are still likely to take up at least a small portion of their time. And as caring parents, it is important that the movies you choose for your children reflect, not only common sense, but also a desire to see your kids learn and grow as individuals.

Along with instilling a sense of values in your kids, the movies you choose should allow for an appreciation of the art of filmmaking and storytelling. By making an effort to share in this experience with them, you can transform the watching of TV into a richly rewarding family event. While *Barney, Blues Clues* and *Sesame Street* may be satisfactory for the little ones, those preteens over six may be harder to please. You may also wish to steer them clear from the coarser material out there that they would, no doubt, watch if they could get away with it. There is nothing sadder than to see parents caving in to the latest trends, regardless of content, or allowing their kids to see inappropriate videos, like R-rated horror films, just so they can plop them down in front of the tube to shut them up. TV should not be used simply as an electronic baby-sitter.

Following is a selection of movies that are not only suitable for kids, but are equally enjoyable, as well, for adults. While we can all decry the lack of wholesome entertainment for children in the media, here is a chance to let them know just how good family movies can be.

* *MICRO COSMOS* (1996)—Directed by Claude Nuridsany & Marie Perennou. For those kids who went crazy for *A BUG'S LIFE* and *ANTZ*, here is a film that gives you the real thing very close up. This European documentary explores life in the bug realm in a way never seen before. Spanning one complete day, we are shown the life and death struggles of a bug-eat-bug world, where butterflies are born, ants toil and an afternoon rainstorm can wreak havoc. At once, alien and familiar, gruesome and magical, the complex lives of these tiny creatures are fascinating and miraculous. This film won a Special Jury Prize at the 1996 Cannes Film Festival. Prepare to be enthralled.

* *THE IRON GIANT* (1999)—Directed by Brad Bird. While Disney has long dominated the feature animation field, and rightly so, in the last decade several other studios have entered this arena with varying results. Recently, Warner Brothers established a feature animation division at its studio, and hit a home run with this sensitive and exciting adventure story. Set in the cold war chaos of Russia's Sputnik success, this film offers more than just the chance to teach baby boomer history to your kids. The story centers on Hogarth Hughes, (enthusiastically voiced by Eli Marienthal) a lonely, fatherless boy, desperate for friendship. His mom (voiced by Jennifer Aniston) waitresses to make ends meet, which means she can't always be there for him. Into this loving, but fractured family arrives The Iron Giant, a 50 foot tall mechanical robot from outer space! A large dent in the metal man's noggin prevents him from remembering his true purpose, which allows Hogarth to step in and befriend him. The two "outsiders" form an uneasy alliance with hip, beatnik artist, Dean, (voiced nicely by Harry Connick Jr.). But, a visitor this large can't stay invisible forever, and soon the army is hot on his trail. The clash of Commie xenophobia and heartfelt empathy allows for a very textured examination of intolerance vs. acceptance, the nature of bigotry, and the healing power of self-sacrifice. The look of the robot is wonderfully realized in a retro-fifties style, and his CGI (computer graphic imaging) animation is fluid and dynamic. To fully appreciate the loving care that went into the look of this film, make sure you get the widescreen version, which preserves the Panavision framing of the original movie.

* *THE SECRET GARDEN* (1993)—Directed by Agnieszka Holland. Though there have been several film versions of the classic Frances Hodgson Burnett children's story, not to mention a successful stage rendition, this 1993 production is far and away the best. From its opening sequence in bright, hot India, to the arrival at the dark and gloomy Gothic mansion, to the vine covered walls of the garden, itself, the movie fairly drips with atmospheric production design. But cool sets, alone, aren't enough to make a classic, and *THE SECRET GARDEN*'s real secret is the stunning performances from its three child stars. As the orphaned Mary, 10 year old Kate Maberly uses her expressive eyes and open face to reveal the pain and longing this child feels to reconnect with her family. Heydon Prowse and Andrew Knott are equally fine as Mary's sickly cousin, Colin, and the groundskeeper boy, Dickon, who become her friends and allies. When they gain access to a long neglected garden, their efforts at returning it to life are mirrored in the healing of old family wounds. Adult actors Maggie Smith, as the strict housekeeper, Mrs. Medlock, and John Lynch, as the brooding and melancholy lord of the manor, are also quite good. Director Holland has a fine eye for composition and staging, and she obviously has a knack for working with children. Finally, the music score by Zbigniew Preisner is heartbreakingly

beautiful. You are not likely to find a classier or better made children's film, which is also equally appealing to adults, than this one.

* *THE INDIAN IN THE CUPBOARD* (1995)—This remarkable movie, based on the novel by Lynne Reid Banks, was written by Melissa Mathison (the writer of E.T., who just also happens to be Mrs. Harrison Ford) and directed by Frank Oz (who just also happens to be Yoda and Miss Piggy!). The story concerns a young boy named Omri (appealingly played by Hal Scardino, blessed with a wonderfully atypical movie face) who receives a most unusual birthday gift from his older brother, a large wooden cupboard in which to keep his toys. Omri places a small Indian figure inside the cabinet and, much to his surprise when he opens it the next morning, the toy Indian has magically become a tiny, living, real human being, an Indian brave who calls himself Little Bear (a charismatic performance by native American rap artist, Litefoot). The relationship between Omri and Little Bear is at the heart of this very beguiling movie. However, their friendship is not without problems, and Omri learns many hard lessons about honesty, responsibility, and respect for other people. At film's end, Omri has grown and matured as a result of his friendship with Little Bear. If this movie teaches us anything, it is that our experiences can, and should, make us better human beings.

There are many other great films out there for you and your family to enjoy, films that don't always have the high profile of the Disney classics, yet are every bit as good. They include: *THE SECRET OF ROAN INISH, THE ROCKETEER, SHILO, A LITTLE PRINCESS, EVER AFTER, JAMES AND THE GIANT PEACH, ANASTASIA, THE PRINCESS BRIDE, CHITTY CHITTY BANG BANG, THE BLACK STALLION, THE NEVERENDING STORY, BLACK BEAUTY,* and *THE BEAR*, to name only a few. These are all films you can be proud to watch with your children. Rather than the usual mindless mayhem and double entendre humor that passes for most of kid's films these days, these movies serve a deeper purpose: they stimulate the creative, the thoughtful, even the intellectual side of your children. And they do it while they entertain.

IN THE GOOD OLD SUMMERTIME: FINDING THE GEMS IN THIS SUMMER'S MOVIES

(June 2000)

Summer's almost here and that means another summer movie season is upon us. And with each passing year, the "season" seems to expand further and further into the spring. The submarine thriller, *U-571*, opened at the end of April, now making that month fair game as a summer movie slot. Like it or not, with so many films set for release, more weekends are needed for these movies to have a chance for success.

The month of May has already seen its first smash hit with *GLADIATOR*, and its first major bomb, *BATTLEFIELD EARTH*. Before the summer is over, there will be many other titles finding their place in one or the other category. Which films will be hits and which ones won't aren't always obvious. This year promises a bizarre variety of films, so predicting the winners won't be any easier. Nevertheless, whatever your tastes, there's bound to be something out there for everyone.

For my part, I've decided to pick one movie from each month that has sparked my excitement and curiosity. While most of us will see many films this summer, I'm sure that only a very few will have the power to stay with us to the end of the year. And, if we're really lucky, there may be one or two that will stay with us even longer, perhaps for years to come.

*JUNE: The summer gets off to a real bang with the June releases. There's the animated sci-fi flick *TITAN A.E.*, Jim Carrey in *ME, MYSELF AND IRENE*, Samuel L. Jackson in *SHAFT*, Mel Gibson in *THE PATRIOT*, George Clooney in *THE PERFECT STORM*, and most bizarre of all, Robert DeNiro as "Fearless Leader" in the live action/animated *ADVENTURES OF ROCKY AND BULLWINKLE*. However, my personal choice for this month is the equally bizarre, and potentially more charming, *CHICKEN RUN*, the clay animation feature film debut from the Aardman Animation team of Peter Lord and Nick Park (creators of the *WALLACE & GROMIT* shorts). *CHICKEN RUN* envisions a small British poultry farm as if it were Stalag 17. The harried hens decide to stage a daring departure a la *THE GREAT ESCAPE*, with the help of an American rooster, voiced by Mel Gibson. Park's and Lord's previous work has shown a great flair for comedic timing, story plotting, clever gadgetry, and witty production design. Given the chance to spread their wings with a feature, these offbeat British animators are sure to rise to the occasion.

*JULY: The first half of July will be dominated by several end-of-June titles, capitalizing on July 4th business. The second half of the month will see Harrison Ford in *WHAT LIES BENEATH*, Eddie Murphy in *NUTTY PROFESSOR II*, the comic book inspired *X-MEN*, and the even more comic documentary *THE EYES OF TAMMY FAYE*, she of the running mascara (lots of nightmare material, there!). However, for pure popcorn entertainment, I'm pulling for *THE HOLLOW MAN*, a sci-fi thriller about invisibility by the intense Dutch master, Paul Verhoeven (*ROBOCOP, TOTAL RECALL, BASIC INSTINCT, STARSHIP TROOPERS*). *THE HOLLOW MAN* stars Kevin Bacon and Elizabeth Shue, who play a couple of scientists experimenting with invisibility. Well, we all know what happens, but the real fun of a movie like this is all the cool "invisible" effects, and Verhoeven has evidently set the bar very high. My favorite effect from the trailer shows Bacon's shimmering outline as he stands, invisible, under a gushing sprinkler. Cool!

*AUGUST: This month offers us yin and yang. There's the macho *SPACE COWBOYS*, with Clint Eastwood, and the feminist indie, *GIRLFIGHT*. We have hunky Matt Damon in *THE LEGEND OF BAGGER VANCE*, and gorgeous Jennifer Lopez in *THE CELL*. Brendan Fraser and Elizabeth Hurley star in a remake of *BEDAZZLED*, and the notorious John Waters is back with *CECIL B. DEMENTED* with Stephen Dorf and Melanie Griffith, plus Waters' regulars Ricki Lake and Patricia Hearst. Though these may seem to be tough competition for most memorable film of the month, I'm going with the character driven, future thriller, *IMPOSTER*, which began life as a 40 minute short (part of a proposed trilogy). During the shoot, however, studio heads at Miramax were so impressed with the footage, the short was quickly upgraded to a feature. Whether this decision will prove successful remains to be seen, but with a first rate character cast that includes Gary Sinise (*APOLLO 13*), Vincent D'Onofrio (*THE WHOLE WIDE WORLD*), Madeleine Stowe (*THE LAST OF THE MOHICANS*) and Mikhi Phifer (*CLOCKERS*), the acting promises to be as much of a draw as the futuristic storyline. I'm just crazy about seeing Sinise and D'Onofrio act together.

Since I've yet to see any of the films I've talked about, it's anyone's guess whether or not they're any good. With so many choices, going to a summer movie is always a gamble. There's nothing quite so disquieting as spending good money on a highly hyped movie, only to be totally disappointed by the actual film. Fortunately, the reverse is also true: there is nothing more exhilarating, or satisfying, than seeing a great movie, especially one that has had little or no pre-release attention. It's like making a great discovery or finding a rare treasure. You, as a moviegoer, get to take credit for the pleasure derived from the movie you chose to see. You get to participate in your own happiness. Whenever you get the chance to do that, it's a wonderful feeling.

THE CELLULOID HOTEL
(September 2000)

Easton, currently, is still in the midst of an economic and artistic renaissance, as a multitude of businesses, creative or otherwise, are investing in our town's future. The most recent development to make headlines was the purchase of the decade dormant Hotel Easton by local businessman Peter Koehler and his New York partner Theodore Kheel. The successful team, who have a track record for renovating properties, including The National Building at 4th and Northampton St. which houses the Irregular offices, have promised to take the late 1920's landmark and "restore it to its ancient glory".

Such romanticism about hotels stems, I think, from the magical, larger than life aspect of their architecture and decor: the ornate ballrooms, lobbies and restaurants; the endless hallways with their rows of doors; even the large work kitchens seem special. It is not surprising, then, that throughout the history of cinema, hotels have figured many times as the prime location for movies.

Some films, like *PLAZA SUITE, HOTEL, SAME TIME NEXT YEAR* and *FOUR ROOMS*, used the hotel setting simply as a location or backdrop for the action and story. A few films, however, allowed the hotel, itself, to literally become a character within the film. As we await the reincarnation of Hotel Easton, and the splendor it promises, let's take a look at a few movies where the hotel took center stage.

* *GRAND HOTEL* (1932)—This best picture Oscar winning film featured a star studded cast that included Greta Garbo, John & Lionel Barrymore, Joan Crawford, Wallace Beery, and Jean Hersholt. The hustle and bustle of the famed German establishment is echoed by the dramas of the many characters who reside there. The Grand's decor features an astonishing circular lobby, with a surrounding spiral balcony that rises to vertiginous heights. At the lobby's center is a beautiful, ringed front desk, where much of the film's early story unfolds. The distinctive, identical looking doors of each room symbolically tie together the various tenants, and their interwoven lives, in a visual display of designed uniformity. The transient nature of hotel residency even allowed for an existential observation at film's end by the long term resident doctor, who muses about people coming and going and nothing ever happening. Ironically, the previous two hours completely contradict that statement. Many things happen at the Grand Hotel, and many lives are changed as a result. But life does go on, even as the film comes to its end. As the characters leave the hotel to get on with their own lives, we are left to wonder who will next come to stay at the Grand. Of special

interest to film buffs is the chance to hear Garbo uttering her famous "I want to be alone" line. Twice!

* *LAST YEAR AT MARIENBAD* (1961)—Made by the brilliant director Alain Resnais from text by Alain Robbe-Grillet, this strange excursion into French existentialism is gorgeous to look at, yet its plot defies any attempt at rational interpretation. The story takes place in a setting that's not just a hotel, but an incredibly ornate chateau. A man (Giorgio Albertazzi) meets a woman (Delphine Seyrig) at the chateau and insists that they've met before, had an affair, in fact, the previous year "...at Frederiksbad, or perhaps at Marienbad". The woman claims to have no memory of this and tells the man he is mistaken. The man continues to reminisce in minute detail about their supposed encounter as the film juxtaposes the concepts of past and present, memory and reality, fact and fiction. Another man (Sacha Pitoeff), who wanders in and out of the story, and may be the woman's husband, raises the creep factor considerably with his gaunt, brooding persona. The visuals in this film are quite simply stunning, as the camera prowls around every nook and cranny of the opulent mansion: "a universe of marble and stucco, columns, moldings, gilded ceilings..." according to the author. Ironically, it is a universe which, though fully occupied, never seems to be really alive; people sometimes stand immobile like statues, while statues seem to be more evocative than the people. Perhaps the inhabitants are all ghosts; or maybe this is actually heaven; or even hell. It doesn't really matter. While the characters ponder and fret over the reality of their thoughts, their past, and their very existence, only the lavish surroundings seem to have any substance or permanence. Controversial at its release, the film was both hailed for its brilliant vision and reviled for its obtuse sense and deliberate obscurity. Where your own opinion falls will depend very much on your patience and willingness to explore new forms of cinematic expression. The funereal organ score by Francis Seyrig is especially effective in maintaining an otherworldly mood.

* *THE SHINING* (1980)—This is, without a doubt, the ultimate "hotel" movie. The story, for those who don't know, concerns a failed writer named Jack Torrance (a very eccentric performance by Jack Nicholson), his wife Wendy (Shelley Duvall), and their young son Danny (Danny Lloyd), who become caretakers at a large Colorado hotel, named the Overlook, during the closed winter season. Virtually cut off from the outside world, Jack begins to succumb to the ghostly incarnations, from the hotel's ignominious past that preys on his own insecurities. Danny has the gift of "shining", and is able to see both past and future events, including the horrific deaths of two little girls whose spectres now haunt the Overlook. Director Stanley Kubrick went to great lengths to design an impressive and labyrinthine hotel set containing a seemingly endless variety of

corridors, a grandiose ballroom, and a cavernous lounge. The production design went a step further to ensure that audiences would react with unease: in some rooms carpet and wallpaper designs were a riot of clashing colors and patterns; in the ballroom, the gold walls added an ominously reflective glow; one bathroom was a startling pure blood red; another (complete with a mischievous ghost) was cool green. Kubrick employed endless tracking shots throughout the hotel interior, using the recently developed Steadicam, a hand held camera harness strapped to an operator that permits smooth camera moves without a dolly or crane. It is especially effective on stairs and over uneven terrain where conventional equipment can't be used. Kubrick even hired Steadicam inventor Garrett Brown to operate the device for his film. One early stand out sequence using the Steadicam has the camera , gliding mere inches above the floor, follow young Danny as he tools around the hotel interior on his Big Wheel. The idea of a single family all alone inside a giant hotel was obviously too tempting for Kubrick to resist. Though he took some liberties with author Stephen King's original book, the movie version has gone on to become a cult classic. It is now regarded as one of the most visually stylish films of all time, due in no small part to the design of its centerpiece attraction, the Overlook Hotel.

Once the Hotel Easton has been reopened, it will no doubt become a vital part of our city's tourism economy. Unlike any other establishment in town, the hotel will be able to host lavish ballroom soirees and upscale business conventions. As in days past, Easton will again have a class act hotel of which everyone can be proud. And, with the growing interest in Easton as a film production community and location site, there's even a chance that, someday, Hotel Easton's own distinct visage, may find its way to the silver screen in a major motion picture. I just hope it gets to play the main character.

SILENT SCREAMS: HORROR FILMS BEFORE "THE TALKIES"
(October 2000)

When it comes to movies, no doubt about it, times have changed. And this is most evident in the evolution of the horror film. However, I'm not talking about the increasing use of gore and violence, though that has had a big impact on the genre, as well. More specifically, I'm talking about when films made the leap from silent to sound. Now, while there have been many extremely good horror films made during the sound era, I believe something was irrevocably lost in cinema when the motion picture gained a voice.

The dawn of movies and the dawn of horror movies came hand in hand. One of the very first narrative films (all sixteen minutes of it) was Thomas Edison's 1910 version of Mary Shelley's novel *FRANKENSTEIN*. Though crude by today's standards, the film had its frightening moments, as well as a very striking monster, the image of which can still haunt one's nightmares.

A decade later, the silent horror movie would be in full flower with the release of *THE CABINET OF DR. CALIGARI* (1919) and *THE GOLEM* (1920). The former was one of the most stunning examples of German Expressionist filmmaking, by director Robert Wiene, adopting an experimental visual style that included painted shadows and off-kilter architecture (there's not a door or window to be found that adheres to right angle geometry). This look adds much to the tale of a mad doctor who runs an insane asylum. *THE GOLEM*, directed by Carl Boese, while dated, still has the power to frighten us through its use of extreme camera angles. The story concerns a clay statue brought to life by a Rabbi to defend his community. The immobile features of the Golem's face, suggesting his inability to be reasoned with, are far scarier to me than any blood-squirting animatronic head seen in today's fare.

What these films share is an overwhelming sense of dread; of things outside our ability to contain, and therefore beyond our control. These movies were frightening for what they implied, rather than what they showed. These films worked on our imaginations to scare us and, at least for a time, they succeeded.

The pinnacle of silent movie horror can be summed up by a pair of films from the first half of the 1920's. In 1922 Germany's master filmmaker, F.W. Murnau, created an indelible horror icon with his rat-like vampire, in *NOSFERATU*. Like much of German Expressionism, there is a heavy reliance on the use of shadows and darkness to convey mood. Though Bela Lugosi's *DRACULA*, a decade later, would set the look and style of vampires for years to come, Max Schreck's rodent-faced monstrosity made the Count fearsome both inside and out. The other Grand masterpiece was Rupert Julian's 1925 opus, *THE PHANTOM OF THE OPERA*, starring Lon Chaney, Sr. in his unsurpassed interpretation of Erik, The Phantom. Chaney was a consummate actor who designed all his own make-ups for the characters he played, everything from the Hunchback to a multiple amputee; a shark-toothed vampire to an ape-man. The Phantom, however, is clearly his crowning achievement, a sort of "living skull" face with upturned nose and pulled-back grimace. Chaney's prodigious abilities with make-up and contortion led him to be known as "the man of a thousand faces". But, what makes *PHANTOM* truly compelling is the tragedy of a man whose soul is as disfigured as his face. What makes it frightening is the thought of such a creature freely running amok throughout the cavernous opera house, an anonymous ghost who haunts every room, but is always just out of reach.

As a society, we are different, now, than when "the silents" ruled the cinema. We can no longer be frightened by such indirect means as a shadow on a wall. Suggestion doesn't scare us anymore. In the 1970's and '80's we were inundated with the gross-out carnage of "Jason" and "Freddie"; and then in the '90's we had the "been there, done that, too jaded and knowing to be scared" hipness of the *SCREAM* franchise. Fortunately, there have been a few recent exceptions: *THE BLAIR WITCH PROJECT* re-acquainted us with the fear of the unseen, while *THE SIXTH SENSE* showed us that a whisper could be as effective as a scream.

While the horror genre has had its ups and downs, its peaks and valleys, I don't think it will ever become obsolete. Getting scared will always be cool, and we'll take it any way we can. Even *THE EXORCIST* has been re-released in theatres, with extra footage. Ironically, while it is known more for its loud soundtrack and gross-out imagery, director William Friedkin borrowed many concepts and tricks from the silent films to make his modern day horror classic (the poster art, itself, is a fine example of German Expressionist lighting and composition).

I know we'll never be able to return to the days when the quaint notions of horror in a silent movie can scare us. We just can't be frightened that way, now. But, nostalgia has its place, too. Wouldn't it be great, this Halloween, to have a "Silent Movie Party", where all the guests have to come dressed up as characters from one of those great old films? And then, to cap off the evening, everyone could sit together and watch an honest to goodness silent horror film, with an appropriate music score and the lights turned down. Imagine the fun of seeing a movie that frightened your grandparents (or even your great grandparents). Imagine seeing a movie where the only screams you hear are the ones you make yourself.

IT'S BEGINNING TO LOOK A LOT LIKE DVD

(December 2000)

The home video market is currently undergoing a revolution that may well prove to be as radical a shift as when we went from renting movies to buying them, and may be as big a deal as the VCR itself. I am talking about the growing proliferation of the Digital Video Disc, or the DVD, as it is more commonly known. Currently, it is the fastest growing technology in the world.

The arrival of home video, in the late 1970's, where you could rent a complete movie and watch it in the comfort of your own home, revolutionized how we watch and relate to movies. Back before the days of videotape, most of us could see movies only in a theatre, and on TV, where you had to endure commercial interruptions along with cuts and trims to the film to accommodate time slots and broadcast standards regarding content. So, it's not surprising that videotape movies caught on, and as prices dropped for VCR's, they became as commonplace in the home as a TV set.

An industry was born. Movie rental places sprung up like weeds, first as Mom & Pop businesses, then as corporate franchises. Soon there were thousands of movie titles from which to select as, one by one, the various studios came on board when they realized they had a ready cash cow residing in their film vaults. Some individuals even purchased movies on tape, but with an initial retail price tag in the $80-$90.00 range, most people opted for renting only. (Back in those days, blank tapes went for $20.00 a pop.)

With the growing acceptance of movie rentals, it was inevitable that a buying market would eventually emerge. Some far-sighted studios began releasing former rental titles at $30.00, and found a public that was eager to buy. Ironically, the genres that saw the greatest immediate acceptance of this practice were children's films and adult porn! But, the die had been cast. Soon other studios fell in line and it became the norm for movies to be priced to sell after they had their run in the rental market. The standard rental window today is about six to eight months. There are the rare exceptions that go directly to sell-through, bypassing the $100.00 rental price. These include most children's films and the occasional PG and PG-13 blockbuster.

As a result of this cinematic bombardment over the last twenty years from the home video industry, the populace has grown more savvy in their knowledge about films and film structure. It may even be the reason that some younger people, raised in a videoized world, have grown disenchanted with conventional storytelling and plots (aka: good movies with depth), and have embraced films that stress form over content, style over substance. While there have been some very good movies of this type (*PULP FICTION, PLEASANTVILLE, DARK CITY*), it has also led to an abysmal variety of cheap, sensationalistic and moronic fare (this may explain Adam Sandler's career). Fortunately, for every *RAMBO* there's also been a *FARGO*.

Just as the audience has become more media savvy, the format, itself has had to grow and change as well. And it looks like DVD will eventually supplant pre-recorded tape as the format of choice. With its sharper picture, cleaner sound, supplemental features, and its random-access menu capabilities, DVD makes your old videotapes look like stone knives by comparison.

Perhaps the most far-reaching supplement on DVDs (and practically becoming a standard issue feature) is the audio commentary track. First developed for the now defunct laserdisc (the connoisseur's format of the '90s) this secondary track features the film's director (and sometimes others, such as the writer, cinematographer, and the actors) in a running commentary as you watch the film. It's almost as if they were on the couch with you as they explain various aspects of the movie. The commentary is generally scene specific to what you are seeing, but there is the occasional tangent about filmmaking in general. These tracks can be quite enjoyable and entertaining (even if you're not a film geek) as well as highly informative about the filmmaking process. They cover everything from casting and location decisions to on-set choices that come up at the last minute. It's a real inside look at the industry, and these commentaries have become very popular with cineastes who have a driving passion for the minutiae of moviemaking.

The bottom line is that DVDs are providing a far richer movie-viewing experience for people who take their movie watching seriously. In addition to audio commentary, this latest arrival on the format front offers such extras as multi-lingual voice tracks, theatrical trailers from the movie, a making of featurette, cast & crew interviews, isolated music score track, still frame gallery of production shots, and even games and extras that can be accessed by the DVD-ROM drive on your computer. As the technology continues to grow, DVDs will grow right along with it, offering viewers an ever increasing bounty of riches.

DVDs have been with us now for a couple of years, but it was only in this last year (2000) that they really took hold. Players are now readily available for under $200.00, and DVDs, themselves, cost only slightly more than tapes. For all the extras you get, it's well worth the added expense. As we prepare to truly enter the next millennium (2001), DVDs promise to become the preferred format for the discerning cineaste. I predict there will be many, many DVD players under the tree this holiday year. Yes, in the world of home video, it's beginning to look a lot like DVD, and that is something about which movie lovers, everywhere, can be happy.

WELCOME ... TO "THE FUTURE": THE COMING OF DIGITAL CINEMA
(February 2001)

Now that we are finally and truly in the 21st Century, it seems like the right time to speculate on what the future of cinema may become. With all the technical advances that have occurred over the years, it is a bit of a shock to realize that the way movies are made and projected today has changed very little from nearly a century ago. The pre- eminent art form of the last hundred years is long overdue for an upgrade.

While film stocks have become more sensitive, allowing a wider range of lighting options, and sound design and special effects have become way more sophisticated, the bottom line is that movies have remained in an arrested development regarding how they're shown. It is still a strip of celluloid with sprocket holes running down the sides that feed through a mechanical sprocketed wheel. The technology that existed in 1912, which showed moviegoers newsreel footage of the Titanic, is essentially the same technology as that used to show James Cameron's 1997 blockbuster movie *TITANIC*.

As we all know, computer technology has become a large part of our everyday lives, its presence increasingly apparent in everything that we do. And, just as the industrial revolution of the 19th Century gave way to the electronic revolution of the 20th, so too will that make way for the "digital age" of the 21st. And this will impact the film industry in a major way. How movies are made and shown is about to change in a manner that is as radically new as was the introduction of sound to silent cinema. Movies on celluloid are about to go the way of the dinosaur. Within ten years there will probably be no more "film" as we know it, as movies are shot and projected digitally.

In point of fact, portions of many movies are already being shot without film, through the use of digital cameras. Many special effects shots are now routinely being created digitally. Instead of images being recorded on film emulsion, they are captured and stored as digital information (1's and 0's) which a computer can then render pictorially as accurately as any traditional camera. The new *STAR WARS* movies are being shot with digital cameras by George Lucas, who has been in the forefront of digital imagery for quite some time. Both *TOY STORY* movies and *A BUG'S LIFE*, made for Disney by Pixar, were created entirely in the digital realm and then transferred to film for theatrical release.

Once movie theatres change over to digital projection, movies will no longer have to be shown on film. Instead, the movie will be contained on a disc, similar to a DVD. The advantages of this system are readily apparent: no film breaks or meltdowns, no jumpy picture, and no muffled sound. While the initial cost to convert theatres will be enormous, the savings at the back end will be even greater. Just how long it takes theatres to embrace this new technology depends on just how forward thinking the film industry is willing to be.

Currently, to make a single print of a feature length movie costs several thousand dollars. Multiply this by 2,000, which is the average number of release prints made for a major mainstream movie, and we're talking about a pretty hefty sum, and that's just for prints. Add to that the cost of trucking all of these prints to all of the movie houses, and you get an idea of the monetary expenditure involved, week in and week out, all year long. The studios could pool their resources and set up a program that would help to fund the conversion of movie houses to digital projection. Both the studios and the theatre chains would benefit as a result, not to mention all of us patrons who just want to see some movies without worrying whether the picture is going to be in frame on the screen.

Already, digital technology has taken over the domain of film editing. Today, most movies are edited digitally (the film is converted to digital information that can be manipulated in a variety of ways without the cut-and-tape mess of old fashioned editing). Once the final edit is completed on the computer, the actual film negative is conformed to the digital edit, and prints are made in the usual way. This method allows for much more experimentation in the editing process, without increasing the man-hours of work that would be necessary in conventional editing.

Every facet of filmmaking has been influenced and/or overtaken by digital technology. Shooting, editing, cinematography, special effects, sound design, and music scoring have all succumbed to this latest innovation. The last great remaining hurdle is the presentation of the final product, itself. Most entrenched industries in this country have been slow to change with the times and "modernize". One only has to look at the auto and steel industries to see what that sort of reluctance has wrought. It is time, then, for the motion picture industry to embrace digital projection as an inevitability, and thus, close the circle.

As we begin our journey into the 21st Century, so begins the era of digital cinema. Like its celluloid predecessor a hundred years earlier, this new medium holds the same promise of magic and wonder. And for those of us who have a passion for movies and the art of cinema, being able to witness the inception of this new era allows us the chance to imagine what it must have been like for the original pioneers of the movie industry, or any new art form for that matter. How great a feeling is that?

WHAT'S UP, DOC? APPRECIATING THE DOCUMENTARY FILM

(March 2001)

With the Academy Awards season upon us, many film buffs have taken to making predictions about which nominated movies will get the golden Oscar. And, of course, we all have opinions on just who or what should win for best picture, director, actor and actress. However, one category that most of us know nothing about is the one for best documentary. Not only are the nominees unfamiliar to us, the odds are we will never have the opportunity to see them, due to limited distribution in theatres and almost universal indifference from the home video market. On rare occasions, an Oscar winner may find its way to a theatrical release or a high profile video campaign, but that is usually the exception. Even rarer is the word-of-mouth success of Michael Moore's Flint, Michigan expose *ROGER & ME* which wasn't even nominated!

The first time the Academy honored a "non-fiction" film was in 1936, when it gave a special award to *THE MARCH OF TIME*. It wasn't until 1942, however, that categories for documentaries were officially created. *CHURCHILL'S ISLAND*, released in 1941, was the first to win a regulation Oscar. Since documentaries rarely have wide, theatrical releases, films eligible for Academy consideration are entered by their producers and are screened by a Documentary Awards Committee which then picks the nominees. Voting is restricted to Academy members who've seen all the nominated films. This process is still adhered to today.

Over the years, there have been complaints about how these films are chosen, and there have been accusations of politics and favoritism. Most surprising, there seems to be a feeling among the Committee that documentaries that do achieve a measure of success should be passed over in favor of those that remain obscure. Well, while we're trying to figure out the merits of the current crop of Oscar nominated documentaries, let's take a look back at some past titles, Oscared and otherwise, that left their mark. These are the ones that have created a stir, pushed the envelope, and above all, made a difference.

NANOOK OF THE NORTH (1922)—Filmmaker Robert Flaherty took his crew to the North Pole, well not exactly, but he did brave northern climes to live with an Eskimo family to record their day-to-day existence. Like much of Flaherty's work (he practically invented the documentary) this film is visually alive with amazing location images and examples of strange local customs that intrigued movie goers of the day. Some scenes were purportedly "staged", such as Nanook wrestling with the unseen, "under the ice" catch on the end of his fishing line. His melodramatic struggle appears designed more for the camera than out of actual necessity. Still, it's all very thrilling, and provides a glimpse into a world that is, even today, unfamiliar to most of us.

TRIUMPH OF THE WILL (1935)—Leni Riefenstahl made some of the most powerful documentary films ever. Unfortunately, they were made as propaganda for Adolph Hitler and his Nazi regime. Leni claimed she was only pursuing her art and was unaware of Hitler's intentions. Others asserted she would have had to have been blind not to know, and that she chose not to see so she could further her career. Regardless, the fact remains that she was a born filmmaker who knew where to put the camera and how to edit for maximum impact. This film, considered her best, chronicles Hitler's 1934 Nuremberg rallies. As a chilling snapshot of history, it is both absorbing and frightening. The perfect companion to this film is 1993's *THE WONDERFUL, HORRIBLE LIFE OF LENI RIEFENSTAHL*, which shows the still vibrant and active Leni still denying she knew what Hitler was up to.

WOODSTOCK (1970)—The documentary film grew up with Michael Wadleigh's three hour extravaganza of the ultimate outdoor hippie rock festival. Employing multiple split screens and stereo sound recording, Wadleigh throws you headlong into the trip of a lifetime. It perfectly captures the "it's-all-happening-at-once" euphoria of a public event with half a million people. The line-up of performers is a who's who of 60's rock icons, from Jimi Hendrix and Janis Joplin, to still active artists Santana, The Who and Arlo Guthrie. To fully appreciate the visual splendor of this mammoth event, be sure to see the widescreen version.

KOYAANISQATSI (1983)—Godfrey Reggio reinvented the documentary format with this hypnotic tone poem to modern civilization. The title, taken from the Hopi Indian language, means "life out of balance." Using over cranked and under cranked cameras, Reggio's film wordlessly explores images from nature juxtaposed with society's encroachment upon these pristine landscapes. As we move into the city, speeded up images are shown with naturalistically panning camera moves, lending an otherworldly realism to the scenes. Philip Glass's repetitive and, at times, frenetic score perfectly complements the visuals. The small screen robs much of the imagery of its power, but it's still a stunning piece of filmmaking bravura.

* *THE THIN BLUE LINE* (1988)—The documentary was reinvented yet again, this time by Errol Morris, in this film about a convict who may have been

wrongfully imprisoned for the murder of a police officer. Morris relies heavily on staged reenactments, multiple versions of events (a la *RASHOMON*), and close-ups of seemingly unimportant details, all of which create a mise-en-scene that is a radical departure from the documentary format. Philip Glass, again, provides a memorable score.

HOOP DREAMS (1994)—This documentary transcends the genre and moves us straight into the realm of drama. Steve James follows two Chicago inner city boys for four years as they pursue the dream of basketball stardom. At once a scathing commentary on society and a tribute to the strength of family, this everyman epic is filled with enough twists and turns to keep you guessing about its outcome. Best of all, you don't have to like basketball (or any sport) to enjoy this fresh and unpredictable film.

There are many other documentary films that are worth checking out, several of which have been made by some of the best feature film directors around. Martin Scorsese's *THE LAST WALTZ* (1978), chronicles the Thanksgiving 1976 farewell concert by The Band. Jonathan Demme's classic *STOP MAKING SENSE* (1984) has been hailed as the best concert movie ever. Michael Apted has invested thirty five years of his life, so far, in an on-going, ever-expanding documentary chronicling the lives of a number of people at ages 7, 14, 21, 28, 35 and 42. Reissued every seven years, the current version, *42 UP* (1999) is an unprecedented look at humanity's journey through life. And German director Wim Wenders' *BUENA VISTA SOCIAL CLUB* (1999) was a compassionate love sonnet about the lives of a group of Cuban musicians and performers, some in their 70's and 80's, who re-established their former glory in a set of concerts.

At a time when so many of us are complaining about how bad most movies are, maybe it's time we take a look at this often overlooked segment of the movie industry. The next time you hear about a film that is playing at the theatre, or you see it on a shelf at the rental store, don't arbitrarily pass it up just because it's a documentary. Who knows, it just might be the best film you'll see all year.

SHAKESPEARE IN THE DARK:
THE BARD ON SCREEN
(April 2001)

In Elizabethan England, the play was the thing, or so Shakespeare's Hamlet told us. And, indeed it was. While actors and playwrights were held in very little esteem (an actor was only one step above a prostitute) the fact remains that the populace at large flocked to the theatre. King and peasant, nobleman and servant, rich and poor, regardless of their standing, the works of Thomas Heywood, John Milton, Christopher Marlowe, Thomas Dekker, Ben Jonson and, of course, William Shakespeare provided entertainment for them all.

Theatre, today, is still alive and well, but for the most part has been supplanted by the movies as the dominant form of mass entertainment. Some contemporary playwrights, such as Tom Stoppard, Harold Pinter, David Mamet, Edward Albee, Sam Shepard, David Rabe and Peter Shaffer, have even seen their work translated to the screen with varying degrees of success. It is somewhat humbling, then, to realize that of all the scribes whose plays have found their way to the cinema, the one who's been the most successful has been the nearly four centuries dead "Bard of Avon" himself, William Shakespeare.

Even before cinema gained its voice, filmmakers turned to Shakespeare to entertain the masses. There was a *TAMING OF THE SHREW* in 1908 followed by *AS YOU LIKE IT* in 1912, *HAMLET* in 1913, *JULIUS CAESAR* IN 1914 and *MACBETH* in 1916. That same year saw the first *ROMEO & JULIET*. There was an *OTHELLO* in 1922 and a second *SHREW* in 1929, embarrassingly bad, but notable for the only screen pairing of real life star couple Douglas Fairbanks and Mary Pickford. This film also contained the infamous credit "by William Shakespeare with additional dialog by Sam Taylor".

A pair of movies from the 1930s helped raise the profile of Old Will on film. *A MIDSUMMER NIGHT'S DREAM* in 1935 starred James Cagney as Bottom and Mickey Rooney as Puck, while George Cukor's 1936 version of *ROMEO & JULIET*, starring Leslie Howard and Norma Shearer, was quite good even if the two stars were a tad too old. As talkies came to dominate the cinema, several theatre-trained actors took a stab at bringing The Bard to the screen, most notably John Gielgud, Lawrence Olivier and Orson Welles.

In 1936 Olivier jumped in as Orlando in *AS YOU LIKE IT*. He then moved on to directing, as well as acting, in several first rate adaptations, including *HENRY V* in 1945, *HAMLET* in 1948, *RICHARD III* in 1955 and *OTHELLO* in 1965. Orson Welles also tried his hand at *OTHELLO*, in 1952, but he first tackled The Bard for the screen with *MACBETH* in 1948. His crowning achievement, without question, was 1966's *CHIMES AT MIDNIGHT*, cobbled together from scenes in five of Shakespeare's plays that dealt with the character Falstaff. Though John Gielgud, the great actor and theatre director, never directed Shakespeare for the movies, he did lend his considerable talents as a performer in the 1954 version of *ROMEO & JULIET* (where he introduced the play). He later worked with Olivier in *RICHARD III,* Welles in *CHIMES* and was in both versions of *JULIUS CAESAR,* in 1953 with Marlon Brando and 1970 with Charlton Heston.

The 1960s proved to be a fruitful decade for Shakespeare. Two versions of *MIDSUMMER* appeared in 1966 and 1968, and Tony Richardson directed a stark and moody *HAMLET* in 1969 starring Nicol Williamson and Anthony Hopkins. However, most notable at the time was Italian director Franco Zefferelli's one-two punch of 1967's *TAMING OF THE SHREW* with Richard Burton and Elizabeth Taylor, and 1968's *ROMEO & JULIET,* considered by many to be the definitive screen version, and blessed with stellar performances by its age-appropriate leads Leonard Whiting (17) and Olivia Hussey (15).This film also featured upcoming British actor Michael York as Tybalt, a scene stealing turn by John McEnery as Mercutio, narration by Lawrence Olivier, and an unforgettable, heartrending score by Nino Rota. After these successes, Zefferelli abandoned The Bard, on screen, for twenty years, but returned full force in 1990 with a powerful, yet sombre adaptation of *HAMLET* starring Mel Gibson, Glenn Close, Alan Bates, Ian Holm and Helena Bonham Carter.

Through much of the 1970s and 1980s, Shakespeare seemed to take a backseat as gritty urban dramas and science fiction dominated the movies; the sole exception was Paul Mazursky's modern day loose interpretation of *THE TEMPEST* in 1982. Starring John Cassavettes, Raul Julia and Molly Ringwold, it sank without a trace. However, in 1989, The Bard was back with a vengeance, thanks to a brash and talented young actor and director named Kenneth Branagh. His first film foray was *HENRY V,* which was bold, exhilaratingly, and had the critics toasting him as the next Olivier. He followed that up with the light comedy *MUCH ADO ABOUT NOTHING* in 1993, and in 1996, an unexpurgated, full-text four-hour 70mm extravaganza version of *HAMLET* that included most every actor of note, from John Gielgud and Charlton Heston to Jack Lemmon, Billy Crystal, Kate Winslet, Robin Williams, Julie Christie and Derek Jacobi. While commendable for its sincerity and devotion to the text, as well as its original flourishes (updated to mid-19th century with a much brighter veneer), there is something to be said for the judicious editing of the text in the 1990 Zefferelli version.

The 1990s found Shakespeare in full bloom again with film versions springing up left and right. Laurence Fishburn appeared in Oliver Parker's 1995 adaptation of *OTHELLO,* which finally depicted an African American in the title role. That year also saw an ingenious retelling of *RICHARD III,* set in a World

War II fascist environment. The following year brought us The Bard's cross dressing comedy, *TWELFTH NIGHT* by Trevor Nunn, and Baz Luhrmann's experimental and highly successful *ROMEO+JULIET* starring Leonardo DiCaprio and Claire Danes. Replacing swords with guns, and tights with hip hop fashions, it proved that iambic pentameter could co-exist with MTV-style editing. Whether this film will have the longevity and staying power of Zefferelli's 1968 masterpiece is questionable, but anything that can open young minds to appreciating great literature is welcome indeed.

In 1999 two more Shakespeare films appeared, miles apart in tone and style, attesting to the range of The Bard's talent. First came a star-studded Victorian remake of *MIDSUMMER* with Kevin Kline, Michelle Pfeiffer, Rupert Everett, Stanley Tucci and Calista Flockhart. Later that year, theatre director Julie Taymor (who brought *THE LION KING* to Broadway) made her film debut with *TITUS* starring Anthony Hopkins and Jessica Lange. Based on Shakespeare's first play *TITUS ANDRONICUS*, this visually stunning and highly stylized feature takes place in an alternate universe that is part Ancient Rome and part Fascist Italy. Cinematic as well as theatrical, it restores one's faith in the power of innovative moviemaking.

To cap off the year 1999, we were treated to another innovative film called *SHAKESPEARE IN LOVE*, ostensively about how The Bard was inspired to pen his most famous play. Funny, romantic and very clever, it reassured a tentative public that you didn't have to know Shakespeare to like Shakespeare. While not based on any of the plays themselves, *ROMEO & JULIET* figures prominently in the storyline. A splendid and smartly conceived concoction, the film went on to win Oscars for best picture, screenplay (by Marc Norman & Tom Stoppard), actress (Gwyneth Paltrow), supporting actress (Judi Dench), costumes (Sandy Powell), and score (Stephen Warbeck).

The year 2000 brought another pair of experimental "time warps" from The Bard's cache. Kenneth Branagh made *LOVE'S LABOUR'S LOST* as a musical comedy set in the 1930s, complete with Astaire & Rogers songs, and it was roundly trashed by the critics and public alike. Better received, though not universally praised, was Michael Almereyda's updating of *HAMLET* to modern-day Manhattan. Though it hoped to do for twentysomethings what Luhrmann's R+J did for teens, it never really clicked with its target audience, despite a solid cast that included Ethan Hawke, Kyle MacLachlan, Sam Shepard, Diane Venora, Bill Murray, Liev Schreiber, Julia Stiles and Steve Zahn.

If a century of cinema has shown us anything about Shakespeare, it's that he's as resilient as he is timeless. And he is infinitely adaptable. Both the classic sci-fi adventure *FORBIDDEN PLANET* 1956, and the unorthodox Peter Greenaway mindbender *PROSPERO'S BOOKS* 1990, owe their inspiration to *THE TEMPEST*. The masterful Japanese filmmaker Akira Kurosawa based

THRONE OF BLOOD 1957 on *MACBETH* and *RAN* 1985 on *KING LEAR*. The Cole Porter musical *KISS ME KATE* 1953, and the teen comedy *10 THINGS I HATE ABOUT YOU* 1999 had their origins in *TAMING OF THE SHREW*. *WEST SIDE STORY* 1961 was culled from *ROMEO & JULIET*, while *INTERNAL AFFAIRS* 1990 took its cue from *OTHELLO*. And that old workhorse, *HAMLET*, was turned into a western *JOHNNY HAMLET* 1973, and a Disney classic *THE LION KING* 1994, while two of its most minor characters found a home of their own in Tom Stoppard's play and subsequent film *ROSENCRANTZ & GUILDENSTERN ARE DEAD* 1990. And even Al Pacino got into the act with his wonderfully quirky documentary *LOOKING FOR RICHARD* 1996. The film chronicles Pacino's exploration of *RICHARD III* through interviews, rehearsals, staging and performances, so completely that one is literally swept up in the pure joy of the play.

So, why does Shakespeare endure? Four centuries after his death, the man and his work are more popular than ever. Interest may wax and wane over the years, but we always seem to find our way back. Certainly the writing is a strong draw, but it seems there must be more. What about his genius for wordplay, and his talent for invention? Why do the tragedies move us, and the comedies make us laugh so? No other playwright has ever captured the public's heart in quite so complete a manner. His ability to hold an audience in rapt attention remains unparalleled. Scholars continue to study his work, searching for clues, but the magic formula remains elusive. And, perhaps that's just as well. We have the stories and that should be enough. For as Shakespeare told us in *HAMLET*, all those years ago, "The play's the thing."

MOMMIE DEAREST: FILMS
ABOUT MOTHERHOOD
(May 2001)

Is there anyone, or anything, better than Mom? Most of us would say, "No way!". Regardless of how much we may love the "old man", there will always be a special feeling toward the woman who bore us. Cinema, also, has had a soft spot for Mom, featuring her in everything from *I REMEMBER MAMA* to *THROW MOMMA FROM THE TRAIN*. In this month of Mother's Day, I'd like to spotlight a few movies that have explored the theme of motherhood in ways that are intriguing and insightful. Whether you rent them or buy them, just be sure that you watch them, with Mom.

* *A CRY IN THE DARK* 1988—What could be more heart-rending for a parent than the loss of a child? Meryl Streep and Sam Neill play a real life Australian couple, Lindy and Michael Chamberlain, whose baby is taken by a wild dingo while on a camping trip. Streep does her usual accent thing to perfection, portraying this mother who must fight to clear her name even as public sentiment turns against her and her husband. Bad as it is to lose a child, imagine being condemned in the court of public opinion as well. Lindy's sincerity as a mother is put to the ultimate test when she must go to prison for her child's death. Director Fred Schepisi strikes just the right balance of personal tragedy and social commentary as Lindy must bear the brunt of her loss through the lens of public scrutiny. This is an absolutely riveting movie that says as much about the strength of motherhood as it does about the weakness of our media-dependent society.

* *THE GOOD MOTHER* 1988—Diane Keaton plays a divorced mother who hooks up with bohemian artist, Liam Neeson. Ironically, the very attributes that make Neeson the perfect mate for Keaton are the same that raise questions of his appropriateness toward, and influence on, Keaton's young daughter. The spectre of sexual impropriety, regarding the child, is handled in an unbelievably subtle manner that leaves you guessing whether there was any wrongdoing. The complexities of juggling one's love life with the responsibilities of parenthood are depicted in all their varied shades of grey, thanks to the fine and sensitive direction of Leonard Nimoy. Best known as *STAR TREK*'s Mr. Spock, Nimoy proved he could make movies without the need of spaceships or special effects.

* *THE JOY LUCK CLUB* 1993—Four mothers, four daughters, two generations of women, one traditional Chinese, the other, assimilated American. Amy Tan's book was beautifully transformed into film by director Wayne Wang, who shows

the chasm between these women as being both cultural and generational. The mother/daughter dynamic provided fertile ground to explore the changes wrought in a society over a single lifetime. History and family are thus seen as one. This simple truth, though widely known, has rarely been illustrated in so moving a way.

Of course, there are many, many other movies that, in whole or in part, deal with the special circumstances of being a Mom. There's Holly Hunter's mute mother in *THE PIANO*, Meryl Streep's anguished concentration camp survivor in *SOPHIE'S CHOICE*, Susan Sarandon's wise and caring rock of strength in *LITTLE WOMEN*, and even Debbie Reynolds' wacky turn in Albert Brooks' *MOTHER*. Whether serious or comedic, movies about Moms touch something within us all. Interestingly, the directors of the three movies profiled in this piece are men. I didn't think it was necessary to seek out films specifically directed by women, since I felt you didn't have to be a Mom to make a good film about a Mom. You only needed to have had one.

THE LONG, HOT SUMMER MOVIE SEASON
(June 2001)

Between Memorial Day and Labor Day, there stretches a hundred day span that is the summer movie season. By an interesting coincidence, Hollywood will release one hundred or so movies during this same period. Even for the serious cinephile, a daily visit to the multiplex would not be enough to exhaust the supply of new movies on the big screen. For most of us, seeing that many movies is an impossibility, both economically and time-wise. So, it is up to us to choose which movies we will see in the theatre and which we will relegate to home video. The "rule of law" dictates that, for most of us, spectacle will win out over quieter fare. The month of May has already seen the arrival of *PEARL HARBOR*, a film that delivers *TITANIC*-level special effects and thrills, along with a sweeping epic love story. Its success has guaranteed that the summer movie season is off to a very good start. Of the hundred-plus films remaining to be released, I have chosen an even dozen that appear to be worth checking out. A few are very high profile; most are a little lower on the hype-o-meter.

J U N E

A.I. ARTIFICIAL INTELLIGENCE—The highest profile movie of the summer is also the most secret, as well as the product of two legendary directors: Steven Spielberg and the late Stanley Kubrick. This sci-fi extravaganza is basically a futuristic Pinocchio story about a robot that wants to be a real boy, played by *SIXTH SENSE* phenom, Haley Joel Osment. Jude Law and William Hurt also star. After Kubrick's death in 1999, Spielberg took over his friend's pet project. Let's hope some of Stanley's cool irony remains to counter balance Spielberg's penchant for schmaltz. And just how successful will A. I. be? Well, the last film which Spielberg released that had initials for a title was a little thing called E.T. This will be the biggest hit Stanley Kubrick never made!

ATLANTIS: THE LOST EMPIRE—Disney tackles the myth of Atlantis in an animated tale worthy of Jules Verne and H. G. Wells. Set in 1914, an expedition goes out to find the lost continent and discovers that it is still inhabited. Voice talent includes Michael J. Fox, James Garner, Jim Varney and Leonard Nimoy. Expect all the usual Disney innovations for pushing the animation envelope. They've also decided to ditch the singing, a move that will, perhaps, set a new paradigm for how to package an animated feature.

SEXY BEAST—Ben Kingsley goes from Mahatma to hit man, dumping his Gandhi persona once and for all. Big Ben comes on strong as a career criminal whose high calibre weapons are matched by his even higher calibre use of profanity. The classically trained Kingsley makes this modern-day British gangster story a cut above the rest.

* *BRIDE OF THE WIND*—Behind every great man is an equally great woman. How often have we heard that one? Such was evidently the case with composer Gustav Mahler and his devoted wife Alma, who was a talented musician in her own right. Jonathan Pryce and Sarah Wynter play the Mahlers in this exquisite drama of love and sacrifice.

J U L Y

PLANET OF THE APES—Easily, one of the most anticipated movies of the summer, stylish director Tim Burton brings his twisted sensibility to this remake of the 1968 classic. For one thing, the apes are portrayed much more realistically, galloping on all fours and leaping dozens of feet at a time. The whole storyline has been refashioned, including a new ending that replaces the Statue of Liberty revelation of the original. Mark Wahlberg plays the stranded astronaut, with Tim Roth and Michael Clarke Duncan as apes, and Helena Bonham Carter as the prettiest damn chimp you ever saw. Original *APES* astronaut, Charlton Heston, makes a cameo as an elderly silverback. That, alone, makes this a must-see movie.

FINAL FANTASY: THE SPIRITS WITHIN—While a movie based on a video game may not seem worth mentioning here, this is, in fact, the first real step to achieving photo real animation for human characters. Though *TOY STORY* and *SHREK* have proven the viability of computer animation, they've pretty much stayed in the realm of caricature. *FINAL FANTASY* attempts to bring us ever closer to replicating a totally believable human. They're not quite there yet, but the level of realism is still amazing and points the way to a future where actors could literally phone in their performances.

THE SCORE—The plot of this film is really secondary (an aging thief agrees to one last job for his mentor). The real reason to see this flick is to partake in the pleasure of the long overdue pairing of Robert DeNiro and Marlon Brando. Add to that the always good Edward Norton as an edgy young thief, and stellar direction by Frank Oz, and you've got a cinema event that just begs to be seen.

JACKPOT—Real life twin filmmakers, Michael and Mark Polish (who starred in and directed the nicely strange *TWIN FALLS, IDAHO*) turn their talents to country music. Their new film is about a singer who leaves his wife to try his luck in karaoke bars. Jon Gries and Daryl Hannah star in what promises to be another meditative mood piece by the talented Polish brothers.

A U G U S T

ROLLERBALL—Another remake, but one that clearly wants to kick the stuffing out of the original. Action director John McTiernan (*DIE HARD*) lays on the thrills and stunt work, bringing the world of *ROLLERBALL* into a flashy, fast-paced, hyper-edited, extreme sport reality that makes the 1975 James Caan original seem tame by comparison. That version, directed by Norman Jewison, is a bit too stately and formalized to appeal to today's gung ho teens. For us older geezers, it might be fun to compare the two films to see which one makes the least sense.

THE CURSE OF THE JADE SCORPION—A 1940s era comedy from the master of all things New York and Jewish, Woody Allen. He stars with Helen Hunt, who plays an efficiency expert hired to remodel the office where insurance investigator Allen works. The cast also includes Charlize Theron, Dan Aykroyd, Elizabeth Berkley, David Ogden Stires and Wallace Shawn. When it comes to Woody, you either like him or you don't. To his credit, though, his films have some of the most interesting characters and situations you are likely to see in mainstream cinema.

BUBBLE BOY—A comedy about an immune-deficient teen who must live in a plastic bubble-like cocoon. Sounds like a laugh riot, huh? Jake Gyllenhaal, who was so good in *OCTOBER SKY*, makes a much appreciated return to the screen opposite the always interesting Swoosie Kurtz. This decidedly offbeat comedy goes heavy on the slapstick and stunts, but it still looks like a lot of fun.

THE DEEP END—Co-directors, Scott McGehee and David Siegel come on strong with this disturbing tale of a mother who helps hide her teenage son's involvement in the murder of his gay lover. Tilda Swinton (*ORLANDO*) stars as the conflicted mom. There is major Sundance Film Festival buzz on this one.

These dozen titles represent little more than a tenth of what will be released this summer. Most of us will be lucky to see even that many. Like every business, the film industry is motivated by money. The films that make the most are the kind that will get made again. Teens and young adults have held sway over the box office for some time now. If we want better films, then we must support them. Some quality films, like *A.I.* and *ATLANTIS* won't need our help, but others, like *JACKPOT* and *BRIDE OF THE WIND* will. It's up to us, all of us, whether this summer is remembered for these films, or for *AMERICAN PIE 2*. Our patronage will determine what the phrase "box-office gross" really means.

THE CHEESE STANDS ALONE:
A SPECIAL BRAND OF
CINEMATIC PLEASURE
(September 2001)

For anyone who loves movies, seeing a truly great one can be a singularly satisfying experience. This holds true for any art form about which one is passionate. When you encounter greatness, when the artist has pushed his or her talents to make their work unique, when the art form, itself, is transformed, such an achievement makes us all better people. And, then, society as a whole has reason to be proud.

But, on the other hand, as much as we like to laud the best and brightest in the arts in our culture, we also have a soft spot in our hearts (and maybe our heads, too!) for the laughable, the absurd, the inept, and even the downright bad; everything from the infamous "Golden Throats" compilation albums of bad celebrity singers to kitsch-art Elvis paintings on black velvet (glitter highlights optional). And, perhaps, best of all in this very specialized sub-genre are really cheesy science fiction and horror movies.

The king of "bad" cinema was undoubtedly Ed Wood, Jr. His no-budget oeuvre included the cross-dressing/sex-change melodrama *GLEN OR GLENDA* (1953), the overwrought mad scientist bomb *BRIDE OF THE MONSTER* (1955), and his magnum opus, the absolutely dreadful sci-fi classic *PLAN 9 FROM OUTER SPACE* (1959), all of which starred a washed-up, drug-addled Bela Lugosi, floundering and overacting his way through the cardboard sets. Wood was notorious for using mismatched stock footage to pad out his films and keep costs down to a bare minimum. As a result, the make and model of automobiles, and even day and night, would change unexpectedly during the course of his films. At times this penchant bordered on the ludicrous, as in *GLEN OR GLENDA* where Wood inexplicably added footage of a buffalo stampede!

Much higher on the competency scale, though equally unique, was William Castle. His main claim to fame was the use of in-theatre gimmicks (with accompanying hokey names) at crucial moments in his films, such as "Emergo"-- (a skeleton on a wire "flew" over the heads of the audience in *HOUSE ON HAUNTED HILL*), and "Percepto"-- (select theatre seats were electrified to give patrons a little jolt in THE TINGLER). Less technical tricks included *HOMICIDAL*'s "Fright Break" where scared patrons could get their money back before the "terrifying ending" was shown, though they would have to sit in a specially designated "Cowards' Corner" in the theatre lobby. Not surprisingly, less than one per cent of the movie-goers opted to endure this humiliation. The reason Castle was able to implement such outlandish stunts was by "four-walling" the theatre, that is, renting the actual theatre outright for his films, and by-passing the regular distribution practices of the day. And his shenanigans earned him much-needed free publicity.

The list goes on and on. There's Roger Corman, who gave Jack Nicholson his start, Bert I. Gordon, who never met a cheap special effect he didn't like, and the Toho Studios in Japan, home to the Godzilla franchise. When it comes to bad cinema, the stinky cheese content remains plentiful. The rarity is to find a movie that, while maintaining a high curd factor, still has a core of intelligence. The pair of films discussed below fall into this category. Both were borne out of 1950s paranoia about UFOs and alien conquest, but they also serve as a handy metaphor for our more deep-seated fears. It's great when a movie is fun to watch, fun to laugh at, yet still holds a kernel of respectability.

THE BLOB (1958)—Twenty-eight year old Steve McQueen plays the world's oldest teenager, as he and his equally long-in-the-tooth girlfriend (Aneta Corsaut, later a regular on The Andy Griffith Show) encounter an old man with a gelatinous mass on his hand. The goo came from inside a metcorite which the old man found when it landed in the woods near his cabin. As the Blob attacks one person after another, consuming them and growing larger, our boy Steve can't find any adults in authority who will believe him; (after all, he's just another one of those crazy teenagers!). But it ends up being the teens who save the day when McQueen figures out how to stop the big bad Blob. Highlights include the Blob invading a movie theatre by oozing obscenely through the slats of a ventilation grate, and later gushing out of the projection booth window ports into the auditorium. Perhaps best of all is the now classic "The End" title morphing into a question mark. The actual Blob prop was made out of the relatively new substance, silicone (insert Hollywood starlet joke here!), and was made to move by putting it in miniature sets, tilting them and allowing gravity to do the rest. Though there's much to laugh at, *THE BLOB* still has its share of real scares, and the effects aren't bad, given the time period and money constraints.

I MARRIED A MONSTER FROM OUTER SPACE (1958)—Though saddled with a risible title, this nifty little tale concerns a man who is captured by aliens the night before his wedding. The groom-to-be is replaced with a doppelganger who quickly adapts to married life. After a year with her dour looking, square-headed hubby, however, his wife suspects things aren't as they should be. His bachelor drinking buddies are eventually replicated as well, and marry unsuspecting, husband-starved women. It turns out the aliens' race has no women anymore, hence the need for human brides. Soon, others become suspicious, like the bartender who wonders why his regular, male customers, who used to knock back prodigious amounts of booze, have become virtual teetotalers and no longer seem to have a taste for the stuff. Though the idea of marriage as a metaphor for the loss of male freedom certainly wasn't new at the time, the novelty of alien abduction as the catalyst provided a nice quirky twist. And since the aliens wanted offspring, the notion of them bedding down with human females, even under the sovereignty of holy matrimony, was kind of lurid and racy for the time. Best moment: the abstract expressionist alien visage is glimpsed on the creature's "human" face during the lightning flashes of a storm. Neatest effect: when the aliens take over a human, the victim is engulfed by a weird, undulating dark cloud.

The 1950s were rife with paranoia, be it the threat of communism, the atomic bomb, or the rash of UFO sightings. In sci-fi films of this time, alien invasions of one sort or another often stood in for our fears about the uncontrollable forces that could destroy the "American way of life". Looking back nearly half a century later, we can easily smile at the ironic juxtaposition of such serious concerns with the ludicrous monsters that represented our deepest fears. Now that our cold war anxieties are largely behind us, many people are looking back to that period and re-examining the politics, the social structures and the psychological profiles of the populace, to see how it impacts on our society today. However we view our past paranoia, we have to acknowledge that it helped give rise to the genre of the cheesy sci-fi movie that we enjoy today. And when it comes to cheesy films, the true movie buff is anything but lactose intolerant.

UNTITLED

(October 2001)

My first column written after the 9/11 attacks. It was a tough one to write and I couldn't even come up with a title for it. Since I'd already decided to make "The Big Cheese" a regular feature category, I took this opportunity to feature the 1976 King Kong film which showcased the World Trade Center in the film's denouement.

October and November are our prime autumn months. The leaves turn and fall from the trees and we prepare for the coming of the Christmas holiday season. But, before we can hang the tinsel we first must carve the pumpkin for Halloween. Given the events we've just suffered in September, it's unlikely that we will embrace the faux-morbidness of this holiday with quite the same abandon as in years past. Still, there are some new films coming out this season that may help us to enjoy the pleasures of "all hallow even" while we work to overcome our current hardships and personal grief.

NEW IN THEATRES

*MULHOLLAND DRIVE—Director David Lynch has always been an acquired taste. Even his most mainstream films (*THE ELEPHANT MAN* and *THE STRAIGHT STORY*) are cloaked in a textured atmosphere of surreal absurdity. In his more outlandish excursions (*ERASERHEAD* and *LOST HIGHWAY*) art and artifice collide head on to create an internal logic that defies any kind of rationalization. Between these cinematic polarities, Lynch's middle ground works (*BLUE VELVET, WILD AT HEART* and *TWIN PEAKS*) explore areas of the unconscious where timeless landscapes of lush, overwrought Americana frequently erupt into geysers of quicksilver violence and deadpan humor. In *MULHOLLAND DRIVE*, Lynch seems to mine elements from all three strata of his cinematic mother lode. Originally conceived as a TV series, the pilot was expanded into a feature, and the added material clearly takes it beyond the bounds of conventional network fare. Set in present day L.A., *DRIVE* has the timeless veneer that encases all of Lynch's films. Here, the characters range from an espresso-loving mobster to a scarily polite cowboy; from a film director and a beehive-hairdo'd actress to a couple of cute lesbians, all L.A. fixtures to be sure, but equally they are all, very much, residents of Lynchville, U.S.A. Explaining the storyline is another matter. Like much of Lynch's work, the plot and meaning of this film will spark endless debates among moviegoers for some time. In a world that produces mostly unsatisfying films, with obvious situations and neatly tied-up resolutions, it is refreshing to experience a movie in which riddles abound even after the closing credits end. Once you've left the theatre after your two-hour plus visit, and you ponder the mysterious runes that Lynch has allowed you to glimpse, you'll realize that the real entertainment this movie has to offer is only now getting ready to kick in.

MONSTERS, INC.—The creatures that lurk in our closets are pretty scary, right? Well, it turns out that they aren't really all that bad. You see, monsters need to harvest the screams of frightened children for energy. But lately, the jaded tots just aren't giving up their shrieks that easily, causing a growing energy crisis in the monster world. That's the inspired premise behind *MONSTERS, INC.*, Disney and Pixar's computer animated answer to *SHREK*. While the DreamWorks megahit certainly had its moments, *SHREK* was also shrill, smug and smarmy, with a hollow, mean-spirited nature unbecoming of a children's film. Being hip shouldn't mean you also have to be nasty. Pixar, maker of the *TOY STORY* films and *A BUG'S LIFE*, infuses their films with a genuine sense of joy, a love for their characters, and a gleeful delight in revealing their secret worlds, whether they be the worlds of toys, insects or, yes, even monsters. In this case, the world is depicted to be much like a corporation, staffed with executives, office workers and secretaries (all of them monsters). Pixar's trademark candy-colored palette is much in evidence, with characters rendered in bold reds, greens and blues. The voice talent (another Pixar touchstone) includes Billy Crystal, John Goodman, James Coburn and Jennifer Tilly. DreamWorks and Pixar went toe-to-toe before, in 1998, when *ANTZ* faced off against the much superior *A BUG'S LIFE*. Here's hoping history will repeat itself.

NEW ON VIDEO

WITH A FRIEND LIKE HARRY—Mix one part Hitchcock with one part Kubrick, and you'll have some idea of the tone that is set with this intriguing French thriller. A married couple on their way home meets up with a man named Harry who claims to be an old acquaintance of the husband. Insinuating his way into their lives, Harry at first appears to have the answers to many of their problems. But, like the deal you make with the devil, when it comes time to pay, you tend to be shocked at the bill. And the price of friendship with Harry is anything but a bargain. Metaphorically, Harry does seem to represent that unconscious, amoral animus we all carry around inside us, but rarely unleash in our civilized society. He makes the selfish choices without regard for the consequences to others. He looks out for number one, even if it means killing numbers two, three, four and five! An extremely haunting and wicked commentary on our social evolution, *HARRY* will delight and disturb you in equal measure.

CLASSIC CORNER (DVD)

CITIZEN KANE—The greatest American movie ever made finally gets the deluxe DVD treatment. What more can really be said about *KANE*? It was made in 1940 by young upstart Orson Welles (at age 25, and his first film, no less!), released in 1941 after a tumultuous struggle to suppress it, and received generally lackluster reviews. Though it completely redefined the way movies could be made, it wasn't until it was rediscovered in televised broadcasts in the 1950s that *KANE* finally blazed the path that led to our current modern cinematic style. Loosely based on the life of newspaper giant William Randolph Hearst, Welles, along with writer Herman Mankiewicz and cinematographer Gregg Toland, totally reinvented the filmmaking process with astonishing results. Anyone interested in the language of cinema need look no further than this film. Like Hitchcock, Welles understood the concept of "pure cinema" (communicating plot and character through images rather than dialogue) and *KANE* abounds in visual flourishes few directors, even today, would dare to attempt; the breakfast table montage is but one example. This two-disc set includes a new digital transfer of the film with revitalized digital audio, two full-length audio commentary tracks by film critic Roger Ebert and Peter Bogdanovich (film director and friend of Welles), a two-hour documentary on Welles' struggle to get the film made and released, interviews with the cast and with associates of both Welles and Hearst, rare footage of Hearst's San Simeon estate and Welles' historic "War of the Worlds" radio broadcast, plus much more. Anyone who considers themselves a film buff should have this movie as part of their collection.

SNOW WHITE-- Disney's first feature length animated film is also being released in a special two-disc DVD edition. Extras include a featurette "The Magic Mirror" hosted by Roy Disney, deleted scenes, a multi-level game, behind-the-scenes footage and more. This is the film that truly launched the Walt Disney empire and established the feature length animated musical fairy tale format. A bonafide classic, this movie is filled with vivid characters, great art design and many memorable songs.

DVD ALERT

THE GODFATHER TRILOGY—Before *THE SOPRANOS* cursed and killed their way into our hearts, there was the Corleone family. In addition to the three films in this set, there is a fourth disc of supplemental extras that includes interviews, documentary footage, screen tests and plenty of other bits of priceless trivia that will surely please fans. The movies, themselves, have been spruced up with improved sound and picture quality, showcasing Gordon Willis' stunning cinematography. Director Francis Coppola does audio commentary for all three films, taking the viewer inside on the problems and challenges he faced in bringing this saga of the Italian-American underworld to cinematic life. Though many people have mixed feelings about the third installment (made fifteen years after the first two) this collection is still an offer you can't refuse.

THE BIG CHEESE

KING KONG (1976)—They don't get much dumber than this big budget remake of the 1933 classic, but it is one of the only movies to feature the World Trade Center as a prime location. Kong climbs these newer, taller skyscrapers instead of the Empire State Building from the original film. Jessica Lange (in her film debut) gets to do the Fay Wray part, and is forced to spout such unbelievable howlers as "You male chauvinist pig ape!" when she reprimands her simian co-star. Jeff Bridges and Charles Grodin, both fine actors, can't bring any dignity to this overripe banana, but they are still fun to watch. The giant ape, himself, though heralded in pre-publicity as being a full-size animatronic robot, in the end was mostly make-up wizard Rick Baker stomping around in a mediocre monkey suit. If nothing else, this expensively bad film serves as a nostalgic reminder to us of the glory days of the World Trade Center while we all wait to see just how big a can of whup-ass George W. plans to open up on Osama bin Laden.

AND SO THIS IS CHRISTMAS:
Movies For A Stressful Season
(December 2001)

Probably not since the attack on Pearl Harbor in December 1941 has our country faced a holiday season rife with such anxiety, fear and misgiving. For the families and friends of the 6000-plus people who have perished in the attacks on our nation, this will indeed be a solemn yuletide. For the rest of us, we will do our best to put on a brave face and try to make the most of the occasion. At the very least, we may appreciate the ties to our family and friends just a little bit more. It is in this spirit that the movies we see this holiday can have the power to help us heal our souls.

NEW IN THEATRES
THE MAJESTIC—Manic comedian Jim Carrey plays it straight and goes for the heart this time, as a 1950s blacklisted screenwriter. After an accident leaves him with a case of amnesia, the residents of a small town mistake him for one of their own (a presumed-dead local war hero). As his memory returns, he must choose which life he wants to live. The schizophrenic nature of Carrey's character somewhat mirrors his own film career; he's careened wildly between over-the-top clowns like Ace Ventura and the Riddler to more down-to-earth types in *THE TRUMAN SHOW* and *SIMON BIRCH*. And in THE MASK he got to do both in one film. For *THE MAJESTIC*, director Frank Darabont openly evokes the spirit of *IT'S A WONDERFUL LIFE* and its director Frank Capra with this strongly emotional journey into a wistful American past that seems to exist only in the movies. Tellingly, the film's title refers to a small town movie house that Carrey helps to re-open. Movies also figure in the story line; as a screenwriter, Carrey's character is responsible for penning "Sand Pirates of the Sahara", a black & white B-movie actioner that makes up the movie-within-the-movie. Given Darabont's penchant for pathos and the sentimental (he directed *THE SHAWSHANK REDEMPTION* and *THE GREEN MILE*), it remains to be seen whether this film will be "Capra-esque" or merely "Capra-corn".

NEW ON VIDEO
MOULIN ROUGE—Aussie director Baz Luhrmann made a name for himself in 1992 with the allegorical musical *STRICTLY BALLROOM* and in 1996 with the MTV-inspired, alternate universe re-telling of *ROMEO & JULIET*. His audacious visual style, coupled with an irreverent taste for settings that are more fanciful than real, finds full flower in his latest. Set in a phantasmagorical Paris at the turn of the century (last century, that is), the eponymous dance hall is re-imagined as

part carnival sideshow and part three-ring circus. In a hyper-active dream state, the camera swoops and soars over the city and through the Moulin Rouge, itself, assaulting your senses from the get-go. Nicole Kidman and Ewan McGregor play starry-eyed lovers who croon modern-day ballads (by Madonna and Elton John, among others), as the spectre of tuberculosis hangs over their future. The impish John Leguizamo shines as stunted artist Toulouse-Lautrec, seen here as a sort of lisping, whirling dervish dwarf, while Jim Broadbent is perfectly over-the-top as Moulin Rouge's sinister master-of-ceremonies. The film's frenetic camera work takes a bit of getting used to, but the pace does eventually settle down, somewhat, allowing one to marvel at the incredibly dense production design. Texture and color are combined in a smorgasbord of influences, everything from Victorian to Moorish to Art Nouveau, evoking a swirling, sensory-overloaded, "fabulist" environment. You will come away from this movie much as you would from a weekend in Paris; you'll be exhausted, but you'll also be satisfyingly sated.

CLASSIC CORNER

BLOOD SIMPLE—In light of the Coen Brothers most recent success, *THE MAN WHO WASN'T THERE*, now seems like a good time to revisit their first film. A neo noir classic from 1984, this sordid tale of adultery, jealousy, ruinously fatal misunderstandings and the seediest private investigator you're ever likely to encounter, is nothing short of miraculous. The Coen's first film is a surprisingly assured piece where they expertly manipulate audience expectations. Their fondness for unsentimental, wickedly clever dialogue is quite evident. And even this early, their visual playfulness is firmly in place: a key piece of evidence, a cigarette lighter, (which ends up being little more than a red herring), is hidden beneath a barbershop quartet of dead fish, their open mouths frozen in mid-croon. The DVD release of this film includes improved picture and sound, and an audio commentary track with Kenneth Loring of Forever Young Films. But, be forewarned, this audio track is essentially a gag; Loring pontificates in great detail about each shot, concocting copious amounts of deliberate misinformation that attempts to be humorous (in an almost Monty Python-esque fashion) but is mostly just tedious. It is also a huge letdown for film buffs who, no doubt, were expecting an honest and informative assessment of a truly wonderful film. While this joke track is a major misfire, the movie itself remains worthy of your attention. Here's hoping that in the future, the Coen brothers will take their fans' interest in their work a bit more seriously.

DVD ALERT

STAR TREK: THE MOTION PICTURE—The first ever *STAR TREK* movie may have been many things, but it certainly wasn't a great film. Born from the fires of Trekkie fandom in the 1970s (where the 1960s series gained popularity in syndication after its cancellation) the journey from TV screen to cinema screen was long and arduous. Fans tried to revive the series, which made its first comeback as a half hour Saturday morning cartoon show in 1973. A live action version was a bit longer in materializing, though it was on the boards to return as either a TV movie or series in the mid-1970s. However, after the phenomenal success of *STAR WARS* in 1977, the long delayed series was bumped up to feature film status. Things looked especially promising when prestigious director Robert Wise was hired to helm the picture, and state-of-the-art special effects were promised. Unfortunately, a rushed shooting schedule, dictated by a locked-in 1979 Christmas release date (and too many cooks stirring the script), conspired to make the finished product a big, plodding, poorly paced, lumbering, mediocre cinematic event. Still, despite poor reviews, the movie made a lot of money and paved the way for eight more films and four more series. Now, in a bold move, Paramount Studios agreed to let director Wise re-edit his movie properly, re-mix the sound, and complete the special effects the way they were intended to look. The result is still a somewhat mediocre film (some things just can't be fixed!) but for Trekkers everywhere, this is the best version of the movie they will ever see. And to the filmmakers' credit, the movie does play much better than it did in its original release. DVD extras include three new documentaries, added scenes and deleted scenes, an audio commentary with Wise, effects supervisors Doug Trumbull & John Dykstra, composer Jerry Goldsmith and actor Stephen Collins, and a text commentary that offers a treasure trove of trivia and facts. Years before it became a Hollywood staple to turn TV shows into movies, this two-disc set offers eloquent testimony about the rigors and hurdles involved in reviving a cult TV classic for the big screen.

THE BIG CHEESE

SANTA CLAUS CONQUERS THE MARTIANS—In 1964, the same year that Disney released its great children's classic *MARY POPPINS*, we also got this film, a real low in the kid flicks genre. Santa and two children are abducted by Martians who need help with their own kids (apparently they're hooked on TV, watching Earth broadcasts!). Swathed in green greasepaint, antenna helmets and unflattering-to-the-waistline body suits, the Martian actors ham it up big time, especially the villain Voldar (who does everything but twirl his mustache) and a comic relief simpleton named Dropo, who is so mannered in his attempts to be funny that it's actually embarrassing to watch him. The production design is sloppy and unimaginative, with a silver-painted cardboard box robot, cheap special effects, a polar bear that is clearly some guy in a costume and sets that look like they were pilfered from a cancelled game show. Add a pitiful, saccharin score to the jawdroppingly bad script and you've got one nasty chunk of smelly green cheese here. You really have to wonder what the filmmakers were thinking when they churned out this mess, which still somehow managed to turn a profit. Regardless, it is definitely the worst Christmas movie ever made. But, with the right group of friends (along with eggnog aplenty flowing freely) this can be a fun evening's entertainment. For added pleasure, seek out the Mystery Science Theater version if you can. Most references to this film mention that Pia Zadora plays one of the Martian tykes, as if that tidbit of trivia has the same omigosh factor as, say, Meryl Streep playing the part. In a season dominated by *HARRY POTTER*, a kid's film that was made the right way with a great deal of care, you can only shake your head at *SANTA/MARTIANS* for blowing what should have been an easy winner: a children's outer space adventure with Santa Claus as the hero.

MYTH AMERICA: American Cinema in the New Era.

(February 2002)

2002 will be the first full year of the new world in which we now live. The events of September 11th have lowered the curtain on one era and raised it on another. America, as a culture, will never be the same again. The rest of the world, it seems, has a love/hate relationship with American culture; they admire and envy our freedom, but feel fear and resentment at the arrogance they perceive in us which such freedom engenders. The myth of the "ugly American" certainly has some truth, but for all our faults, we still embody the lifestyle most others want to achieve. The 20th century was America's century; we rose from upstart nation to world power. It remains to be seen what our role in the 21st will be. The last century was also the century of cinema, an art form dominated by America in general and Hollywood in particular. The films listed below are all, in one way or another, purely American, not in the flag-waving, pseudo-patriotic vein, but in the sense that they could not have come from anywhere else.

NEW IN THEATRES

BELOW—While *BLACK HAWK DOWN* is getting the lion's share of press coverage as the war film du jour, this creepy little number directed by David Twohy is slinking into theatres under the radar. Co-written by *REQUIEM FOR A DREAM* director Darren Aronofsky, this bizarre World War II thriller concerns a submarine full of American soldiers preparing to do battle with the Nazi ships that are floating above them. Adding to their woes, they discover there are some malevolent supernatural beasties swimming in the depths beneath them. Bruce Greenwood, who was so excellent and charismatic as President Kennedy in *THIRTEEN DAYS*, stars in what may best be described as an *X-FILES* version of *DAS BOOT*.

NEW ON VIDEO

ATLANTIS: THE LOST EMPIRE—Much has been made about the success of computer generated, or "dimensional", animation films like *SHREK* and *MONSTERS, INC.* So much so that the regular "flat" animation movie is said to be in danger of disappearing. That would be a shame, since traditional animation has its own distinctive charms. Disney's *ATLANTIS* even uses dimensional imagery to complement its flat cel art work, a technique they've judiciously employed in most of their animated features from *THE GREAT MOUSE DETECTIVE* in 1986 on. As imaginative entertainment, *ATLANTIS* delivers, with a delicious blend of Jules Verne adventure and New Age mysticism. Young cartographer Milo Thatch (voiced by Michael J. Fox) heads a ragtag submarine crew in 1914 to locate the lost civilization of Atlantis. Others who lend their distinctive vocal talents include James Garner, Leonard Nimoy and Jim Varney. Visually audacious and thoroughly enchanting, this may be one of the last big-budget flat animated features for some time to come. Some critics even seem to revel in *ATLANIS*'s less-than-blockbuster grosses, hailing 3-D computer animation as the next great thing. While this may actually be true, there's no reason the success of one has to be at the expense of the other. Are flat cartoons, even those as lavish as the ones made by Disney, becoming obsolete? I sure hope not. We may gain an extra dimension, but we'll be losing a whole lot more.

CLASSIC CORNER

THE HOT ROCK—Thanks to the success of recent films like the *OCEAN'S 11* remake and *THE SCORE*, the "heist" flick is back in vogue. This 1972 movie finds Robert Redford, in full anti-hero mode, as a just-released convict who can't seem to stay out of the business. He joins up with George Segal and Ron Leibman to steal a large gemstone which, after the heist, has a habit of remaining continually just beyond their grasp. Every generation has its own form of hip, glib humor, and *THE HOT ROCK* is clearly ensconced in its 1970s milieu. Writer William Goldman, who won a 1969 Oscar for his *BUTCH CASSIDY & THE SUNDANCE KID* screenplay would later work with Redford again on *THE GREAT WALDO PEPPER* (1975) and *ALL THE PRESIDENT'S MEN* (1976). For *THE HOT ROCK*, he provided some great character interplay as well as several ridiculous situations. One of his best bits is the phrase "Afghanistan bananastan", which is used as a post-hypnotic suggestion at a key point in the movie. I doubt that many other 30-year-old films can boast of having a catch phrase that is, both, still humorous as well as relevant to current events.

DVD ALERT

TWIN PEAKS: THE FIRST SEASON—In 1990 this eccentric series, created by David Lynch and Mark Frost, burst upon the television world with its eclectic mix of cherry pie, damn good coffee, unforgettable characters, and the central mystery about just who killed teen homecoming queen, Laura Palmer. This first season DVD box set (minus the pilot program, unfortunately) contains the first seven episodes which spawned a TV viewing frenzy not seen since everyone wondered who shot J.R. on *DALLAS*. *TWIN PEAKS* was a watershed series whose trademark quirkiness paved the way for everything from *NORTHERN EXPOSURE* and *PICKET FENCES* to more extreme fare like *THE X-FILES*. *PEAKS* articulated its 1990s sensibility beneath a 1950s veneer. The small town innocence concealed its tawdry Peyton Place antics. The show's duality extended far beyond its name; hidden agendas and double crosses abounded. No one was who they first appeared to be. From its hunting lodge decor to its finger-snapping, jazzy beatnik soundtrack, this deliberately overwrought melodrama constantly teased our baby-boomer sensibilities, evoking a less cynical era. For true *PEAKS* fans this collection is a must. The high definition transfers are immaculate, showing off the series' warm palette and striking cinematography as never before. Extras are abundant, including present day interviews with series creator Mark Frost and most cast members, audio commentary with episode directors and crew, plus much more. Though David Lynch's fingerprints are all over the series, he chose not to contribute to this set, no doubt due to his preference to let his work speak for itself. A bigger loss than Lynch's no-show is the absence of the two-hour pilot which launched the series. Not only are the characters established in that pilot, but the show's iconography and visual framework are introduced in a very specific manner that allows it to resonate during each episode. Without the pilot, these visual touchstones lose some of their force, as do the dynamics between the characters. The pilot was released in Europe as a stand-alone movie (with added sequences that wrap up the murder in a different manner than the series would eventually do). Parts of this wrap up do appear in episode three (directed by Lynch, as was the pilot) in a dream sequence where they were used to better effect, making that the most talked about episode in the entire season. The Warner Brothers tape of the pilot/movie is currently out of print, but an import DVD can still be had.

THE BIG CHEESE

THE QUICK AND THE DEAD—Not all cheese is bad cheese; some of it can be mighty tasty. Nor must it be a moldy oldie. This thoroughly arch and wickedly revisionist genre offering takes the classic western and turns it on its ear. Producer and star Sharon Stone, invoking the spirits of Peckinpah and Leone, appropriates the "spaghetti western" and gives it a decidedly feminist slant. Director Sam Raimi, meanwhile, opts for a sunset saturated patina to envelop his comic book compositions. Stone, herself, assumes Clint Eastwood's "man-with-no-name" role and plays it to the hilt, complete with raspy voice, the "Clint squint" and even his trademark cheroot. She enters the town of Redemption to take on its corrupt owner, Herod, played with extra relish by Gene Hackman. The squalid town is populated with every cliché character from every western ever made: there's the black-clad gunslinger (Lance Henriksen at his oily best), the escaped convict, the noble Indian, the blind merchant boy, the killer-turned-Preacher (an as-yet unknown Russell Crowe), and the charismatic hot shot "kid" (a pre-*TITANIC* Leonardo DiCaprio). The movie is essentially a series of quick-draw shoot-outs, each filmed in a heightened, exaggerated style for maximum effect. Raimi's signature style was forged in the blast furnace heat of his *EVIL*

DEAD films and can be seen again this summer in the highly anticipated *SPIDERMAN*. In *QUICK*'s cartoony tableau, a victim is as likely to learn that he's been shot by seeing a little dot of sunlight nestled within the confines of his own shadow as by the pain. Raimi uses every gimmicky camera set-up in the book to taunt and tease the viewer. Keith David gets what is perhaps the most visually outrageous coup-de-grace death scene ever committed to celluloid. Composer Alan Silvestri contributes a note-perfect, Latin-tinged pastiche score, flavored with mariachi guitars and horns, and a whistling accompaniment punctuated by whip cracks, that hovers just short of parody. The script by Simon Moore even has a classic twist ending that has become a cliché, itself. While the movie pays homage to literally dozens of older films, its subversive whimsy clearly marks it as a contemporary work. *QUICK* uses the conventions of the classic western, and pokes fun at it, without ever straying beyond its bounds, unlike the broad farcical style Mel Brooks adopted in *BLAZING SADDLES*.

POST OSCAR RESPITE: The Calm Before The Summer Storm.

March/April 2002

As the awards season winds down with the presentation of the Oscars, we find ourselves in that strange twilight zone that sweeps over us each spring, prior to the big summer movie season. Like the fall, this is a time of smaller, more thoughtful movies, though the line of demarcation between light and dark, good and bad, is becoming fainter with every passing year: not all big budget extravaganzas are mindless, and not all low budget independents are smart. Finding the good stuff still takes work. But it is a duty we cannot shirk, otherwise the mindless junk will prevail. We must all do our part to support smart, innovative movies so that they will continue to be made.

NEW IN THEATRES

THE TIME MACHINE—In 1960, sci-fi fantasy filmmaker George Pal made a lavish cinematic version of the classic 1894 novel. The main character was a Victorian scientist who invents a time machine, travels to the far future and witnesses the decline of the human race into two factions: the childlike "Eloi" and the bestial "Morlocks" (mutant primitives who prey on them).The movie starred Rod Taylor and Yvette Mimieux, and was a resounding success, both artistically and financially. Fast forward thirty-two years and we find this marvelous remake, using state-of-the-art special effects that George Pal would never have dreamed were possible. First time director Simon Wells is actually the great grandson of the novel's author, H. G. Wells, a bit of serendipity that was not concocted for its publicity value. (Wells, the younger, was sent the script without anyone being aware of his famous linage.) It has become almost routine for Hollywood to remake past successes that are deemed in need of a new coat of paint so they will appeal to the newer generation of movie goers. From the sublime (*LITTLE WOMEN*) to the ridiculous (*PSYCHO*- talk about a misfired attempt!) nothing is above being tinkered with. However, in this case, the effort seems to have paid off. For all its wonderful imaginings, the original *TIME MACHINE* has, ironically, become dated. The effects, while clever, are a bit cheesy looking by today's standards, and the genre, itself, is now taken more seriously than it was then. The casting is also superb, with the very intense, yet likable, Guy Pearce (*MEMENTO*), the smoothly villainous Jeremy Irons (*DEAD RINGERS*), who gives all his roles an extra dimension, Mark Addy (the fat bloke in *THE FULL MONTY*) who seems quite at home in the Victorian world, and newcomer Samantha Mumba, as the blended-race Eloi girl. Look also for original TM cast member Alan Young (Wilbur on TV's *MR. ED*) in a cameo as an elderly flower vendor.

NEW ON VIDEO

JOY RIDE—When two brothers on a cross country road trip decide to play a CB radio prank on a horny trucker, they get a lot more than a few laughs for their effort. Much like surfing on the internet, talking on a CB radio has a certain element of anonymity to it that encourages some people to explore their darker side. Without overburdening this slick thriller with too much psychological baggage, one can interpret the mostly unseen trucker as a personification of the brothers' unconscious id. Still, even without the subtext, this is one nifty and entertaining movie. The great Steve Zahn (*THAT THING YOU DO, OUT OF SIGHT*) and hunky/wholesome Paul Walker (*PLEASANTVILLE, THE FAST AND THE FURIOUS*) are the brothers, while the vivacious Leelee Sobieski (*THE GLASS HOUSE, EYES WIDE SHUT*) is their innocent female friend who finds herself in the middle of the boys' ongoing nightmare.

CLASSIC CORNER

LA JETEE—Time travel movies often run into problems of logic and believability. In 1962, this thirty minute French film, which translates as *THE JETTY*, provided a powerfully original and audacious technique that both subverted and extended the film watching experience as we know it. The movie was made up entirely of still photographs (with narration) that formed a document of the time travel experiments conducted by scientists in a post-war future. When photography came into existence in the mid-1800s, cameras were seen, rightly so, as sort of like "time machines", in that they could literally stop time and save it for future examination. In the film, time travel was accomplished with the use of powerful drugs, rather than a machine, which raises the question of whether the journey was just all in the participant's mind. This short film was later adapted into the 1995 feature length movie, *TWELVE MONKEYS*, directed by Terry Gilliam (*BRAZIL, THE FISHER KING*), starring Bruce Willis, Brad Pitt and Madeleine Stowe. This was one of the very few examples where a remake was as artistically successful as the classic upon which it was based. *MONKEYS* retained most of *LA JETEE*'s plot strands, expanding and enlarging them for a feature length story. And Gilliam added his own visual flourishes, guaranteeing that his film would be a true original. For those who appreciate smart films, and smart filmmaking, both of these cutting edge movies are extremely satisfying.

DVD ALERT

ROLLERBALL—This is the original 1975 film, not the dumbed down remake currently in theatres. Directed by Norman Jewison (*FIDDLER ON THE ROOF,*

MOONSTRUCK) and starring James Caan, this tale of a corporate-run world that salves its cultural ennui through a sort of gladiatorial roller derby is far from a perfect film. Some of the plotting is clunky, and the futuristic look of the movie has become very dated, but the rollerball sequences are nicely staged and edited, and are exciting to watch. And where the film fails in accuracy, it still works nicely as metaphoric prophecy. What makes this title an entry in the DVD ALERT category is that this disc is a great example of how satisfying and inexpensive a DVD film can be. Retailing for $15.00, you not only get an excellent widescreen transfer of the movie, but also a thoughtful and informative audio commentary track with Jewison and a short making of featurette. For true movie buffs, these extras are an invaluable look inside the film right from the source. There are many other titles, old films and new, in this price range with similar extras, so you need not go broke building up your DVD collection, nor give up those extra features that make watching movies so much more of an enriching experience.

THE BIG CHEESE

THE TIME TRAVELERS—There are certain movies that are so bad, some people would walk out on them even on an airplane! But, for us cheese lovers, these films are pure gold. In this bubbly 1965 fondue, a group of scientists, engaged in a top secret project to create an observational time window, instead open a doorway into the future. Once they pass through it, they are trapped in a barren, post-apocalyptic world. There they meet up with a clutch of humanity who are building a spaceship to travel to another star system and begin life anew. The war-ravaged earth is much too ruined for mankind to remain, not to mention being overrun with radioactive mutant humans! While working on their rocketship, the futurists, holed up in an underground enclave, show off their technological advances to the visiting time travelers, which include robot androids (who do most of the work), a teleportation device, female health spas (really just an excuse to display scantily clad women), and a musical light organ where lovely young ladies can entice young men by playing really mediocre tunes. The publicity for the movie refers to this device as "The Love Machine", but don't get your hopes up; it's as lame as all get out. The android repair factory, however, is a real hoot, looking more like a warehouse for mannequins, with heads on shelves, arms and legs mounted on walls, and trays of eyeballs carried around like they were hors d'oeuvers. The music in the factory scene (which sounds like it belongs in *WILLIE WONKA*) is so wrong in style and tone that you'd gladly puncture your own eardrums if you could only stop laughing. One of the selling points of this film was the use of super-secret breakthrough special effects-- a "live" robot gets a head change, shown in one continuous shot with no edits, and a teleportation demonstration where the occupant disappears (again, on camera with no edits) only to reappear elsewhere. Both these "effects" are clearly derived from magician stage tricks, but are still pretty decent in their execution. The acting is almost totally of the stilted variety, and the attempts at humor are uniformly witless and lowbrow: one of the time travelers (a young Steve Franken), has set his sights on a pretty technician in the robot factory. When she hands him a tray of robot eyes, he looks down at them, looks up at the camera and quips, "I thought I was giving her the eye." Groucho Marx, no doubt, would have been proud. Why *MYSTERY SCIENCE THEATER 3000* never tackled this turkey remains one of the great unknowns in the universe.

WADING INTO SUMMER
(May 2002)

Though it's still only spring, the summer movie season is already upon us. From now until Labor Day, the big budget "fun" movies will be coming at us, fast and furious. First out of the gate is Sam Raimi's *SPIDER-MAN*, followed closely by *STAR WARS EPISODE 2: ATTACK OF THE CLONES*. As the summer rolls on, the variety increases to include Steven Spielberg's sci-fi thriller, *MINORITY REPORT*, starring Tom Cruise, a live action *SCOOBY-DOO* flick, and sequels to *MEN IN BLACK, AUSTIN POWERS* and *SPY KIDS*. There will also be some counter programming with a bit more meat like *POSSESSION* with Gwyneth Paltrow, *THE IMPORTANCE OF BEING EARNEST* with Reese Witherspoon, *ROAD TO PERDITION* with Tom Hanks, and the supernatural thriller, *SIGNS* with Mel Gibson. No matter how many (or few) of the sixty-plus releases you see this season, it promises to be one of the most lucrative summers on record. Whatever your preferences, choose wisely.

NEW IN THEATRES
INSOMNIA—After wowing the public with two low budget indie productions (*FOLLOWING, MEMENTO*), maverick director Chris Nolan steps up to the A-list plate with this remake of a 1998 Scandinavian thriller. The $50 million budget also allows Nolan to work with A-list Oscar winners like Al Pacino, Hilary Swank and Robin Williams (doing his latest in a recent string of villainous turns). Set in Alaska, this crime drama follows visiting cop Pacino as he investigates the murder of a teen-age girl. While the plot sounds run-of-the-mill, Nolan's past work guarantees that this will be a cut above the standard issue storyline. Whether or not he employs his trademark structural tinkering, though, remains to be seen.

NEW ON VIDEO
WAKING LIFE—During this year's Academy Awards, the new category of Best Animated Feature was seen largely as a horse race between *SHREK* and *MONSTERS, INC.* Curiously missing from the nominees (much to the shame of the Academy) was this breathtakingly original film that certainly advanced the art of the animated movie. Director Richard Linklater (*TAPE, BEFORE SUNRISE*) added animation on top of live action footage, resulting in some trippy cartoon images that swim and flow with fluidity and color, yet look eerily real. Even more remarkable is that the animation was accomplished with simple software on a home computer, thus liberating the feature animation movie from the domain of major studios and putting it within reach of just about anyone. The DVD release

includes audio commentary with Linklater and over 25 of the animators, plus an animation software tutorial, a featurette and two short films.

MEMENTO SPECIAL EDITION—While it's true this innovative film was released on home video last year, this new DVD is the special, limited edition, 2-disc set loaded with extras the original DVD lacked, including audio commentary with director Chris Nolan, anatomy of a scene, the shooting script, production stills and more. The film has also been remastered in high definition. This is the movie that many people felt should have won Best Picture at the Oscars, but it wasn't even nominated in that category. If you missed this breakthrough movie, pick it up and see what all the fuss is about. It's the first truly classic film of the 21st century.

CLASSIC CORNER

SCHOOLHOUSE ROCK—We all know about "Conjunction Junction" and that "Three Is A Magic Number". Anyone who grew up in the 1970s and 80s would be all too familiar with these cartoon songs that helped us learn math, grammar, history and science. Conceived by David McCall, Tom Yohe and George Newall, with music and lyrics written mostly by jazz great and local legend Bob Dorough, the Schoolhouse Rock cartoon "bumpers" appeared on Saturday morning TV between the regular kids' shows. Now, after a successful run on videotape, the whole kit and caboodle of them are being released on DVD (with audio commentary, as well, no less!). So now we can all groove along with 'My Hero, Zero", "I'm Just A Bill" and "Interplanet Janet". Thanks to these wonderfully animated musical gems, learning the basics has never been more entertaining or endearing. And why not? After all, that's their function!

DVD ALERT

ERASERHEAD—How can anyone explain the phenomenon that is David Lynch's first feature film? This brilliant, abstruse, radically strange celluloid dream came directly from Lynch's own murky subconscious. Filmed over a period of four years, starving art student Lynch assembled a loyal cast and crew that included actor Jack Nance, sound designer Alan Splet and cinematographers Frederick Elmes & Herbert Cardwell. Together they toiled on the American Film Institute grounds with an initial $10,000 grant, building strange sets and props that comprised the director's peculiar vision. Finished in 1976 and released the following year, *ERASERHEAD* was largely responsible (along with *THE ROCKY HORROR PICTURE SHOW* and *EL TOPO*) for creating the midnight movie culture. Long out of print on VHS (rental store copies "disappeared" years ago) this unique cinematic nightmare returns to home video with a vengeance. David Lynch (who owns the film, outright) has chosen to release the movie on DVD, exclusively through his website (www.davidlynch.com). On the plus side, the film has been meticulously cleaned, rendering the luminous black & white cinematography in all its glory. Packaged in a special 8" x 8" box, the disc includes a 20-page booklet, put together by Lynch, himself, though sadly there are no other extras to speak of. (That's the negative side!) The quirky director is notorious for limiting the content on his DVD releases (you can be sure he'll never do a commentary track). Still, it is the movie that's the main prize, and it's a genuine oddity, a total original, a film that boldly revels in its uncommercial content, defying you to decipher its cryptic meaning. For those who've never seen the movie and think that Lynch's later, marginally more commercial works, like *LOST HIGHWAY* and new video release *MULHOLLAND DRIVE* are baffling, all I've got to say to you is that you ain't seen nothing, yet! *ERASERHEAD* is, perhaps, the closest that cinema has ever come to putting an actual dream on film. And that, I think, is the secret to enjoying Lynch's movies. Don't even try to understand them; just settle back and dream the dream.

LEGEND: ULTIMATE EDITION—Thanks to the success of Peter Jackson's first installment of his *LORD OF THE RINGS* saga, the epic fantasy genre is once again a viable cinematic commodity. In 1985 British director Ridley Scott (*GLADIATOR, BLACK HAWK DOWN*) created his own take on the mythic fairy tale, which starred Tom Cruise, Mia Sara and Tim Curry (unrecognizable in demon make-up). The lavish film was released in Europe at 114 minutes with a musical score by Jerry Goldsmith. In America, however, it was cut down to 90 minutes and the original score was replaced with one by the innovative synthesizer band Tangerine Dream. Neither version did well, though the Euro-cut has been touted as the better of the two. Now you'll have a chance to find out. This special 2-disc set offers both versions along with many other extras, including audio commentary with Scott, a making of documentary, lost scenes, an alternate opening, three featurettes, a music video and DVD-ROM features that include the movie script. Scott's sumptuous visual sense has always been the driving force in his movies (especially *ALIEN* and *BLADE RUNNER*), so the chance to see him take on a full out fantasy is not to be missed.

THE BIG CHEESE

DEVIL DOLL—When it comes to movies with "so bad they're good" type storylines, you just can't go wrong with the old "evil living ventriloquist dummy" bit. And this 1964 black & white low budget thriller is the tastiest slab of British cheese this side of Wensleydale. Bryant Haliday plays "The Great Vorelli", a smooth, yet snooty, mesmerist/ventriloquist, who has a scary looking dummy named Hugo that seems to be alive! But, just what is the terrifying secret of the Devil Doll? That's what American reporter Mark English (played by William

Sylvester, who would go on to play Dr. Floyd in *2001*) wants to know. There are some genuinely creepy moments in this little seen flick, which has just been released on DVD in a special edition. There are also some hilariously lame sequences as well, including Vorelli's stage act where he drinks wine while his dummy companion chatters on, and hypnotizes Sylvester's girlfriend Maryann (Yvonne Romain) into (gasp!) dancing the twist on stage. Everyone reacts as if the hypnotist had transformed her into Isadora Duncan, when in fact her moves would scarcely raise eyebrows on Lawrence Welk, much less American Bandstand. However, when the arrogant Vorelli makes the dummy walk unassisted to the footlights of the stage to take a bow, it does make you wonder just what the heck is inside the little guy. While there's little that is truly frightening by today's standards in *DEVIL DOLL*, it's still worth seeing for a few laughs, not to mention an insight into the low budget British film industry during the period when The Beatles were busy conquering America and the world.

A YEAR UNDER A CLOUD:
LIVING WITH TERRORISM
(September 2002)

This month marks the first year anniversary of the attacks we faced in the United States by terrorists. It has been a hard year for many people, especially those who lost loved ones. Somehow we pressed onward. Clean up at the World Trade Center site is over, and the city is making plans to erect a memorial for those who perished. The Pentagon and the field in Pennsylvania where the other tragedies occurred are also contemplating their own tributes to the innocent victims of 9/11. And while things are far from resolved, America has gotten back to the day-to-day routines that define our culture and society. And that includes watching movies. The terrorists are still out there, but we have chosen to go on living.

NEW IN THEATRES
CITY BY THE SEA—Robert DeNiro plays a cop who is investigating a murder. (Yawn). But wait, his estranged son is the prime suspect! (Ho hum.) Why should you give this fact-based, but routine, crime drama the time of day? Well, first, it IS DeNiro, but perhaps more importantly, the director, Michael Canton-Jones, previously worked with the star in the 1993 film, *THIS BOY'S LIFE*. That taut and intense drama, also based on true events, showcased a young up-and-comer named Leonardo DiCaprio. Canton-Jones clearly has an eye for talent and a knack for this kind of material. Also, it's been a long time since DeNiro has had the opportunity to blow us away with a great performance. The pairing of these two talents bodes well for all of us who love good movies.

NEW ON VIDEO
MONSTERS, INC.—DreamWorks' *SHREK* may have the distinction of winning the first Oscar for Best Animated Feature, but for my money, Disney/Pixar's *MONSTERS, INC.* is the real champ. Their insistence on story and character, over smug humor and cheap jokes, resulted in a true children's classic that is fun for adults as well. In its first ten minutes, this film was already more clever and imaginative than all of *SHREK*, and it only got better. Billy Crystal and John Goodman provide voice talent for Mike and Scully, a pair of working class monsters. The duo labor on the "scare floor" at Monsters, Inc. where they have access to every child's closet in the world. Harvesting the screams from scared kids is how the monsters collect energy for their own world. Things go awry when top kid frightener Scully returns from a job with a three-year old girl named

Boo inadvertently clinging to his shaggy back. Children are considered toxic to the monster world, and Boo's intrusion causes panic among the inhabitants. The twist in the plot is that it's really the monsters who are afraid of kids! Things eventually work out for everyone, but there are plenty of thrills and laughs along the way. Pixar has always had its heart in the right place, and *MONSTERS, INC.* may be their most touching film yet. The two-disc DVD version contains plenty of extras on how the movie was made, including an informative and entertaining audio commentary track with the animators. Both the DVD and videotape come with the animated short, *MIKE'S NEW CAR*, which was made exclusively for the home video release.

CLASSIC CORNER

A HARD DAY'S NIGHT—When The Beatles' first film came out in the 1960s, it firmly cemented the "fab four" as that era's icons of rock and roll. Conceived as a fast track quickie to capitalize on the group's burgeoning popularity, the film was shot in March and April of 1964 and released later that summer. To everyone's surprise the movie garnered overwhelmingly positive reviews from the critics, who hailed it as "the *Citizen Kane* of juke box musicals" and referred to The Beatles, themselves, as latter day Marx Brothers. And it was true; the film is a cinematic gem. American director, Richard Lester, caught "lightning in a bottle" with his innovative editing and camera work, not to mention having a first rate script by British playwright Alun Owen. The film effectively captured the band's cheeky freshness before the first blush of fame could wear them down. The decision to shoot the movie in black & white helped it achieve a timeless, classic look that color photography might have negated. It is ironic that the only reason the movie was green-lighted in the first place was so the studio could put out a soundtrack album! (To the execs, who just wanted a piece of the "Beatlemania" pie, making the movie was merely a necessary step to that end.) The fact that the movie ended up being a modern classic is a tribute to those who took the challenge more seriously than the bean counters, who only wanted to cash in on a fad. It is a real triumph of art over commerce. A new two-disc DVD release comes with many extras, including audio commentary, interviews and a new documentary, all of which are sure to please Beatles fans here, there and everywhere.

KOYAANISQATSI—Back in 1983, documentary filmmaker Godfrey Reggio released this mesmerizing aural/visual collage that used time lapse photography to depict our world in a way it had never been seen before. With no discernible plot, no actors, and no dialog, the images tumbled forth, one after another, all to the hypnotic strains of composer Philip Glass's minimalist score. The title comes from the Hopi Indian language and translates as "life out of balance". While much of the imagery in the film has been copied by countless commercials and other movies over the last two decades, this cinematic poem still has the power to hold you spellbound. Having been out of circulation on video for a number of years, it finally makes its debut on DVD, a medium that can really do justice to the striking photography. A follow-up film titled POWAQQATSI (the second installment of a proposed trilogy) came out in 1988 and is also being released on DVD. While lacking the impact of the first film, the sequel (which uses a lot of layered, multiple exposure images) still has its strong points, especially the music score, again by Philip Glass.

DVD ALERT

*LORD OF THE RINGS SPECIAL EDITION—Australian director Peter Jackson has made what many people consider to be THE definitive "Ring Trilogy" film epic. The story recounts the adventures of gentle hobbit Frodo Baggins, played by Elijah Wood (whose angelic face helps make up for the distraction of his badly bitten fingernails). Also in the cast are Ian McKellen as Gandalf the Wizard, Ian Holm as Frodo's uncle, Bilbo Baggins, Cate Blanchet as the Elvan Queen Galadriel, and Christopher Lee as the evil sorcerer Saruman. If you are a fan of this first installment, titled THE FELLOWSHIP OF THE RING, and plan to own it on DVD, you might want to pass up the version released in August and hold out for this special edition director's cut set to arrive in November. The four-disc set includes a longer (by 45 minutes) director's cut of the movie, four audio commentary tracks, and a plethora of behind-the-scenes featurettes, all in a package that resembles an ancient leather bound book (a nod to "Rings" literary origins). Even better is the five-disc set which includes everything in the four-disc set, plus an extra disc with the National Geographic special, BEYOND THE FILM, and a set of custom bookends (designed after the "Pillars of the Kings", the gigantic statues that flank the river entrance seen in the film). When the other two movies in the series are released on DVD in similar book packaging, you can then display all three between the bookends. How cool is that?

*THE CIVIL WAR—In September 1990, filmmaker Ken Burns changed the way we looked at documentaries when PBS ran his long format, eleven hour examination of the American war between the states. Up until that time, Burns was best known for his series of hour-long documentaries on subjects like the Brooklyn Bridge and the Statue of Liberty. With THE CIVIL WAR, he established a new way to chronicle history, one that was both entertaining and educational. Utilizing lush location photography, interviews with historians, voice-over readings of diaries, letters and newspaper accounts, and intense scrutiny of thousands of period photographs, Burns captivated the world with his mix of scholarly research and heartfelt empathy; (the reading of the last letter that Maj.

Sullivan Ballou sent to his wife Sarah before he died in battle was especially heartbreaking and caused a wave of emotional outpouring from PBS viewers everywhere). Burns continued making documentaries on American history, including two more long form extravaganzas, *BASEBALL* and *JAZZ*. For most fans, however, *THE CIVIL WAR* remains the best of Ken Burns' epic length endeavors. And, finally, it's on DVD. Here is your chance, literally and figuratively, to own a piece of history.

CHICK CHIC: Embracing the Feminine Side of Movies

(October 2002)

Women's films, or "chick flicks", more often than not get a bad rap from male movie goers, who can't conceive of calling a film good unless there are car chases, gun fights, and at least a dozen or so big explosions punctuating the action. As much fun as all that mayhem may be, I'm here to tell you that there is more to life than these testosterone fantasies. For every *FAST AND FURIOUS* that rakes in a fortune, there are ten or more movies out there about falling in love, being true to a friend, or just dealing with issues that women find appealing, that barely break even. The real problem is that women are willing to go see movies that are about guy things, but men won't go see films about girl things. And that has to change. Women make up half the population, and it's time they take a stand about choosing the kind of films they see with their husbands and boyfriends. And guys, not all chick flicks are about ladies sipping tea and crying into their hankies, though some of those can be really good, too. There are others like *JACKIE BROWN, AMELIE, THE PIANO, LEGALLY BLONDE* and even *POSSESSION* that are female driven, yet totally satisfying, whether you're male or female. So, let's all work together to span the cinematic gender gap and start promoting more films about women. The end result will be better movies, and a better movie going experience, for all of us.

NEW IN THEATRES

FRIDA—Theatre director Julie Taymor (who had wowed the public with *THE LION KING* on Broadway) made a big splash with her debut movie *TITUS*, starring Anthony Hopkins and Jessica Lange, based on Shakespeare's first play, *TITUS ANDRONICUS*. She follows this up by collaborating with actress/producer Salma Hayek to bring to life the story of Mexican artist Frida Kahlo. The beautiful Hayek managed to replicate the look of the severely-eyebrowed artist with a minimal makeover. A bio pic of Kahlo had been on the agendas of several actresses, including Madonna and Laura San Giocomo. The pairing of Hayek and Taymor, along with co-stars Alfred Molina, Geoffrey Rush, Edward Norton and Ashley Judd, makes it seem as if the best of all possible *FRIDA*s got made. Perhaps this film will do for Hayek what *MONSTER'S BALL* did for Halle Berry. Maybe it's time to start thinking about a film on the life of Georgia O'Keeffe.

NEW ON VIDEO

ABOUT A BOY—At first glance, a movie with this title would seem out of place in a column about "chick flicks," but in fact, this Hugh Grant comedy/drama about a perpetual bachelor is just that. Grant plays Will Freeman, a rakish womanizer, living off the royalties from a ditty his late father bequeathed to him. As a result, he's never had to grow up and face the realities of being an adult. His Peter Pan world is turned upside down when, while pretending to be a single parent, to score a date at a support group, he is side-tracked into the lives of Megan and her son, Marcus. Though he really wants to date the neighbor of Megan, fate, instead, throws him a mighty curve. After a failed suicide attempt by Megan, Will finds that Marcus has latched onto him as a sort of surrogate father figure. The growing relationship between these two characters, and the redemption they both receive, is at the heart of this touching film. The title applies equally to both these lost "boys" who each find a new meaning in what had been fairly empty lives. What makes this movie especially chick-friendly, of course, is that the shallow Will changes for the better, thanks to his relationship with a child, something most women already know in spades. And the fact that Will looks like Hugh Grant is just icing on the cake.

CLASSIC CORNER

THELMA & LOUISE—Director Ridley Scott, best known as a visual stylist (*ALIEN, BLADE RUNNER, LEGEND*) proved he had what it took to do a strong, yet engaging, character-driven story. Writer Callie Khouri picked up a best screenplay Oscar with this tale about a couple of oppressed women who take to the road to have a good time, but find they still must contend with male arrogance and authority along the way. Geena Davis and Susan Sarandon have great chemistry together as the reluctant rebels who find an inner strength during the course of their travails. While not at all an anti-male diatribe, the film did serve as a sort of primal scream therapy for the frustration that many women felt about living in a man's world. With its mix of heightened realism and archetypal myth, the humor and drama are played against one another in a tone that is similar to another rebel classic, *BONNIE & CLYDE*. Shot on the back roads and desert vistas of the American west, Scott strove for a visual elegance in the landscapes that culminates at the Grand Canyon. The non-distaff side of the cast includes Harvey Keitel and Michael Madsen, both playing against type as sympathetic male figures, and a boyish Brad Pitt, who seduces Geena Davis (and the audience), in a flashy, career-making performance as a charming drifter named J. D. (Rumor has it he beat out an equally young George Clooney for the role.) The DVD (priced at a very reasonable $15.00) includes an entertaining and informative commentary track with the director that reveals some interesting insights into what the filmmakers were trying to achieve.

DVD ALERT

BEAUTY AND THE BEAST—Lately, Disney has taken the lead in offering special edition DVDs of their movies, everything from the three-disc sets for the FANTASIA ANTHOLOGY and the TOY STORY ULTIMATE TOY BOX to deluxe editions of most of their other titles. For the release of their masterpiece, BEAUTY AND THE BEAST, they've pulled out all the stops. Not content to merely issue the regular movie, the folks at Disney added a newly animated sequence for a song that was to appear in the original film. The song, called "Human Again", was cut (and the scene abandoned while still in the planning stage) because the story team couldn't figure out how to solve a time problem that the song created: Belle's father would have had to have been lost in the woods for weeks the way the song was used. However, when the movie was adapted as a stage play, someone figured out how to solve that problem and the song was put back in. For the DVD release of the film, it was decided to restore the song to a newly animated segment done by the original animators. The result is a BEAUTY AND THE BEAST that's even better than the one we all fell in love with over a decade ago. The two-disc set includes three separate versions of the film, plus all the usual Disney extras that we've come to expect from these special editions.

THE BIG CHEESE

EARTH GIRLS ARE EASY—Remember when Geena Davis actually had a career? (See "Classic Corner" above.) Hot off her successes in THE FLY, BEETLEJUICE, and THE ACCIDENTAL TOURIST, Davis took the time to make this hilarious, kitschy send up of the sci-fi alien genre. The lovely Geena plays a ditsy California manicurist whose world is turned upside down when an alien spaceship (looking like a 1950s carnival ride) crash lands in her pool. The space monkey crew, clad in primary-hued fur, takes a shine to their earthly host and agrees to total makeovers by Davis' salon co-worker, Julie Brown. Stripped of their crayon colored body hair, the aliens turn out to be none other than Damon Wayons, Jim Carrey and Davis' then husband, Jeff Goldblum (guess which one she has the "hots" for?). Michael McKean adds considerable laughs as a part-time pool man (and full-time surfer dude) named, Woody, who takes the aliens out to the beach. You don't need to have a nail fetish to love this movie, with its funky production design and razor-sharp wit. At times the satire is as pointed as the brightly colored talons on the ladies' hands: Julie Brown's song (yes, it's also a musical!) "'Cause I'm A Blonde" is a real bimbo basher. Directed with great, campy flair by Julien Temple, who nurtured his appetite for visual excess doing music videos in the early 1980s. That style serves him very well, here. It's nice to see a film that is not afraid to be smart, even when it's about a bunch of not-so-bright people. Hollywood, take note.

A BOUNTIFUL FALL YIELDS
A THANKFUL THANKSGIVING

(November 2002)

The fall movie season is off to an excellent start thanks to a crop of early good films. From *THE FOUR FEATHERS* to *RED DRAGON* to *WHITE OLEANDER*, Hollywood has come out swinging. Add to that such offbeat fare as *THE GREY ZONE* and Werner Herzog's *INVINCIBLE*, and you've got one hot autumn. And it looks like things will only get better. Still waiting in the wings is the musical *CHICAGO* with Catherine Zeta-Jones, *THE LIFE OF DAVID GALE* with Kevin Spacey and Kate Winslet, *THE HOURS* with Meryl Streep and Ed Harris, a new *STAR TREK* movie, and the second installments of *HARRY POTTER* and *LORD OF THE RINGS*. In other words, there's a movie out there for everyone, and that's something for which we can all be thankful.

NEW IN THEATRES

*THE CORE—Though this sci-fi adventure flick seems more suitable as summer fare, its appearance now in the fall guarantees that it will get noticed. Oscar winner Hilary Swank takes a break from her serious cinematic roles to have some fun. She heads a group of "terranauts" on a trip to the center of the Earth to save the planet. Other cast members include Aaron Eckhart, Stanley Tucci and Alfre Woodard. As the intrepid team makes its way to the Earth's core, shifting tectonic plates and wayward magnetic fields wreak havoc on many famous landmarks and structures. The final result is a film that's sort of a cross between *INDEPENDENCE DAY* and *EARTHQUAKE*.

NEW ON VIDEO

*SPIRIT: STALLION OF THE CIMARRON—DreamWorks Studios has been trying to make its mark for a number of years in the traditional animation field, which has been almost exclusively dominated by Disney. Their past efforts, *THE PRINCE OF EGYPT* and *THE ROAD TO EL DORADO*, did only mild business compared to Disney, but with *SPIRIT*, DreamWorks has finally arrived. Combining breathtaking animation with a strong story, about a captured wild stallion that yearns to be free, the film is a total delight from beginning to end. Matt Damon provides the narrated thoughts of the title character, while Daniel Studi voices the Indian brave who befriends him.

CLASSIC CORNER

GLENGARRY GLEN ROSS—Playwright David Mamet won a Pulitzer in 1984 for his play about real estate sharks who specialize in swamp land swindles. Though an accomplished filmmaker, himself, this 1992 movie version of Mamet's most famous play was, instead, directed by James Foley, working with an extraordinary cast that included Jack Lemmon, Al Pacino, Ed Harris, Alan Arkin, Kevin Spacey, Alec Baldwin and Jonathan Pryce. Mamet, however, did write the screen adaptation, and even added a new scene (with Baldwin) that sets up the story in a stronger fashion and gives the audience a more tangible glimpse of the characters' plight. For its 10th anniversary debut on DVD, the two-disc set features audio commentary with Foley, cast interviews and a tribute to the late Jack Lemmon. Everybody involved is at the top of their game, here, and you'd be hard pressed to find a finer example of ensemble acting than in this riveting drama.

DVD ALERT

SPIDER-MAN—Few popcorn movies have been as universally embraced, by critics and public alike, as this 2002 summer blockbuster. Directed with manic flare by Sam Raimi, who cut his teeth on the *EVIL DEAD* movies, this film hit all the right notes. Tobey Maguire plays the webbed boy wonder, while Kirsten Dunst and Willem Dafoe give terrific performances as the love interest and villain, respectively. But it's character actor J. K. Simmons, as the cigar chomping newspaper editor J. Jonah Jameson, who nearly steals the show. Columbia has wisely chosen to make this their Christmas video of choice to own, releasing it in a two-disc set complete with audio commentary, a making of featurette and other extras. For the serious fan, however, there is the limited edition collector's set that includes an extra DVD on Spider-Man creator Stan Lee, a reprint of Amazing Fantasy #15 (the first comic in which Spider-Man appeared), a limited edition lithograph reproduction by Spider-Man artists John Romita, Sr. and Jr., and more, all packaged in a special collector's box. My spider senses are definitely tingling.

THE BIG CHEESE

SHOCK CORRIDOR—Cult melodramatic filmmaker, Sam Fuller, made a name for himself in the 1950s with harsh, hard bitten fare that included everything from westerns, *FORTY GUNS*, to crime dramas, *PICK UP ON SOUTH STREET*, to war pictures, *THE STEEL HELMET*. Sam gloried in exposing man's baser emotions, coupled with the ironies of life and death. His populist outlook, however, wasn't really appreciated in his day. As a result, by the early 1960s, a down-on-his-luck Fuller found himself making this quickie exploitation flick (shot in ten days, mostly on a single set). The tale involved a newspaper man, played by Peter Breck, who gets himself committed to an asylum so he can write an expose about conditions there, and maybe pick up a Pulitzer along the way. The "loony bin" setting allowed Fuller free reign to explore the contradictions in society in his usual, outrageous style. One of the most disturbing is a black patient (Hari Rhodes) who thinks he's a white racist! His anti-black diatribe is all the more astonishing, issuing as it does from a black man. Being confined with these oddballs, Breck finds his own grasp of reality crumbling. Though the plot has more holes than a slice of Swiss cheese, the movie revels in some lurid "madness" set pieces where the characters chew the scenery as they climb the walls. The DVD is somewhat lacking in extras, but it does boast a high quality black & white transfer that includes the rarely seen color sequences (taken from Fuller's own home movie travel footage) and the original theatrical trailer. You won't go mad watching this snake pit potboiler, but you'd be crazy to pass it up.

CHRISTMAS TIME IS HERE, AGAIN!
(December 2002)

It's been a banner year for the film industry, with record box office numbers, due in no small part to *SPIDER-MAN, STAR WARS*, the indie surprise *MY BIG FAT GREEK WEDDING, HARRY POTTER* and *LORD OF THE RINGS*. On home video, the DVD market has taken hold in a big way, and is fast becoming the format of choice for videophiles everywhere. The studios can't seem to release new titles fast enough to keep up with demand. And while other businesses are experiencing an economic slump, the season has never looked brighter for movies than now, in whatever form they're viewed.

NEW IN THEATRES

GANGS OF NEW YORK—Martin Scorsese's long-delayed saga about the immigrant turf wars in 19th century New York finally arrives just in time for the holidays. Starring Leonardo DiCaprio, Daniel Day-Lewis and Cameron Diaz, this movie truly has the look and scope of a grand epic masterpiece. Though Scorsese has been a cinematic fixture in the business for over thirty years, with work as varied as *TAXI DRIVER* and *THE AGE OF INNOCENCE*, he has yet to win an Oscar as director. *GANGS* represents his best chance in years to rectify that oversight.

NEW ON VIDEO

LILO & STITCH—They say politics makes strange bedfellows, but imagine Walt Disney hooking up with Elvis Presley! That unlikely scenario is at the heart of this hip, irresistible animated treat from Disney Studios. Set in Hawaii, lonely, little girl Lilo, who is being raised by her older sister, makes friends with a strange looking pooch at the local pound. The wacky canine, in fact , is actually an alien on the run from space authorities who have been charged with tracking him down. There is an immediate bond between these two outsiders from different worlds, something with which most children can readily identify. The color palette of this film is extraordinary, with vibrant watercolor washes in deep, stained-glass hues. The irreverent tone of the movie owes much to such varied modern kiddie fare as the Powerpuff Girls, SpongeBob, Ren & Stimpy and even Disney's own recent *THE EMPEROR'S NEW GROOVE*. The capping element to this film is the decision to use the music of Elvis Presley. One wonders what "Uncle Walt" would think of collaborating with "The King." Is he spinning in his grave (or shivering in his freezer as the legend goes), or is he kicking back on a cloud with Elvis and saying, "Why didn't we think of doing that?" All I have to say to the studio heads who gave this project the go ahead is, "Thank you, thank you very much".

CLASSIC CORNER

THE PRODUCERS—Before it was a smash hit on Broadway, this yarn about a down-on-his-luck theatre producer who concocts a scheme to put on the worst play ever (and make a killing off the investors once the play is canned), was in fact a hilarious film directed by Mel Brooks and starring Zero Mostel and a very young Gene Wilder, who snagged a best supporting actor nomination. The movie actually won an Oscar in 1969 for best original screenplay, beating out such contenders as John Cassavetes' *FACES* and Stanley Kubrick's *2001: A SPACE ODYSSEY*. The special edition DVD comes with a new documentary, deleted scenes and more. Even in today's outrageous culture, it's hard to top the play's centerpiece song, "Springtime For Hitler", for sheer wit and insanity.

DVD ALERT

BACK TO THE FUTURE TRILOGY—Along with the Indiana Jones trilogy, this is one of the most requested titles for release on DVD by movie fans. The first of these films, released in 1985, made TV actor Michael J. Fox a movie star, and established director Robert Zemeckis as a major force in Hollywood; his previous movie, *ROMANCING THE STONE*, had also been a big hit. The time travel flick did so well that Zemeckis put together a pair of sequels, shot back to back, which were released in 1989 and 1990. While all three films are inventive and clever, most people consider the first one to be the best. The other two tend to rely on special effects, rather than character or story, for their crowd pleasing moments. Still, the entire trilogy, which also stars Christopher Lloyd, Lea Thompson, James Tolkan and Thomas Wilson, is loads of fun, and the DVD comes with many extras to please even the most discriminating DVD fan. Zemeckis, among others, provides a very informative audio commentary track, plus there are behind the scenes featurettes, interviews, special effects secrets and much more.

THE BIG CHEESE

THE YEAR WITHOUT A SANTA CLAUS—What's a Christmas season without a good old-fashioned, cheesy Christmas TV special? One of the best of this bunch comes from Rankin & Bass, who made many of these during the 1960s and '70s. Starring the voice talent of Mickey Rooney and Shirley Booth, this 1974 stop-motion animated classic recounts the tale of an under-the-weather Santa who decides to pass up his holiday duties, feeling no one really cares about Christmas, anyway. Mrs. Claus sends a couple of elves out to find proof that people still care so her chubby hubby will change his mind. By today's standards, the animation looks a bit clunky and dated; recent fare such as *THE NIGHTMARE BEFORE CHRISTMAS, WALLACE & GROMIT* and *JAMES & THE GIANT PEACH* have raised the bar, considerably, for stop-motion, while the CGI technology used in *TOY STORY, JURASSIC PARK* and *MONSTERS, INC.* has all but eliminated the use of this very labor-intensive format. For that reason alone, watching these quaint old shows from the *GUMBY* era can be a real pleasure. For *THE YEAR WITHOUT A SANTA CLAUS* you also get some great songs by Maury Laws and Jules Bass, especially the Snow Miser and Heat Miser tunes that practically steal the show. Whatever the charm of this special, it continues to be a big hit on video at Christmas time. This year, a merchandising blitz has been added, with dolls, mugs, clothing and more, all showcasing the characters. The DVD includes, along with the 50 minute feature, two extra animated shorts: *NESTOR, THE LONG-EARED CHRISTMAS DONKEY* and *RUDOLPH'S SHINY NEW YEAR*, all for a very reasonable $20.00. Whether you're trying to recapture your past, or you just dig old shows, this is one tasty and enjoyable hunk of holiday cheese.

THE SACRED AND THE PROFANE: RATING THE YEAR'S MOVIES

(January 2003)

It's been another crazy year at the movies, and now with the start of the new year, it's time to take stock of the films of 2002. Why does it always seem as if the past year was worse than the one before? It's not that films are getting worse, it's just that the really good ones don't get released until the end of the year or the beginning of the next. This is done primarily to position the best of the best for Academy Award consideration. While *THE ROAD TO PERDITION, SIGNS* and *INSOMNIA* came out mid-year, most of the others with serious pedigrees— *FAR FROM HEAVEN, SOLARIS, THE HOURS, GANGS OF NEW YORK, THE LORD OF THE RINGS: THE TWO TOWERS, THE QUIET AMERICAN, ARARAT, CHICAGO*—are recent arrivals or have yet to go into wide release. No matter which films you think are best, or which gems get overlooked, it's still fun to follow which movies will make the cut and end up on Oscar's short list.

NEW IN THEATRES

THE 25TH HOUR—Most January movie releases are really just late December releases finally making it into wide distribution. Such is the case, here. Director Spike Lee (in desperate need of a comeback hit) works with a largely white cast—Edward Norton, Barry Pepper, Philip Seymour Hoffman and Anna Paquin—to tell the tale of a Wall Street broker enjoying his last day of freedom before serving a seven-year prison sentence for drug dealing. Based on the novel by David Benioff, the film explores the nature of friendship when the main character begins to suspect that his girlfriend and buddies may have set up his drug bust. Like most of Lee's films, this one takes place in New York, but don't call him "the black Woody Allen" or "the black Martin Scorsese."

NEW ON VIDEO

SIGNS—Director M. Night Shyamalan is fast becoming the next Steven Spielberg. With only three films the Philadelphia native has established a style (and a knack with children) that is positively Spielbergian, and yet, still wholly original. His latest, and best, effort has Mel Gibson as a farmer and former minister who has lost his faith when his wife died. The grieving widower is thrust into what seem to be supernatural events when a crop circle mysteriously appears on his property. Joaquin Phoenix is his younger brother, who has come home to help with the rearing of Gibson's two children. The casting of Mel and Joaquin as brothers is inspired, as the two quite resemble one another. Shyamalan casts himself in a small, but pivotal role that proves he is a capable actor in his own right. The "signs" of the title refers to much more than the crop circles that set the story in motion. While all of Shyamalan's films have a neat twist built into their finale, here it serves a purpose beyond being merely a clever stunt. The DVD release includes deleted scenes, Shyamalan's first alien film, and an exclusive six-part documentary that covers such areas as scriptwriting, set design, special effects, the score, marketing the film, and a making of featurette. What's missing is audio commentary by the director, something he seems reticent to do, since none of his films have it. It's a trait (or phobia) he evidently shares with Spielberg. Still, the extras are plentiful, making this a must-have DVD.

CLASSIC CORNER

WAR AND PEACE—Forget about James Cameron's *TITANIC* or the Taylor/Burton 1963 *CLEOPATRA*; when it comes to figuring out what was the most expensive movie ever made; hands down the winner is this 1968 mammoth production from Mother Russia, herself. Based on Leo Tolstoy's epic novel, and clocking in at an exhaustively impressive 7 hours and 11 minutes, the film took five years to make with a price tag of over 100 million dollars. To mount such an endeavor, today, would cost at least five times as much. The only production even remotely similar is Peter Jackson's *LORD OF THE RINGS* trilogy. The Russian film boasts some truly impressive stats: 300 speaking parts, 120,000 extras (no computer-generated battle scenes here, my friend), 35,000 costumes and 273 sets (indoor and outdoor). The four-disc DVD released by Image offers a restored widescreen picture; a behind-the-scenes featurette; interviews with the cinematographer, two of the actors and the head of Mosfilm Studios; a Tolstoy documentary and studies of the art direction and set designs. Stay away from the slightly shorter 403 minute three-disc version available from Kultur, which lacks the picture clarity and extras of the Image release, and is minus the widescreen presentation. An Oscar winner for Best Foreign Film of 1968, this powerful motion picture is the very epitome of "epic."

DVD ALERT

THE GOOD GIRL—Despite glowing reviews from the critics, this touching little film did only minor business at the box office. Jennifer Aniston de-glams herself and proves that a cast member from FRIENDS can actually make a decent movie if they just put their mind to it. The low key story involves working class clerk, Aniston, becoming involved with a young, sensitive co-worker, played nicely by Jake Gyllenhaal. The impish John C. Reilly adds some considerable weight as Aniston's cuckolded husband. The DVD includes writer/director commentary as well as commentary with Aniston, herself, who is being touted as a possible Oscar contender.

THE BIG CHEESE

JESUS CHRIST, VAMPIRE HUNTER—Just in time for the post-Christmas season, comes this tasty, action musical morsel. The sandaled savior teams up with pro wrestler El Santos, and together they use their kung fu skills against an army of the living dead. The image of a high kicking, Bruce Lee-inspired King of Kings makes one wonder if action figures aren't far behind. If you'll recall, a company in the Midwest a while back, released a series of porcelain figurines of Jesus playing football, baseball, basketball and even tennis, all with children, as a way to encourage spirituality in youngsters. I guess the message, there, was that Jesus is so cool He can shoot hoops with the best of them. While the knickknacks were unintentionally humorous, the movie clearly has its tongue in its cheek. Throw in some deleted scenes, audio commentary and interviews, and you've got a winning package. This new release is just another example of how even a modern day "cheese-in-a-can" snack can be as delicious and satisfying as the finest aged 1950s rubber monster cheddar. Amen to that!

COURTING OSCAR: THE AWARDS SEASON BEGINS

(February 2003)

With Christmas a fading memory, Hollywood replaces its warm and fuzzy countenance with the aggressive promotion of their product for awards consideration. From the Golden Globes to the People's Choice and the sundry film critics' picks, the business seems to thrive on the bestowing of awards and the acknowledgment to one another of the artistry of their craft. Some of it is hype and some is genuine, but the bottom line is that this is the publicity grease that keeps the industry wheels turning. While everyone has his or her idea of what the best film/actor/etc. was for last year, we are still drawn to see what the film community thinks of itself. Later this month the Oscar nominations will be announced, and the awards will be given a month after that. We may agree or disagree, be pleased or not, and argue our own feelings about it, but we will not be indifferent. For those of us who love movies (or even just like them) we will most definitely be interested.

NEW IN THEATRES

HE LOVES ME, HE LOVES ME NOT—What would February be without a good romance movie? While you might want to skip *JUST MARRIED* (aka "Dude, Where's My Honeymoon?") you might want to check out this French confection. Audrey Tautou, the adorable sensation from *AMELIE*, stars as a young student who falls in love with a married doctor. Directed by Laetitia Colombani and co-starring Samuel LeBihan, the film promises a journey that is both conflicted and bittersweet. However, any chance to see the lovely Ms. Tautou again is reason enough for most of us.

NEW ON VIDEO

THE ROAD TO PERDITION—Though released during the summer of 2002, this handsomely mounted drama is a likely candidate for a best picture Oscar nomination. Directed by Sam Mendes and starring Tom Hanks, Paul Newman, and newcomer Tyler Hoechlin, this period gangster flick was based on the graphic novel of the same name. Mendes, who cut his teeth in the theatre, managed to impart a sense of the theatrical (much of the action occurs "in the wings") but in a more subtle manner than his previous Oscar winning film, *AMERICAN BEAUTY*. Much has been made of the fact that Hanks, in portraying a hit man, was trying to break out of his nice guy image. Don't you believe it. He may be with the mob, but he only kills other mobsters, and is a man of honor who will do anything to protect his family once they are threatened. He is the least bad guy in this film. Jude Law provides a bit of kinky darkness as a creepy news photographer who takes crime scene pictures of dead people. The look of the movie is exquisite, thanks to cinematographer extraordinaire Conrad Hall, who cloaks his depression era tableaux in the mantle of mythic grandeur. With just two movies, Mendes has proven that he is one of the most formidable talents working in the cinema today.

CLASSIC CORNER
BEAUTY AND THE BEAST—One of the most sublime movie fantasies ever made finally comes to DVD. This 1946 French classic by Jean Cocteau speaks volumes about the power of cinema as an art form. Shot in luminous black & white, this live-action masterpiece gives the Disney feature a run for its money. Released by Criterion, the special edition includes commentary tracks, an interview with cinematographer Henri Alekan, stills gallery, the original trailer and a reprint of Madame Leprince de Beaumont's original fable.

DVD ALERT
ONE HOUR PHOTO—Fans of Robin Williams who liked the comedic actor in his whirling dervish mode were in for quite a surprise in 2002. Williams made a number of films where he explored a darker, more subtle performance style. In *INSOMNIA*, he contained his manic persona to play a quiet killer who always seemed to be one step ahead of cop Al Pacino. For *ONE HOUR PHOTO*, a film that came and went, Williams expanded on the still-waters-run-deep idea to play a bland photo processor who becomes obsessed with a picture perfect family. For him, their photos have taken the place of a genuine life with genuine relationships. Sporting short blonde hair and large glasses, Williams personifies a quiet, almost pathetic blankness that is the sad residue of a life unlived. Co-star Connie Nielsen (*GLADIATOR, MISSION TO MARS*) plays the mom with whom Williams becomes fixated. Nielsen has a great facility for melting into her roles, to the point that she seems unrecognizable from film to film. The DVD includes an incisive audio commentary track with the director and Williams, along with featurettes, interviews and more. While *INSOMNIA* was, I think, a better film, Williams' performance, here, is the one that deserves Oscar's consideration.

THE BIG CHEESE
SILENT RUNNING—This 1971 ode to ecology and long-haired radicalism makes it to our cheese board mainly because of its wildly unorthodox premise that in the future they will put all of the earth's forests in gigantic domes and hurl them out to Saturn for safe keeping. And to top it off, let's throw in some Joan Baez songs as well. What at first blush might appear to be a case of too many

film execs smoking too much weed was in fact a very ambitious and visually audacious sci-fi fable. Made for a paltry $1.3 million, the movie has the scope and breadth of a major Hollywood production. First time director Douglas Trumbull, who made his name as one of the effects supervisors on Stanley Kubrick's *2001: A SPACE ODYSSEY*, learned well from that experience and found ways to cut corners without sacrificing the epic scale. The spaceship sets were shot inside a decommissioned aircraft carrier, which was modified for the film. The results were very realistic sets that looked like several million bucks because that's what they were worth. Trumbull also employed front projection techniques, which had been used in *2001* for the opening African segment, to create the domed background on his forest sets as well as the star fields for his model shots. Finally, he resurrected his "slit scan" device, which he'd developed for the "star gate" sequence in *2001*, to create a trip through Saturn's rings that were quite impressive. The film starred Bruce Dern as spaceman/botanist Freeman Lowell, who revolts when the order comes to blow up the domes and head home. After taking over the mission his only companions are three pre-R2D2 robot drones who he dubs Huey, Dewey, and Louie. Even though Dern kills his fellow crewmen, this is a far cry from his maniac/psycho characters for which he is best known. The DVD has some great extras including an hour-long documentary about the film and audio commentary with Trumbull and Dern that is fun and informative. The ecological theme of the movie seems more relevant than ever. So, after grooving on this cosmic wake-up call, break out the old tie-dyes, put on a Joan Baez record, and go hug a tree.

OSCAR, OSCAR EVERYWHERE: SEEING BEYOND THE ACADEMY HYPE.
(March 2003)

It's real. The Oscar nominations have happened and the real race for Hollywood's golden boy is under way. While there are some clear front runners—*Chicago, Gangs of New York, The Hours*—there have also been surprises and disappointments. *Road to Perdition* managed five nods, but only one (Paul Newman) in a major category. Meryl Streep was cited a record thirteenth time as a performer yet Robin Williams, Leonardo DiCaprio and Dennis Quaid were overlooked, even though all turned in strong, multi-film performances. And it looks like Spielberg gets to sit this year out, despite making two highly touted movies. The most pleasant surprise is *Frida* being recognized with six nominations. Even if it wins nothing, it has accomplished a great deal. As we approach Oscar night, the media frenzy will only get more intense. And once it's all over, later this month, we'll wonder why we cared so much. Such is the magic of Hollywood and its hype, as well as our love of movies, that we give ourselves over to this mania year after year.

NEW IN THEATRES
Lost in La Mancha—Tilting at windmills is nothing new for director Terry Gilliam. The former Monty Python alum has made a career by tackling unusual film projects that put him at loggerheads with studio execs. Both *Brazil* and *The Adventures of Baron Munchausen* had their share of problems while being made, yet went on to be critical, if not commercial, successes. Gilliam's most recent endeavor was to be a retelling of *Don Quixote*, but the multi-million dollar project fell apart after only a week of filming. However, another film crew was following Gilliam, lensing a making-of featurette. Nearly every Gilliam film has had such behind-the-scenes coverage, which has provided an illuminating look inside the filmmaking process. This time, however, the documentary was the only element to survive, and in an ironic twist worthy of Cervantes, himself, has taken the place of the original movie. Gilliam, always a champion of the underdog, has given this film his hearty endorsement, if only so the public can see for themselves the problems inherent in the movie industry. Given Gilliam's talent, and obvious affinity for the source material, one can only hope that he will get the chance to do his version of Cervantes' classic story. If any filmmaker can "dream the impossible dream," it is Terry Gilliam.

NEW ON VIDEO

The Grey Zone—Based on true events, this film chronicles a special squad of Jewish prisoners during World War II who staged the only armed revolt at the infamous Auschwitz prison camp. This riveting drama stars Steve Buscemi, Harvey Keitel, Mira Sorvino and David Arquette, and was written and directed by Tim Blake Nelson. Best known for his roles in *O Brother Where Art Thou?* and *Minority Report*, Nelson has proven to be a capable director with such films as *Eye of God* and *O*, the high school basketball version of Shakespeare's *Othello*. The DVD release of *Zone* includes a director commentary as well as one with the cast and crew. While there may be some who are weary of yet another Nazi/ Holocaust film, the fact remains that there are still many stories to be told. *The Grey Zone* is one that is worth your time.

CLASSIC CORNER

Metropolis—Fritz Lang's 1927 masterpiece about a future world of haves and have nots has been a seminal part of film history. But, for most of us, our experience with this imaginative sci-fi epic has been through bad prints that are scratched, washed out and, most importantly, incomplete. Now, thanks to a state-of-the-art restoration by Germany's Murnau Foundation, *Metropolis* has been returned to its original glory. The DVD includes a newly recorded version of the original Gottfried Huppertz music score, along with a wealth of supplements including audio commentary with film historian Enno Patalas, documentaries on the film and its restoration, plus a stills gallery of production sketches, costume designs and vintage posters. German Expressionist filmmaking was at its height in the late 1920s, and Lang was a master among masters. While the movie is dated in its style and tone, this restored DVD *release allows us to see just how great the cinema had become prior to the introduction of the "talking picture."

DVD ALERT

"*Who Framed Roger Rabbit?*—One of the most entertaining movies of the 1980s finally makes it to DVD in this special edition two-disk package. Director Robert Zemeckis has spent his entire career creating visually audacious films, everything from the *Back to the Future* trilogy, *Forrest Gump, Contact* and most recently, *Cast Away*. Known for his visual slight-of-hand, Zemeckis inserted Tom Hanks into footage with John Kennedy, helped Jodie Foster travel to the ends of the universe, and convinced us that Gary Sinise was a legless war veteran. In *Roger Rabbit*, the director seamlessly integrated live action characters with animated ones, in a world of "toons" and humans. Bob Hoskins, Joanna Cassidy and Christopher Lloyd provide in-the-flesh performances while Charles Fleischer and Kathleen Turner are the vocal inspiration for the toons in trouble. Extras include three *Roger Rabbit* shorts, a pair of documentaries about the film, a deleted scene, a "facts and trivia" commentary and much more.

THE BIG CHEESE

"Logan's Run—"Welcome to the 23rd century" was the tag line for this 1976 sci-fi movie that starred Michael York and Jenny Agutter. As it turned out, the future looked a heck of a lot like a shopping mall (which is where a large chunk of the film was shot) and was filled with casual sex, legal drugs and beautiful people, including a pre-*Charlie's Angel*s Farrah Fawcett. The only down side is that when you reach your 30th birthday, you must die! There is a sort of hocus pocus renewal ritual called carousel, wherein you may be reincarnated, but not everyone believes it. Logan and his friend Francis are part of the police unit, called "sandmen" that tracks down these 30 year old doubting Thomases and kills them on the spot. When the central computer assigns Logan to go undercover as a "runner," he is forced to leave the safety of the domed city and ends up in the wilderness of a vine-covered, overgrown Washington, D.C. There he meets the oldest man in the world (Peter Ustinov, delightfully hamming it up) who agrees to go back to the city. Logan's plan is to show all the young, beautiful people that you can live past 30 and become old and decrepit and senile. While touted at its release as a big budget, extravaganza, the film nevertheless has a closed, cheap feel to it, and moves along at a sluggish pace. Still, it can be a lot of fun to watch. There is a stirring score by Jerry Goldsmith, a nice villainous turn by Richard Jordan as the single-minded sandman, Francis, and the first use of holography in a movie when Logan is interrogated. The DVD contains audio commentary with director Michael Anderson and Michael York, both of whom are still quite pleased with their effort, and seem oblivious to its cheesy shortcomings. Personally, I like the irony of Logan having a life-changing epiphany by going from one mall (the domed city) to another (D.C.)

POST OSCAR MALAISE: DESPERATELY SEEKING DISTRACTION
(April 2003)

With the Oscars behind us, movie buffs everywhere must search for new cinematic rituals upon which to fixate. The awards are over, the trophies have been handed out and it's time to move on. Though the summer season is a ways off, there are plenty of new movies to see in theatres. And the DVD industry continues to grow by leaps and bounds, offering up a cornucopia of old and new titles, some released for the first time, some in newly packaged special editions, all catering to our ongoing hunger for movie entertainment. If the theatre experience can be said to be the chief art form of the 20th century, it is beginning to look like the home viewing experience may be the art form of the 21st. Couple that with the growing sophistication of computers, which provide instant access to an immense amount of information and product, and it looks like we will be spending more and more time glued to our screens, searching for ever more entertaining distractions amid the sea of troubling times in which we find ourselves.

NEW IN THEATRES

Phone Booth—If the movie *Speed* could be called *Die Hard* on a bus, then this film might best be described as *Speed* in a phone booth. Shot in a remarkable ten days, this story about a guy (dark Irish hunk Colin Farrell) who answers a ringing public phone only to be told that if he hangs up, the caller will shoot him from his sniper's nest. Directed by Joel Schumacher (*Tigerland*) the movie was originally supposed to be released last fall, after sitting on the shelf for a year, but was delayed, again, due to the D.C. sniper. Rounding out the cast are Ron Eldard (as the sniper), Forest Whitaker and Katie Holmes. This project has bounced around Hollywood for a number of years with such names as Mel Gibson, Will Smith and Jim Carrey attached to it. Now with Farrell red hot thanks to his recent roles in *Minority Report* and *Daredevil*, we can see if Schumacher has redeemed himself from those awful *Batman* movies he made in the 1990s.

NEW ON VIDEO

Far From Heaven—The biggest oversight in the best picture category this past Oscar season was for Todd Haynes' *Far From Heaven*, an audacious take on melodramas from the 1950s. Starring Julianne Moore and Dennis Quaid (another overlooked category as best supporting actor), the movie explored the notion that in the 1950s, movies were unable to deal with subjects of race and sex as they were being played out in real life. Haynes chose to shoot his story about a couple who must confront these matters in the style of 1950s Hollywood, specifically, the films of Douglas Sirk. Using the same camera set ups, over saturated colors and lens choices of the time, Haynes achieved a unique synthesis of two worlds in collision in a work of stunning art that is also a wry commentary on our culture, past and present.

CLASSIC CORNER

The Day The Earth Stood Still—In the 100-plus year history of cinema, you can count on one hand the number of science fiction movies that have transcended the genre and achieved greatness. At the top of this short list would be *2001: A Space Odyssey*, *Forbidden Planet*, the original *Invasion of the Body Snatchers* and this 1951 movie directed by Robert Wise. An alien saucer lands in Washington, D.C. causing panic and apprehension from the populace. When a strangely attired man emerges from the craft, along with a nine foot tall robot, well, what's a cold war culture to do? The man is accidentally shot (by a nervous army grunt) and taken away. He later escapes from the military hospital and takes the name "Mr. Carpenter" (the Christ allusion is intentional). At its heart, this is a cautionary tale about the madness of war and aggression, topics that are more relevant than ever. Starring Michael Rennie, Patricia Neal, Sam Jaffe and Billy Gray, the film, written by Edmond H. North, was intelligent and high-minded, an unheard of concept in sci-fi at the time. Another first was the use of the theremin by composer Bernard Herrmann to create an otherworldly effect. The instrument would later become something of a horror movie cliché. The newly released DVD by Fox Studios includes audio commentary with Robert Wise and Nicholas Meyer, a 70-minute documentary, the shooting script and much more.

DVD ALERT

Red Dragon—With this movie, Anthony Hopkins completes his Hannibal Lecter trilogy. Based on the first book by author Thomas Harris, this story was previously filmed as *Manhunter* by noted director Michael Mann in 1986. That movie was a moderate success with Brian Cox as Hannibal. However, when the movie version of Harris' second book, *The Silence of the Lambs* was released in 1991, starring Jodie Foster and Anthony Hopkins, it became a huge hit, winning Oscars for best picture, director Jonathan Demme and both leads. The movie made Hopkins a star, effectively reviving his career, and helped forge Hannibal Lecter as a cult anti-hero. He went on to play Lecter again in Ridley Scott's operatic and under-appreciated *Hannibal*. For *Dragon*, screenwriter Ted Tally fleshed out, if you'll pardon the pun, the relatively small part that Lecter had in the story. Director Brett Ratner (*Rush Hour*) working more in the style of *Lambs* surrounded Hopkins with top notch co-stars, including Ed Norton, Emily Watson and Ralph Fiennes. The DVD release will be available in a bare bones single disk or an extras packed two disk set. For the true Lecter fans out there, the choice is clear. Fava beans and Chianti are optional.

THE BIG CHEESE

Dick—What is it about former President Nixon that inspires satirists to keep digging at him? Richard Milhouse Nixon (aka "tricky Dick") resigned from office in 1974 under threat of impeachment and left the White House in disgrace after the fiasco of Watergate came to light. His administration came to represent everything that is despised in corrupt politics. But that didn't stop people from having fun with him, then or now. This most recent jab at our 37th commander-in-chief can best be described as *Clueless* meets *All the President's Men*. A couple of dim bulb teen-age cuties (Kirsten Dunst and Michelle Williams) find themselves involved in the Watergate cover-up, after an innocent school tour of the White House. Dan Hedaya is terrific as the prez, while Saul Rubinek does an outstanding turn as Henry Kissinger. Dave Foley is suitably nerdy as White House chief of staff H. R. Haldeman. *Saturday Night Live*'s Will Ferrell and Bruce McCulloch provide some balance to the humor as an inept Woodward and Bernstein (the Washington Post reporters who first broke the story). To best appreciate the jokes and situations that are lampooned, be sure to watch the original *All the President's Men* video prior to screening *Dick*. To those who thought that they no longer made movies that engage in political satire, all I have to say to you is that you don't know . . .   this film.

SPRING FEVER AND THE RETURN OF
THE MATRIX
(May 2003)

The budding flowers of May are a clear sign that spring has sprung, but it is also a harbinger of the summer movie season to come. Ever since *Star Wars* opened in May 1977, this month has been a proving ground for potential summer blockbusters. This year is no different. Several movies will vie for your time and money this month, none more anticipated than the second installment of *The Matrix* trilogy. (Number three will bow in November.) These two seasonal tent poles in the film industry help sustain the market during lean times The spring/summer pole has traditionally been the domain of mindless, testosterone-driven fare, with little Oscar-calibre contenders in evidence (that's for the other pole). Still, a few gems show some promise, such as *The Matrix Reloaded*, which appears to have genuine originality on its mind, a rare commodity in the business. Who could forget the slew of films that copied the signature "moving freeze frame" technique from *The Matrix*, rather than create their own look. Whatever new bells and whistles come with *Reloaded*, you can be sure that you will see variations of them in the next wave of films that are presently being made. It's as inevitable as flowers in the spring.

NEW IN THEATRES
Finding Nemo—The wizards at Pixar Studios, who in the past were responsible for such great computer animated classics as *Toy Story*, *A Bug's Life* and *Monsters, Inc.*, have done it again with this, their latest effort, a literal fish-out-of-water tale. It seems that Nemo, a tropical clown fish, has been taken from his ocean environs and is now a resident in a dentist's aquarium. It is up to Nemo's dad (voiced by Albert Brooks) to track him down and bring him back. All the usual Pixar elements are here: strong story, memorable characters, vibrant colors, humor (one of the characters is a vegetarian shark!) and lots of heart (after all, it is about a father searching for his missing son). The cast also includes Ellen DeGeneres and Pixar regular John Ratzenberger. Given the past record of this studio, we're all in for a whale of a good time.

NEW ON VIDEO
Catch Me If You Can—Leonardo DiCaprio plays Frank Abagnale, a teenage con artist who impersonates an airline pilot, a doctor and a lawyer, all the while kiting fake checks to maintain an upscale lifestyle. Tom Hanks plays the spectacled FBI man out to nab him. Though the story seems preposterous, it's all true, as shown

in the faux *To Tell The Truth* episode at the film's beginning that sets up the story. Director Steven Spielberg evokes the early 1960s perfectly, from the opening animated credit sequence to the Mancini-esque score by longtime collaborator John Williams. Set design and costumes are also right on the money, all of which help to create a jet set world of Frank Sinatra songs, Pam Am stewardesses and a sense of public decorum that has long since vanished. The supporting cast includes Martin Sheen and a surprisingly sympathetic Christopher Walken as Frank, Sr., the always proud father who could never quite make his own scams work. Over the past decade, Spielberg has learned to reign in his trademark sentimentality in favor of honest emotion. As a result, this is one of his most entertaining, and least cloying, films to date.

CLASSIC CORNER

Dances With Wolves—Say what you will about Kevin Costner, whose star seems to have dimmed of late, but back in 1990, he took quite a gamble when he directed and starred in this epic western with the strange title. Advance word was not good; westerns weren't in vogue, it had a three-hour running time, and the Indians' dialogue was subtitled. Costner stood by his epic which insiders were calling "Kevin's Gate", a reference to the Michael Cimino western, *Heaven's Gate* that flopped a decade earlier. When released, *Wolves* was a spectacular hit, garnering seven Oscars, including Best Picture as well as one for Costner as Best Director. It re-established the western as a viable art form and led the way for a more serious treatment of Native Americans in films. For this special edition DVD, MGM has pulled out all the stops, creating an extended version of the movie that runs nearly four hours, two audio commentary tracks, a making-of featurette, a retrospective documentary and much more.

DVD ALERT

The Cat's Meow—For some reason, this little gem slipped past the public when it played in theatres. Thanks to home video, however, it has a chance for a second life. Based on the play by Steven Peros (which, in turn, was based on Hollywood gossip) it's about an incident that occurred during a party given by William Randolph Hearst on his yacht in 1924. While hosting a birthday bash for producer Thomas Ince, Hearst became convinced that his young bride, Marion Davies, was having an affair with waggish party guest Charlie Chaplin. In the accompanying audio commentary, director Peter Bogdanovich tells how the legendary Orson Welles (who did his own version of Hearst in *Citizen Kane* in 1941) first related this tale to him in the early 1970s. On a tight budget, Bogdanovich assembled a first rate cast that includes Kirsten Dunst (Davies), Edward Herrmann (Hearst), Cary Elwes (Ince) and in a bit of inspired casting, Eddie Izzard as the impish and randy Chaplin. While the truth behind this scandal may never be known, this film offers a most entertaining best guess, as well as a look inside the gaudy world of Hollywood in the 1920s.

THE BIG CHEESE

Freeway—Before Reese Witherspoon was *Legally Blonde*, before she was the victim of *Cruel Intentions*, even before she took up residence in *Pleasantville*, she made this nifty, one-of-a-kind thriller satire that is, in essence, a white trash version of *Little Red Riding Hood*. As a foul-mouthed teenage illiterate, with shoplifting priors, our plucky heroine has a crack whore for a mom (Amanda Plummer) and a no count stepdad with designs on her. When her folks get busted, Reese escapes her hillbilly hell and heads for grandma's house (trailer, that is). While hitching to get to her destination, our gal Reese is picked up by a kindly shrink (Kiefer Sutherland). The caring counselor turns out to be more psycho than psychiatrist, turning into the big, bad wolf. Reese, however, turns the tables on him, showing her wildcat side that leaves the lout all but dead. And that's just the first half. First time director Matthew Bright, working from his own screenplay, takes great delight in such lurid settings as redneck squalor and women's prison. The DVD has a great audio commentary with Bright where he speaks with unbridled enthusiasm for his underclass wastrels and has little sympathy for authority. In one sense, he is the west coast cousin of Baltimore's John Waters (*Pink Flamingos, Hairspray*), though Bright is clearly a better filmmaker. While *Freeway* is not for everyone, if you have an adventurous spirit, this is one road trip that will definitely leave you breathless.

10 THINGS TO LOVE ABOUT
THE SUMMER MOVIE SEASON
(June 2003)

As the summer movie season truly begins, it's time to take stock of just what is so good about these films. Like summer reading, summer movies are about lightness and fun. No heavyweight fare like *The Pianist* if you please. Instead, it's all about escapism. Hold it! Stop right there! The fact is that while most films this season are about lightweight entertainment, there are still some quality movies out there to see. For every *Charlie's Angels* abomination there is something else that you won't be ashamed to admit you saw. By summer's end, with a little bit of luck, there could well be ten movies that were worth your time and money, as well as your passion for high quality cinema.

NEW IN THEATRES
Down With Love—One of the latest trends in Hollywood is the revival of the "jet set" era of the early 1960s. Everything from Spielberg's recent *Catch Me If You Can* and the Bob Crane biopic *Auto Focus* to the Tom Hanks-directed pop band comedy drama, *That Thing You Do*, Hollywood has fallen in love with this hip, pre-hippie period in American pop culture. This latest effort (and a musical, to boot) stars Renee Zellweger and Ewan McGregor, who proved they had the pipes for the job from their previous work in *Chicago* and *Moulin Rouge*. A total throwback to the sex comedies that used to star Doris Day and Rock Hudson, they even managed to dig up Tony Randall who appeared in these kinds of flicks 40 years ago. Whether this film will one day be a classic on the order of *Breakfast at Tiffany's* or *Pillow Talk* is yet to be determined. However, the cast looks great, as do the clean lines and bright colors of the production design. The real test will be whether or not Renee and Ewan have good chemistry together.

NEW ON VIDEO
The Hours—Trying to pick one movie as the best of the year is a nearly impossible task. The fact remains that there are always several films that are quite good, and choosing just one becomes a matter of apples and oranges. Such was the case last year, with work as wide ranging as *Far From Heaven*, *The Pianist*, *Chicago*, *Adaptation* and this one. All were outstanding, and all, in their own way, were great. Based on the Pulitzer winning novel by Michael Cunningham, *The Hours* skillfully wove together the threads of three separate stories into a fascinating tapestry about life, death and the creative spirit. Nicole Kidman, in a tangled wig and sizable false nose, plays tormented author Virginia Woolf,

beginning to write her novel, *Mrs. Dalloway*, in 1923, and fighting the demons that would ultimately cause her to take her own life years hence. Julianne Moore is Laura, a 1950s wife and mother who is reading Mrs. Dalloway yet feels smothered by the constraints of her seemingly blissful domesticity. Finally, Meryl Streep plays Clarissa, a modern day New York professional who is hosting a party for a literary friend. The merging of these three tales is miraculous and borders on the poetic. Profound and intensely moving, the film is a true work of art, and an example of just how powerful moviemaking can be. The DVD includes audio commentary with the three actresses who weigh in on the experience of being a part of this one-of-a-kind movie.

CLASSIC CORNER

Miller's Crossing—While many people have commented on the mythic qualities in the movie, *Road To Perdition*, it was not the first gangster film to mine such territory. A dozen years earlier, the Coen brothers (*O Brother, Where Art Thou?*) tackled similar ground in this epic masterpiece about Irish gangsters in 1920s Chicago. Starring Albert Finney, Gabriel Byrne, Jon Polito, Marcia Gay Harden and John Turturro, this stylish drama envisioned a hard, cynical world of crime bosses and flunkies, yet managed to imbue it with a wit and humor that remains unmatched to this day. By turns lyrical and brutal, the film's central metaphor is best illustrated in the opening credits which shows a man's hat blowing through a wooded glade. At its heart, the movie is about the roles people play in life, the hats they wear and the forces of fate that blow and buffet them about. Blessed with a stellar cast and a haunting score by Coen regular Carter Burwell, *Miller's Crossing* is one of the truly great films of our time. This first time DVD release (along with another Coen classic, *Barton Fink*) has been much anticipated by fans of this remarkable filmmaking team.

DVD ALERT

The Right Stuff—Little did Tom Wolfe realize when he wrote his book about mid-20th century test pilots, that its title would one day become a catch phrase for all things heroic. The book became the basis for this 1983 motion picture by off beat writer/director Philip Kaufman. Working with a dynamic cast that included such then up and comers as Sam Shepard, Ed Harris, Dennis Quaid, Fred Ward, Scott Glenn, Jeff Goldblum, Pamela Reed and Barbara Hershey, director Kaufman delivered a quirky and entertaining film about the formative years of the American space program. The DVD is finally being re-released in a beautiful two disk set that includes documentaries, audio commentary and more. For those who have yet to see this uniquely original movie, all I have to say is you're in for quite a surprise. *Apollo 13* this ain't.

THE BIG CHEESE

Capricorn One—Between the time that O.J. Simpson was a Heisman Trophy winner and a multiple murder suspect, he managed to squeeze in a relatively lucrative film career, filling out small parts in such flicks as *The Towering Inferno* and *The Naked Gun*. One of his more successful, yet totally inane, efforts was this 1978 big budget sci-fi flick about a bogus trip to Mars set up by the government that goes horribly wrong. O.J. plays an afro'd astronaut, along with Sam Waterson and James Brolin. Major technical problems with the space hardware causes NASA to fake a Mars landing (so they won't lose their funding) and the three astronauts are coerced into going along with the sham. While an empty rocket is launched into space, our three heroes cavort about in a soundstage rigged to look like the red planet. Things get dicey, however, when the returning rocket burns up during re-entry, on live TV, and our guys must now be killed to sustain the ruse. They escape into the desert, but are hunted down by the Feds. During all of this, reporter Elliott Gould becomes suspicious about the authenticity of the mission. A major faux pas involves a space conversation between the astronauts and their wives on earth, without regard for the time delay that would actually occur (who's running things here anyway?). To create some urgency, there are car crashes, an aerial chase through the desert in a small plane and way too much bad dialogue. By the film's end, when Elliott Gould saves James Brolin, no one really cares anymore, despite the heroic music and slow-mo photography. Ironically, as outlandish as the story may be, it pales in comparison to the fact that these two men would one day share a unique place in celebrity history: each one said "I do" to Barbra Streisand. And you gotta love a flick where a former "Mr. Babs" saves the life of a future "Mr. Babs."

10 THINGS TO LOVE ABOUT
THE SUMMER MOVIE SEASON
(July 2003)

> For some reason, I have this second version of the June 2003 column for July. I'm guessing the previous one didn't run and I adapted it for July. I've decided to simply run them both so the reader can see the minor and major differences I made to the text. There was enough new material to warrant this.

As the summer movie season truly begins, it's time to take stock of just what is so good about these films. Like summer reading, summer movies are about lightness and fun. No heavyweight fare like *The Pianist* if you please. Instead, it's all about escapism. Hold it! Stop right there! The fact is that while most films this season are about lightweight entertainment, there are still some quality movies out there to see. For every *Charlie's Angels* abomination there is something else that you won't be ashamed to admit you saw. In addition to the already released *Down With Love* and *Finding Nemo*, promising new and upcoming releases include the New Zealand import *Whale Rider*, Luke Wilson and Kate Hudson in Rob Reiner's *Alex & Emma*, Nick Nolte and Daryl Hannah in the eccentric *Northfork*, *Dirty Pretty Things* with *Amelie* star Audrey Tautou, Nicholas Cage in Ridley Scott's *Matchstick Men* and *The Secret Lives of Dentists* with Campbell Scott and Denis Leary. By summer's end, with a little bit of luck, there could well be ten movies that were worth your time and money, as well as your passion for high quality cinema.

NEW IN THEATRES
Seabiscuit—At the top of the serious summer list is this true story, based on the best seller by Laura Hillenbrand which taps directly into the underdog spirit that Americans find so endearing. The movie stars Tobey Maguire as Red Pollard, the half-blind jockey who, along with owner Charles Howard (Jeff Bridges) and trainer Tom Smith (Chris Cooper), took a crooked-legged horse and made him into a winner, which struck a chord with the common-man ethos of Depression-era America. Directed by Gary Ross, who previously examined American culture and values in *Pleasantville*, this epic saga of a bygone era in racing promises to satisfy moviegoers' hunger for some counter programming in this season of fluff.

NEW ON VIDEO
The Hours—Trying to pick one movie as the best of the year is a nearly impossible task. The fact remains that there are always several films that are quite good, and choosing just one becomes a matter of apples and oranges. Such was

the case last year, with work as wide ranging as *Far From Heaven, The Pianist, Chicago, Adaptation* and this one. All were outstanding, and all, in their own way, were great. Based on the Pulitzer winning novel by Michael Cunningham, *The Hours* skillfully wove together the threads of three separate stories into a fascinating tapestry about life, death and the creative spirit. Nicole Kidman, in a tangled wig and sizable false nose, plays tormented author Virginia Woolf, beginning to write her novel, *Mrs. Dalloway*, in 1923, and fighting the demons that would ultimately cause her to take her own life years hence. Julianne Moore is Laura, a 1950s wife and mother who is reading Mrs. Dalloway yet feels smothered by the constraints of her seemingly blissful domesticity. Finally, Meryl Streep plays Clarissa, a modern day New York professional who is hosting a party for a literary friend. The merging of these three tales is miraculous and borders on the poetic. Profound and intensely moving, the film is a true work of art, and an example of just how powerful moviemaking can be. The DVD includes four featurettes plus two audio commentary tracks, one with the director and writer, and the other with the three actresses who weigh in on the experience of being a part of this one-of-a-kind movie.

DVD ALERT

Solaris—The pairing of George Clooney and director Steven Soderbergh has yielded such fine films as *Out of Sight* and *Ocean's Eleven*. And, on his own, Soderbergh has shown himself to be unafraid of tackling unusual and experimental projects, everything from *Kafka* in 1991 to *Full Frontal* last year. One of his most artistic, if not financially successful, endeavors is this remake of the Russian classic, based on the novel by Stanislaw Lem. The story concerns a psychiatrist (Clooney) sent to investigate the goings on at a space station where the crew seems to be insane. The station is in orbit around the planet, Solaris, which is covered by a living, sentient ocean that can interact with the minds of the crew. The result is that any thought a person has can be given tangible reality, including, as it turns out, Clooney's memory of his dead wife (Natasha McElhone). It is not often that cinematic sci-fi explores such substantial realms as religion and philosophy; usually they settle for monsters, explosions and space battles. In addition to a unique production design, color palette and an intriguingly haunting score by Chris Martinez, Soderbergh adds his trademark story structure and editing style, creating a look and feel that is truly original. Like *2001: A Space Odyssey* and *Contact, Solaris* has a depth and sophistication that is generally missing from most other sci-fi movies. That, alone, makes it worth your while.

Winged Migration—Though originally released last year, this Oscar-nominated documentary is only now making it to the Lehigh Valley; it will be shown at the newly refurbished 19th St Theatre in Allentown July 19-23. Shot over a four-year period, this extraordinary movie literally takes flight as it follows the migration odyssey of many avian species from our planet. Using a variety of airborne cameras, the filmmakers put the viewer in intimate contact with these remarkable birds in a series of visually stunning tableaux. Director Jacques Perrin previously got up close and personal with the bug world as producer of the 1996 breakthrough feature *MicroCosmos*. For *Winged Migration* he has truly outdone himself with a film that is destined to be a timeless classic.

A BREATH OF FRESH AIR: LOOKING AT THE FALL MOVIE SEASON
(September 2003)

Now that the lightweight summer movies are behind us, it is time for the serious films to arrive, heralding the start of the Oscar-worthy movie season. Of course, there will still be a fair percentage of mediocre and bad films since, as the saying goes, "90% of everything is crap." However, with the coming of the fall, the ratio of good to bad cinema, does seem to edge up slightly on the side of the good. Those that look especially interesting include *The Human Stain* with Anthony Hopkins and Nicole Kidman; *Dummy* starring Adrien Brody (*The Pianist*) as a put upon ventriloquist; *Under The Tuscan Sun*, a romantic comedy with Diane Lane; *Mystic River* starring Sean Penn, Marcia Gay Harden and directed by Clint Eastwood; *In The Cut*, an erotic thriller by Jane Campion (*The Piano*) based on Susanna Moore's best-seller and starring Meg Ryan and Jennifer Jason Leigh; *Master And Commander: The Far Side Of The World* an historic sea epic with Russell Crowe and directed by Peter Weir; Tim Burton's quirky circus flick *Big Fish*, starring Ewan McGregor, Albert Finney and Helena Bonham-Carter; and the first installment of Quentin Tarantino's Hong Kong action flick, *Kill Bill* starring Uma Thurman and David Carradine. How many of these films will turn out to be good is anybody's guess at the moment, but it's nice to know that the percentage of quality cinema has gone up.

NEW IN THEATRES

INTOLERABLE CRUELTY—Art house cult filmmakers, Joel and Ethan Coen (aka the Coen Brothers) try to break into the mainstream with this farcical dark comedy. George Clooney (who previously worked with the Coens in one of their few breakout hits *O Brother, Where Art Thou?*) here plays sleazy divorce lawyer, Miles Massey, who is not above rigging a trial for his millionaire client, Rex Rexroth (Edward Herrmann). The ex Mrs. Rex (Catherine Zeta-Jones) is understandably furious at the outcome, and makes it her mission in life to get back at Clooney. Sparks fly when the two combatants start falling for one another amid the heat of battle. Also starring are Billy Bob Thornton and Geoffrey Rush. The Coens are known for their snappy, clever dialog and subversive sense of humor, and they have flirted with the screwball genre before in the underrated *The Hudsucker Proxy*. How will they fare with mainstream viewers? Some may resist them since the Coens are the Coens are the Coens, and are an acquired taste. But, for the rest of us who know that these brothers are among the most original and talented filmmakers out there, we say, objections overruled. In other words, go see it. Case closed.

NEW ON VIDEO

RUSSIAN ARK—It is rare these days when a movie comes along which blends form and content in a manner that borders on the magical. Russian director Alexander Sokurov's latest effort does just that. The story concerns a modern filmmaker who finds himself drifting through three hundred years of Russian history as he wanders the sumptuous interior of a palatial museum. Unseen by the audience, we hear the time traveler's thoughts as we watch the movie through his eyes. Curiously, he also remains unobserved by the various characters in the film, save one fellow who, it appears, is equally unstuck in time. The film's conceit has the main character's point of view unfold as a single, uninterrupted shot with no editing. Previous films have played with the "one take" concept, the most famous being Hitchcock's *Rope* in 1948, but in fact they merely disguised their edits to create the appearance of a single shot. This was necessitated by the fact that film cameras can hold only about ten minutes of film at a time. For *Ark*, the filmmakers used a digital camera with an expanded hard drive to accommodate a feature length film. Months of planning and preparation led to a one-day shoot at the Russian Hermitage Museum with over 900 actors. The palace location provided an astonishingly opulent and textured backdrop for the film story, and would have been impossible to build as a set. The title cleverly embraces the notion of a vessel which contains the cultural treasures of Russia, as well as tracing the country's own arc through history over time. The DVD includes audio commentary with producer Jens Meurer, interviews, a making of featurette and a documentary about the stunning Hermitage location. Visually breathtaking, artistically rich and dramatically weighty, *Russian Ark* provides the viewer with a satisfying journey through culture and history where, ultimately, the goal becomes one of self-discovery.

CLASSIC CORNER

FARGO—When the DVD industry first began, most studios rushed into release a number of recent catalog titles they had on hand. In those halcyon days, special editions with extra features were a rare commodity, so most of these early DVDs were bare bones affairs with little more than a trailer to pad out the disc. Now, with DVDs firmly entrenched as the home video format of choice, and special editions as plentiful as multiplexes, many of those early releases are getting deluxe makeovers. Such is the case with this 1996 film by the quirky Coen Brothers. When released in theatres, this frostbitten thriller became a surprise hit, garnering seven Oscar nominations, including best picture, and winning for best actress (Frances McDormand) and best original screenplay. Dark and humorous, the story about a desperate car salesman who hatches a kidnapping plot that goes horribly awry, and the pregnant police chief investigating the case, struck a chord with the public and made "Yeah, sure, you betcha" a catchphrase. Extras include a new documentary *Minnesota Nice*, interviews with the Coen Brothers and Frances McDormand, audio commentary with cinematographer Roger Deakins, a trivia track, collectable packaging and other surprises. Should you rush out and purchase this latest special edition of a Coen Brothers classic? Well, as William H. Macy's car salesman character says, "You're darn tootin'".

DVD ALERT

THE LION KING—Released into theatres nearly a decade ago, this "circle-of-life" musical classic by Disney went on to become the highest grossing animated film of all time. (Only recently has it been surpassed by Disney/Pixar's fishy fantastic *Finding Nemo*). Epic in scope and drama, the Hamlet-inspired storyline follows Simba, a lion cub who must come to terms with his father's death (for which he feels responsible) and who ultimately becomes a strong leader to the animals in his kingdom. Played against the vast landscapes of Africa, The Lion King was a total triumph for Disney, from the stellar voice cast of James Earl Jones, Jeremy Irons, Matthew Broderick, Moira Kelly, Nathan Lane, Whoopie Goldberg and Robert Guillaume, to the songs by Elton John and the moving African-inspired score by Hans Zimmer. For its debut release on DVD, Disney has concocted an extravagant two-disc set worthy of this animated classic. In addition to making of featurettes and audio commentary, the animators have added a new sequence and song (ala the *Beauty and the Beast* DVD last year) making this a must-have title for anyone's collection.

THE BIG CHEESE

MONTY PYTHON AND THE HOLY GRAIL—The British comedy troupe which called itself *Monty Python's Flying Circus* first made a splash on TV in the late 1960s and early '70s. The next logical step for these loony comedians was to jump into films. Armed with a miniscule budget and boundless enthusiasm, they tackled the Arthurian legend in what would become one of the funniest movies ever made. As they did on their skit TV show, the six-man team (Graham Chapman, John Cleese, Terry Gilliam, Eric Idle, Terry Jones and Michael Palin) played nearly all the parts, giving each member three or more roles. Shooting at real castles and moody Scottish locations, the two directors in the group, Jones and Gilliam, brought a rich visual style to their no-budget production. They even turned one economic concession (no horses) into a major comedic asset by having the characters mime galloping while their squires followed behind banging together cocoanuts to simulate hoof sound effects. Visually, the movie evokes a very realistic historical ambience, with mud-spattered characters and dank stone castles, though the story is anything but traditional. There's a killer rabbit, a three-headed knight who bickers with himself (themselves?), a holy hand grenade, a shrubbery that serves as a bargaining tool, plus encounters with rude Frenchmen, a band of zealous witch-haters, a persistent Black Knight and a wizard named Tim. As much fun as the movie, itself, is, the special edition DVD comes loaded with a wealth of extras including two audio commentary tracks with the cast, an on-set making of featurette, a new documentary where Jones and Palin revisit the castles and locations, plus a Lego version of one of the movie's musical numbers. All in all, a tasty treat that proves that some of the world's best cheese comes from merry old England.

GOOD CHEER AND GOOD MOVIES
THIS CHRISTMAS SEASON
(December 2003)

December can be one of the most intense months for new film releases. The studios let loose with their Oscar hopefuls, inundating the theatres with some of the best movies of the year. The biggest guns in this final month include such varied fare as Tom Cruise's *The Last Samurai*, the conjoined-twin comedy *Stuck On You* starring Matt Damon and Greg Kinnear, the Vermeer-inspired *Girl with a Pearl Earring* with Colin Firth and Scarlett Johansson, the Civil War drama *Cold Mountain* starring Nicole Kidman, Jude Law and Renee Zellweger, the 1950s-era collegiate drama, *Mona Lisa Smile* starring Kirsten Dunst, Julia Stiles and Maggie Gyllenhaal as a trio of Wellesley co-eds and Julia Roberts as their art history professor, and the final chapter in the *Lord of the Rings* saga, *The Return of the King*.

Conversely, given this wealth of movies, December is also the month when most people find they have little free time for the multiplex, what with the approaching Christmas holiday. Still, enough folks do make the time, and in any event these films usually carry over into January. So, while you're anticipating what presents you'll be opening on Christmas morning, don't forget the wonderful cinematic gifts that also await you.

NEW IN THEATRES

BIG FISH—As the title might indicate, this is a movie about tall tales. Director Tim Burton is no stranger to the fantastic, with films as varied as *Beetlejuice, Edward Scissorhands, Mars Attacks* and *Sleepy Hollow*. Here he creates the isolated, off-kilter world of Spectre, Alabama. The one-street town serves as a dreamscape memory lane for dying patriarch Albert Finney, who spins tales of his younger self (played by Ewan McGregor). Part fable, part family drama, the screenplay by John August allows Burton to weave his usual brand of magic realism and gothic iconography, as he paints in broad strokes to illustrate one man's life as he might wish to remember it. Along for the ride are Billy Crudup, Danny DeVito, Jessica Lange, Steve Buscemi, Alison Lohman and Helena Bonham Carter.

NEW ON VIDEO

NAQOYQATSI—With this film, director Godfrey Reggio completes what has come to be known as the "qatsi" trilogy. These non-story, non-dialogue, non-actor tone poems about life on Earth are, in equal parts, cryptic and inspiring.

Back in 1983 Reggio, along with cinematographer Ron Fricke and composer Philip Glass, created *Koyaanisqatsi*, the groundbreaking aural/visual experience that showed western society's dependence on, and interconnectedness to, technology. The title, taken from the Hopi Indian language, translates as "crazy life" or "life out of balance" and was chosen for its lack of associative baggage. Originally, Reggio wanted to use an image or symbol instead of a title, since he was trying to bypass language, but a film studio requires a title (even an unconventional one) in order to market its product. Reggio and Glass collaborated (without Fricke) on the second installment called *Powaqqatsi*, released in 1988, which covered the Southern hemisphere cultures, in contrast to the first film's Northern bias. (Fricke went on to direct his own visually spiritual film called *Baraka* in 1992.) With *Naqoyqatsi*, Reggio and Glass have completed their trilogy, collaborating with editor and visual designer, Jon Kane. Using found footage and computer animation, Kane brings a very different look to this film, yet stays true to the series. All three movies are now available on DVD and contain interviews with the principle creators about their creative odyssey.

CLASSIC CORNER
CHITTY CHITTY BANG BANG—Based on the fantasy novel by James Bond author Ian Fleming, this 1968 children's classic has long been overdue for a DVD special edition. Starring Dick Van Dyke as a widower/inventor with two kids to raise, the family's home is a funhouse collection of Rube Goldberg contraptions that do everything from make breakfast to clean house. The centerpiece of the film is the titular jalopy, cobbled together by Van Dyke, which turns into a magical flying car that carries off the main characters on a grand adventure. The casting of Van Dyke seems clearly inspired to hearken back to his success in 1964's *Mary Poppins*. He shows off his phenomenal performance skills in numerous dance numbers, none more astonishing then his impersonation of a dancing marionette that is so flawless, you'd swear he were hanging from wires. Though *Chitty* is no *Poppins*, comparisons to the Disney classic are inevitable; both films are about damaged families that need fixing, in both films the songs were written by Richard and Robert Sherman, and both are filled with magical moments and great musical set pieces. The elaborately choreographed "Me Ol' Bamboo" recalls *Poppins* rooftop number, "Step in Time", while the gentle "Toot Sweets" is reminiscent of "Chim Chim Cher Ee" and "A Spoonful of Sugar". The standout tune, however, is the title song, which is both catchy and memorable. The two-disc special edition DVD includes hours of extras plus a 34-page photo-packed storybook, all in a beautifully designed case. And this movie has something that even *Mary Poppins* doesn't have... a Dick Van Dyke performance minus the fake cockney accent!

DVD ALERT

THE SINGING DETECTIVE—Though recently remade with Robert Downey Jr. that is currently in theatres, the original, 1986 British TV miniseries is the one to check out. The story, about a writer afflicted with a grotesque case of psoriasis, is based on the screenplay by Dennis Potter (who suffered a similar skin condition). The series chronicles pulp writer Philip Marlow's treatment in a hospital for his affliction and how he deals with it. His raw, nearly untouchable skin is the perfect metaphor for his own soul. As he lies in agony, Marlow reminisces about his childhood, and fantasizes himself as the main character in his noir novel, *The Singing Detective*. In his miserable state, he sees the hospital staff periodically burst into song and dance as his mind seeks some relief from his hellish condition. Fact and fantasy, past and present, blur, mix and intertwine as Marlow tries to make some sense out of his life and the mistakes he has made. Michael Gambon (*Gosford Park, Sleepy Hollow*) is in brilliant form as the tormented writer, and he is ably assisted by co-stars Joanne Whalley, Janet Suzman, Patrick Malahide, Lyndon Davies and Jim Carter. This miniseries has been called (and rightly so, I think) the greatest drama ever made for television. The DVD includes an illuminating audio commentary with director Jon Amiel and producer Kenneth Trodd, a documentary on the life and career of Dennis Potter and much more. This is truly "must see TV".

CHRISTMAS CLASSIC

A CHRISTMAS STORY—Who would have ever believed that Bob Clark, the director of the raunchy *Porky's* films, could make such a heartwarming, funny and touching Christmas movie, one that would go on to become a perennial classic, no less beloved than *A Christmas Carol* and *Miracle On 34th Street*? Released into theatres in 1983, with little fanfare and less marketing, the film did scant business on its initial release. But, thanks to TV and home video, this slice of holiday cheer has found a home in nearly everyone's heart. Based on humorist Jean Shepherd's autobiographical book, *In God We Trust, All Others Pay Cash*, (and narrated by Shepherd, himself) the movie recounts young Ralphie's (Peter Billingsley) 1940s childhood when all he wanted for Christmas was a Red Ryder BB rifle. Much of the homespun humor derives from Ralphie's relationship with his parents (Darren McGavin and Melinda Dillon, both splendid) and younger brother, as he tries to ensure he'll get his Christmas wish. Evoking a simpler time, the film still finds plenty of edgy humor to contemporize its Norman Rockwell tableaux. Though previously available on VHS tape and DVD, the movie has been newly re-released as a special two-disc set, loaded with extras. Especially good is the audio commentary with director Clark and a now grown-up Billingsley. Also included is a new documentary with the cast, more Christmas stories by Jean Shepherd and some amusing background information on the Red Ryder air rifle and the notorious "leg lamp". All in all, there's enough here to satisfy even the most Scrooge-like curmudgeon around.

OSCAR MIRED

(February 2004)

In our ever increasingly bustling world, the pace of life just moves faster and faster. Hollywood has, evidently, taken notice of this and responded by shortening the time span between Oscar nominations and the awards ceremony. I guess they figured that since the studios no longer had to distribute movies by covered wagon, or acquire ballots through the pony express, the seven-week window could be essentially cut in half and still leave enough time to campaign in the trade papers and on television. The real reason for this accelerated schedule is so the Oscars can remain competitive with the various other awards announcements, and will hopefully translate into better T.V. ratings for the Academy Awards telecast. It's ironic that the motion picture Academy now depends so strongly on the television medium (once considered an arch rival) for its public relations and that it's become the single most important element in its advertising promotion.

*NEW IN THEATRES

KILL BILL VOL. 2—After a six-year spell away from the director's chair, quirky auteur Quentin Tarantino returned, literally, with a vengeance last fall with his chop socky action epic, *Kill Bill, Vol. 1*. Originally conceived as a three-hour plus opus, Miramax Studios persuaded the director to release the movie in two parts (hence the volume number). Starring Uma Thurman as a double crossed hit lady who returns from a coma set upon revenge, the movie's giddy indulgence of over-the-top carnage split the audience into two camps of either love it or hate it. As was typical in all of Tarantino's work, Reservoir Dogs, Pulp Fiction and Jackie Brown, the movie riffed on 1960s and '70s exploitation flicks along with obscure music from the period, most notably "The Green Hornet Theme" and the Latino/disco rendition of "Don't Let Me Be Misunderstood" by Santa Esmeralda. The box office proved that Tarantino's style-over-substance blend of ultra-violence and female empowerment clicked with a public eager for anything even remotely original. As Miramax sighed with corporate relief, the release of Vol. 2 was looked upon with great anticipation. The saga now continues with Uma's character, "The Bride", as she is referred to in the credits, working her way up her lethal "to do" list. Having terminated Vivica A. Fox and Lucy Liu (along with a hundred or so henchmen) in part one, she is now set to dispatch Daryl Hannah and Michael Madsen on her way to David Carradine's "Bill", the head honcho/former lover of 'The Bride", who's actions against her set the whole story in motion. What tricks Tarantino has up his sleeve is anybody's guess, but we can all be sure it will be a stylish concoction set to the coolest music this side of Nancy Sinatra's "Bang Bang (My Baby Shot Me Down)."

NEW ON VIDEO

LOST IN TRANSLATION—Every once in a while, a little gem of a movie sneaks in under the radar, surprising audiences and critics alike. Such is the case with Sophia Coppola's latest film, only her second feature as director. Her first, *The Virgin Suicides*, though a cult hit, was a mixed bag, at best, and showed little indication of what was to come. Bill Murray, in one of his finest performances, plays a washed up actor who has sold out to cash in on a big paycheck by hawking booze to the Japanese. The world weary Murray wears his age and life lessons like a well-tailored suit; the smart aleck from *Saturday Night Live* has transformed over the years into a wry cynic who doesn't suffer fools gladly, least of all, himself. Holed up in a Tokyo hotel, he makes the acquaintance of another lost soul, (Scarlett Johansson), whose photographer husband is always off to a photo shoot one place or another. The two form an odd bond, strangers in a strange land who connect despite their 30-year age difference. Ms. Coppola's cinematic pedigree (her dad is Francis Coppola of *Godfather* and *Apocalypse Now* fame) has, until recently, been restricted to weak performances in daddy's movies, *Rumble Fish* and *Godfather 3*, the latter where she was unmercifully singled out for her bad acting and unfairly blamed for that movie's failure. Taking the axiom that what doesn't kill you makes you stronger, Ms. Coppola has concentrated her efforts behind the camera as a writer and director and proven that the best revenge is success. This movie heralds the arrival of a major talent.

CLASSIC CORNER

INGMAR BERGMAN'S GOD TRILOGY—The revered Swedish director, Ingmar Bergman, has left a legacy of dozens of great films during his half century in the movie industry. His considerable oeuvre includes such classics as *The Seventh Seal*, *Wild Strawberries*, *The Virgin Spring* and *Fanny & Alexander*. His cinematic journey reached a profound apex in the early 1960s with the release of three films that came to be known as "The God Trilogy." The unrelated storylines focused on the director's own search for spiritual meaning in an otherwise indifferent world. The first, *Through a Glass Darkly,* concerns a family dealing with isolation and madness while attempting to maintain their religious conviction. The second film, *Winter Light*, is an exceedingly bleak study of a pastor who has lost his faith, yet continues on despite the meaninglessness of his life. Finally, *The Silence* is a visual tone poem illustrating nothing less than the emotional collapse of society, itself. What makes these intensely painful stories endurable and compelling is the sheer artistry of the director, the luminous black and white photography by cinematographer Sven Nykvist and the uniformly excellent acting by Bergman regulars Max von Sydow, Harriet Anderson, Gunnar Bjornstrand and Ingrid Thulin. In lesser hands this material could degenerate into maudlin posturing, but Bergman is mining a deeper vein here, one that goes straight to the soul. The three films have recently been released on DVD in a special edition package by Criterion and include a wealth of extras befitting these classics. Whether you're a newcomer to Bergman's films or an old timer, this collection is a great way to appreciate the depth and artistry of one of cinema's grand masters.

DVD ALERT

ED WOOD—The timing could not be better for the release of this special edition modern classic. Director Tim Burton's current flick, *Big Fish*, is reeling in rave reviews and respectable box office, while actor Johnny Depp has never been hotter, thanks to his back-to-back hits, *Once Upon a Time in Mexico* and *Pirates of the Caribbean*. With this in mind, the time is ripe for a rediscovery of this overlooked jewel. When first released in 1994, this fanciful tale of the 1950s grade Z filmmaker was a critics' darling but a box office dud. Even an Oscar for Martin Landau's astonishing turn as the over-the-hill Dracula star, Bela Lugosi, did little for the film's bottom line. Most people, it seems, had no interest in a movie about the world's worst filmmaker. What these people failed to realize was that this was really a story about a man who loved movies; that he lacked the talent to make good films, himself, was no impediment to his belief in his own abilities. And, the motley crew of talent-free associates who made up his luckless troupe gave his cause a quixotic flair, illustrated most forcefully in Mr. Depp's performance as the ebullient and ever optimistic Wood. In addition to the aforementioned Landau, supporting players include Sarah Jessica Parker, Patricia Arquette, Bill Murray and Burton regular Jeffrey Jones. Beautifully photographed in black and white by Stefan Czapsky, the film totally captures the look and feel of 1950s Los Angeles. The terrific, upbeat Latin-tinged score by Howard Shore is equally effective. (Tim Burton's usual composer, Danny Elfman, must have been on vacation.) The two-disc set is a welcomed upgrade from the previous bare bones single disc. If this one sells well, perhaps we can look forward to future reissues from Burton's catalogue.

A PASSION FOR MAKING MOVIES
(March 2004)

There are many stories from Hollywood about filmmakers taking 10 to 20 years to get a pet project made. Scheduling and money are usually the stumbling blocks that hold things up, and it generally takes great fortitude and personal commitment to keep these celluloid dreams alive during their gestation. None were more personal than Mel Gibson's decade-long desire to illustrate his Catholic faith on the big screen with *The Passion of The Christ*. Putting up $30 million of his own money, Mr. Gibson was determined to see his vision become reality.

Biblical films have had a difficult time finding success, given the polarizing nature of religion. Martin Scorsese's *The Last Temptation of Christ* ignited a firestorm of protest in 1988 over its depiction of Jesus' life. As a result, religious people stayed away in droves. By contrast, Gibson's film takes a more traditionalist view of Christ (though augmented with much more graphic violence) that has the religious community lining up en mass.

Judging by his past work as a director, Mr. Gibson is more intuitive than analytical, given more to emotion than reasoned thought. That raises the issue of whether or not *Passion* is pretentious. His work on *Braveheart* showed a director who was very self-assured and unafraid of honest emotion. Is that sort of style akin to pandering or stacking the deck? Is Mel an artist or merely a proselytizer? Is it art or just propaganda? Can it be both? Just think how rare it is for a film, any film, to provoke such questions. Whatever the answers turn out to be, it's nice to hear the questions being asked.

NEW IN THEATRES

ETERNAL SUNSHINE OF THE SPOTLESS MIND—Screenwriting is perhaps the least appreciated craft in the filmmaking community. For the last five years one of the quirkiest and most original voices in this field has been Charlie Kaufman. His scripts for *Being John Malkovich, Human Nature, Confessions of a Dangerous Mind* and *Adaptation* have been a breath of fresh air for those who appreciate unique storytelling. His latest effort reteams him with *Human Nature* director Michel Gondry in a tale about a man (Jim Carrey) who can't get over the break-up with his ex. When he learns she has undergone a procedure that can wipe clean specific memories (in this case, him) he opts for the same in hopes of moving on with his life. The irony and satire come fast and furious (as is generally the case in a Charlie Kaufman screenplay) in this film who's wordy title might best be distilled down to "ignorance is bliss." The film is blessed with a great cast that includes Kate Winslet, Kirsten Dunst, Mark Ruffalo, Elijah Wood and Tom Wilkinson.

NEW ON VIDEO

21 GRAMS—With its obscure title and preview clips of a haggard, dressed down Naomi Watts, some people assumed this film was about drug addiction. The title actually refers to the speculated loss of weight a body incurs at the time of death-literally, the weight of one's soul. The fragmented, convoluted plot directed by Mexico's Alejandro Gonzalez Inarritu, who worked in a similar style in his 2000 release, *Amores Perros*, finds Sean Penn, dying of a heart condition, receiving a transplant from Watts' dead husband. Meanwhile, ex-con, Benicio Del Toro is trying to find some spiritual meaning in his life, even as it tears his family apart. The convergence point of these "lost souls" is a tragic car accident that impacts all their lives. The film, itself, feels as though it were a part of this collision, with its scrambled, out-of-order plotline that unfolds like a Cubist, Rorschach jigsaw puzzle. All the actors give riveting performances that you will not soon forget.

CLASSIC CORNER

JESUS OF NAZARETH—The controversy over Mel Gibson's *The Passion of The Christ* has caused many to look again at other movies about Jesus. Everything from *The Greatest Story Ever Told* to *Jesus Christ Superstar* are seeing renewed interest from the public. One of the very best ever made was this 1977 mini-series by British author Anthony Burgess (*A Clockwork Orange*) and Italian film director Franco Zeffirelli (*Romeo & Juliet, Hamlet.*) This 6½ hour opus features an all-star cast that includes Anne Bancroft, Christopher Plummer, Stacy Keach, James Farantino, Laurence Olivier, James Mason, Donald Pleasence, Ian Holm, James Earl Jones, Rod Steiger, Michael York, Peter Ustinov and, in an astonishing portrayal, Robert Powell as Jesus, who looks like he stepped right off a holy calendar. Lacking the overwrought histrionics of many religious films, Zeffirelli chose a more tasteful and low key approach while retaining the full spiritual nature of the material. Eschewing the Technicolor excesses of most Biblical epics, the filmmakers opted for a more muted palette of beiges and browns. Everything from sets and costumes to music and photography are first rate and work in the service of the story. The lengthier format is a big plus, also, and allows for a more leisurely and in-depth telling of this "Greatest story."

DVD ALERT

SCHINDLER'S LIST—Though Steven Spielberg is undeniably the most popular and successful filmmaker of our time, with such notable box office winners as *Jaws, E.T.* and the *Indiana Jones* films under his belt, it wasn't until

1993 with the release of this Holocaust drama that he moved beyond his popcorn pretensions into the realm of serious film director. The same year he gave the world computer generated dinosaurs in *Jurassic Park*, he explored this dark chapter in his Jewish history. And no one was more surprised than he when his gritty, black-and-white three-hour drama (complete with full-frontal nudity) became a huge box office phenomenon. The movie was based on the bestselling book by Thomas Keneally about Catholic businessman and war profiteer, Oskar Schindler (Liam Neeson), who risked his reputation, his fortune and even his life to save over 1000 Jews destined for the Nazi death camps. Co-stars include Ben Kingsley, Embeth Davidtz and a frightening, star-making turn by Ralph Fiennes as a vicious Nazi commandant. The movie swept the Academy Awards with seven Oscars for Best Picture, Director, Screenplay, Art Direction, Cinematography, Editing and Music Score. For its premiere on DVD, in addition to a standard issue disc, there is also a special edition box set that includes a Holocaust documentary, the original soundtrack CD, *Images of the Steven Spielberg Film* book, a framed Senitype film clip and a certificate of authenticity, all in a specially designed Plexiglas case. Though Mr. Spielberg has gone on to make other highly-lauded films, this Holocaust drama stands as his finest work and is the movie of which he is most proud.

THE BIG CHEESE

SUPERCAR—Mention the name Gerry Anderson and most people will remember his British sci-fi T.V. series from the 1970s such as *UFO* and *Space: 1999*. However, prior to these live action offerings, he first made a name for himself in the 1960s with a number of marionette shows like *Fireball XL5*, *Stingray*, *Thunderbirds* and the granddaddy of them all, *Supercar*. These special effects laden series fired up many a little boy's imagination with heroic characters that had such cool macho names as Mike Mercury, Steve Zodiac and Troy Tempest. With their oversized heads and creepy caricatured features, these puppet stars had faces that only a ventriloquist could love. Anderson called his process "Supermarionation", which was kind of like Howdy Doody on steroids; realistic sets and flashy effects put these shows way ahead of anything else. *Supercar* concerned the exploits of scientists Prof. Popkiss and Dr. Beaker, test pilot Mike Mercury, along with their young friend Jimmy Gibson and his pet chimpanzee, Mitch, who have built a flying and submersible vehicle at their secret Nevada desert lab. Adventures ranged from spies trying to steal the machine to politically incorrect encounters with native headhunters. That silliness aside, nothing was quite as bracingly cool as Mike Mercury charging up the engines on the aptly named vehicle. Most of Gerry Anderson's shows are available in re-mastered DVD box sets and are loads of fun to watch. Though the strings are glaringly visible and lip synch is hit or miss, these old shows are a gentle reminder of just how much fun innocent adventure could be. As Dr. Beaker would say, "Satisfactory, most satisfactory."

LET THE 2004 MOVIE SEASON BEGIN
(April 2004)

Now that the Oscars are behind us, the movies of 2004 can finally take center stage. As the season truly begins, it's nice to see some really fine films emerge. The eclectic Coen brothers are back with *The Ladykillers* (a remake of the 1955 Alec Guinness comedy) starring Tom Hanks and Marlon Wayans, plus *Dogville*, another unique offering from Lars von Trier, which stars Nicole Kidman. For the comic book crowd there's *Hellboy* with Ron Perlman and Selma Blair, and *The Punisher* with Thomas Jane, John Travolta and Rebecca Romijn-Stamos. Distaff choices include *Mean Girls* with Lindsay Lohan (*Freaky Friday*) and SNL's Tina Fey (who adapted the screenplay from Rosalind Wiseman's *Queen Bees & Wannabes*); *13 Going On 30* with Jennifer Garner in the Tom Hanks *Big* role; and *Ella Enchanted* with Anne Hathaway (*The Princess Diaries*) under a spell in which she can refuse no commands. And for big laughs there's Jack Black and Ben Stiller in Barry Levinson's comedy, *Envy*, co-starring Christopher Walken and Rachel Weisz. So, as you can see, there's something for everyone, which is a great way to start off the new movie-going season. Here's hoping it bodes well for the rest of the year, too.

NEW IN THEATRES
THE ALAMO—Originally scheduled for release at Christmas 2003, this movie was, instead, bumped to the spring 2004 line up. A remake, of sorts, of the 1960 epic which starred and was directed by John Wayne, this new version was helmed by John Lee Hancock (who stepped in when original director Ron Howard stepped down.) The high-powered feature cast includes Dennis Quaid (who previously worked with Hancock in *The Rookie*) as Sam Houston, Billy Bob Thornton as Davy Crockett (the John Wayne role) and Jason Patric as Jim Bowie (of Bowie knife fame.) The production built a full-scale replica of the legendary fort on a 50 acre site and strove for authenticity in every detail. Perhaps second only to the gunfight at the O.K. Corral in western lore, this 1836 event nonetheless looms large in Mexican and American history. And while the John Wayne original still casts a large shadow, it remains to be seen whether or not this will be an *Alamo* to remember.

NEW ON VIDEO
MASTER AND COMMANDER: THE FAR SIDE OF THE WORLD—Two generations of Australian movie talent come together in this great 1800s sea epic based on the novels by Patrick O'Brian. Director Peter Weir (*Gallipoli*, *The Truman Show*) and actor Russell Crowe join forces for the first time, though

hopefully not the last, to tell this tale of two British naval officers, the other played by Crowe's *Beautiful Mind* co-star, Paul Bettany. Weir, who has been making visually powerful films for 30 years, has always blended form and content in interesting and provocative ways. Here, he tackles the historic sea epic with gusto and bravura, but never lets the human story become overwhelmed by the effects. Crowe delivers another first rate performance, proving again that he is one of the finest actors of his generation. The DVD release includes a deluxe edition with loads of extras designed to satisfy the most demanding movie buff.

CLASSIC CORNER

THE PINK PANTHER COLLECTION—In 1964 director Blake Edwards (*Breakfast at Tiffany's*, *10*) and actor Peter Sellers (*Lolita, Dr. Strangelove*) created movie magic with the release of *The Pink Panther*, a jewel heist comedy with Sellers as the bumbling French Inspector, Jacques Clouseau. The success of the film spawned an instant sequel that same year, *A Shot in the Dark*. A decade later saw *The Return of the Pink Panther* revive the franchise, which led to three more films over the next seven years: *The Pink Panther Strikes Again*, *Revenge of the Pink Panther* and *Trail of the Pink Panther*, the latter cobbled together in 1982 from existing footage after Sellers' death. The 6-disc box set puts together five movies and a bonus disc of extras. Unfortunately, 1975's *Return* (one of the best of the series) is inexplicably omitted, perhaps due to legal problems, but can be purchased separately. That caveat aside, this is a beautiful set packaged in a customized fold-out case illustrated with original, panoramic art work. There is a terrific audio commentary track with Edwards on the first film, and a new documentary, *The Pink Panther Story*, that brings to life the history of the *Panther* films. Rounding out this lavish set are six *Pink Panther* cartoon shorts and a featurette on the origins of the colorful feline.

DVD ALERT

GHOSTS OF THE ABYSS—After the phenomenal success of the movie *Titanic* in 1997/98, Oscar-winning director and self-proclaimed "King of the World", James Cameron took a hiatus from the director's chair. However, the lure of the great ship proved to be irresistible to the formidable filmmaker, who returned to this most famous of shipwrecks in 2001. Armed with newly-designed underwater robotic cameras, Cameron shot footage for this awesome documentary in areas inside the Titanic not seen since its maiden voyage in 1912. Shown in IMAX Theatres in 3-D, *Ghosts* is Cameron's very personal odyssey about the Titanic in which he was able to photograph and explore the sunken luxury liner in unprecedented detail. (An interesting side note: on September 11, 2001 Cameron was on his way to the bottom of the ocean to photograph the wreck when he heard about the attacks on the World Trade Center. Talk about a "Where were you?" story!) This month commemorates the 92nd anniversary of the great ship's tragic demise and the loss of 1500 lives. For those who thought they 'd O.D.'d on Titanic mania in the wake of the '97 mega film, this documentary is a reminder of just how much the great ship and its legacy can still move us.

KID STUFF

BROTHER BEAR—The proliferation and success of computer animation films such as *Toy Story* and *Finding Nemo* has caused some to fear the end of traditionally-drawn animated movies. The poor box office results of recent films such as *Treasure Planet*, *Sinbad* and this latest Disney effort has done little to dispel this death knell mentality. However, all is not lost; the success of *Lilo & Stitch*, *The Lion King 1½* and the buzz for *Home on the Range* proves there is still hope for the struggling format. With that in mind, home video is the perfect opportunity to re-examine this tale of a boy (voiced by Joaquin Phoenix) who is transformed into a bear cub. Comic relief is provided by a pair of Canadian moose (Dave Thomas and Rick Moranis reviving their *Second City* McKenzie Brothers routine, "How's it goin', eh?".) Despite the laughs, there is a serious message about redemption, forgiveness and walking a mile in someone else's shoes (or paws as is the case, here.) The 2-disc, kid-friendly DVD includes games, a making of featurette and a moose audio commentary. Beauty, eh?

SUMMER MOVIES, START YOUR ENGINES!
(May 2004)

The month of May brings a wide range of cinematic offerings, helping to kick off the pre-summer movie season. Roland Emmerich, the director of *Independence Day*, wreaks more havoc in *The Day After Tomorrow*. Dennis Quaid, Jake Gyllenhaal and Ian Holm endure tidal waves and other freaks of nature in this disaster film to end all disaster films. Horror buffs can rejoice in *Van Helsing* where *The X-Men*'s Hugh Jackman faces off against all the monsters made famous by Universal Studios in the '30s and '40s, including Frankenstein, the Mummy, the Wolf Man and, of course, Count Dracula. Sexy Kate Beckinsale is along for the ride, as well. For kids, everyone's favorite green ogre is back for some more smarmy fun in *Shrek 2*. Mike Myers, Eddie Murphy and Cameron Diaz reprise their roles from before, along with new characters voiced by Antonio Banderas, Julie Andrews and John Cleese. Former "'tween" cuties the Olsen twins, Mary-Kate and Ashley, are all grown up as they try to woo an older audience in *New York Minute* with some help from comic master Eugene Levy. Finally, Dutch director Pieter Jan Brugge has the serious-minded kidnapping drama *The Clearing* with Robert Redford, Willem Dafoe and Helen Mirren lending their considerable talents. Even though it's still only spring, with this slate of films set for release, it already feels like summer.

NEW IN THEATRES

TROY—The success of *Gladiator* a few years back created a scramble in Hollywood to plunder ancient history for another blockbuster. Enter Homer's *The Iliad*, whose title means "a poem about Ilium" (i.e. Troy, which makes for a better movie title). For those who don't know this Greek tragedy (or slept through it in class) it concerns Achilles (Brad Pitt), a warrior and leader of the Myrmidons, one of the largest contingents of the Achaean (Greek) army. Early on, our conflicted hero (who is also a half god) is at odds with King Agamemnon (Brian Cox), but later reconciles with him and turns his rage upon the Trojan leader Hector (Eric Bana). Agamemnon's brother, King Menelaus (Brendan Gleeson), learns that his wife Helen (Diane Kruger), she of "the face that launched a thousand ships" fame, has been abducted by Hector's brother, Paris (Orlando Bloom). In response, Menelaus launches those thousand ships, with Achilles at the helm, to affect her return.

Director Wolfgang Petersen (*Das Boot*, *The Perfect Storm*), creates a sweeping spectacle worthy of this timeless classic with some help from screenwriter David Benioff. All the elements are here: the Trojan Horse, the gates of Troy, the aforementioned 1K of ships, clashing armies, love, desire, betrayal and heroism. This is the story that became the template for so many others. And while the lesson of the Trojan Horse may have been "beware of Greeks bearing gifts", this film version of Homer's epic tale is truly a gift worth embracing.

NEW ON VIDEO

GIRL WITH A PEARL EARRING—Films about artists can be risky undertakings, even when much is known about the subject in question. In the case of Vermeer, where little is known about the 17th century Dutch painter, director Peter Webber, working from a script based on Tracy Chevalier's best seller, concentrates on a single painting and speculates freely on how it came to be. Whether or not you buy into this premise (that Vermeer used a servant girl as his model), the fact remains that the finished film is a glorious celebration of Vermeer's talent and his determination to find meaning in his life and art. The cast includes the always dependable Colin Firth (*Bridget Jones' Diary*), the luminous Scarlett Johansson (*Lost in Translation*) and the masterful Tom Wilkinson (*In the Bedroom*). Cinematographer Eduardo Serra, who created such memorable imagery in *What Dreams May Come*, uncannily captures the buttery patina and balanced compositions of Vermeer's work (every shot looks like a painting). Even though by the film's end the characters remain pretty much enigmas, we are nonetheless left with the insight that all those musty old paintings in the Louvre, or wherever, each has a hidden story to tell. Some may never be known, but after seeing this movie, you can't help but wonder what secrets lie within those ornate frames.

CLASSIC CORNER

ROOM WITH A VIEW—The movies of Merchant/Ivory have become a genre unto themselves. Beginning in the early 1960s producer Ishmail Merchant and director James Ivory, along with screenwriter Ruth Prawer Jhabvala, carved out a niche in cinema of mostly Edwardian drawing room dramas. Titles such as *Howard's End*, *The Remains of the Day* and *Maurice* chronicled life in Britain among the upper class (usually as it played out against the lower). Released in 1984, *Room* was Merchant/Ivory's breakout hit, setting the standard for much of their later work, and making stars of its young cast: Helena Bonham Carter, Daniel Day-Lewis and Julian Sands. The story, based on E. M. Forster's novel, follows a group of Englanders traveling abroad (in this case, Florence), who bring along their attendant baggage of manners and mores. Though Sands is, ostensibly, the male lead, it is Daniel Day-Lewis who steals the movie with his bravura performance as the effete snob, Cecil Vyse, paving the way for his stunningly diverse career. This special edition two-disc set includes a feature length audio commentary track with Merchant and Ivory, actor Simon Callow (the Reverend Mr. Beebe) and director of photography Tony Pierce-Roberts, plus archival interviews with Callow and Day-Lewis and a curious 1970 BBC tribute/obituary of Forster.

DVD ALERT

PANIC ROOM—By his own admission, director David Fincher (*Alien 3*, *Seven*, *Fight Club*) considers this film to be simply a nail-biting thriller. "It's not Ingmar Bergman." Jodie Foster and her 12-year old daughter take refuge in their new home's "panic room" on their first night there when three burglars (Forest Whitaker, Jared Leto and Dwight Yoakam), who thought the place was empty, show up. So, why make a three-disc special edition of this slight confection? Well, according to Fincher, sometimes B movies resonate more than "important" films. "I remember aspects of *The Road Warrior* more than *Gandhi*." That said, though *Panic Room* has a somewhat detached feel, very cold and impersonal, it is a textbook example of the classic thriller structure, executed in a dynamic fashion. Brimming with style and panache, the movie was preplanned to within an inch of its life, all of which has been documented for this set. While the film suffers slightly from its hermetically sealed perfectionism, the precision of Fincher's mobile camera work is stunning to behold. The exhaustively comprehensive extras include three commentaries: one with Fincher, another with cast members Foster, Whitaker and Yoakam, and a very informative track with screenwriter David Koepp. There are numerous featurettes, running several hours, that detail every aspect of the making of the movie from pre-production through post-production., guaranteed to satisfy the most demanding film geek out there. Fincher is a major filmmaking talent, and this set is the perfect tutorial for gaining access to the creative process he employs.

THE BIG CHEESE

JASON AND THE ARGONAUTS—In the annals of fantasy filmmaking, there is a universal reverence for stop-motion animator extraordinaire, Ray Harryhausen. During a long career spanning the films *Mighty Joe Young* in 1949 to *The Clash of the Titans* in 1981, he single-handedly re-invented the fantasy genre, and made movie history with some of the most imaginative, horrific and exciting films ever seen. His crowning achievement, by most accounts, is this ancient Greek extravaganza about the search for the Golden Fleece. The story, directed by Don Chaffey, pits Jason (Todd Armstrong) and his band of adventurers against such formidable foes as a pair of menacing winged "harpies," the seven-headed hydra dragon and an army of skeletons that became the talk of the industry for the next twenty years. It's hard to believe in this age of special effects (with credits that read like the population rolls of a small nation), but Mr. Harryhausen created his stop-motion magic virtually alone. While effects have certainly become more sophisticated since the introduction of the computer, few are as heartfelt and engaging as the work of this gentle genius. Though the limited budgets often resulted in stilted performances by actors on skimpy sets, Ray's work always shined through, raising the level on films that would otherwise be pure cheese. So, while you revel in the glories of the mega-priced *Troy* at your local theatre this month, and marvel at how far the adventure epic has evolved, check out this little gem and see what was possible in the long-ago 1960s on a budget that would barely cover the catering bill on today's film sets.

SUMMER MOVIES IN FULL FLOWER
(June 2004)

The first wave of summer movies has crashed upon the shore of the '04 season, drenching the populace for better or worse. Now we find ourselves in the thick of things as, week after week, we are deluged by dozens of new releases. Though the "feast or famine" days of targeted movie seasons seem long gone as plentiful movie titles bombard us year round, the summer is still one of the key release periods where studios bank on higher attendance. *Troy, Shrek* and *The Day After Tomorrow* have already landed, starting things off with a bang, and they will soon be followed by such high profile titles as *Harry Potter, The Terminal, Spider-Man, I Robot, King Arthur, Catwoman, The Village, The Manchurian Candidate, Thunderbirds, Shall We Dance, Collateral* and *Exorcist: The Beginning*. When the summer is over and we head into the fall, the question we should ask ourselves isn't how many of these cinematic confections have remained with us, but how many have wilted?

NEW IN THEATRES

THE STEPFORD WIVES—Back in the Dark Ages of 1975, the feminist movement was in its early stages of pursuing equality for, and recognition of, women as participants in our society. A reaction against this growing "feminization" of our culture came from Hollywood in *The Stepford Wives*. In the story, based on the novel by Ira Levin, the town of Stepford, Connecticut is home to a group of upscale men and their perfect, beautiful, devoted wives. It turns out the wives are automatons (created by a former Disney animatronic designer no less) that have replaced the real wives of the town's chauvinistic husbands. The new remake is directed by Frank Oz (Miss Piggy) and stars Matthew Broderick and Nicole Kidman as the newly arrived couple, and Glenn Close, Bette Midler and Faith Hill as "the wives." Playing the diabolical leader of the Stepford men is Christopher Walken (perfect casting, yes?). The original film had a dark, downbeat ending, typical of the 1970s, where we see all the robot wives mindlessly shopping, their individuality and humanity hopelessly squashed. What sort of denouement will this new version have? If this one has a happy ending does that make it a "Stepford Wife" of *The Stepford Wives*? Well, I guess that's one reason to go to the theatre and check out this latest incarnation.

NEW ON VIDEO

MONSTER—By now everyone knows about the extraordinary transformation endured by gorgeous South African actress, Charlize Theron, to become real life serial killer, Aileen Wuornos. Sporting thirty extra pounds, brown contacts, prosthetic teeth and a ruddy complexion under a tangled wig, Ms. Theron totally suppressed her natural statuesque beauty and literally embodied this raging maniac who posed as a hooker in order to kill men. That performance earned her a Best Actress Oscar this past spring along with widespread praise from audiences and critics. While the politics behind the actions of the now executed Wuornos remain clouded and contradictory, she was obviously a very disturbed person. It is, therefore, to Theron's credit (along with writer/director Patty Jenkins) that we are able to see the humanity beneath the calloused exterior of this brutalized brute. The result is a compelling drama about a sad, wasted and misused life. Playing off the primal scream antics of Theron, Christina Ricci gives an equally heartfelt performance as Wuornos' timid young lover, who is kept largely in the dark about the hellish acts of her beloved.

CLASSIC CORNER

UNIVERSAL MONSTER LEGACY COLLECTIONS—While the new horror/action flick, *Van Helsing*, does its grave robbing best to revive the Universal horror monsters for a new generation of film goers, some of us old timers believe it's just old wine in new bottles. Worse still, the wine has turned to vinegar! For a truly sumptuous horror movie feast, then, I recommend revisiting the originals which have recently been re-issued in three beautiful DVD boxed sets. They include five Dracula movies, five Frankensteins and four Wolfmans. The Dracula set includes the original 1931 Bela Lugosi classic (with and without the newly added Philip Glass score), the Spanish language *Dracula* (shot at the same time as the Lugosi version on the same sets, but with a different cast and crew) plus the lesser known sequels *Dracula's Daughter* '36, *Son of Dracula* '43 and *House of Dracula* '45. Extras on all three sets include a behind-the-scenes look at how *Van Helsing* director Stephen Sommers was influenced and inspired by the original movies, and film scholar audio commentaries which delve into the history of the films.

DVD ALERT

EXISTENZ—The *Matrix* films have, no doubt, made a huge impact on sci-fi in the movies. Unfortunately, the buzz surrounding the first film, when it was released in 1999, seriously eclipsed this far darker offering from the twisted imagination of Canadian filmmaker, David Cronenberg (*The Fly, Dead Ringers*). The intriguing premise postulates a near future where immersive video games are played using organically grown control pods that are umbilically wired into a "port" in your spine. Like much of Cronenberg's work, the imagery is intentionally sexual and disturbing. The plot really kicks in when celebrity game designer Allegra Geller (Jennifer Jason Leigh) survives an assassination attempt and flees with novice security guard Ted Pikul (Jude Law). The two then enter the virtual world of Allegra's latest game, eXistenZ, where they encounter some very strange situations. The American DVD release of Cronenberg's film was a bare bones affair, unworthy of the director's artistry. Fortunately, there is a Canadian edition DVD (available from northamericandvd.com) that is a treasure trove of extras. In addition to an hour long documentary on Cronenberg's production designer, Carol Spier, there are three, count 'em three, audio commentary tracks that dissect all aspects of the movie. *The Matrix* is a lot of fun, but visiting the world of *eXistenZ* is a trip that will stay with you forever.

THE BIG CHEESE

REEFER MADNESS—Originally made as a warning to America's youth (circa 1938) under the title *Tell Your Children*, about the evils of marijuana, its simple naiveté became a source of great entertainment in the hippie trippy days of the late 1960s. "The times they are a changin'" sang Bob Dylan, who was known to inhale a doobie or two, so it's no wonder this flick, retitled *Reefer Madness*, has remained a teen favorite for over sixty years. The basic premise of the film has a group of depression era drug dealers, living in a swank Art Deco apartment, recruiting some teen squares into trying their demon weed. The grass may not have been greener for these hard-boiled drug lords, but it sure was more potent. One puff is enough to send these Jazz age potheads reeling into chaotic abandon and eventual madness. Part of the hilarity derives from casting actors who are well beyond their teen years as the young innocents.

In a bold stroke of creative marketing, the DVD release of this cult classic has been colorized in a slightly over-the-top fashion that plays off the message the filmmakers intended. The innocent family lives in a sea of beige blandness, while the drug dealers' pad is a smoking hot pink. And since everyone's drug high is personal to their character, each individual's toke on their "Mary Jane" elicits its own particular shade of second hand smoke: baby blue for the innocent, purple for the crazed, etc. Extras on this "special addiction" include a comic commentary by Mike Nelson of *Mystery Science Theater 3000*, though without his robot pals he seems to be just talking to himself, rendering his quips a bit flat. More entertaining is the commentary by the colorists who provide insight into their choices. An accompanying short, titled *Grandpa's Marijuana Handbook*, is mildly amusing.

In Supertramp's *Goodbye Stranger* they sang "Goodbye Mary, goodbye Jane. Will we ever meet again?" Well, now you can, safely and legally, as you indulge your "sweet leaf" passions with this uber-cheesy DVD classic. Just don't forget the popcorn in case you get "the munchies."

TRADING SEASONS:
Say Goodbye to Summer
(September 2004)

It's certainly been a summer of surprises. There were the usual sure things like *Spider-Man* and *Shrek*, but *Catwoman* proved to be a dog and *Fahrenheit 9/11* was the hottest ticket this season. Likewise, M. Night Shyamalan's *The Village* under-performed while Jonathan Demme's *The Manchurian Candidate* turned out to be a worthy remake, both films defying predictions and expectations. Now that we're entering the fall, a new slate of pictures is waiting in the wings; some will soar, others will crash. From the highbrow of *Vanity Fair* with Reese Witherspoon, to the lowdown humor of Bernie Mac in *Mr. 3000*, there is something for everyone. In this election year, even political films come in various guises, from the teen comedy *First Daughter* to John Sayles' satiric drama *Silver City*. And that's just this month. As the start to a new movie season, this first wave looks very encouraging.

NEW IN THEATRES

SKY CAPTAIN AND THE WORLD OF TOMORROW—Anyone who saw the preview for this astonishing-looking film this past spring couldn't help but be bowled over by its absolute originality and unique mise-en-scene. Originally scheduled to be released this past summer, but instead pushed back to the fall, this highly stylized, Art Deco fantasy stars Jude Law, Gwyneth Paltrow and Angelina Jolie (talk about a gorgeous-looking cast) in a World War II-era comic book world of giant flying robots and swooping enemy airplanes with wings that flap like menacing bats. Visually unlike anything you've ever seen, the movie is reminiscent of German Expressionist films of the '20s and '30s as well as Nazi and Stalinist propaganda of the time. As an added textural flourish, the stark compositions are bathed in a luminescent sepia glow that helps soften the tone of the movie's Teutonic grandeur.

First time director Kerry Conran put together this high concept project by creating a six-minute short on his computer, showcasing the cutting edge visuals he had in mind. Based on that, he was able to convince Paramount to put up the money and attract an A-list cast. To keep costs down, the movie was shot entirely on a blue screen stage with no practical sets; costumes and props were the only real elements to interact with the performers. With so many cookie-cutter films out there, and remakes of remakes, sequels of sequels, etc. etc., it is refreshing to see a movie that has such a singular look. And, for once, the style is in service of the story, not the other way around.

NEW ON VIDEO

THE LADYKILLERS—This southern fried remake of the 1955 British classic, about a motley group of bungling thieves who meet their match in a trusting landlady, is a welcome return for the filmmaking duo, the Coen Brothers, to the world of the eccentric. Most recently, they tried their hand at more conventional fare with *Intolerable Cruelty*, but anyone who is a fan of the Coens, knows that their true strength lies in worlds of heightened strangeness, filled with quirky characters: *Raising Arizona, Fargo, The Man Who Wasn't There*. For their latest endeavor, the Coens team with Tom Hanks, who brings his considerable skills into playing one of the strangest characters in his oeuvre, a mellifluous, southern gentleman con artist with a nasal cackle and prominent teeth, who is out to swindle a floating casino. Standing in the way of Hanks and his henchmen, including Marlon Wayans and J.K. Simmons, is a Bible-quoting holy roller of a landlady, Irma P. Hall, who is oblivious to the shenanigans going on under her roof. The Coens push the envelope with some pretty salty language, as they did in *Fargo* and *The Big Lebowski*, so the easily offended need to know this is not your typical Tom Hanks flick. Still, for those who can get past the language, or who might even embrace it for that matter, the film delivers some solid laughs and has moments of poetic beauty that serve as ironic counterpoint to its lowbrow antics. While you're at it, check out the 1955 version, now available on DVD, which stars Alec Guinness, Herbert Lom and Peter Sellers, the latter two who would later team up in the *Pink Panther* films. What's most surprising about seeing these two films is how much of the original plot the Coens were able to retain, despite the shift from 1950s England to 21st century American south.

.

DVD ALERT

THE PASSION OF THE CHRIST—Who could have guessed that Mel Gibson's pet project—a film about Christ's last hours, spoken in Latin and Aramaic—would end up being the blockbuster of the year? Of course, it didn't hurt to have a bit of controversy about the film being anti-Semitic (it isn't) to help keep it in the news. Gibson, who previously proved his directing chops with *The Man Without a Face* in 1993 and *Braveheart* in 1995 (the latter winning five Oscars including Best Picture and Director), brings his own passion to this project and invests this potentially overwrought material with some wonderfully poetic touches. Actor Jim Caviezel (*The Thin Red Line, Frequency*), as Christ, brings his trademark spiritual charisma to a part he was born to play. This anxiously-awaited DVD is, unfortunately, a bare bones affair with virtually no extras. A special edition is supposedly in the works for either Christmas or Easter. Given the controversial nature of the film, and Gibson's absolute determination to make it, this is a home video release crying out for audio commentaries, making of featurettes and interviews. Those who are interested in having more than just the movie may wish to wait for this later edition.

THE BIG CHEESE

VALLEY GIRL—Ah, the nostalgia for the Reagan-era 80s; it was a time when malls (and young republicans) ruled, when feathered hair and pastel colors were the norm, while the burgeoning punk/new wave movement fought for recognition. Hard to believe it's been more than 20 years since Martha Coolidge directed this low budget teen comedy classic (which was shot in a mere 20 days).

This tale of valley girl Julie (Deborah Foreman) finding true love with wild new waver Randy (a dreamy-looking 17-year old Nicolas Cage) is a total 80s time capsule of Southern California culture. Julie's shopping-obsessed friends want her to remain in the valley fold with her blonde jock boyfriend Tommy (Michael Bowen), while her hippie parents (Frederic Forrest and Colleen Camp), who, naturally run a health food store, tell her to follow her heart. Coolidge front loads this cotton candy confection with lots of "valley speak" ("tubular," "grody," "omigod!," "gag me," "totally") in the first 10 minutes, then backs off to allow the timeless Romeo & Juliet story to unfold along the schism between Hollywood and "the Valley." While all the young actors turn in acceptable performances, it is Cage who is the stand out, and his soulful expression brings to mind, today, the visage of Jake Gyllenhaal.

Though the low budget precluded the use of tunes by The Police or Talking Heads, the rad soundtrack does sport the Modern English hit *I Melt with You*, and features performances by hot club band, The Plimsouls and the delightful Josie Cotton doing her 80s anthem to sexual ambiguity *Johnny, Are You Queer?* The 20th anniversary DVD includes an hour of featurettes and three commentary tracks that are like "totally bitchin'." While it's fun to look back and laugh at the empty-headed silliness of the valley girl phenomenon, this film reminds us that even a cheesy era like that can produce some fine artistry. Fer sure!

THE SCARIEST MOVIE STORY EVER!
(October 2004)

"Gather round and you shall hear the scariest movie story of the year." Though it's Halloween season, I'm not just talking about some scary movie or anything like that, I'm talking about *Exorcist: The Beginning*. Not the film, mind you, but what the studio did is what scared me. Oscar-winning screenwriter and noted director, Paul Schrader, was tapped to direct this "prequel" to the 1973 classic. After completing the film, however, the studio execs were unhappy with it, so they fired Schrader and hired Renny Harlin (*Cutthroat Island*) to reshoot the entire movie. The resulting finished product was released and received some of the worst reviews of the year (what is it with this franchise, anyway?).

So, how bad could the earlier version have been? Granted, Schrader has fallen on hard times, with low budget releases ranging from brilliant (*Mishima*) to banal (*Forever Mine*) to interestingly creepy (*Auto Focus*.) But the man who wrote *Taxi Driver* and *Raging Bull*, and directed *American Gigolo* and the remake of *Cat People*, deserved, at least, to have his movie released, instead of being pushed aside for the formulaic work of an undistinguished director like Harlin. The fact that it happened, the fact that Schrader's film, no matter how bad, may never see the light of day, well now, that's truly frightening. In this season of cinematic scares, there is nothing out there capable of chilling me like that. Maybe they should turn that into a movie.

NEW IN THEATRES

TEAM AMERICA WORLD POLICE—The creators of the nasty cult cartoon, *South Park* (Trey Parker and Matt Stone), have branched out in their assault on what was a children's entertainment genre, and have now invaded the realm of marionettes. Once the sole domain of Gerry Anderson and his "Supermarionation" TV shows like *Thunderbirds, Supercar* and *Fireball XL-5,* Parker and Stone have taken the concept of an adventure show rescue team and sacrificed its innocence on the altar of hard R-rated comedy, much as they did with cartoons on *South Park.*

For their version of "naughty puppet theatre," the iconoclastic filmmakers have kept the low-tech look (with visible strings), but have pumped up the action with fast paced editing, grisly violence and lots of cursing (these puppets have attitude!).And while Parker and Stone are exceptionally talented, they are also angry: angry at the left, angry at the right, downright angry at the whole freakin' world. So, it's no surprise that these two anarchists take gleeful pleasure in bashing everyone in sight, from Michael Moore and Tim Robbins on the left to George W. on the right, to terrorists and other "foreigners" out to bring America down. This take-no-prisoners style of humor can be a bit exhausting, but boy is it funny. And for those of us who grew up watching those old Supermarionation shows on TV, this new, amped up, very un-PC big screen version being rolled out in this political season is bound to be bracingly entertaining. No strings attached.

NEW ON VIDEO

FAHRENHEIT 9/11—Starting with his breakthrough documentary on corporate wrongdoing, *Roger & Me,* back in 1989, maverick filmmaker, Michael Moore, has made a career out of sticking his pudgy thumb into the eye of authority. He won an Oscar in 2003 with *Bowling for Columbine* in which he explored America's fascination with guns. What sets Moore apart from the usual polemicist is his ability to impart humor into his work without diminishing the seriousness of the message. His latest effort, about the Bush administration's corrupt dealings in the Mid-East, and how it has affected our culture, has been his most successful (and divisive) film yet, raking in over $100 Million and causing a schism among the public along clearly ideological lines. I don't recall Errol Morris' *The Fog of War* or even Moore's own *Columbine* eliciting such anger as has happened with *9/11*. When was the last time a filmmaker got death threats and needed personal security? This DVD release, loaded with extras, is much anticipated by both sides. Hopefully it will find an even larger and wider audience who missed it in theatres. Ironically, with the recent repeal of the assault weapons ban, maybe it's time to take another look at *Columbine*, too.

CLASSIC CORNER

THE GHOST AND MRS. MUIR—This Halloween, how about curling up with a ghost story that's not the least bit scary. There are tons of films out there that will scare the pants off you or gross you out or do whatever it is that passes for horror these days. But, there are very few movies that can take the genre and mold it into something that is warm, funny, inviting, touching, heartbreaking and finally, just achingly beautiful. Thanks to director Joseph L. Mankiewicz and screenwriter Philip Dunne, such is the case here. Starring Rex Harrison and Gene Tierney, respectively in the eponymous roles, it concerns a young widow who takes up residence in a seaside cottage that is inhabited by the ghost of an ornery, yet dashing, sea captain. Both actors are perfectly cast and bring a great deal of charm and charisma to their characters. Shot in 1947 in glorious black & white, this is a textbook example of old Hollywood filmmaking at its best. The DVD contains a beautifully rendered transfer and has two audio commentary tracks, one with Greg Kimble and Christopher Husted, and the other with Jeanie Bassinger and Kenneth Geist., all of whom have much to say about the making of this cinematic treasure.

DVD ALERT

ALADDIN and *MULAN*—After the modest release on home video last month of *Home On the Range*, Disney comes out swinging this month with the one-two punch of *Aladdin* and *Mulan* in special edition DVDs. Released in theatres at the height of Disney's '90s animation renaissance, *Aladdin* was a hilarious magic carpet ride, boasting a frenetically funny turn by Robin Williams, whose stream-of-consciousness, quicksilver persona was expertly transferred to animation as the constantly morphing Genie. The two-disc set bows on DVD with a king's ransom of extras. It is also available in a Collector's set with accompanying book and artwork, ala *The Lion King* release

Previously available only in a bare bones edition, *Mulan* gets the two-disc upgrade it richly deserves. Based on an ancient Chinese folk tale about a girl who disguises herself as a soldier to help fight the invading Hun army, Disney crafted a work that is both visually lush and emotionally satisfying. And, thanks to Eddie Murphy's performance as a diminutive but determined dragon, Mushu, it's also extremely funny. The voice cast also includes Donny Osmond (honest!), Pat Morita, Harvey Fierstein, George (*Star Trek*) Takei, Miguel Ferrer and Ming-Na Wen as Mulan. Legendary composer, Jerry Goldsmith's wondrous score, and the memorable songs by Matthew Wilder and Easton's own David Zippel, complete this near-perfect classic.

THE BIG CREEP

VIDEODROME—Just about anything from director David Cronenberg is bound to leave you feeling disturbed and unsettled. If he has a unifying theme in his work, it might be "the revolt of the body," be it the mutation of Jeff Goldblum in *The Fly*, the diseased osmosis of the twin gynecologists in *Dead Ringers*, or even the betrayal of memory in *Spider*. In this, one of the director's best early works, it is the effect of media on the body of society, itself. For Cronenberg, metaphor is only a means to actualization. As such, we have televisions that pulsate with living energy and then explode to reveal their organic entrails. And in the case of TV cable programmer James Woods, who is obsessed with a pirated channel of torture and abuse called Videodrome, he finds his body transmogrifying in extraordinary and unnerving ways. As always in Cronenberg's work, there are underlying sexual politics at play that inform the characters and their motivations. This newly released Criterion DVD is loaded with extras, including commentary tracks with the director, several making of featurettes and plenty of ghoulish wonder to get you through this Halloween season.

WE WISH YOU A MOVIE CHRISTMAS
(December 2004)

For many people, Christmas is a time of mixed feelings; some love the holiday season, others reflect on their spirituality, and still others are turned off by the hectic pace and rampant commercialization that seem to go hand in hand. Part of that also includes a vigorous movie season, as the studios position their Oscar films for the year. November has already seen the release of Kevin Spacey as '60s crooner Bobby Darin in *Beyond the Sea*, Rene Zellweger returning for seconds in *Bridget Jones: The Edge of Reason*, Liam Neeson and Laura Linney starring in *Kinsey*, and Colin Farrell heading Oliver Stone's epic, *Alexander*. In the world of animation, Pixar hit another homerun with *The Incredibles*, while Robert Zemeckis re-teamed with Tom Hanks for the hauntingly beautiful *The Polar Express*.

December is just as packed, with everything from Adam Sandler in *Spanglish* to Leonardo DiCaprio as Howard Hughes in Martin Scorsese's *The Aviator*. Rounding things out this month are Andrew Lloyd Webber's *The Phantom of the Opera*, Bill Murray in Wes Anderson's *The Life Aquatic*, George Clooney back for *Ocean's Twelve*, Sigourney Weaver and Jeff Daniels exploring the dark side of suburbia in *Imaginary Heroes* and Kevin Bacon, Kyra Sedgwick and Benjamin Bratt dealing with their sordid past in *The Woodsman*. Certainly all these film releases won't make your Christmas holiday any less hectic, but some of them just might make the season a little bit more interesting.

NEW IN THEATRES
CLOSER—Veteran director Mike Nichols returns to the world of sexual politics that recalls such earlier works of his as *The Graduate* and *Carnal Knowledge*. Based on the devastating play by Patrick Marber, this dark story concerns four protagonists on a sexual battlefield of mix and match relationships as they engage in payback with one another. This reckless love rectangle stars Julia Roberts, Jude Law (in one of six new films he is in this season), Natalie Portman and Clive Owen (last seen in *King Arthur*) as the attractive, but not very likable, foursome which doesn't hesitate to go for the jugular when it suits them. Like Paul Mazursky's 1960s classic *Bob & Carol & Ted & Alice*, Nichols and Marber have crafted their own updated take on our sexually obsessed culture with all its petty insecurities. This time it's Jude & Julia & Clive & Natalie as Dan & Anna & Larry & Alice. Definitely not recommended as a first-time date movie.

KING ARTHUR—The legend of King Arthur has provided the raw material for countless plays and films, everything from *Camelot* to *First Knight*. The myth has proven to be both resilient and malleable, allowing a variety of filmmakers to put their personal stamp upon it. John Boorman's *Excalibur* took a decidedly mystical view while *Monty Python and the Holy Grail* milked the legend in a mostly absurdist vein. Enter uber-producer Jerry Bruckheimer who was determined to do an historically-accurate version. Set during the Roman Dark Ages, and divested of all its mysticism (no wizards, magic sword or Holy Grail), this gritty drama, as directed by Antoine Fuqua, downplays the Arthur/Guinevere/Lancelot love triangle in favor of dirt-under-the-nails realism. Clive Owen is a somewhat dour Arthur, but he does have the smoldering presence to be a star (perhaps even the next James Bond), while Ioan Gruffudd (A&E's *Hornblower*) does what he can with an underwritten Lancelot. The stand out is Keira Knightley as a feisty, Pagan wild child Guinevere who proves to be as much warrior as maiden. This revisionist Arthur may not be for everyone, but it is interesting to see this oft-told tale stripped of its familiar accoutrements and presented as fact with all the you-are-there realism of an archeological dig. In addition to the tamer PG-13 theatrical version, the DVD is also available in an extended, unrated director's cut containing more intense action. There are also deleted scenes, commentary with director Fuqua, an alternate ending, an extensive making of featurette, a "Round Table" commentary with the cast and filmmakers, plus a pop-up trivia track containing even more information on the movie.

CLASSIC CORNER

GONE WITH THE WIND—When talking about truly classic American films, at the top of the list, along with *Citizen Kane* and *Casablanca*, one has to include this long, sprawling Civil War-era Gothic melodrama. Whether you consider the story of spoiled Southern belle Scarlett O'Hara and her relationship with waggish cad Rhett Butler to be the greatest movie ever made or just an overblown soap opera with good production values, the fact remains that this was an example of "Golden era" Hollywood filmmaking at its finest. Produced in 1939 by the legendary David O. Selznick and directed by Victor Flemming (who also directed *The Wizard of Oz* that same year!), it was shot entirely on sets at MGM studios and fulfilled the Hollywood dream of bringing Margaret Mitchell's novel to the big screen. It made a star of then unknown British actress Vivian Leigh and gave screen icon Clark Gable his most famous role. And for pop culture fanatics, you get to see future 1950s TV Superman, George Reeves, in a brief role as one of the Tarleton twins who try to woo Scarlett in the film's opening scenes. A lavish four-disc DVD special edition finally does justice to this seminal work of overwrought cinema. In addition to a digitally restored print of the nearly four hour saga, spread over two discs, there are two more discs of extras, including interviews, screen tests and a special 1989 documentary, *The Making of a Legend*, about the famous epic. Everything about this movie, from the sweeping strains of Max Steiner's memorable score to such classic lines as "Frankly, my dear, I don't give a damn." and "As God is my witness, I'll never go hungry again." has been burned into our collective psyche. Even those who've never seen the film seem to know it by osmosis, such has its essence been embedded into the cultural zeitgeist.

DVD OF THE YEAR

THE LORD OF THE RINGS—The concluding chapter of director Peter Jackson's mammoth *Lord of the Rings* trilogy, *The Return of the King*, finally makes its way to the 4-disc, extended edition DVD. Containing nearly an hour more story than the theatrical, and earlier DVD, release, this new extended edition includes a cornucopia of extras sure to please fans of the film. As in the previous two DVD extended editions, this one comes with four commentary tracks plus two discs of featurettes (about six hours) covering every aspect of the making of this monumental epic. For the truly hard core fan there is also a limited edition gift set which includes a CD of new score pieces by composer Howard Shore that were used in all three extended editions, plus a highly detailed resin sculpture of Minas Tirith, the fabled city glimpsed briefly in parts one and two, and where, in part three, the story culminates in the said "Return of the King." Although the film received major accolades upon its release, not to mention racking up 11 Oscars, including Best Picture and Director (which was a way for the Academy to acknowledge the entire trilogy), it still took a few lumps for having too many endings. However, all in all, the movie was highly praised and was deemed an appropriately lavish finale to the Tolkien classic. And with this extended edition concluding chapter, Peter Jackson's film saga trilogy can now stand beside *Lawrence of Arabia*, *War & Peace* and *2001: A Space Odyssey* as one of the greatest epic achievements in cinematic history. It is truly one film to rule them all.

SIZING UP THE MOVIES OF 2004
(February 2005)

With the whirlwind of the Christmas season behind us, it's time to take stock of the movies of 2004. As in times past, what seemed to be a thin year for good films has now swelled into a bountiful cinematic smorgasbord. The year-end dam burst has flooded theatres with many great new titles, adding to the smattering of others that populated the year. Most top ten lists include such well-received movies as *The Aviator, Hotel Rwanda, The Incredibles, Sideways, Million Dollar Baby, Finding Neverland , Kill Bill Volume 2, Closer, Vera Drake* and *Eternal Sunshine of the Spotless Mind.* Some less well-received and/or lesser known movies that I feel deserve recognition for, at least, trying to be unique include *Sky Captain and the World of Tomorrow, A Very Long Engagement, The Ladykillers, The Polar Express* and the much maligned *The Village.* Add to that such hot button titles as *Fahrenheit 9/11, Super Size Me* and *The Passion of the Christ* and you've got one heck of a movie year.

NEW IN THEATRES
IMAGINARY HEROES—Originally scheduled for release in December of last year, this dark, quirky drama was repositioned from the Christmas season to now, all the better to liven up the dreary late winter. The film stars Sigourney Weaver and Jeff Daniels as a couple who must deal with a family suicide. First time writer-director Dan Harris makes a splashy debut, helped, no doubt, by his top notch cast. Given the subject matter, the move from Christmas was probably a smart one.

NEW ON VIDEO
THE NOTEBOOK—Just in time for Valentine's Day comes this sweeping romantic drama about a pair of young lovers (Rachel McAdams and Ryan Gosling) who are caught in the turmoil of World War II. The story unfolds in flashback as the elder version of these characters (played brilliantly by Gena Rowlands and James Garner) recall their life together thanks to the musings jotted down in a journal (i.e. the notebook). This engaging film made a respectable showing in the summer movie shuffle, but for those who missed it, now is the perfect time to rediscover this gem that explores the fragility of memory and unabashedly pulls at your heartstrings. Based on the 1996 novel by Nicholas Sparks, the screenplay was written by Jeremy Leven and directed by Nick Cassavetes (son of co-star Gena Rowlands and maverick filmmaker John Cassavetes).

CLASSIC CORNER

SHAME—Though Swedish director Ingmar Bergman is known more for brooding, introspective work like *The Seventh Seal* and *Winter Light,* he did take a stab at social commentary, as it relates to war, in the late 1960s with this devastating indictment on man's inhumanity to man. Bergman regulars, Max von Sydow and Liv Ullmann, play a farmhouse couple who find themselves in the middle of a civil war in which they have no vested interest. As tensions escalate they see their world crumble around them and find their humanity slipping away as their survival instincts take over. Given the current quagmire of the world today, Bergman's Vietnam-era meditation on war and aggression is just as relevant now as it was when it was first released. Extras on the DVD include a commentary track with Bergman biographer, Marc Gervais, and a featurette, *Search For Humanity*, containing interviews with Bergman, Ullmann and Gervais.

DVD ALERT

FANNY & ALEXANDER—In his 50-plus year career as a writer and director, acclaimed Swedish filmmaker, Ingmar Bergman, has left a body of work unmatched in artistry, depth and introspection in the world of cinema. From early masterpieces like *Smiles of a Summer's Night, The Seventh Seal* and *Wild Strawberries* to his later, more mature works, *Cries & Whispers* and *Autumn Sonata,* Bergman proved he was a complete master of the film medium. His penultimate cinematic achievement, released in 1983, was a cogent distillation of the themes that ran through most of his collective oeuvre. The story of *Fanny & Alexander* concerns two children whose widowed mother (an actress) remarries to a stern, repressed minister which causes a dark cloud to fall over what had been a creative and loving family environment. Criterion has come out with two editions of this masterpiece—a two-disc set of the 197-minute theatrical release, and a five-disc set that includes the Swedish mini-series version which runs considerably longer. If you've never seen a Bergman film, you can do no better than to start here. And for Bergman connoisseurs, this special edition package is indeed a treat that is long overdue.

PANNING OSCAR'S GOLD: WHAT VALUE DOES AN OSCAR WIN BRING?
(March 2005)

The Academy Awards are over and with them, the publicity campaigns employed to acquire the "golden boy". Each year millions are spent by the studios in an effort to gain the prestige that an award brings to their movies. In many cases, an Oscar win can translate into huge profits for under-performing films. But beyond that is the cache the award carries in perpetuity. Thanks to home video, movies now have a shelf life (and revenue stream) that was virtually non-existent 25 years ago. The ability to add "Oscar Winner!" to the box art has become nearly as important as the names of the lead actors. For those who care about movies, and have acquired a sizable video collection, an Oscar imprimatur certainly adds some status to their hobby and to themselves by association. It's just another bit of magic the movie industry casts over the public. And it pays off handsomely.

NEW IN THEATRES
BE COOL—It's been ten years since John Travolta played the part of Elmore Leonard's movie-loving, small-time mafia thug in *Get Shorty*. Well now Chili Palmer is back, this time to wreak havoc on the music industry. Along for the ride is Travolta's *Pulp Fiction* dance partner, Uma Thurman, who again tears up the rug with her sexy co-star. Also lending their support are Vince Vaughn, Cedric The Entertainer, Bethlehem's own Dwayne "The Rock" Johnson and *Shorty* alums Danny DeVito and Harvey Keitel. While the previous film was directed by Barry Sonnenfeld (*Men in Black*), this sequel was helmed by F. Gary Gray, who proved he could cut the mustard with his hip remake of *The Italian Job*.

NEW ON VIDEO
THE INCREDIBLES—It's no secret that Pixar Studios practically invented computer animated movies. Starting in 1993 with the release of *Toy Story,* the company has a stellar track record for technical innovation AND heartfelt storytelling. The sincerity they bring to their scriptwriting and the richness and diversity of their characters has kept Pixar head and shoulders above their competitors at DreamWorks (*Shrek*) and Fox (*Ice Age*). In the spirit of their ongoing desire for new horizons to conquer, Pixar brought in Brad Bird (*The Iron Giant*) who pitched this story, about a family of superheroes now trying to cope in the world as average citizens, which seriously raised the bar for animated features. While the tony Ayn Rand/Nietzschean philosophy at the beginning

surprised many, the story arc ultimately softened this notion as the characters realize that a tolerance of others is essential if they are to function in society. Whereas Pixar's earlier films were aimed primarily at young children, this latest effort skewed more toward teens and adults, with more intense action and some consequential violence. In staking out territory once ruled by live action fare like *Indiana Jones, James Bond* and *Spider-Man*, Pixar has taken a quantum leap in the respectability given to animation. Mention should also be made of the fantastic vocal performances (another Pixar hallmark) from Craig T. Nelson, Holly Hunter and Samuel L. Jackson. As usual with Pixar, the DVD release is chock full of extra features, from commentary to production design featurettes that leave you dizzy over the amount of creative work that went into the making of this masterpiece.

CLASSIC CORNER

JESUS CHRIST SUPERSTAR—Remember a time when "hippies" and Christ went together like bread and wine at the Last Supper? Back in the late 1960s/early 1970s, these "Jesus freaks," as they were affectionately called, could be found on street corners singing the praises of the Lord. This new-found youth "Passion" made its way to live theatre in the musical productions of *Godspell* and *Jesus Christ Superstar*. In the case of *Superstar*, which started life as an album, then made it to the boards, the result was artistically satisfying and musically sophisticated. The 1973 movie version, directed by Norman Jewison (*Fiddler on the Roof*) and starring Ted Neeley, was shot on location in Israel and proved you could capture the spirit in spirituality without the leaden overtones of past Biblical epics like *King of Kings*. Recently re-released on DVD, the movie holds up rather well, and recalls a time when films could be stylistically experimental. The audio commentary with Jewison and Neeley is a warm and friendly encounter between two old colleagues, reminiscing about a project they remember fondly. Neeley, especially, seems genuinely moved by "revisiting" the various cast and crew members (including recently deceased co-star, Carl Anderson, who played Judas), all of whom he remembers by name. Jewison, too, has personal anecdotes, as well as some interesting comments about the technical challenges he faced in bringing this story to the big screen. There is also an exclusive interview with lyricist Tim Rice, who puts the musical he created with Andrew Lloyd Webber into historical context.

DVD ALERT

I AM CURIOUS—The mid to late 1960s was a seminal period in the history of American cinema. It marked a time when the desire for more frank and realistic depictions of sex, violence and language in films was forcing a re-examination of what was acceptable. Paving the way were such mavericks as *Who's Afraid of*

Virginia Woolf?, *Bonnie & Clyde* and *Midnight Cowboy*. The foreign cinema, which was already ahead of this American curve, now found a new market for its more erotic fare, be it Ingmar Bergman's *The Silence* or Vilgot Sjoman's "curious" double feature, *I Am Curious (Yellow)* and *I Am Curious (Blue)*. Curious, indeed! The *Yellow* version became a huge sensation in America (where it was initially banned), due to its sexually explicit scenes, mixed in with its anti-fascist/anti-war story line. Viewed today *Curious* is certainly a curiosity, where sexual freedom is linked directly to political freedom. In our own jaded time, where, sexually speaking, there are no boundaries and seemingly anything goes, such purity of expression seems downright quaint. Criterion has put together both films (*Blue* and *Yellow*) in a two-disc set that includes interviews, commentary, trailers and more. For those who want to experience libido fulfillment through intellectual and political awakening (you got that?) you just might find this Swedish oddball your cup of tea. The question you have to ask yourself is "Am I curious?" Well, are you?

THE BIG CHEESE

GALAXY QUEST—"Never give up, never surrender!" This is the mantra of starship commander Peter Quincy Taggart on the hit sci-fi TV series, *Galaxy Quest*. Flash forward two decades, add an army of fanboy geeks, and the once bracing credo has become the hollow catchphrase employed by over-the-hill actor, Jason Nesmith (Tim Allen). The man who once played Taggart now spends his time on the sci-fi convention circuit trying to reclaim his glory days while fending off the icy stares of contempt from his former cast mates who jealously languish in the second billing shadow of his star presence. However, when a cadre of desperate aliens mistake the actors for their TV counterparts, the celebs find they are called upon to do more than sign autographs and answer dumb trivia questions. Let me make one thing perfectly clear: this is not about *Star Trek* or William "Captain James T. Kirk" Shatner. Yeah, right! The truth: this is an on-the-nose parody of the celebrity purgatory that the *Star Trek* cast endured for 30 years, a not-unfamiliar typecasting phenomenon that has bedeviled many an actor (e.g. Max "Jethro" Baer). It is also a sincere love letter to the classic show (and to sci-fi fandom in general). Director Dean Parisot's clever casting (Sigourney Weaver as the blonde babe; Alan Rickman as the long-suffering Brit who feels humiliated playing the "alien crewmember") allows you to laugh at the cheesy nature of televised sci-fi while still honoring its legacy in our culture. And, just as Shatner (currently seen on *Boston Legal*) has proved with his recent Emmy win for his role on *The Practice*, there is indeed life after pop icon idolatry. But, you must embrace your fame rather than fight it. The lesson learned here is (say it with me) "Never give up, never surrender!"

SATISFYING YOUR MOVIE THEATRE "JONES"

(April 2005)

I still get a jolt when I go to the movies. Most of the time I end up seeing stuff at home on DVD (Thank you, Netflix!) but nothing beats the theatre-going experience for transporting you to another world. Unfortunately, other than offering the big screen/big sound package, there is something that many of the mega multiplexes have forgotten—ambience. Whether it's an old time movie palace like the Boyd in Bethlehem or the 19th Street in Allentown, or1970s era rehabs like 25th St. in Easton, these lesser "players" are striving to keep the movie theatre ambience alive.

Most recently, the Marquis Theatre (formerly Cinema Paradiso, United Artists and Eric) has been doing its part to compete with the multiplex big boys while maintaining the charm of the old style movie houses. Starting with the elegant makeover from the Paradiso days, Marquis owner John Halecky has overseen the installation of new projectors and screens, an upgraded sound system and, most important of all, a commitment to restoring a family friendly atmosphere of an old fashioned movie theatre. And with a diverse program schedule covering everything from mainstream and family to art house and independent, the Marquis is setting the standard for how a theatre should be run. Thanks, John, for believing in movies, the public, and most of all, Easton, itself.

NEW IN THEATRES

SIN CITY—This summer promises to be a big year for comic book action films. June heralds the return of the *Batman* franchise (thankfully Schumacher-free), while July offers up the debut feature of *The Fantastic Four*. Prior to these high profile flicks comes Robert Rodriguez's take on Frank Miller's *Sin City* graphic novel. Here, the two men share directing billing (along with an unbilled directing cameo by Quentin Tarantino), for a film that promises to be an eclectic blend of Miller's noirish visuals jazzed up with Rodriguez's trademark staccato editing. And it doesn't hurt that Rodriguez, himself, is a comic illustrator and devoted fan of the form. The film boasts a definitively edgy cast as well—Bruce Willis, Mickey Rourke, Clive Owen, Jessica Alba, Brittany Murphy, Nick Stahl, Rosario Dawson and well, you get the idea. Rodriguez is one of the few true mavericks working in the mainstream, so you know this is going to be something special. Teaming up with Miller (who previously reinvented Batman in the '80s with his *Dark Knight* series), bodes well for the *El Mariachi* and *Spy Kids* director. What he did for those genres he is now going to do for the comic book movie.

- 181 -

NEW ON VIDEO

VERA DRAKE—Those who are familiar with the work of British filmmaker, Mike Leigh (*Secrets & Lies, All or Nothing*), know that his movies carry a heady dose of intense emotionalism that fairly crackles on screen when the characters interact. Whether it's the nihilistic Johnny, from *Naked,* fighting off the outside world so that he can remain secure in his relationship-free cocoon, or songwriters, Gilbert and Sullivan, at odds with one another over the nature of their collaborations in *Topsy-Turvy*, Leigh likes to put you through the wringer. With *Vera Drake*, the story of a 1950s housewife (Academy nominee, Imelda Staunton), who goes on trial for providing illegal abortions, or as she puts it, "Helping young women who are in trouble," the class-conscious Leigh has, again, found a provocative subject to mine. Whatever side of this very divisive issue you are on, you can't help but feel for this woman whose heart is in the right place as she battles against the hypocritical politics of the time.

CLASSIC CORNER

BACKBEAT—While on its surface, this small movie is about two Liverpool art school buddies, at its core, it's really the story about the Beatles before they became "The Beatles." Before they were John, Paul, George and Ringo, they were John, Paul, George, Pete and Stuart. Though drummer Pete would later be replaced with Ringo, the story of Stuart Sutcliffe—art student and school chum of the Beatles founder, John Lennon—has gone largely untold. The shy artist was coerced by his soon-to-be-famous friend into buying a bass guitar and joining the fledgling band. They headed off to Germany, where they thrashed out their sets of raucous rock & roll in the smoke-filled music clubs of post-war Hamburg. The innocent lads from Liverpool quickly transformed into hardened rockers, fueled by copious amounts of booze, sweat and pills. However, their hellish nights on stage were leavened, somewhat, by the arrival of a sweet, German angel named Astrid Kirchherr, an artist, photographer and hip purveyor of the sophisticated beat movement in Germany. The blonde beauty took an instant liking to these British invaders, none more so than the shy Stuart, who ended up walking away from what would become the most famous musical group in the world. This 1993 slice of Beatle history finally comes to DVD in a special edition that includes audio commentary with director Iain Softley and actors Ian Hart (Lennon) and Stephen Dorff (Stu). There are also interviews with the director and a conversation with Astrid, herself.

DVD ALERT

SIDEWAYS—Call this one "the little movie that could." It may not have won the Oscar for Best Picture, but this indie sleeper about two middle-aged men on a road trip through California wine country is as satisfying and refreshing as a glass of chardonnay. Paul Giamatti, who made a big splash in 2003 in *American Splendor*, and who has previously stolen the show as third and fourth bananas in such films as *Private Parts, The Negotiator* and the remake of *Planet of the Apes*, here plays Miles, a down-on-his-luck would-be novelist, still nursing the wounds from his two-year old divorce. He teams up with his actor friend, Jack (Thomas Haden Church), an aging, narcissist who still gets by on his fading charm, and who decides to use his weeklong wine-tasting road trip with Miles as an excuse for one last fling before his impending marriage. Along the way, the pair of bonding buddies hook up with a couple of female wine enthusiasts (Virginia Madsen and Sandra Oh), and find that the mutual attraction extends to more than just the vino swirling in their goblets. This thoughtful and very funny movie was written and directed by Alexander Payne (*About Schmidt, Election*) and is based on the somewhat autobiographical novel by Rex Pickett, who came seriously close, himself, to being destitute during his checkered writing career. The success this movie has had, and the rewards that its participants are now reaping, gives one hope for the future of small independents in the industry. In summing up the piquant pleasures of this sweet little number, let me put it into terms that any wine connoisseur can appreciate—great clarity, a spicy bouquet with a rich aftertaste that leaves you satisfied, yet wanting more. Very good nose. Cheers.

THE BIG CHEESE

CANDYMAN—While the lovely Virginia Madsen is currently basking in the glow of her recent Oscar nomination for *Sideways* (see above), she has paid her dues, toiling in the backwater of mainstream cinema for twenty-plus years in everything from David Lynch's *Dune* to this unusual, yet effective horror flick. Based on the short story "The Forbidden" by Clive Barker (*Hellraiser*), the plot concerns an urban legend, hook-handed murderer haunting a Chicago public housing tenement. Madsen plays Helen, an academic out to study the legend of a long-dead serial killer known as "Candyman." The imposing Tony Todd plays the supernatural menace who seems to hold dominion over swarms of bees, which willingly do his bidding. Stylishly directed by Bernard Rose (*Paperhouse, Immortal Beloved*), who also appears in the film as "Archie Walsh," this is one of the less cheesy horror flicks to come out in the last two decades. It is also blessed with one of the most beautiful scores (by Philip Glass) that you are ever likely to hear (too bad it's not on CD). The DVD was recently reissued in a special edition which includes a cool audio commentary with the director, along with some nifty featurettes on Clive Barker and the Candyman Mythos. You might even want to pair this flick with *Sideways* to do a Virginia Madsen double feature, for the ultimate "wine & cheese" film festival.

LET THE MOVIE FEAST BEGIN
(May 2005)

While it's true that the month of May heralds the start of the pre-summer movie season, it's especially notable this year for the final installment of the *Star Wars* series, along with other highly anticipated fare as *Monster-In-Law* with Jane Fonda, and the CGI animated *Madagascar*. However, there is another wave of films that will be finding its way to you in the home video market. Thanks to a crowded Christmas, there are many new titles vying for your attention. Some good films got lost in the holiday release schedule, like *Kinsey, The Merchant of Venice* and *The Life Aquatic*, plus there are plenty of favorites and blockbusters due out now that are sure to satisfy, such as *Phantom of the Opera, The Aviator, A Very Long Engagement* and *The Sea Inside*. So, whether you hit the multiplex or kick back at home, May has become one of the hottest months for checking out movies. It's just a matter of finding the time.

NEW IN THEATRES
KINGDOM OF HEAVEN—Famed director Ridley Scott has always made films with an epic grandeur, whether it was the gothic claustrophobia of *Alien*, the noirish sci-fi of *Blade Runner*, the chic feminism of *Thelma & Louise* or the sublime decadence of ancient Rome in *Gladiator*. Now Mr. Scott turns his practiced eye on the clash between Christians and Muslims that defined the insanity known as the Crusades. Starring Liam Neeson, Orlando Bloom and Jeremy Irons, the film concentrates mainly on the third Crusade (circa 1127-1193) which included such legendary characters as Richard the Lion-heart and King Saladin of Egypt. Given the world situation today, and the rise of fundamental extremists on both sides, was there ever a more relevant time for a movie to confront such a hot button issue? If nothing else, the visual stylist in Mr. Scott insures that this will be one of the most striking-looking films this year.

NEW ON VIDEO
THE LIFE AND DEATH OF PETER SELLERS—Though not shown in theatres, here, this made-for-HBO movie is as good as anything you'll see in the multiplex. As the subject of a film bio, actor Peter Sellers presents a fascinating enigma—a man who, it seems, never grew up, or even had his own persona. He was a little boy in a movie star's body, a Peter Pan with a Captain Hook temper, and that immature child had access to all the excesses that came with celebrity fame. Starring Geoffrey Rush (*Shine*) in an uncanny, transformational performance, the movie chronicles Sellers' rise from pudgy, live-radio comedian to a superstar film actor who worked with such major directors as Stanley

Kubrick (*Dr. Strangelove*) and Blake Edwards (*The Pink Panther*). Along the way he acquired several wives (Emily Watson, Charlize Theron) and a reputation for philandering and self-loathing that drove the people who knew him nuts. Rush bravely plays the part with all the warts intact, yet still manages to find sympathy for this pathetic man who, despite his flaws, was an awesome talent. As the directors in Sellers' life, Stanley Tucci captures the spirit, if not the look, of Kubrick, while John Lithgow does a fine job as the flamboyant Edwards, who seems to have been the closest thing the actor had to a friend, despite their stormy relationship. Visually, the movie has fun replicating the "swinging sixties" hey day of Sellers' career, along with classic moments from several of his films (the "war room" from *Strangelove* is the best). The movie also trades on Sellers' chameleon-esque behavior and cipher-like personality by having Rush portray many of the main characters in "soundstage" versions of scenes previously shown with the regular actors. It is a mannered conceit, but it mostly works, especially in illustrating how Sellers lived outside his world, and drew on others to define him. It's not for nothing that one documentary on him was titled, *Peter Sellers: The Mask Behind the Mask*.

CLASSIC CORNER

CHARIOTS OF FIRE—Cinematically speaking, the 1970s officially came to an end during the Academy Awards in the spring of 1982. The split of Best Picture and Director clearly illustrated the passing of the torch from one decade to the next when Warren Beatty won as director for his very seventies sympathetic look at Communist history in the sprawling epic, *Reds*, while the British invasion of American cinema was inaugurated with a Best Picture Oscar to this little movie about Olympic runners. First time feature director, Hugh Hudson, and veteran producer, David Puttnam, joined forces to tell the story of Eric Liddell and Harold Abrahams—a Scottish Christian and a Cambridge Jew, respectively— who brought glory and recognition to the United Kingdom at the 1924 Olympics. The movie was a surprise hit, and is now best remembered for its use of slow-motion photography to stretch out the short running sequences (the races were barely half a minute, and sometimes shorter), and the stirring, Oscar-winning score by Vangelis. The cast was equally impressive, with Ian Charleson and Ben Cross as the intensely driven runners, plus great supporting turns by Ian Holm, Nigel Havers, John Gielgud, Nick Farrell and Alice Krige. A special edition, 2-disc DVD has recently been issued which includes current-day interviews with many of the participants and an informative commentary track with the director. Certainly, the success of this "veddy British" film led to a more open acceptance of the Merchant/Ivory type movies (those set mostly in England in the early 20th Century) that came to the forefront in the eighties and nineties.

DVD ALERT

THE TWILIGHT ZONE—This classic series from the 1960s has previously been available on DVD in single discs and in box sets that randomly packaged together various episodes of the groundbreaking show. Finally, someone got the bright idea to do seasonal box sets, and added a slew of extras worthy of this one-of-a-kind phenomenon. So far, only the first two (out of five) seasons are available, but they're winners. In addition to pristine transfers of these glorious black & white programs, the sets, called "The Definitive Editions," include interviews and commentaries on selected episodes, and even isolated scores, that add a layer of resonance to these timeless treasures of a bygone era in television. The Season One set also includes the book, *The Twilight Zone Companion*, by Marc Scott Zicree, the definitive guide which gives you a complete history of the show, along with detailed descriptions of each episode. For those who can appreciate what writer and creator, Rod Serling accomplished with this series, these DVD box sets are a validation of his effort. Rod said it best, himself, in his classic opening monologue which began each episode: "There is a fifth dimension beyond that which is known to man. It is a dimension as vast as space and as timeless as infinity. It is the middle ground between light and shadow, between science and superstition, and it lies between the pit of man's fears and the summit of his knowledge. This is the dimension of imagination. It is an area we call the Twilight Zone." Truer words were never spoken.

THE BIG CHEESE

THE REAGANS—This two-part mini-series was originally set to premiere on network television, but they caved in to pressure from conservative groups who balked at the notion of portraying "Saint Ron" as anything other than godlike. The brouhaha led, ultimately, to the film being re-cut as a one night movie event on ABC's pay cable sister channel, Showtime. The results were less than overwhelming. Now out as a 3-hour DVD, the movie about this most dysfunctional of first families reveals itself to be much more even-handed, and less of a hatchet job, than the Republican right would have you believe. James Brolin (Mr. "Babs!" Oh, the scandal!) does a credible job impersonating Mr. Reagan, while the fantastic Judy Davis (who previously wowed TV viewers with her turn as Judy Garland), brings great dimension and, yes, warmth to her portrayal of Ronnie's better half, Nancy (Davis) Reagan. Note: I seriously doubt the two women are related. Following standard issue TV biopic procedure, the movie presents us with a greatest hits collection of Reagan moments, none more memorable than those from his Presidency: his quips about trees causing pollution, the assassination attempt and the Iran Contra debacle. Along the way, we're also treated to Ron & Nancy's parenting skills, as demonstrated by their brood of now-famous children—Michael, Maureen, Patti and Ron Jr. Though the far right would, no doubt, prefer to whitewash the lives of these troubled and complex offspring, the movie doesn't shy away from Patti's drug use; however, it does tend to gloss over the question of ballet dancer Ron's sexual orientation. On the whole, Republican and Democrat, alike, will find this inoffensive bio-drama a fun viewing experience, seeing it through their own partisan eyes. An audio commentary with the filmmakers, and an interview with Brolin, offer surprising insight into the production, yet doesn't detract from enjoying the film as a cheese ball guilty pleasure. And, as for Brolin's second outing impersonating a movie icon (previously he played Clark Gable in 1975's *Gable & Lombard*), all I have to say is, "Well, there you go, again."

SECOND HELPINGS: GORGING ON SUMMER MOVIES

(June 2005)

The summer movie season is upon us. While the onslaught of films began last month, those releases were merely the entree to the main course. The summer months are a true smorgasbord of mostly empty calories, designed to sate our ever ravenous appetite. This year's slate is no different, and includes such eagerly awaited titles as *Mr. & Mrs. Smith, The Honeymooners, Batman Begins, War of the Worlds, Dark Water, Fantastic Four, Charlie and the Chocolate Factory, Bewitched, An Unfinished Life, The Island, The Brothers Grimm, Asylum, Domino, Red Eye, Valiant* and more. Those waiting for *The Pink Panther*, however, will have to wait; it's been pulled from release and is being rescheduled for September 2006. Still, every summer it seems the menu gets bigger. But like any "all-you-can-eat" buffet, it's best to proceed with caution. Certainly partake of your favorites, but don't be afraid to try a new dish or two. And, above all, go easy on the "cream puffs" (movies so light weight they have no substance at all); I know it's summer, but too many of these gooey confections and you're bound to end up with a serious stomach ache.

NEW IN THEATRES

CINDERELLA MAN—Director Ron Howard and company engage in a bit of counter programming designed to offset the mostly mindless offerings this summer. Starring Russell Crowe (back with Howard after their successful work on *A Beautiful Mind*), this Depression-era tale follows the true story of heavyweight boxer Jim Braddock. Renee Zellweger (*Chicago*) plays his faithful rock of a wife, Mae, and the wonderful Paul Giamatti (*Sideways*) lends his considerable talents as Braddock's manager and trainer. This is normally the kind of fare you'd see in the fall, laden as it is with "*Rocky*-esque" Oscar potential. Thankfully the filmmakers have chosen to release it now, ensuring that at least one major release this summer will be about something other than just whiz bang euphoria. This is the kind of film that Howard is really good at, so it's not surprising that he's elected to throw it out there, toe-to-toe with the summer blockbusters. Here's hoping he scores a knockout.

NEW ON VIDEO

MILLION DOLLAR BABY—"Go ahead, make my dilemma." That is a phrase that Clint Eastwood's character might have said in his surprisingly downbeat Oscar-winning drama. The film stars Hilary Swank as a young woman determined to rise above her white trash, trailer park existence, and sees boxing (under trainer Eastwood's tutelage) as her ticket to a better life. A lot of fuss has been made over the dark turn the movie takes, but it was a necessary element to provide the spiritually-conflicted trainer with a moral dilemma, the kind of which he often posed to dismiss the religion he'd felt had failed him. Morgan Freeman brings his considerable gravitas and bearing as an over-the-hill boxer who holds onto his dignity in a world that no longer cares about him. While the film is long and bleak, it is one of Eastwood's most powerful works, which garnered Oscars for himself (as director), as well as Freeman and Swank.

CLASSIC CORNER

CASINO—Director Martin Scorsese's three-hour meditation on the 1970s Las Vegas numbers racket was looked upon by many as merely a warmed over rehash of the goons from *Goodfellas*. While it was co-written by Nicholas Pileggi, who'd also penned the *Goodfellas* source book, *Wiseguys*, *Casino* dealt with a totally different milieu. The director's stable of regulars, including Robert DeNiro and Joe Pesci, along with a stellar cast of supporting players (Sharon Stone, Kevin Pollak, James Woods, Alan King, Don Rickles and even Dick Smothers) contribute to the film's overall sense of menace and glamour. Scorsese perfectly captures this tawdry era of Vegas before it was transformed into the mega-billion dollar theme park it is today. The two-disc special edition finally does justice to this overlooked gem. While the director is currently flying high over the critical praise he garnered for last year's spectacular hit, *The Aviator*, this movie reminds us of just how versatile a master of the medium he could be. Hopefully the motion picture Academy will someday realize it, too, and give the man his Oscar.

DVD ALERT

STAR TREK: INSURRECTION—This is the ninth of the *Star Trek* movies to get the two-disc treatment (*Star Trek: Nemesis,* the tenth and last film in the franchise, still remains in need of an upgrade from its initial release). By *Trek* standards, *Insurrection* is a lesser effort, lacking the verve that made the even numbered films, generally, the best. This time the story concerns the *Trek* team coming upon a planet of eternally youthful inhabitants who are threatened by outsiders. Despite fine work by the cast and guest stars F. Murray Abraham and Anthony Zerbe, the story just never takes flight. Still, for *Star Trek* fans, this is a must-have title, if only to have the complete set. As in the other special editions, extras include audio commentary, interviews, featurettes and an amalgam of *Trek* history. Though it's hard to believe, *Star Trek* will celebrate its 40th anniversary next year. With no current show or movie in the pipeline, these DVDs are all the fans have. Has the *Star Trek* phenomenon finally run out of steam (the last movie and series both failed to hit their mark)? Though it's been counted out before, my guess is that the people involved have something up their sleeve for the near future. The franchise will indeed "live long and prosper."

THE BIG CHEESE

SPACEBALLS—A decade after the 1977 release of the original *Star Wars*, and four years after the trilogy's concluding chapter, *Return of the Jedi*, funnyman Mel Brooks released this sci-fi send up. Following in the tradition of his earlier genre parodies, *Blazing Saddles* (westerns), *Young Frankenstein* (horror) and *High Anxiety* (Hitchcock), Mr. Brooks scored another hit with this on-the-nose satire of sci-fi in general and *Star Wars* in particular. Beginning with booming music and a three-paragraph intro crawling up the screen, Brooks knows that getting the background right is important, from an overly-detailed spaceship model moving endlessly past the camera, to the roaring sound effects and flashy editing associated with *Star Wars*. Brooks also hits on a few other movie classics including *Alien, Planet of the Apes, The Wizard of Oz* and *Lawrence of Arabia*, all to good effect, though he still has a tendency to fall back on bathroom humor and rude innuendoes. The casting is equally eclectic, a mix of then new faces (Bill Pullman and Daphne Zuniga), and seasoned professionals (John Candy, John Hurt, Dick Van Patten and Rick Moranis as the hilariously schizophrenic nerd/bully "Dark Helmet"). Brooks saved his most pointed barbs for the, even then, ever increasing reliance by moviemakers on merchandising tie-ins. Playing the wise, Yoda-esque, and very Jewish "Yogurt," Brooks waxes lovingly on the plethora of *Spaceballs* memorabilia he hawks, everything from dolls and lunchboxes to a working flame thrower. Throughout the film, every manner of tie-in is displayed, bearing the movie's title ("*Spaceballs*: the shaving cream"). Even the movie is called *Spaceballs: The Movie*. Now, eighteen years later, it seems that Brooks, himself, has been seduced by the dark side. What with a new film version of his hit Broadway play, *The Producers* (which was based on his earlier film version), now in the works, and a new, two-disc special edition DVD of *Spaceballs* coincidentally timed for release as the final *Star Wars* commercial, I mean movie, hits theatres, there indeed appears to be a definite disturbance in the force. Still, Brooks has certainly paid his dues, with more than half a century in show business, so go out and get this latest edition of the last good film he made and let the "farce" be with you.

LOOKING AT MOVIES... SERIOUSLY
(September 2005)

With the arrival of fall, there generally follows an increase in the number of "serious" movies released to the public. While the summer had its share of satisfying fare (*Batman Begins; Cinderella Man; Charlie & the Chocolate Factory* and *March of the Penguins* to name a few), September is the real beginning of the serious movie season, with such promising mainstream titles as *Capote* with Philip Seymour Hoffman; *Just Like Heaven* with Reese Witherspoon; and *Oliver Twist* with Sir Ben Kingsley and directed by Roman Polanski. And now, thanks to John Halecky at the Marquis Theatre on South Third Street in Easton, there is another new venue for art house movies as well. Starting this past August, the 25-seat mini-theatre at the Marquis, called "The Screening Room," has offered such award-winning (but rarely seen outside of New York) titles as *Short Cut to Nirvana; Walk on Water; Palindromes; Paheli* and *Schultze Gets the Blues.* September promises even more interesting fare, such as *Voices in Wartime; Saraband* (see review below)*; Rize; The Animation Show 2005; Nomi-Song*—a semi-biography about Germany's eccentric glam rocker, Klaus Nomi, and *Mondovino*—an entertaining documentary that takes you on an inside look at the wine industry. Though seating is limited, this is a good first step in bringing quality art house films to Easton. Let's all do our part to make it a success.

NEW IN THEATRES
SARABAND—Three decades after the release of Ingmar Bergman's meditation on married life, *Scenes From a Marriage*, the famed Swedish director and his cast (Liv Ullmann and Erland Josephson) revisit these characters in a stunning new film that proves the old filmmaker still has a few tricks up his sleeve. After a 30-year separation, Marianne and Johan revisit at Johan's mountain cabin, in a reunion that is anything but serene and loving. The long-divorced couple may be older, but seem far from wiser. The metaphoric title refers to a stately court dance, which is one way to look at how these people go through the motions of civility, while deeper passions are held in check. Though Bergman had sworn that *Fanny & Alexander* (1986) would be his last film (he did do a TV movie in 1998), the lure of bringing these two characters back, and the actors who played them, after so many years must have been irresistible. Thankfully, for all of us, he took the bait. And it's nice to know that, even in his old age, Bergman has lost none of his sting. (Scheduled for the Marquis Theatre this month.)

CRASH—Not to be confused with David Cronenberg's 1996 "auto-erotic" thriller, this ensemble film, starring Don Cheadle, Matt Dillon, Sandra Bullock, Ryan Phillippe, Thandie Newton and Brendan Fraser, finds a disturbing metaphor in the head-on collisions between racial cultures and their class struggles through the social intercourse of car crashes. During Christmas in L.A. (the center of car culture), racial tensions are played out through various vehicle-related vignettes, involving the intertwined lives of the principal players. First time director, Paul Haggis (who wrote *Million Dollar Baby*), has as good an eye for composition as he has an ear for dialogue, some of it shockingly frank and provocative. We all know that sickening feeling we get in the pit of our stomachs when we realize we're about to be in an accident; this film drives home the notion that racial and cultural tensions hold the same destructive potential as the dumb brute power of colliding automobiles. Honk if you love good movies.

CLASSIC CORNER

BULLITT—For more than thirty years, the anti-hero, cool cop movie has been a genre unto itself. We've had Mel Gibson in *Lethal Weapon,* Bruce Willis in *Die Hard,* Al Pacino in *Serpico,* Clint Eastwood in *Dirty Harry* and Gene Hackman in *The French Connection.* But, before any of them pinned on a badge, there was Steve McQueen as Frank Bullitt. The low-key actor perfected his minimalist style over the 1960s in everything from *The Magnificent Seven* to *The Great Escape* to *The Sand Pebbles.* For *Bullitt,* McQueen created one of his most iconic characters, from the dark turtleneck, with accompanying shoulder holster, to his Ford Mustang that figures prominently in the still thrilling car chase through San Francisco. Other highlights include a foot chase on an airport runway amongst taxiing jets, and a creepy cat-and-mouse search for the villain in a hospital morgue. Don Gordon and Robert Vaughan provide strong performances in supporting roles. The two-disc special edition is a vast improvement over the bare bones single disc that was previously issued. In addition to a great commentary track with director Peter Yates (a Brit, no less!), there are a pair of feature length documentaries—one on film editing and the other on McQueen, called *The Essence of Cool,*—plus a vintage 1968 featurette on the making of the film. A great package all the way. At a time when the counter culture viewed police (some say accurately) in an unflattering light, McQueen decided to gamble that he could make this tarnished profession look hip and cool. Boy, did he ever succeed.

DVD ALERT

A VERY LONG ENGAGEMENT—How do you follow-up on the success of *Amelie*, the adorable French fable starring Audrey Tautou that was written and directed by Jean-Pierre Jeunet? Well, you can't, really; that movie was a one-of-a-kind treat, a delectable piece of French puff pastry with the most satisfying filling imaginable. Instead, Jeunet took his *Amelie* star and went off in a different direction, melding the beauty and romance of that earlier gem with the unspeakable harshness of "The Great War" (aka: World War I). Tautou plays Mathilde, a young woman who is in deep denial over the death of her fiancé, Manech, in the war. What follows is a detective story about this woman's search through the facts and fallacies that point in many directions. Part *Amelie,* part *Paths of Glory*, and even a little bit of *Rashomon* thrown in, Jeunet has conjured up another winner that is darker and more complex than his previous film, yet just as beautiful to look at (thanks to his *Amelie* cinematographer Bruno Delbonnel and of course the lovely Ms. Tautou). The two-disc DVD has commentary by Jeunet (in French with subtitles), and some entertaining making-of material. One special highlight of this movie is the wonderfully evocative score by composer Angelo Badalamenti, who is best known for his atmospheric work with David Lynch (*Blue Velvet, Twin Peaks*). Also, look for Jodie Foster (speaking flawless French), in a small supporting role.

THE BIG CHEESE

THE OUTER LIMITS—"There is nothing wrong with your television set. Do not attempt to adjust the picture. *We* are controlling transmission." So says the solemn "control voice" at the beginning of each episode of this classic 1960s sci-fi anthology series. The show, which lasted only two seasons, first aired in the years between that of two other classics of the period, *The Twilight Zone* (1959-1964) and *Star Trek* (1966-1969), but never really caught on as they did. The hour-long episodes were well written by such established names as Harlan Ellison and Joseph Stefano (who also co-produced), and well-acted by the cream of 1960s acting talent (who would later make names for themselves) that included William Shatner, Martin Landau, Sally Kellerman, Ed Asner, Robert Duvall and Carroll O'Connor. The major drawback to this series' success was its reliance on cheesy monsters and effects that were at odds with the fine scripts, overshadowing their integrity. Also, coming on the scene right after the huge success of Rod Serling's *Twilight Zone*, with its streamlined half-hour format, twist endings, catchy theme music and the presence of Serling, himself, *Outer Limits* could never match *Zone*'s snazzier appeal. The entire series is available on DVD in two, seasonal box sets that wonderfully showcase the luminous black-&-white episodes (many shot by the great Conrad Hall), but entirely lacking in any extras (thanks, guys!). Of the 49 total episodes, there were very few clunkers, which mean these sets are a real treat. The best of the best include, *The Sixth Finger* (with David McCallum), *Demon with a Glass Hand* (with Robert Culp), *I, Robot* (with Leonard Nimoy), *Soldier* (with Michael Ansara) and fan favorite,

The Zanti Misfits (with Bruce Dern). This was some of the best writing ever to appear on network television; the cheesy packaging just adds to the pleasure, now.

THE SCARIEST MOVIE STORY EVER, PART 2

(October 2005)

Last October, I wrote that Paul Schrader's movie prequel to 1973's *The Exorcist* was shelved and entirely re-shot by another director, Renny Harlin. The re-done version got some of the worst reviews, ever, and I wondered just how bad Schrader's version could have been. Since then, in a bittersweet victory, Schrader's *Exorcist* prequel, *Dominion*, was released, perfunctorily and without much fanfare, to middling reviews (as opposed to the scathing ones Harlin's version got). Well, now, thankfully, it's coming out on video, just in time for Halloween. Schrader's work has always been a bit high-minded for the masses, tinged as it is with intellectualism, metaphor and obscure literary references. They are really films designed for adults, and well-read ones at that; a minority to be sure. Still, there is usually enough "filler" for mainstream tastes to have a hearty meal. His version of *Cat People* still packs a wallop, even if you don't pick up the allusions to Dante and Campbell. And, given how bad most horror films have been of late, I'll take Schrader's rarified elitism over the formulaic bilge that floods the multiplexes any day. I'd rather support that. If you disagree, then that's the scariest movie story I've ever heard.

NEW IN THEATRES

GOODNIGHT AND GOOD LUCK—For his follow-up to the highly entertaining *Confessions of a Dangerous Mind*, his debut feature (as director) about the shady life of game show creator, Chuck Barris, George Clooney decided to tackle the story of one of his (and his father's) heroes, broadcast journalist, Edward R. Murrow. The brilliant CBS newsman, with his ever-present burning cigarette, proved you could be a liberal and a patriot (hear that, Mr. President?) when he stood up to Joseph McCarthy during those paranoid years in the 1950s of the "Red scare" communist witch hunts. Befitting the period, Clooney shot his film in stark black & white; most of our memories of Murrow come from just such monochromatic television and grainy newsreels of the day. A steadfast liberal, himself, Clooney said this story hit particularly close to home, since his father, Nick Clooney, was also a broadcaster for television news. The great character actor, David Strathairn, was tapped to play Murrow, and the lanky performer easily slipped into the gaunt newsman's persona. While the film's title derives from Murrow's signature sign-off, it can also be seen as Clooney's own feelings about our current political situation. It's gratifying to know that there are still some people with clout, out there, willing to put their reputations on the line for something they believe in. Clooney could just as easily cashed a big paycheck making *Ocean's 13*; instead, he chose to do this. That's called putting your money where your mouth is.

NEW ON VIDEO

BATMAN BEGINS—Holy re-invention, Batman! Back in the late 1980s, director Tim Burton, fresh off his success with *Beetlejuice*, recreated the Batman story as a "Dark Knight" mythology (from Bob Kane's graphic novel), which resulted in two pretty good films. Unfortunately, in the 1990s, the reins were handed over to Joel Schumacher, who ruined the franchise with a pair of cheesy, over-the-top offerings that made the 1960s camp TV series look tame by comparison. Thankfully, the Batman name has been redeemed with this truly dark and serious drama, written by David Goyer and directed by Christopher Nolan (*Memento, Insomnia*).The result is the best Batman movie, ever, and damn near the best superhero one, as well. The extraordinary cast, led by Christian Bale as "the Dark Knight," includes Michael Caine, Liam Neeson, Morgan Freeman, Gary Oldman, Katie Holmes, Cillian Murphy, Rutger Hauer and Tom Wilkinson. Nolan keeps the fantastical elements of his film grounded in firm reality, and does true justice to the comic crime fighter's legacy. The two-disc set arrives just in time to join a re-release of the other four *Batman* movies in similar DVD sets. So, wherever your tastes run to in caped crusader fare—Burton, Schumacher or Nolan—there is a DVD version with loads of extras just for you.

CLASSIC CORNER

TITANIC—Eight years after director James Cameron proved that he was the "King of the World," with his epic, tragedian drama about the most famous shipwreck in maritime history, he finally delivers the goods for this special edition DVD set. The story of Jack and Rose on that ill-fated ocean liner was previously released in a bare bones theatrical cut at the dawn of the DVD era. However, Cameron had hinted that he would one day release a longer version for the home video market, but this ain't it. What had once seemed a radical idea in home video is now almost commonplace in the industry. Perhaps emboldened by the success of the "extras-heavy" special editions of *Lord of the Rings* on video, Cameron has put together a three-disc DVD special edition of his most successful movie to date. In addition to the theatrical cut (which Cameron now deems is the best, and only version he'll release), there is a wealth of extras about the work that went into this awesome production which netted the 1997 film epic 11 Oscars to tie the record for the most wins. All I have to say is, "Jim, it's about time."

DVD ALERT

NAKED—British director Mike Leigh's oeuvre of mostly contemporary working class dramas has proven to be a genre unto itself. From *Secrets & Lies* to *Career Girls*, Leigh finds both the heart and the fire that burns in the grey landscape of English life. One of his darkest forays was this 1993 existential study starring David Thewlis in a mesmerizing performance as Johnny, the anarchic drifter who swoops down into the lives of his old girlfriend and her vulnerable roommate. The raging Johnny, an alcoholic, womanizing scarecrow with a chip the size of the British Isles on his lean shoulder, embarks on an all-night odyssey into the underclass world where he spews his caustic bitterness at whoever stumbles into his path. Though this is undoubtedly the bleakest entry in Leigh's canon, it is also one of his best. Criterion is finally bringing out this dark masterpiece on DVD, which includes an audio commentary with Leigh and the cast, interviews and a Leigh short called *The Short and Curlies*, featuring a young Thewlis as a reedy nerd with a penchant for very bad jokes. For those who can handle it, *Naked* is a brilliant excursion into the very heart of pessimism and despair.

THE BIG CHEESE

H.G. WELLS' WAR OF THE WORLD—No, this isn't the Tom Cruise/Steven Spielberg extravaganza, nor is it the 1953 George Pal production starring Gene Barry. What we're talking about, here, is a "no-budget" attempt to tell this classic story in its proper Victorian England setting. Unfortunately, this version's ambitions are stunted by its non-existent budget and uneven amateur talent. Photographed, edited and directed by Timothy Hines, it's clear he had a strong desire to tell the complete tale of Wells' classic in its correct time period, something no other film (or radio) adaptation had done. But the director and his crew are clearly out of their depth. While there is some clever design work afoot, regarding the Martians and their lethal war machines, the effects are of the low-calibre, desktop computer variety that would look more at home on an episode of the old *Dr. Who*. And the "synth" orchestral score is just a further example of the lack of capital at hand. This seems even to extend to the casting; Anthony Piana, in the dual roles of "the writer" and "the brother," is distinguished mainly by the wearing of a mustache for one of the parts. What the film does have going for it is a real sense of heart and a loving respect for the source material. Most of the acting, except for Mr. Piana, is dreadful, and set design is catch as catch can. It also appears that they only had the use of horses for about a day, since most carriage shots are framed to exclude the animals. But, despite all this, and a glacial sense of pacing, this wedge of Victorian Velveeta is a curiosity worth checking out. At the very least, you and your friends can make fun of all the running scenes in the film.

'TIS THE SEASON TO WATCH MOVIES
(December 2005)

Christmas time means many things—getting together with family and friends, sharing in the holiday spirit and checking out some good movies. This end-of-the-year season promises to have many excellent offerings to please the cinephile in all of us. There's the John Smith/Pocahontas saga, *The New World*, directed by Terrence Malick and starring Colin Farrell; *Chicago* director Rob Marshall's *Memoirs of a Geisha*; Steven Spielberg's *Munich*; the gay cowboy drama, *Brokeback Mountain* by Ang Lee; Nathan Lane, Matthew Broderick and Uma Thurman in *The Producers*; Woody Allen's *Match Point*; and Jude Law and Sean Penn in the classic political drama, *All The King's Men*. Oh, yes, there is, of course that 800 lb. gorilla of a flick, Peter Jackson's epic remake of *King Kong*. Based on advanced word, the director of *Lord of the Rings* is evidently out to prove he is also Lord of the Apes. With a killer cast that includes Naomi Watts, Adrien Brody and Jack Black, Jackson may just have another blockbuster hit to add to his considerable resume. There are plenty of other choices at theatres this month, so you're bound to find something that will make this an especially memorable holiday. After all, 'tis the season.

NEW IN THEATRES
THE CHRONICLES OF NARNIA: THE LION, THE WITCH AND THE WARDROBE—With the *Lord of the Rings* trilogy a thing of the past, the film industry has been looking for the next great fantasy franchise. If Disney has its way, C.S. Lewis will be the new J.R.R. Tolkien, and *Narnia* the new *Rings*. The devout Lewis, a friend and contemporary of Tolkien, wrote many books with Christian themes—*The Screwtape Letters, Mere Christianity*—none more beloved than his series of fantasy tales set in the magical land of Narnia. The first book (though the second, chronologically) is *The Lion, the Witch, and the Wardrobe,* about the Pevensie children who enter the world of Narnia through a magical wardrobe chest. There they are plunged into a battle between good: Aslan, the lion (voiced by Liam Neeson) and evil: Jadis the White Witch (Tilda Swinton). Directed by Andrew Adamson (the *Shrek* films) on location in New Zealand and the Czech Republic, this live-action Disney version has the same scope and mythic grandeur as the *Rings* trilogy, while maintaining its own look and originality. Many of the people who worked on *Rings* worked on this as well. With seven books in the *Narnia* series, the success of this first film could lay the groundwork for a whole new movie franchise about fantasy and magic. *Harry Potter* fans, take note.

NEW ON VIDEO

THE POLAR EXPRESS—Director Robert Zemeckis and actor Tom Hanks joined forces (after previously working together on *Forrest Gump* and *Cast Away*) to create a new kind of animated movie, using the new medium of "motion capture." This cutting edge technology (which was used to great effect for Gollum in *Lord of the Rings*, allows live-action performances to be recorded by a computer and then applied to computer generated characters, giving them a realism unmatched in traditional animation. The result of their effort was a hauntingly beautiful telling of the classic children's book by Chris Van Allsburg. Initially, the film garnered some mixed reviews due to its sombre tone and slightly mannequin-esque characters (a side effect when you apply photo-real techniques to animated humans). However, the film is still a quantum leap in the use of this new technology, which was perfectly suited to recreating the rich, painterly look of the book's artwork. Zemeckis and Co. had to expand the story a bit to fill it out to feature length, adding a robust song-and-dance routine with the train's waiters and an overlong exploration of the North Pole factory near the end, but the film is still touching and heartfelt, and the production design is absolutely stunning. The two-disc DVD comes packed with the usual making-of features that have graced Zemeckis's other video releases, including coverage of the motion capture work that allowed Hanks to play many of the characters, from the young boy to a ghostly tramp and even Santa, himself. An elaborate gift set is also available. All aboard!

CLASSIC CORNER

THE WIZARD OF OZ—Who hasn't fallen under the spell of Dorothy and her friends from the magical land of Oz, thanks to untold viewings of this genuine American classic on TV and home video over the years? It's hard to believe now, but the film failed to turn a profit for the studio when it was released in 1939 (it was popular, but so costly to make that it took a decade to recoup its budget); today it is considered to be the *Gone With The Wind* of fantasy films (ironically, both were credited to Victor Fleming, though several other directors actually had input on them, too). *Oz* was previously released on DVD in a lavish special edition package only a few years ago, but the makers of this version found a way to top it. Using new computer software they were able to realign the three separate Technicolor elements, creating an image sharper than any seen before. The two-disc set has many making of featurettes, audio commentary and deleted scenes. The three-disc set has all of that plus the 1925 silent version, lobby card reproductions and much more. For the legions of fans out there who adore this timeless classic, this is the version you've been waiting for. So, curl up in front of your TV with family and friends and keep telling yourself while watching this bona fide heart warmer, "There's no place like home."

DVD ALERT

SHADOWLANDS—With the arrival of the film version of C.S. Lewis's *The Chronicles of Narnia: The Lion, the Witch and the Wardrobe,* some people may be interested in looking back on the life of this learned Oxford Professor who had his own tragedies to deal with in his life. As played by Anthony Hopkins, Lewis is a man of faith and devotion, and a bit of a creature of habit. Into his well-ordered life comes Joy Gresham, a young, headstrong poet and struggling parent (Debra Winger), who clearly has her eye on more than just the professor's curriculum. Not simply a love story for intellectuals, the stodgy Lewis ends up bonding with Joy's young son as well, played by Joseph Mazzello (*Jurassic Park*), when tragedy throws them together. Finely acted by all, the film is a treat for anyone who wants to glimpse the creative mind behind the *Narnia* tales. The current DVD is devoid of any extras (perhaps a special edition is in the works for release when *Narnia* comes out on DVD next year), but, for now, the movie, itself, is well worth your time. By the way, Joy's son, Douglas Gresham, would grow up to become the keeper of Lewis's estate, and spent 20 years trying to bring *Narnia* to the big screen.

HOLIDAY PICK

THE MUPPET CHRISTMAS CAROL—Everyone has their favorite version of Dickens' *A Christmas Carol,* whether it's the one with Alastair Sim (arguably the best), George C. Scott or even Mr. Magoo. While I love them all, I have a special place in my heart for this one, which features Kermit the Frog as Bob Cratchit; Miss Piggy as his wife; Gonzo as Charles Dickens (no kidding!) and Michael Caine as Scrooge. This version has as much heart and sincerity as any I've seen, mixing live actors with Muppet characters in a tale brimming with Victorian charm, endearing songs (by Paul Williams) and just enough whimsy and wit to give this fire-roasted old chestnut a fresh originality. It helps that Caine plays his part totally straight, never once winking at the camera. The DVD is thankfully back in circulation, just in time for the Muppets' 50th anniversary. So banish the humbug and add some much-needed cheer to your holiday this season. As Tiny Tim would say, "God bless us, everyone!"

OSCAR DAYS ARE HERE, AGAIN!
(February 2006)

With Christmas and New Year's behind us, it's time to plunge, headlong, into the Oscar movie season. As is generally the case, the best movies were held till the end of the year (and some not even going into wide release until now), so the studios can cash in on the "Oscar buzz" while their films are still in theatres. I'm writing this prior to the nominations, but the obvious contenders include such varied fare as *Capote; Brokeback Mountain; Good Night, and Good Luck; A History of Violence; The New World; Crash; Munich; Match Point; The Constant Gardener; The Squid and the Whale;* and even *King Kong.* There are always a few curve balls thrown by the Academy voters, so expect some surprises as well.

NEW IN THEATRES

MANDERLAY—In the second part of his proposed trilogy about the contradictions and hypocrisy in American society (part one was 2003's *Dogville*), Danish director Lars von Trier now tackles race relations. Starring Bryce Dallas Howard (*The Village*) and Willem Dafoe performing on minimalist stage sets, this 1930s-era drama concerns a plantation where black laborers are still treated like slaves. At once bracingly honest and heavy handed, von Trier's films still have an artistry and truthfulness that keeps them from being mere polemics. That said, I must add that despite our nation's shameful past history, and the director's sincerity, virtually every country has its share of skeletons in their collective closets, and ours are far from being the fullest.

NEW ON VIDEO

PRIDE AND PREJUDICE—This latest version of the Jane Austen classic (it had previously been done in 1940 with Greer Garson and Laurence Olivier, the 1995 BBC mini-series with Colin Firth, and 2004's "Bollywood" incarnation, *Bride and Prejudice*), this is the most sumptuous and artful of them all. The ravishingly beautiful Keira Knightley plays Elizabeth Bennet who, along with her four sisters, is on the prowl for true love with a man of good standing. The object of their desire (an imposing and dashing figure named Darcy played by Matthew Macfadyen) and Elizabeth's misunderstanding about his demeanor, becomes the heart of the story. The impeccable ensemble cast includes Rosamund Pike, Jena Malone, Simon Woods and, as the Bennet elders, Brenda Blethyn and Donald Sutherland, both in top form. The biggest criticism that can be made of this version is that the gorgeous Ms. Knightley fails to convince viewers that she is the plain Jane sister she insists she is. A minor quibble to be sure.

CLASSIC CORNER

GALLIPOLI—Australian filmmaker Peter Weir has made some of the most pictorially interesting movies ever over his 30-year career. Everything from 1975's *Picnic at Hanging Rock* to 2003's *Master and Commander* reveals an artist totally at ease with his facility for visual storytelling. In 1981 he brought his talent to bear on this account of the World War I battle of Gallipoli. Starring a young and dreamy Mel Gibson and first-time actor Mark Lee, it relates the tale of two Aussie runners who stake their skills in pursuit of military careers which ultimately leads them to one of the most horrific chapters in the annals of modern war. Using music by Jean-Michel Jarre as counterpoint in stunning set pieces, Weir demonstrates his penchant for lyrical interludes to establish story and character in a commanding, yet unobtrusive, style. The DVD extras on this newly-released special edition include a 6-part documentary on the making of this watershed film, which reveals that the star, male model Mark Lee, was originally hired only for a stills shoot to help attract financing. It was only when the film was ready to go a year later that they remembered him and brought him back for a screen test. The rest is history.

DVD ALERT

TURTLES CAN FLY—In the days leading up to the Iraqi war, three wandering orphans (an armless boy, a suicidal girl and a toddler), enter a tent-city village made up mostly of derelict children who eke out a living by digging up land mines and selling them to the local traders. The savvy, young teen leader called "Satellite," because he has a way with modern electronics far beyond the capabilities of the ruling elders, is drawn to the girl and tries to befriend the trio, especially when he learns the armless boy is said to have the gift of prophecy. This co-production between Iraq and Iran was directed by Bahman Ghobadi, who previously dealt with the hardships of the Middle East in *The Year of Drunken Horses* in 2000, and *Marooned in Iraq* in 2002. In his latest, he eloquently shows the ravages of a war-torn society by concentrating on the struggles of the youngest and least culpable members of that culture. His genius is that he never panders to our sentimental urges, even as we bond with these hardy child survivors. And while the story is mostly apolitical in its depiction of the impending American invasion, it's clear the director believes that whatever the interests of America might be, it has little to do with the plight of the general populace.

THE BIG CHEESE

TIM BURTON'S CORPSE BRIDE—What can you say about a film whose plot gives new meaning to the phrase, "Till death do us part?" In Tim Burton's latest stop-motion fever dream (previously he gave us *The Nightmare Before Christmas* in 1993), he takes a gun shy groom-to-be (voiced by Johnny Depp) and weds him (accidentally, I might add) to a festering, not quite inanimate corpse bride (Helena Bonham Carter). This clever premise, which admittedly doesn't develop much further, is still a joy to watch. In the ensuing years since *Nightmare* was released, Burton and his effects team have learned a few new tricks to raise the stop-motion bar. Some of it will leave you awestruck, while the morbid Victorian production design is beautifully realized in its quirkily Goth-like fashion. The DVD comes with production sketches, making-of featurettes, interviews and much more. For those who feel Burton's animated universe may be a little too twisted for their tastes, try *Wallace & Gromit: The Curse of the Were-Rabbit*. Though this Aardman animated homage to the horror genre is more "old school" than Burton's film, Nick Park's cheese-loving romp through the underbelly of British vegetable gardens is pure gold. Ralph Fiennes and Helena Bonham Carter (again!) are along for the ride, lending their vocal talents to this very "family friendly" horror show.

LEGENDS OF THE FALL: An Autumn of Stellar Movies

(October 2006)

The fall movie season is in full bloom and promises to be one of the best in many a year. We've already had a taste last month with such varied offerings as *Hollywoodland, The Black Dahlia, All The King's Men* and *Children of Men*. Continuing the trend this month are more good prospects such as *The Departed*, a cop/mobster drama directed by Martin Scorsese and starring Leonardo DiCaprio, Matt Damon and Jack Nicholson; *Fast Food Nation*, Richard Linklater's fictionalized version of Eric Schlosser's expose of the burger industry; *Flags of Our Fathers*, Clint Eastwood's take on the battle of Iwo Jima; Darren Aronofsky's *The Fountain*, a multi-era drama which finds Hugh Jackman in a centuries-long quest to find the fountain of youth; *Infamous*, the other Truman Capote flick about the writing of "In Cold Blood" and *Marie Antoinette*, Sophia Coppola's re-imagining of France's most scandalous Queen starring Kirstin Dunst, Jason Schwartzman and Judy Davis.

November brings even more treats, including *The Hoax*, directed by Lasse Halstrom and starring Richard Gere as author Clifford Irving who tried to pass off a bogus autobiography of billionaire recluse, Howard Hughes, as the real thing; *A Good Year*, which re-teams director Ridley Scott with Russell Crowe as a London Banker who inherits a family vineyard; *Fur*, Steven Shainberg's film of photographer Diane Arbus, starring Nicole Kidman and Robert Downey, Jr. and *Casino Royale*, the latest James Bond flick starring Daniel Craig as the newest James Bond and directed by Bond alum, Martin Campbell. If this is what the fall is like, I can hardly wait for Christmas.

NEW IN THEATRES

THE PRESTIGE—This is the second film this year to deal with Victorian-era prestidigitators (the other one was September's *The Illusionist* with Ed Norton). Here, a pair of magicians (Hugh Jackman and Christian Bale) square off against one another in an escalating series of performances. The title refers to the concluding "reveal" of the trick, known as 'the prestige." Supporting players include Michael Caine, Scarlett Johansson, David Bowie and Andy (Golem) Serkis. Helmed by Christopher Nolan (*Batman Begins, Insomnia, Memento*) you can be sure this film will have more up its sleeve than just smoke and mirrors.

*CARS—That old Pixar magic is very much in evidence in this heartfelt animated tale of a world populated by anthropomorphic automobiles and other sundry internal combustion vehicles—even the insects are tiny VW "Beetles!" When a NASCAR hotrod named "Lightning McQueen" is sidetracked along Route 66 on its way to a big race-off, the city slicker show car gets some much-needed life lessons from the rusty, ragtag denizens of Radiator Springs (in Carburetor County, no less!). Though the roadmap by which this story travels is mostly familiar territory, the Pixar people still manage to provide enough twists and turns along the way to make this a road trip worth taking. Giving life to these chrome-plated characters are the voice talents of Owen Wilson, Bonnie Hunt, George Carlin, Tony Shalhoub, Cheech Marin and a wonderfully grizzled Paul Newman. Director John Lassiter brings his passion for autos and Route 66 to the fore, working with effortless ease in both the fast-paced world of auto racing and the laid back, laconic nostalgia and faded postcard ambience of "the Mother Road." As usual, the Pixar animators are working at peak perfection, rendering sunbaked desert landscapes, dusty rural roads, high-tech NASCAR glitz and lots of shiny, reflective surfaces, all with the panache and gloss of the finest showroom finish this side of a tricked-out, metal-flaked muscle car. (Nov. 7)

DVD ALERT

*ADVENTURES OF SUPERMAN—Thanks to the success of last month's *Hollywoodland*, about the mysterious death in 1959 of *Superman* actor George Reeves, this classic TV series has become a part of the public's consciousness again. Most "boomers" have vivid recollections of watching this show in the early 1960s on weekday afternoons after school. Fast forward a few decades and you can now own the complete series, released in seasonal box sets which include commentaries and interviews with *Superman* experts as well as surviving cast members Jack Larson (Jimmy Olsen) and Noel Neill (Lois Lane). The best of the series was definitely the first two seasons, where the storylines were geared as much for adults, and the black-&-white cinematography was straight out of film noir thrillers. Season one, with Phyllis Coates as Lois Lane, was especially lurid, and featured violent criminals and scary situations; (the later, color years were more kid-oriented and got a bit too silly at times). Seeing these episodes again, it is clear that, for many of us, George Reeves will always be the one and only Superman.

CLASSIC CORNER

*APOCALYPSE NOW: THE COMPLETE DOSSIER—When it was first released in 1979, Francis Coppola's Vietnam epic was greeted as a stunning masterpiece with a flawed last act. While the hallucinogenic, montage-style mise-en-scene of Capt. Willard's journey up river into the heart of darkness was generally praised, the third act appearance of Marlon Brando as the bloated, mumbling enigma, Col. Kurtz, left critics and movie goers a bit bewildered. Still, the film was always considered to be a major work of art by a major director, and put such catch phrases as "I love the smell of napalm in the morning," "Terminate with extreme prejudice" and "Charlie don't surf" into our cultural lexicon. In 2001, a longer "Redux" version, which added 40-odd minutes of story to the film, including the much-debated French plantation sequence, was released in theatres, and then on a bare bones DVD. Finally, both versions are now available together in this deluxe 2-disc set with commentary by Coppola and over an hour of informative documentaries about the making of the film and the groundbreaking sound design it inaugurated. For those who have been waiting for more than the previous DVD releases had to offer, this is the one. Call it Redux Deluxe.

KID VID

THE LITTLE MERMAID—Disney's domination of the animation field has endured for 70-plus years thanks to their constant striving for innovation and quality—synchronous music in *Steamboat Willie*, Technicolor in the *Silly Symphonies*, feature length in *Snow White* or multi-track stereo in *Fantasia*. The studio's modern renaissance can be pegged to the release in 1989 of this literal fish tale about a headstrong mermaid who longs to be human. Its success paved the way for a string of hits—*Beauty and the Beast, Aladdin, The Lion King,* et al, that completely reinvigorated the Disney canon and marked a level of sophistication in animation that remains unrivaled. With the advent of DVD, the mouse house was quick to offer their wares, though these tended to be no-frills editions. Slowly, the studio has been re-issuing these titles in deluxe, 2-disc sets and they've finally gotten around to the movie that put them back on top. This tale about a child railing against the family's status quo became the template from which many other Disney features would be drawn. Being first, it has a looser, freer quality, more child-oriented and less self-consciously important than the later films. The music by Alan Menken and the late Howard Ashman (who would also do the same for *Beauty and the Beast* and *Aladdin*) is fun and infectious. The 2-disc special edition is loaded with the usual Disney extras, from interviews and documentaries to games for the kids. For Disney fans everywhere, this is the best version you can own either over or under the sea.

HALLOWEEN TREAT

THE WICKER MAN—While most people this Halloween season will be flocking to the multiplexes to catch *Saw 3* or *The Grudge 2*, those who plan to stay home and rent a fright flick might want to try this nifty little confection from

1973. Though not scary in the traditional sense of modern horror (for that there's Neil LaBute's remake released last month starring Nicholas Cage), the original, directed by Robin Hardy from a script by playwright Anthony Shaffer concerns a Scottish police Sgt. (Edward Woodward) investigating the disappearance of a young girl from an island community of practicing pagans. Christopher Lee is the patriarchal figure, Lord Summerisle, who controls the island's populace and is the spokesman for the cult's philosophy. As the Sgt. continues his investigation of the town folk, he's convinced that the child is being held for use as a virgin sacrifice. What follows is a surprising revelation that provides an elegantly ingenious twist to what you thought was a straightforward crime thriller. Though the film does not register high on the fright meter, it is still disturbing enough to stay with you a long time. Eerie and engrossing, it is a fine example of psychological horror. Seek out the 102 minute director's cut which restores about fifteen minutes that was snipped from the theatrical version.

I GOT GAME: Checking Out Sports Movies

(November 2006)

The high you get from watching a great sports movie can be almost as exhilarating as the high you experience from participating in the real thing. And it doesn't even matter which sport since all have at least one great film to represent them. With the football season upon us, it would be too easy to settle on a slate of titles from that particular branch to ooh and ash over, but that would be a serious disservice to the others. Instead, I want to comment on films in a number of sports categories as a way to pay tribute to the superhuman efforts of those athletes who make the field of sports one of the great spectacles of achievement, physical or otherwise.

Seeing how this is football season, let's start here. Most people would agree that *North Dallas Forty* (1979) is the best football movie there is (and one of the best all-around sports films, as well). Directed by Ted Kotcheff and starring Nick Nolte, Mac Davis, Charles Durning and Bo Svenson, the plot is about labor abuse in the NFL, though done in a serio-comic vein that makes for very entertaining viewing. Right behind it is *The Longest Yard* (1974), with Burt Reynolds and Eddie Albert, and directed by Robert Aldrich. Reynolds plays a convict and former pro-footballer who pits his team of ruffians against Warden Albert's own team. Hilarity ensues. For flat out emotion, there's director David Anspaugh's inspirational *Rudy* (1993), starring a pre-hobbit Sean Astin as the diminutive college underdog who makes good. Plus, it's based on a true story. Finally, for those whose tastes run to edgier fare, there's Oliver Stone's *Any Given Sunday*, starring Al Pacino, Cameron Diaz, Dennis Quaid, Jamie Foxx and James Woods. The in your face style and jagged editing wear on you after a while, but for some fans it perfectly exemplifies the modern sports era.

In the realm of basketball, two titles stand tall—the crowd-pleasing *Hoosiers* (1986), starring Gene Hackman and Dennis Hopper, directed by *Rudy*'s David Anspaugh, and the brilliant and deeply affecting *Hoop Dreams* (1994), Steve James' documentary about inner city Chicago kids with dreams of making it big in the world of professional basketball. A must see.

The alpha and omega of boxing movies are defined by *Rocky* (1976) and *Raging Bull* (1980), while in the world of auto racing it's a toss-up between *Grand Prix* (1966) with James Garner and *Le Mans* (1971) with Steve McQueen. For golf enthusiasts, you can take your pick from Ron Shelton's *Tin Cup* (1996) with Kevin Costner and Rene Russo, Robert Redford's nicely rendered *The Legend of Bagger Vance* (2000) with Will Smith, Matt Damon and Charlize

Theron, or the Harold Ramis romp, *Caddyshack* (1980) with Chevy Chase, Rodney Dangerfield and Bill Murray. Similarly, hockey offers us *The Mighty Ducks* (1992) with Emilio Estevez, *Mystery, Alaska* (1999) with Russell Crowe and Burt Reynolds, or *Slap Shot* (1977) with Paul Newman in a film that took everyone by surprise.

Finally, there is baseball, our national pastime. There are more movies about this sport than any other. Some are funny—*Major League* with Tom Berenger and Charlie Sheen; *Bull Durham* (1988) with Kevin Costner Susan Sarandon and Tim Robbins; others more serious—*The Pride of the Yankees* (1942) with Gary Cooper; the mythic *The Natural* (1984) with Robert Redford; *The Rookie* (2002) with Dennis Quaid; and still others cover historical ground—women's baseball in *A League of Their Own* (1992) with Geena Davis, Tom Hanks, Lori Petty, Madonna and Jon Lovitz; *Eight Men Out* (1988) about the infamous "Black Sox" scandal, starring John Cusack, Charlie Sheen, John Mahoney and David Strathairn, and directed by John Sayles. All of these are good, but for my money the all-time champ is *61** (2001).

This HBO original has to rank as one of the most passionate and heartfelt movies ever made about sports. Directed with deep sincerity by comic actor Billy Crystal, the film taps directly into this Yankee fan's love affair with the era of Mickey Mantle and Roger Maris, and chronicles their friendship as they chased after Babe Ruth's homerun record in the season of 1961. The asterisk in the title denotes that, since the number of games played per season had increased, beating Ruth's record of 60 homeruns required a footnote to explain the difference. Thomas Jane and Barry Pepper, respectively, play Mantle and Maris, and not only capture the look of these two men to an astonishing degree, but also deliver first rate performances, both on the field and off. As directed by Crystal, the film is infused with scenes that echo images which are familiar to those who remember the long-ago days of early 1960s broadcasts. And while he grounds his actors in the reality that these exceptional athletes were, in fact, mortal (and fallible) human beings, Crystal is smart enough to retain the mythic dimension as well (the "7" on Mantle's back is as iconic a symbol as any superhero insignia). Crystal, who became close friends with Mantle in his later years, obviously retains a hero worship for his idol, but he is not afraid to show the drinking and womanizing side of the man. The result is that Jane's portrayal of Mantle is fully rounded and not a one-note performance, something that carries through with all the actors involved in this project, including such dependable names as Richard Maser, Bruce McGill, Chris Baur, Donald Moffat, Michael Nouri and Seymour Cassel. Crystal's own daughter, Jennifer Crystal Foley, does a nice job, as well, as Maris' wife. Whether or not you like sports, this is one movie that completely transcends the genre and resonates as a satisfying and complex drama. And if you do love sports, well, so much the better.

But, what about the genres in sports that I haven't covered; what about skiing, surfing, horse racing, the Olympics or chess? There are movies about them, too. There are even movies about sports that don't yet exist, such as... *Rollerball* (the 1975 version, with James Caan, of course). I could go on and on, but I think it's best to save these thoughts for another column.

BRING ON THE AWARDS SEASON
(January 2007)

Christmas is over, the new year has begun and it's time to reflect upon the films of 2006 and see which ones might be headed toward Oscar gold. As usual, there is the year-end rush of serious movies, some of which won't go into wide release until this month, all the better to cash in on Oscar's cache, should they win. Out of the gate earlier this year was the solemn and riveting *United 93* about the passengers and crew on the plane that went down in Pennsylvania on September 11, 2001. Directed with great sensitivity by Paul Greengrass, it is one of the strongest contenders for best picture. More recently maverick director, Oliver Stone, put his *Alexander* debacle behind him with his own 9/11 film, *World Trade Center* about two Port Authority officers (Nicholas Cage and Michael Pena) who were caught in the collapse of the twin towers and were the last living persons to be pulled from the rubble. Other high profile contenders include Martin Scorsese's ultra-violent cops and mobsters drama *The Departed*; Clint Eastwood's double whammy *Flags of Our Fathers* and *Letters From Iwo Jima* which tells both sides of that decisive WWII conflict; the South African political thriller *Blood Diamond*; Steven Soderbergh's homage to 1940s-style filmmaking *The Good German* with George Clooney and Cate Blanchett; the musical *Dreamgirls* by Bill Condon and the complexly-structured *Babel* by Alejandro Gonzalez Inarritu

While blockbusters rarely get best picture nods, they sometimes pick up nominations in lesser categories. *Superman Returns, Pirates of the Caribbean 2: Dead Man's Chest, The Da Vinci Code, The Devil Wears Prada, Borat* and the Pixar animated smash, *Cars*, are all bound to be recognized. On the downside, it wasn't a good year for the Ridley Scott/Russell Crowe comic trifle *A Good Year* and M. Night Shyamalan's watery fable, *Lady in the Water,* sank without a trace. My personal dark horse favorites which I fear may get slighted in the larger categories include the George Reeves Superman story, *Hollywoodland*, and Darren Aronofsky's seriously underrated, epoch-spanning fantasia, *The Fountain*. Regardless of what gets nominated and which films win, it's important to remember that while the awards season is fun, it is not the final word on the artistic merit of any given film. We'll leave that to history.

NEW IN THEATRES
BABEL—The previous movies of Alejandro Gonzalez Inarritu (*Amores Perros* and *21Grams*) shared a similar structural style, wherein multiple narratives were exploded and the fragments of each were stitched back together, creating an interwoven tapestry that placed various characters, classes, etc. side by side so

that the viewer could more readily discern the similarities (and differences) between these disparate worlds. *Babel* is no different and, in fact, shows the filmmaker's growing maturity with his chosen methodology. Here, it is the interconnecting tendrils that come attached to a gun purchase that reveals the links across the miles and cultures, and how, truly, in our global society, nothing occurs in a vacuum of isolation anymore. Of the four storylines that comprise the film, the one featuring Brad Pitt and Cate Blanchett has received the most coverage, not unusual given their high profile stardom. But, all the stories, and the actors in them, are just as attached to one another as that self-same gun. This ranks as one of the most serious and original films of the year and a clear front runner for Oscar consideration.

NEW ON VIDEO

LADY IN THE WATER—There was a lot on the line for writer/director M. Night Shyamalan's latest foray into fantasy. Eschewing the formulaic twist with which he'd made his name in *The Sixth Sense*, and had subsequently been chasing with varying degrees of success in *Unbreakable, Signs* and *The Village*. Night, as he is known, revealed that his tale about a water nymph who shows up in an apartment complex swimming pool was based on a bedtime story he made up for his children. Starring Bryce Dallas Howard (daughter of Ron) and Paul Giamatti, it tanked big time when it was released, garnering the director some of the most scathing reviews of his career. That said, curiosity is bound to get the better of some of us (and Mr. Giamatti is always worth watching), so seeing this apparent misfire in the comfort of one's own home, sans the $9.00 ticket price, the $6.00 popcorn and $3.00 coke, one can then find out if it is a pleasant diversion or a verification that Mr. Shyamalan was indeed all wet. Either way, it won't have cost you much.

CLASSIC CORNER

WHO'S AFRAID OF VIRGINIA WOOLF?—Back in the good ol' days of the mid 1960s, cinema was starting to grow up. The outdated Hays code, used to monitor a movie's content, was effectively dead and Hollywood was doing its best to make movies that reflected the real world. This adaptation of Edward Albee's best known play, about a henpecked college professor, George, his shrewish wife, Martha, and the games they like to play with unsuspecting guests whenever they get an alcoholic buzz on, was considered shocking at the time. The literate text contained frank sexual dialogue, liberally sprinkled with the expletive "goddamn" that must have rang out like gunshot reports in movie houses, then. Mike Nichols, heretofore known primarily as a comic performer and writer, made an auspicious directing debut, harnessing the considerable talents of real life couple Richard Burton and Elizabeth Taylor in the lead roles.

The quartet character piece (the other two roles went to George Segal and Sandy Dennis) still holds up, thanks to Ernest Lehman's astute script adaptation and Nichols' unfussy direction. The movie garnered thirteen Oscar nominations (including all four actors) and took home five, two of which went to the women's performances. In retrospect, Ms. Dennis' turn, as the skittish, easily inebriated young wife, seems highly mannered when viewed today, but Ms. Taylor's braying harpy lush is still great; a full-blown monster of almost Shakespearean proportions; she gained twenty pounds, donned a salt and pepper fright wig and seriously curtailed her stunning beauty. The movie has recently been reissued on DVD with commentary and other extras, affording young film aficionados the chance to see what highbrow cinema was like in the swinging sixties. More to the point, it's a fine example of transposing a play successfully to film, while retaining all the sharp edges of theatre.

THE BIG CHEESE

FORBIDDEN PLANET—For classic-era sci-fi fans, you can't do better than this 1956 extravaganza. Taking on a genre that toiled mostly in the backwater ghetto of B-movies, the formidable MGM Studios (which had previously given us *Gone With The Wind* and all those lavish, high-gloss musicals) pulled out all the stops for this big-budget space epic. Loosely based on Shakespeare's "The Tempest" (I kid you not!) and boasting a grocery list of sci-fi staples (spaceships, mad scientists, robots, alien planets, invisible monsters, ray guns, Anne Francis in a micro-miniskirt and a handsome, young Leslie Nielsen in the "Captain Kirk" role of Commander Adams), it also holds the distinction of having the first truly electronic score ever made for a film. Just in time for the film's 50th anniversary comes this two-disc special edition DVD which includes a fine transfer of the movie (alas, no commentary), along with a second movie, *The Invisible Boy* (1957) that also featured "Robbie the Robot" from *Forbidden Planet*. In addition, there is a nice tribute documentary with appearances by stars Francis, Nielsen and Warren Stevens, plus a look at the groundbreaking special effects and how Robbie was built. A super deluxe collector's edition contains the two-disc set and comes in a beautiful, embossed metal box that also houses a miniature Robbie along with a set of lobby card reproductions from both movies. There is even a certificate for a free *Forbidden Planet* movie poster and information on how to purchase a full size electronic Robbie for your very own. As Dr. Morbius tells the visiting astronauts, when they are about to be shown the marvels of the alien Krell technology, "Prepare your minds for a new scale of physical scientific values, gentlemen." This may be cheese, but it's gourmet all the way.

ALL ABOUT THE OSCAR: CHASING THE ACADEMY'S GOLDEN BOY
(February 2007)

Another Oscar Season, another race for the golden idol. As I write this, the Academy Award nominees have not yet been named, and, with the shortened voting window, the Oscars will be over by the end of this issue's month. The best bets for best picture include *Babel, The Departed, Dreamgirls, Letters From Iwo Jima* and *The Queen,* though one or more of these titles could be switched out with *Flags of Our Fathers, Little Children, United 93* or *Volver.* In the acting category it appears to be another good year for black males like Forest Whitaker, Eddie Murphy, Djimon Hounsou and Will Smith, all of whom did very fine work. For actresses, a number of over-fifty women—Meryl Streep, Helen Mirren, Judi Dench—gave stellar leading performances in successful films, proving that passing the half-century mark need not be a career death sentence for women. It's about time they got cut the same slack as the men.

For those who care about directors, the big question is: "Will this finally be Martin Scorsese's year?" Having been the perpetual bridesmaid for over thirty years, which saw such amazing work as *Taxi Driver, Raging Bull, Goodfellas, The Age of Innocence, Gangs of New York* and *The Aviator* get overlooked, he is certainly due. And while *The Departed* is an excellent film, it may be too brutal and testosterone-driven to win for best picture. We therefore have to hope that the Academy will split the picture/director picks so Marty can at last be properly acknowledged. Whatever happens, we'll all know the outcome on the evening of February 25th.

NEW IN THEATRES

HANNIBAL RISING—It was only a matter of time before someone decided to do the Hannibal Lecter origin story. Having risen through the ranks in popularity in Thomas Harris' novels, from bit player in "Red Dragon" (made as *Manhunter* by Michael Mann in 1986 with Brian Cox) to supporting character in "The Silence of the Lambs" (directed by Jonathan Demme in 1991 with a tour de force performance by Anthony Hopkins) to the leading role in "Hannibal" (directed by Ridley Scott at his baroque best with Hopkins back on board), it was inevitable that the studio heads would want to continue the franchise. While waiting for Harris to complete his next installment of "The Lecter Chronicles," the producers managed to squeeze out a remake of *Manhunter* under its original title, *Red Dragon*, with Hopkins in place to lay claim to being Lecter in all three stories. For the origin tale, an obviously younger man was required, who was found in the person of French actor, Gaspard Ulliel (*A Very Long Engagement*). The book and screenplay were created simultaneously, and the publication window for the hardcover edition of the novel lasted a scant few months prior to the film's release. It didn't even matter that the book was vilified by the critics who felt that Harris had traded his storytelling skills since *Lambs* to revel in gruesome, pointless sadism. It won't matter; this is Hannibal Lecter, everyone's favorite cannibal, we're talking about. Like Batman and Superman and even James Bond, we all want to know how he got to be who he is. Cox gave us a chilly creepiness while Hopkins imbued the character with a wry, intellectual nature that was both terrifying and oddly endearing. The real question is, what will Ulliel bring to the table besides Fava beans and a nice Chianti? Bon appetit!

NEW ON VIDEO

HOLLYWOODLAND—While this taut little drama about the low rent side of tinsel town never really caught on at the box office, this story about George (Superman) Reeves' decline from promising leading actor to emasculated "kept man" was one of the best movies of the year. Ben Affleck, perfectly cast as the square-jawed hunk, certainly knows a thing or two about how media typecasting can make or break a career. As Reeves, he taps into his own inner knowledge of fame's dual-edged sword, where success does not always translate into fulfillment. Diane Lane, as the older woman who makes Reeves her boy toy, totally earns our sympathy as she fights a losing battle against encroaching middle age. After Reeves is found dead in his home from a gunshot wound (was it murder, suicide, an accident?) a freelance investigator played by Adrien Brody (a fictional character in this otherwise true story) decides to dig beneath the surface when he's convinced that the official police determination of suicide doesn't add up. The fact that Brody's character needs to prove his own self-worth carries the movie's theme that this is a story about failure and unrealized potential; about people living along the margins in this land of opportunity. In short, it is "Hollywoodland." The movie maintains a nice 1950s period flavor and the recreated scenes, showing the shooting of the *Superman* series, are a real hoot. In some shots Affleck bears an uncanny resemblance to the real George Reeves, especially in his horn-rimmed guise of Clarke Kent. Beyond that, the film is an informative look into the tawdry doings that lurk behind Hollywood's shiny facade; where, even with looks and talent, promising careers can be slapped down, or come to a tragic end, faster than a speeding bullet.

CLASSIC CORNER

STAR TREK: THE ANIMATED SERIES—When the classic *Star Trek* series was cancelled in 1969, after a three-year run on NBC, it appeared as if the good ship Enterprise would not get to complete its stated "five year mission."

However, while the original show found a second life in syndication, something occurred in 1973 that was unheard of in the television industry—the fans managed to get the series back on the air, albeit on Saturday mornings as a half hour animated show. Nevertheless, it was *Star Trek* and it included the voice talents of the seven principal actors, plus scripts by many of the original show's writers. While the animation, by Filmation, was done in a rudimentary fashion due to budget and time constraints, the writing was unusually literate for Saturday morning fare, referencing such subjects as Shakespeare, religion and bigotry, that would give even prime time shows a run for their money in the quality department. By being animated, the show was able to feature environments and creatures that would have been impossible to do as live-action. The twenty-two episodes which comprise the cartoon series were released on VHS tape in the 1990s, but only now are they available on DVD, with commentary on selected shows, plus a nice retrospective featurette. Packaged in a handsome plastic case, similar to the design used for the original series live-action DVD box sets, the release of this long sought after series perfectly fills the gap between the classic, live-action shows and the movies which followed later. For true fans of *Star Trek*, this is a must-have addition to your DVD library.

THE BIG CHEESE

THE BIBLE, IN THE BEGINNING—Made with an earnestness that rivaled the biblical epics of the 1950s, this 1966 endeavor unfortunately inherited its predecessors' penchant for bombast and self-importance. While there is a great deal of scope in the direction by John Huston, who was also blessed with an incredible cast (George C. Scott, Ava Gardner, Richard Harris, Peter O'Toole and Stephen Boyd), the film is ponderous and turgid. Huston was smart enough to save several key roles for himself (he does a wonderful turn as Noah and puts his deep, resonate voice to good use as, both, the narrator and the voice of God). Evidently, producer Dino De Laurentiis originally planned to film the entire Bible, but faced with the reality that such a project would be the length of ten movies and cost an equivalent amount, he settled on doing the first 22 chapters of Genesis; even pared down to that, the finished film still runs nearly three hours. Despite all the nitpicking, however, this film is still fun to watch. The opening "creation of the earth" is pretty cool and is an example of mainstream abstract filmmaking ahead of its time. The dialogue in the Adam and Eve segment is unintentionally funny, but the nudity is handled fairly tastefully. The scenes with Huston as Noah have just the right balance of seriousness and comedy, and the Tower of Babel is properly epic in its scope. George C. Scott has the biggest role as Abraham, and he seems to relish chewing up the scenery at every opportunity. The movie laid a pretty big egg when it came out, despite a few good reviews, but today it can be viewed as Hollywood's attempt to market "culture" to the masses at a time when our society was in transition from bohemian intellectualism to the hippie counter-culture. And if Mr. De Laurentiis can be accused of any transgression against God, it might be for not heeding His most important commandment: "Thou shalt not make boring, bloated movies." Amen to that!

SPRINGING FORWARD: A LOOK
AT WHAT'S AHEAD IN 2007
(March 2007)

With the Oscar race safely behind us (I hope everyone was happy with the outcome), it's time to jump full force into the films of 2007. And a wide assortment there is, too. From the gore spattered, effects heavy *300*, by Frank Miller based on his graphic novel about the said number of Spartans who duked it out with the superiorly-numbered Persian army, to the very kid-friendly *Meet The Robinsons*—a Disney CGI animated adventure about a whiz kid inventor and his dysfunctional family, there's something here for everyone. Adam Sandler goes super serious (and looks more than a little like Bob Dylan) in *Reign Over Me*, a post 9/11 psychological drama that also stars Don Cheadle and Liv Tyler. India's Mira Nair directs Bollywood superstar Tabu in *The Namesake*, about an Indian couple trying to raise a family in America. Mark Wahlberg, capitalizing on his *Departed* buzz, stars in *The Shooter*, a conspiracy thriller where he plays an ex-Marine sniper engaged by our government to stop an assassination plot. Finally, hard-edged director, Paul Verhoeven, tries for a comeback (after his critical drubbing for *Showgirls* and *Hollow Man*) by returning to his Dutch roots for *Black Book*, a WWII drama set in Holland which follows a young Jewish woman who joins the resistance and ends up falling for the German officer she is assigned to seduce. On the whole, it looks like a good beginning to the 2007 movie season.

NEW IN THEATRES

ZODIAC—Fans of filmmaker David Fincher can rejoice over the release of his first movie since *Panic Room* back in 2002. This time, however, the eclectic director of such startling and uneasy works as *Alien 3, Seven* and *Fight Club* has scaled back his visual audacity for a more conventional look in this true story about the "Zodiac killer" who terrorized San Francisco in the late 1960s and early '70s. Fincher's obsession with the still-unsolved case led him to do his own sleuthing, much of which ended up in the film. The low-key approach he chose works well for the movie's time period, as does the pitch perfect cast which includes Jake Gyllenhaal, Mark Ruffalo, Robert Downey, Jr. and Chloe Sevigny. While for some Fincher may be an acquired taste, it must be said that he is one of the few filmmakers out there who is exploring new ways to make movies, rather than just churning out hack work like so many others. He is also quite good with actors, consistently eliciting remarkable performances (think Brad Pitt in *Seven* and Edward Norton in *Fight Club*). In a genre that is rife with mediocrity and sensationalism, Fincher, like Hitchcock, brings a measure of artistry which makes his films compelling to watch, even as you squirm in your seat.

NEW ON VIDEO

FAST FOOD NATION—In 2001, when Eric Schlosser's book about the fast food industry was released, it was a wake-up call to the world about how the friendly burger stand of the long-ago innocent 1950s and '60s had morphed into a corporate behemoth whose tentacles reached into every area of business and society, and not always to our benefit. The book was a best seller (even being compared to Upton Sinclair's expose, "The Jungle," about the Chicago meatpacking industry in the 1920s), and was ripe for a documentary film makeover a la *An Inconvenient Truth*. Instead, director Richard Linklater (*Dazed and Confused, A Scanner Darkly*), working with Schlosser, decided to use the ideas behind the book and tell a fictional story about a McDonald's-like company and how it has impacted all areas of society. The low-budget film still managed to attract some big names—Greg Kinnear, Ethan Hawke and Bruce Willis— along with sturdy supporting players Wilmer Valderama, Luis Guzman and Bobby Cannavale. Will this movie turn you against your taste for Big Macs and Whoppers? Probably not. But the important point, here, is that both the book and movie will open your eyes to the real cost involved in "having it your way." What you do after that is up to you.

CLASSIC CORNER

FIDDLER ON THE ROOF—Even if you've never seen Norman Jewison's film version of Joseph Stein's musical, you're sure to have heard the signature tune, "If I Were a Rich Man." That song alone would make the film a classic, but there is so much more. The tale of the poor Jewish milkman, Tevye (played wonderfully by Topol), as he tries to balance the financial woes of providing for five unmarried daughters and his opinionated wife in an increasingly anti-Semitic Czarist Russia, makes for surprisingly rousing and heartfelt entertainment. Based on stories by noted Yiddish author, Sholom Aleichem, with music and lyrics by Jerry Bock and Sheldon Harnick, it is essentially a meditation on the generational (and universal) change that occurs in our society, where some traditions stay and others pass away. After a phenomenal run on Broadway, the hit musical was a natural to be made into a film. Ironically, Norman Jewison, who was not Jewish (go figure), was hired because the producers thought he was. Fortunately, they kept him on, even after he revealed his true heritage. The 2-disc collector's edition DVD is jam-packed full of extras that will satisfy the most rabid movie buff. There's a commentary with Jewison and Topol, a half dozen making-of featurettes, new interviews with the cast and crew, an hour-long documentary on Jewison's career up to 1971 and historical pieces on Jewish culture and

Aleichem's writings. All in all, it's a remarkable edition of a superb movie that, once you've seen it, will leave you feeling like a million bucks, whether or not you actually are a rich man.

THE BIG CHEESE

CASINO ROYALE—No, not the new Daniel Craig Bond film due out on DVD this month, but the bloated, expensive 1967 Hollywood spoof version of the Bond series, directed by John Huston. Suave Brit David Niven (playing an aging Bond who passes the torch to his nebbishy nephew Jimmy—Woody Allen), heads a huge cast which includes Peter Sellers, Ursula Andress, Orson Welles, Deborah Kerr, William Holden, Charles Boyer, George Raft, Jean Paul Belmondo and a very young Jacqueline Bisset, none of whom can save this mess. The producers threw tons of money into this overdone turkey, most of which actually ended up on the screen, but to little avail. The finished film is wildly uneven in tone with large chunks of it being very unfunny. Burt Bacharach's score provides the only real solace, and features the hit tune, "The Look of Love." Despite its lowbrow pedigree, this swinging sixties romp still has a modicum of nostalgic charm. Certainly Mike Myers was inspired by this send up (along with Michael Caine's "Harry Palmer" films) for his own *Austin Powers* triad (even to using Burt Bacharach!), so it might be fun to compare them. Only don't go mistaking Orson Welles for "Fat Bastard!"

THE FIRST FLOWERS OF
THE 2007 MOVIE SEASON
(April 2007)

With winter firmly behind us, and the warm spring weather giving rise to the rebirth of trees and flowers, it's time to embrace the return of another movie season. Cinematic rebels Quentin Tarantino and Robert Rodriguez team up for the ultimate cheesy, schlock double-feature, *Grindhouse*, which mines both the sci-fi and horror genres in a loving homage to the drive-in staples of decades ago. Then there's Jamie Foxx, Jennifer Garner and Chris Cooper in *The Kingdom*, a thriller about an American housing compound in Saudi Arabia that is bombed. *The Nanny Diaries* brings together Scarlett Johansson, Paul Giamatti and Laura Linney in a satiric story, from the makers of *American Splendor*, about a young college grad who becomes a nanny for a rich family. Christina Ricci dons a pig snout (!) to play the deformed character in *Penelope*, which also stars James McAvoy (who had his own animal make-up experience as the faun, Mr. Tumnus, in *Narnia*). Finally, there's *The TV Set*, starring former *X-Files* lead, David Duchovny and Sigourney Weaver, about the making of a television pilot. A few laughs, a bit of drama, some scares and a dollop or two of cheese. All tolled, it looks like there's something this month for everyone.

NEW IN THEATRES
THE HOAX—Originally slated for release last year, the true story of writer Clifford Irving's "fake" biography about famed recluse Howard Hughes back in the 1970s heralded the arrival of a fraudulent cultural virus that continues to permeate our society today (paging James Frey and Stephen Glass). Richard Gere, at his snarky best, plays Irving as a seductive con man who's not afraid of a little hyperbole—"the greatest book of the century!"—and finds people who are only too willing to lap it up. The book came out, was a huge success and was then found out to be a total fabrication, much to the embarrassment of the publishers. Irving subsequently went to jail and became the celebrity swindler who may not have written the book of the century, but who certainly pulled off the con of the century. Directed by Lasse Hallstrom, who has previously given us such wide-ranging films as *What's Eating Gilbert Grape, The Cider House Rules* and *Chocolat*. Co-starring with Gere are Hope Davis, Alfred Molina, Marcia Gay Harden, Julie Delpy and Stanley Tucci.

NEW ON VIDEO

TWIN PEAKS: SEASON TWO—It's time to break out the cherry pie and a cup of that "damn fine coffee" as the second season of David Lynch's classic television series finally makes it to DVD. The quirky drama starring Kyle MacLachlan as FBI special agent Dale Cooper and Michael Ontkean as town sheriff Harry S. Truman, who investigate the murder of local homecoming queen Laura Palmer (Sheryl Lee), created a sensation when it premiered in 1990. Lynch's mix of surrealism, "Peyton Place" melodrama, retro-'50s ambience and a seriously overwrought style gave iconic status to such everyday objects as lonely stoplights, Douglas firs swaying in the breeze, the aforementioned pie and coffee and knotty-pine paneling. The series was also the launching pad for such new talent as Madchen Amick, Dana Ashbrook, Lara Flynn Boyle and James Marshall, as well as a safe haven for such seasoned actors as Ray Wise, Peggy Lipton, Everett McGill, Russ Tamblyn and Piper Laurie. Though on the air for only a scant two seasons, the show set a standard for strangeness that was a definite influence on such later hits as *The X-Files* and, most recently, *Lost*. While the first season buzz made *Peaks* "must-see TV," it is generally acknowledged that the series lost some of its focus (and much of its audience) during its sophomore year. It regained its momentum in the second half, but by then it was too late. Still, for die-hard fans, the release of this long-overdue second season DVD box set is as welcome a sight as a cup of hot coffee and a slice of cherry pie. On second thought, make that two.

CLASSIC CORNER

JESUS OF MONTREAL—Hovering around the edges of contemporary cinema in which the story of Jesus is told is this 1989 French/Canadian gem that is worth your while to seek out. Written and directed by Denys Arcand (*The Barbarian Invasions* 2003), it utilizes the conceit of a troupe of actors, who are putting on a Passion play, as a way to comment on modern society. In this respect the film has a close cousin in the 1956 movie, *He Who Must Die*, and perhaps even Norman Jewison's 1973 version of *Jesus Christ Superstar*. But Arcand has found his own original take on this material which allows it to resonate in a unique manner. In the film, the Church asks a local actor named Daniel to restage their annual Passion play with an eye toward reviving interest in the congregation. The result is a somewhat radical adaptation that is a success with the people, but an embarrassment to the Church. Inevitably, the forces of art and institutionalism must square off, with Daniel (who plays Christ) taking a stand which leads him toward a conclusion that finds life imitating art imitating life. For those who are looking for a spiritually entertaining movie without the verbal bombast or baked desert mien of so many other "biblical" stories, this heartfelt, funny, secular satire will absolutely fill the bill.

EASTER BASKET

THE PASSION OF THE CHRIST—Whatever one may think of Mel Gibson's drunken, anti-Semitic tirade of last year, my guess is that it was fueled as much by his pro-Catholic beliefs as by any lingering racism with which his Holocaust-denying father may have tainted him. Having created the ultimate Passion play (in Latin and Aramaic, no less), with the most graphic depiction of Christ's suffering ever committed to celluloid, Mel reaped a fortune at the box office with what he had sown. Its initial release on DVD, however, was a disappointingly bare bones edition, lacking the sort of extras this controversial film certainly warranted. Well, seek and ye shall find. A two-disc Definitive Edition has finally been released which includes a feature-length documentary on the making of the movie, four commentary tracks, one of which features Gibson and several priests discussing the film's theological merits, and an additional, longer cut of the film. Gibson's sincerity (and the movie's artistry) is unimpeachable, even if you don't agree with him. Artists are rarely paragons of virtue, but you cannot and should not dismiss someone's talent simply because of a human failing. And, though, I personally consider the 1977 mini-series, *Jesus of Nazareth*, to be the best overall cinematic version of the life of Christ, Mel's film, and this DVD edition, will stand the test of time, as well.

SEQUEL-ITIS: THE SEQUEL
(May 2007)

It isn't the first time, and it won't be the last, but prepare yourselves for another summer of movie sequels. Some will be good (*Spider-Man, Harry Potter*), some are still a question mark (*Pirates, Shrek*), but thanks to name recognition and a penchant for a frenetic style that makes any semblance of a plot seem unnecessary, all are bound to be profitable. Hollywood's continued reliance on name-branding their product through sequels, remakes, retreads and "re-imaginings" of old movies and even older TV shows has led to a sausage factory mentality of endlessly churning out safe, predictable entertainment that not only all tastes the same, but which evaporates from your consciousness within a month, a week or even a day of having been seen. On the other hand there is the "cinema of the outrageous" where filmmakers will do something bold, new and crazy, regardless of whether it makes any sense. To use our food analogy again: "Tired of that same old sausage? Well, try our new chocolate covered pig brains ala mode! Bet you've never had that before?" Uh, that's right, and I don't think I want to, either! The point is there has to be a middle ground where originality serves a purpose in advancing the arts as well as in stemming the rising tide of movie sequels. Cinematic franchises have always been with us from *The Thin Man* to *Blondie* to *Ma & Pa Kettle*. We've had *James Bond* for forty-five years and *Star Trek* for forty. The trick is to do it well, as *Casino Royale* recently proved. And if occasionally we need an *Ocean's Thirteen* to help underwrite something as truly innovative as *The Fountain*, well, that's a compromise I'm willing to make.

NEW ON VIDEO

THE PAINTED VEIL—Based on the novel by Somerset Maugham about an idealistic doctor (Ed Norton) who takes his young wife, Kitty (Naomi Watts) to Shanghai in the mid-1920s to set up his practice. A marriage of convenience for both of them, due to the conventions of the day, which held that a professional man should be married and a woman most certainly must be, the spark of love and passion fails to materialize. Kitty, instead, enters into a smoldering liaison with a smooth-talking, but married, acquaintance (Liev Schreiber). Once found out, the cuckolded Norton drags his wife with him into the heart of rural China on a death wish act of humanitarian hubris to help fend off a cholera epidemic. Both characters must then find their lost humanity and strip away the mask of convention (the painted veil?) which had concealed their true selves. Produced by Norton and Watts, and shot on location in China, the film revels in showcasing the rolling hill mountainscapes so identifiable with that country. The cinematography proves equally impressive when it settles on intimate close-ups of the two leads in all their beautiful splendor. There's nice supporting work, also, from Diana Rigg as an elderly French nun, and by Toby Jones (*Infamous*) as the almost dwarfish neighbor of the couple. Directed by John Curran (whose previous film, *Praise*, used landscapes in a similar manner to evoke a dream-like quality) with a script adapted by Ron Nyswaner (*Philadelphia*), this film captures the terrible beauty of a world of overwhelming environments where the climate, political and otherwise, threatens to suffocate the inhabitants with its stifling heaviness. Perhaps that notion, that idea, of a country masking a harsh reality behind its own visual beauty, is a metaphorical echo of the characters in this tale. Perhaps that, too, represents a painted veil of sorts.

CLASSIC CORNER

THAT THING YOU DO!—Judging by the release in 1990 of *Bonfire of the Vanities*, that decade did not get off to a good start for rising star Tom Hanks. As it turned out, however, the '90s *would* prove to be a watershed period for the actor with *A League of Their Own*, *Sleepless in Seattle* and the one-two Oscar punch of *Philadelphia* and *Forrest Gump*, propelling him to the very top of Hollywood's A-list. Ahead lay such stellar achievements as *Apollo 13* and *Saving Private Ryan*. But in 1996 Mr. Hanks decided to cash in on his success and stature by writing, directing and acting in this sweetly quirky little bauble that drew heavily on his own small town growing-up years in the 1960s when The Beatles changed our ideas about music and every kid wanted to be in a rock-and-roll band. The movie stars Tom Everett Scott, Johnathon Schaech, Steve Zahn and Ethan Embry as "The Wonders," a quartet of Erie, Pa. musicians who experience a momentous rise to success with their song, "That Thing You Do!" A pre-elfin Liv Tyler plays Schaech's muse-like girlfriend, Faye, while solid character actors Bill Cobbs, Alex Rocco, Kevin Pollak, Chris Ellis and Holmes Osborne, Jr. fill out the supporting line-up. Future Oscar winner, Charlize Theron, makes her film debut as Scott's feckless girlfriend, and singer/songwriter Chris Isaak does a brief cameo as "Uncle Bob," who helps the boys record their catchy little tune. Hanks handily plays the band's manager, Mr. White, a no-nonsense professional who guides them through the dizzying maze of success that must have been all too familiar to the star/director. While this sweet fable doesn't have the standard happy ending (the band makes it to national television, but then falls apart afterwards), it's anything but a downer. A coda lets us know that at least some of the band members went on to bigger and better careers.

As a first-time director, Hanks displays an easy, yet sophisticated, versatility with his material, layering in stylistic flourishes which are faithful to the period, but that never overwhelm the narrative structure. To ensure the realism of the musical performances, he had his actors train for months with their instruments to the point where they could've gone out as an actual group. Even more outstanding was his decision to use all original, newly-written pop songs (several for The Wonders, and a number of others in various idioms that recall girl group Motown, mellow jazz, teen surfer music and even a fifties hipster lounge song, complete with a *Peter Gunn*-style riff), all of which are dead-on copies of the real thing. In many cases these new "retro-tunes," some of which were written or co-written by Hanks, are even better. While the low budget dictated an alternative to employing pricey '60s-era songs, the decision was also an artistically smart one since it gives the film a fresh, immediacy instead of a musty, time-capsule feel that can creep in whenever real period songs are used.

Now, over a decade after its release, comes this special, two-disc Director's cut loaded with extras about this extremely entertaining movie (previously there was only a bare bones theatrical version). So, whether you're an old fan or a newcomer, here's your chance to relive the glory days of that long ago wonder group, The Wonders. I know that the movie is actually fiction, but Mr. Hanks does such an impeccable job, you'll swear that The Wonders actually existed.

THE BIG CHEESE

COLOR ME KUBRICK—As if the life of reclusive film director Stanley Kubrick wasn't unusual enough, it turns out that in the early 1990s, a gentleman named Alan Conway went around London pretending to be him. Mr. Conway (who looked nothing like Kubrick, by the way), perpetuated this ruse to scam free drinks, hospitality and gay sexual escapades from his unwitting marks. As played by John Malkovich, the predatory Conway is a pathetic nobody whose slow-talking, heavy-lidded lizard-like bearing occasionally rises up into spasms of foppish delight. Director Brian Cook and screenwriter Anthony Frewin spent decades working for Kubrick (as, respectively, his assistant director and personal assistant) so they bring an insider's knowledge to the proceedings, even though Mr. Kubrick, himself, is never portrayed. The main fun of this minor trifle of a movie resides in the numerous in-jokes, most notably the use of music cues from Kubrick's past films, *A Clockwork Orange* and *2001*. Along for the fun are Richard E. Grant and Robert Powell, plus cameos by Marisa Berenson (who was in Kubrick's *Barry Lyndon*), director Ken Russell and Peter Sallis (the well-known British character actor and voice of Wallace in the *Wallace & Gromit* films). The DVD has a lengthy featurette on the making of the film, including interviews with Cook and Frewin, and there's even a bit of footage of the real Alan Conway who, in a *Twilight Zone*-ish bit of irony, died only three months before Mr. Kubrick passed away.

THE SUMMER MOVIE BLITZ
(June 2007)

The summer juggernaut of movie releases is upon us and, for those who wish to partake, it becomes a matter of choosing which films from the more than 100 that will be vying for our attention between Memorial Day and Labor Day are worth seeing. As usual, there are good films and bad and some in between. Based on the hype the studios put out they'd have you believe they're all great. In any event, unless you have unlimited time and money, you'll have to settle for picking a small percentage of what is out there. (Note: This article was written in May, prior to the release of any June titles.)

JUNE

Of the 48 films scheduled for release in June (including sequels to *Hostel* and *The Fantastic Four*), about half of which look pretty good, the following five have the potential to be real winners. First out of the gate is *Ocean's Thirteen* which hopes to put back the pizzazz of *Eleven* that was missing from *Twelve* (you got that?). The usual suspects are back—George Clooney, Brad Pitt, Matt Damon, Don Cheadle, Bernie Mac, Elliott Gould, et al—along with some fresh faces (Ellen Barkin and Al Pacino). Director Steven Soderbergh promises a return to form and there's no reason to doubt him. Steve Carell is back for *Evan Almighty*, the follow up to Jim Carrey's hit *Bruce Almighty*. Morgan Freeman returns as God and commands Evan to do the Noah thing. Angelina Jolie goes serious as Mariane Pearl (wife of slain reporter Daniel Pearl) in *A Mighty Heart*, while Michael Moore throws his considerable weight against our failing health care industry in *Sicko*. Rounding out the month is Pixar's *Ratatouille* (Rat-a-too-ee) about a gourmet food-loving rat in a Parisian restaurant. Expect all the usual Pixar touches of well-defined characters, clever humor and heartfelt storytelling. Directed by Brad Bird (*The Incredibles*), with vocal talent provided by Brad Garrett, Patton Oswalt and Peter O'Toole, this film is the one sure bet this summer.

JULY

The heart of summer movies has always been July where the blockbusters come fast and furious. Among the 30-plus releases that include *The Transformers* and *Hairspray*, there is a nice mix of high art and high concept. The fifth installment of *Harry Potter* finds our young charges maturing into angst-ridden adolescents. While the young actors have grown nicely into their parts, the real treat with this series is seeing top notch British thespians in the supporting roles. Ralph Fiennes, Robbie Coltrane, Helena Bonham Carter, Michael Gambon, Jason

Isaacs, Maggie Smith, Gary Oldman, Alan Rickman, Emma Thompson, David Thewlis and, well, you get the idea. Serious scares are provided in *1408*, another haunted hotel tale from Stephen King, starring John Cusack and Samuel L. Jackson. Lowbrow laughs can be found in *I Now Pronounce You Chuck and Larry* with Adam Sandler and Kevin James as a pair of macho firemen who pretend to be a gay couple to get domestic benefits. Don't ask, just go and enjoy it. Romantic drama comes courtesy of *No Reservations* starring Aaron Eckhart and Catherine Zeta-Jones about a famous chef who becomes the guardian of her nine year old niece. Directed by Scott Hicks (*Shine*), it could be this summer's sleeper hit. Finally, there is *The Simpsons Movie* which, though highly-anticipated, still must convince people to spend money to see something they already get for free on TV. Not to worry, the talented minds behind the show's 15-year success know a thing or two about pleasing their fans. Besides, who doesn't want to see Homer on the big screen?

AUGUST

Traditionally this month has been the dumping ground for the movie dogs of summer. Certainly a number of the 40 or so films set for release, here, will come with fleas aplenty, but there also promises to be a few that could be genuine winners. Separating the wheat from the chaff, there is Matt Damon in *The Bourne Supremacy*, the thinking person's action franchise, followed by Josh Hartnett and Samuel L. Jackson in *Resurrecting The Champ*, about a former boxing great who has fallen on hard times. For the ladies there is *Becoming Jane* (as in Austen), starring Anne Hathaway and James McAvoy that blows the dust off of literary romance. In *Stardust*, a fantasy not unlike *The Princess Bride,* Charlie Cox and Claire Danes play the young love-struck leads, while Michelle Pfeiffer, Peter O'Toole and Robert DeNiro lend their mature gravitas to the mix. Last, but not least (I hope!), there's *The Invasion*, with Nicole Kidman and Daniel Craig in a new adaptation of Jack Finney's "The Body Snatchers," which has been incarnated at least three times since the mid-1950s. The previous versions have all been good and this latest one, relocated to Washington, D.C., seems both a fitting and timely entry into the series.

Hopefully there will be more good films besides the fifteen titles highlighted here, though many of the smaller releases may not even play in this area. Add to that the inevitable reshufflings, drop-outs, etc. to further complicate things, and it seems easier to just wait for everything to come out on DVD. However, there's still something to be said for going out to the movies. Choose wisely and you may yet have a memorable movie experience this summer.

NAUGHTY AND NICE: A MERRY MOVIE CHRISTMAS

(November 2007)

> This sizable gap of several months was due to the latest shake-up in the running of the paper. Control and operation of the publication had changed hands several times over the years and often resulted in gaps in the monthly output. In some cases I had already written my column, only to learn that it would not run. In some cases I was able to port over what I'd written to another column. That might mean having to adjust a "New in Theatres" piece for "New on DVD." It's all part of what a writer must deal with.

Never let it be said that Hollywood doesn't give us choices. At a time of year you would expect only light fluff entertainment, filmmakers are offering up movies that both delight and disturb. That's as it should be. Movie goers should have the option to see all kinds of films with all kinds of storylines. While the holiday season will mean different things for different people, the one thing all cultures seem to have in common at this time of the year is a penchant for sharing and giving. In the realm of movies you'll have the chance to do both as you share time at the multiplex seeing some great films and then giving someone you love just the right DVD to make their holiday special.

IN THEATRES

NOVEMBER—Director Ridley Scott is the first out of the gate with *American Gangster*, starring Denzel Washington and Russell Crowe about Harlem drug dealers. Jerry Seinfeld joins with DreamWorks for the hip animated *Bee Movie*. *The Kite Runner*, based on the Afghanistan bestseller by Khaled Hosseini is directed by *Finding Neverland*'s Marc Foster. *Fred Claus,* with Vince Vaughn and Paul Giamatti, tells the story about Santa's older, ruder brother in this comedy by the director of *Wedding Crashers*. The quirky Coen Brothers go dead serious in *No Country For Old Men*, an intense thriller starring Javier Bardem, Josh Brolin, and Tommy Lee Jones. Robert Redford directs and stars with Tom Cruise and Meryl Streep in *Lions For Lambs*, a liberal meditation on the nature of modern war. Robert Zemeckis, who brought us *The Polar Express*, returns to the computer animated, motion capture arena with *Beowulf,* featuring Ray Winstone, Crispin Glover, Angelina Jolie and Anthony Hopkins. Family entertainment comes courtesy of Dustin Hoffman and Natalie Portman in *Mr. Magorium's Magical Emporium*. Live action and animation are mixed in *Enchanted*, starring Amy Adams, Susan Sarandon and Patrick Dempsey, about a fairy tale princess who is banished to modern-day New York. Talk about your "poisoned apple!"

Woody Allen returns to England for *Cassandra's Dream* where Colin Farrell and Ewan McGregor play Cockney brothers seduced by femme fatale Hayley Atwell into committing a crime. Finally, this month, there's *Thomas Kinkade's Christmas Cottage*, based, one assumes, on the popular illustrator's artwork. Starring Peter O'Toole, Marcia Gay Harden and Jared Padalecki as the artist, himself.

DECEMBER—Following in the shadow of *Harry Potter* and *Narnia* comes *The Golden Compass*, based on Philip Pullman's fantasy novels and starring Nicole Kidman, Daniel Craig, Eva Green and Dakota Blue Richards. Author Richard Matheson's *I Am Legend* is dusted off for the third time (*The Last Man On Earth, The Omega Man* were the previous incarnations) with Will Smith in the lead, fighting off zombie vampires. Brian DePalma gives us more nastiness in *Redacted*, about rape and murder in Iraq, which covers the same themes as *Casualties of War*, his Vietnam war-crime saga. Frances Ford Coppola returns to the director's chair after a ten-year absence with *Youth Without Youth* starring Tim Roth as a Romanian professor recalling his experiences leading up to World War II. Artist/filmmaker Julian Schnabel gives us *The Diving Bell and The Butterfly*, based on Jean-Dominique Bauby's autobiographical novel about the paralyzing stroke he suffered at 43. Macabre director Tim Burton is back with Johnny Depp and Helena Bonham Carter in *Sweeney Todd* based on the musical about the blood-thirsty barber of Fleet Street. Mike Nichols directs Tom Hanks and Julia Roberts in *Charlie Wilson's War*, about the Afghan revolt during the Soviet occupation. Finally, Paul Thomas Anderson directs Daniel Day-Lewis in *There Will Be Blood*, adapted from Upton Sinclair's 1927 novel, *Oil!*

ON DVD

THE STANLEY KUBRICK BOX SET—Just in time for the holidays is this exceptional box set reissue from Warners of some of director Stanley Kubrick's most popular films. A visionary filmmaker who passed away in 1999, Kubrick created some of the most unique movies in the history of cinema during his nearly fifty-year career. This new set includes lavish, 2-disc special editions of *2001: A Space Odyssey, A Clockwork Orange, The Shining* and *Eyes Wide Shut*, plus a single disc special edition of *Full Metal Jacket*. In addition to numerous documentaries and interviews, four of the five films have audio commentary, a first for the filmmaker's canon and a real treat for Kubrick fans. *Eyes*, instead, includes the unrated European cut which dispenses with the computer-generated figures which were added to obscure several key sex scenes in the R-rated version. Rounding out the set is the previously-available feature-length documentary, *Stanley Kubrick: A Life in Pictures*, which was made by Jan Harlan, Kubrick's brother-in-law and a producer on his last five films. Though not part of this set, two other Kubrick films—*Lolita* and *Barry Lyndon*—are being released separately in upgraded special editions as well. The only title from the previous box set not included in this new makeover series is *Dr. Strangelove*, which is currently still available, separately, in a very fine 40th anniversary 2-disc set.

RATATOUILLE—Pixar Studios has done it, again. While every other animation studio's slate of releases vary in quality, meaning you never know what you're going to get, Disney/Pixar remains the Rolls Royce in the industry, consistently delivering one beautifully handcrafted masterpiece after another. From *Toy Story* to this current release, which for the uninitiated is pronounced "Rat-a-too-ee," every film has pushed the technological envelope while maintaining the filmmakers' stance of providing truly heartfelt entertainment. Director Brad Bird (who previously raised the bar with his astonishing *The Incredibles*) outdoes himself with this delightful culinary tale of a rat named Remy who just happens to have gourmet aspirations. The characterizations are, as usual for Pixar, superb, with such actors as Patton Oswalt, Brad Garrett, Janeane Garofalo, Ian Holm and Peter O'Toole giving voice and depth to their animated counterparts. The visuals are jaw-drop stunning, especially a floor level, "rat's eye view" of a bustling kitchen where gargantuan food carts rumble overhead and people the size of office buildings shuffle by. And don't even get me started on the photo-real backgrounds or the delicate, backlit fine hairs along the rats' ears; suffice it to say that every shot is perfect. The DVD release is another notch in Pixar's home video belt, providing a wealth of information on the film's creation from production design to the voice talent. A real Christmas treat for young and old alike.

BLADE RUNNER ULTIMATE FIVE-DISC EDITION—Though this landmark sci-fi movie from 1982, starring Harrison Ford, Rutger Hauer and Sean Young, did only middling business at the box office during its initial release, it has gone on to become a cult classic and is considered one of the most stylistically influential films of all time. Director Ridley Scott's rain-soaked wet dream future-noir dystopia of hard-boiled detectives, killer replicants and flying cars remains the definitive example of using art direction as a way to immerse the viewer in a completely new world. Based on Philip K. Dick's novel, *Do Androids Dream of Electric Sheep?*, the film failed to find an audience at a time when *Star Wars* was still the rage. Scott also had to contend with studio meddling in the form of an unwanted voice-over narration by Ford's character and a tacked on happy ending that mitigates the original script's ambiguities. Scott did get to release his own preferred "Director's Cut" version on VHS and laser disc (and eventually DVD) in the 1990s, but these have been bare bones editions lacking any extras (like commentaries or making-of retrospectives) that would put the film into its proper historical context. In a bit of home video overkill, Warners is releasing this ultimate five-disc set that has everything (and a little more) that any fan of this classic movie could possibly want. To start with, there are five versions of the film, including Ridley Scott's ultimate, final director's cut (which had a brief run in theatres this fall) and a rare work print edition. There is a feature-length documentary and over an hour's worth of deleted scenes. The whole shebang comes packaged in a special limited edition, numbered briefcase which also contains such memorabilia as a spinner car replica, a unicorn figurine and a lenticular motion film clip in Lucite. (For the less enthusiastic, there is a scaled-down two-disc edition.) Unless Harrison Ford shows up at your house with an actual flying spinner car, this five-disc set is the ultimate *Blade Runner* edition to own.

OH, THOSE GOLDEN GLOBES!
(February 2008)

It's been quite a movie year. As usual, it wasn't until the dam-burst finale that most of the great films came tumbling out. The two dozen-plus contenders for 2007's best of the best include *There Will Be Blood, No Country For Old Men, Atonement, Sweeney Todd, Michael Clayton, I'm Not There, Zodiac, American Gangster, Enchanted, Charlie Wilson's War, Across The Universe, Into The Wild, Eastern Promises, Juno, The Kite Runner, A Mighty Heart, Hairspray, Ratatouille, The Savages, The Simpsons Movie, The Diving Bell and The Butterfly, Before The Devil Knows You're Dead, 3:10 To Yuma* and *The Assassination of Jessie James by the Coward Robert Ford*. Out of this collective, the various award agencies will bestow their blessings.

Even though the writers' strike has cut sharply into the awards season this year, it has been clear to those of us who pay attention that the Golden Globes are finally coming into their own. In years past this Hollywood foreign press award was simply one of the numerous also-ran ceremonies that wanted desperately to escape from Oscar's shadow and be taken seriously. But like the film critics' awards from various cities, the People's Choice Awards and even the Cannes Film Festival, there wasn't enough coverage to make the general public sit up and take notice. That has now begun to change. The film industry has gone global and the revenue stream has grown exponentially, meaning that publicity campaigns for even these smaller events can translate into huge profits for everyone. The bottom line is that, while the Oscars are still the last word in the movie awards season bacchanalia, the Golden Globes (and others) are fast becoming a valuable measuring stick for determining which movies will be looked upon as worthy of Oscar's gold. As such, the studios (and stars) are diverting more resources (and attention) to this once, largely ignored segment of the movie industry congratulatory club.

NEW ON DVD
ACROSS THE UNIVERSE—2007 has been a good year for music in movies, from *Sweeney Todd* and *Hairspray* to *Once* and the eclectic score in *There Will Be Blood*. And then there is Julie Taymor's hippie trippy Beatles musical. As experienced through the lives of its protagonist couple—the British Jude (Jim Sturges) and the American Lucy (Evan Rachel Wood)—the story of *Universe* is the story of the 1960s boomer generation, from pre-war innocence through the flower child summer of love and finally to the inevitable post-radical burnout. And while there was a lot of differing music then, the through-line soundtrack of that era was The Beatles. The trick Taymor and her music maestros, Elliot

Goldenthal and T-Bone Burnett, use to keep the movie from seeming like "golden oldies" night is to find fresh ways to present the mostly-familiar 30-plus songs; so we have a female character sing "I Want To Hold Your Hand" while she gazes longingly at . . . another female, putting a decidedly different spin on what had been a traditional love song. Stylistically, even though Ken Russell's *Tommy* and Pink Floyd's *The Wall* are invoked, Taymor (Broadway's *Lion King*, cinema's *Titus* and *Frida*) finds her own visual sense through period appropriation, as in the Richard Avedon-inspired solarized acid trip with Dr. Robert (Bono) in "I Am The Walrus" and the rooftop concert which is taken directly from The Beatles' own film, *Let it Be*. And the Eddie Izzard "Mr. Kite" Victorian segment deliberately uses bad blue screen compositing right out of the 1960s. Taymor also knows to layer in plenty of in-jokes for the fans, whether it's having a number 9 on a door or using a strawberry (instead of an apple) as a logo. When someone asks about a new face in the apartment he's told matter-of-factly, "She came in through the bathroom window." All that's missing is the rim shot. You may roll your eyes, but it will be with approving affection. If nothing else, the film reveals just how awesome the Beatles' catalog of music actually is. It's a soundtrack that any musical producer (or filmmaker) would kill to have. Julie Taymor knows this and fully honors the privilege she was lucky enough to receive. Love is all you need, indeed.

CLASSIC CORNER

EL CID—Back in 1959, director Anthony Mann was fired from *Spartacus* by actor/producer Kirk Douglas, which turned out to be a break for then up and comer, Stanley Kubrick. Mann, meanwhile, licked his wounded pride and went on to direct this epic production, starring Charlton Heston and Sophia Loren, about the 11th century Spanish warrior who drove out the Moors. Though not held in quite the same esteem as the Kirk Douglas opus, it is still regarded as one of the better historical epics of the early 1960s. This new, two-disc DVD finally does justice to the movie and includes an audio commentary track and making-of featurettes sure to satisfy any passionate fan. And while some people might look askance at Heston portraying a Spaniard, it might be well to remember that Orson Welles beat Mann to the punch when he cast Chuck as a Mexican in his 1958 noir masterpiece, *Touch of Evil*. Ole!

THE BIG CHEESE

FUTURAMA: BENDER'S BIG SCORE—While *The Simpsons Movie* was busy burning up the screens in the local multiplexes during the summer of 2007, creator Matt Groening and his creative team were also planning an end run parallel project with this direct to video feature. Based on the 30th Century Fox animated series (that's no typo; it's set in the year 3000. Get it?) which was cancelled after four seasons, this movie is the first of four that will be released over the next year or so. A possible return as a series is also in the works. For fans of the show, this is the best news ever. The plot, which involves a fair amount of time travel, is rich and complex, and about ten times more convoluted than all three *Back to the Future* movies put together. A thoroughly enjoyable commentary track with cast and crew brings you inside the creative process and shows just how passionate everybody is about the show and its characters. And as for the cheese content, well, any film where a robot character drinks, smokes, swears and isn't above a little bit of chicanery, is sure gonna get my Velveeta vote.

IT'S A DVD WORLD AFTER ALL
(March 2008)

With the Oscar race over and the 2008 theatrical films just getting underway, the studios use this time to bring out many high profile DVDs. Because a large number of big films are released in theatres near the end of the year (to position themselves for the Oscars), many are ready for the home video market by February, March and April. All of which is good news for those movie couch potatoes out there who may have missed some of these great flicks when they played in theatres. Recently released discs, or those on their way, in the new film category are such titles as *Michael Clayton, No Reservations, Beowulf, Enchanted, My Kid Could Paint That, Walk Hard: The Dewey Cox Story, I'm Not There* and of course *No Country For Old Men*. Supplementing these fine selections, the studios also have an impressive slate of older films set for the DVD market, either for the first time or in upgraded new editions. Some that are especially noteworthy include special editions of *Bonnie & Clyde, The Ice Storm, Eight Men Out*, Ingmar Bergman's *Sawdust & Tinsel*, Humphrey Bogart's *The Black Legion, Lost Highway* and *Gattaca*. So while we get ready for the real start of this year's films in theatres and await the restart of our favorite shows on TV, now is a great time to see some of the very best, old and new, that the cinema has to offer in the comfort of your home.

NEW ON DVD

SLEUTH—This is a remake of the 1972 film, which was itself based on Anthony Shaffer's hit play, about a mystery writer and his wife's lover who play out a series of mind games on one another. This, however, is a remake with a curious twist; in the original, the older cuckolded writer was acted by Sir Laurence Olivier, while the younger cad who's stepping out with the wife was played by Michael Caine. Fast forward thirty-five years and we now find Mr. Caine in the old fellow part and the ridiculously handsome Jude Law in the Caine role. Astute movie fans will recall that Mr. Law had previously essayed Mr. Caine's signature turn in the remake of *Alfie*. Given the source material and Mr. Caine's participation here, the filmmakers prove to be up to the challenge of remaking a classic. Director Kenneth Branagh (who remade Olivier's version of *Henry V*, based on another great play I might add) obviously has the talent to pull this off even if his track record behind the camera has been a bit spotty. As for the notion of Jude Law being typecast as a Michael Caine surrogate, it can only be considered a plus. Regardless of the limited box office success this film had, given Mr. Caine's vast cinematic oeuvre, Mr. Law can be assured of a steady stream of acting jobs for decades to come. Just be sure to pass on the remakes of *The Swarm* and *Jaws the Revenge*.

CLASSIC CORNER

2001: A SPACE ODYSSEY—With the exception of 2006's *The Fountain*, no other mainstream film, sci-fi or otherwise, has approached the level of experimentation and integrity as Stanley Kubrick's 1968 masterpiece. The four million-year history of mankind—from ape-like proto-human to 21st century astronaut—is shown to be the product of some godlike, alien intervention in the form of a mysterious black monolith. The vignette structure of the movie was somewhat novel for its day, but recent stylistic trends in cinematic storytelling clearly prove that *2001* was simply ahead of its time. Now, with its signature year long past and its 40th anniversary upon us, the Kubrick estate and Warner's has finally saw fit to release a two-disc special edition (part of a five film box set available since late 2007) of this one-of-a-kind motion picture experience. Previous DVD releases were unaccountably skimpy in the extras department, given the pedigree of this sci-fi *Citizen Kane*. This new edition includes several new featurettes which reexamine the cinematic legacy of Kubrick's most unique film, along with a vintage short on the movie's production. There is also an entertaining commentary track with lead actors Keir Dullea and Gary Lockwood who, while forthcoming with personal anecdotes about their work on *2001*, still occasionally get some of their facts wrong. Rounding out the extras is an audio interview with the director done in 1966 which provides interesting insight into Kubrick's thought process while he was in the midst of the movie's creation. For a generation of film fans raised on *Star Wars* who have never seen Kubrick's epic on the big screen, your loss is greater than you can possibly imagine. However, this new two-disc DVD should give you at least an inkling of how important and groundbreaking *2001* was (and still is) in the annals of cinema history.

THE BIG CHEESE

300—As in Spartans, that is. Based on Frank Miller's graphic novel of the same name, about the Grecian battle against overwhelming numbers of Persians at Thermopylae, director Zack Snyder replicated the comic with great fidelity, which turns out to be both its blessing and its curse. Stilted, but visually arresting, this surprise hit from 2007 unfortunately suffers from its own overwrought sense of gravitas. The sluggish pace is amplified by an inordinate use of slow motion, as if the whole thing were being filmed underwater. And dirty water, at that, given the sepia palette which saturates nearly every shot—a chocolate-colored ocean under a chocolate sky (could this be the sequel to *Vanilla Sky*?), chocolate blood geysering from chocolate wounds, chocolate dirt, chocolate armor, chocolate damn near everything. Life may be like a box of chocolates, but this movie isn't just the box, it's the whole dang candy store. And despite the filmmakers' desire to create a large-canvas epic, they are unable to escape the claustrophobia engendered in having shot the entire film in a studio environment where the backgrounds were created digitally. In contrast, *Sky Captain and the World of Tomorrow* (done in a similar fashion) had a sense of scale that is lacking here. Still, there is no denying that director Snyder has a knack and affinity for the comic book mien (he is currently making the film version of *Watchmen* set for release in 2009). And while *300* has its share of problems, it is still better than *The 300 Spartans*, made in 1962 with Richard Egan, Ralph Richardson and Diane Baker; except maybe for the cinematography which, as I recall, had less chocolate.

APRIL SHOWERS BRING NEW MOVIES
(April 2008)

While it may seem there isn't much happening in movies this year until the late spring release of *Indiana Jones 4* next month, the fact is there are several noteworthy films awaiting your attention. *Leatherheads*, the 1920s-era romantic comedy/football film directed by and starring George Clooney, looks to be a winner. Co-starring Rene Zellweger and *The Office's* John Krasinski, Clooney does for the screwball comedy genre what he did in his previous directing efforts in drama and mystery. Next up, *Shine A Light* brings together The Rolling Stones with master filmmaker Martin Scorsese in a concert film to beat the band. *Smart People* finds a remarkable cast—Dennis Quaid, Sarah Jessica Parker, Thomas Haden Church and the terrific Ellen Page—dealing with sexual politics and family trust under the direction of Noam Murro. Finally, for those whose tastes run to the kinkier side of life, *The Tourist* boasts a steamy look at the New York City sex club underworld. Ewan McGregor, Hugh Jackman and Michelle Williams, along with first-time director Marcel Langenegger, are our guides to this unsavory tale.

NEW IN THEATRES
MY BLUEBERRY NIGHTS—Asian director Won Kar Wai made his name with such Hong Kong classics as 1994's *Chungking Express* (a touchstone for Tarantino) and the cryptically beautiful *2046* in 2004. For his English language debut he's chosen this tale about a waitress (singer Nora Jones) who embarks on a road trip through Nevada in which she meets up with some interesting characters. If his previous work is any indication, *Nights* has the potential of being a solid hit, propelling the director into the Hollywood mainstream, much as *Sense and Sensibility* did for Ang Lee. In addition to Jones, the eclectic, and attractive, cast includes Jude Law, Rachel Weisz and Natalie Portman, who gets to be the bad girl for once.

NEW ON DVD
SWEENEY TODD—There are few filmmakers with as identifiable a visual style as Tim Burton. From his debut, *Pee Wee's Big Adventure*, back in 1985 through his singularly loopy canon that includes *Beetlejuice, Batman, Edward Scissorhands, Batman Returns, Ed Wood, Mars Attacks!, Sleepy Hollow, Planet of the Apes, Big Fish, Charlie & the Chocolate Factory* and the animated *Corpse Bride*, he has proven to be a master at fusing the macabre with a sweet innocence that is both startling and reassuring. It is easy to see, then, why he was drawn to Stephen Sondheim's cannibalistic musical (!) about a Victorian barber who

commits a series of murders and then turns the bodies into meat pies. Reuniting with his longtime leading man, Johnny Depp (*Todd* marks their fifth collaboration), what could have been a disastrous flop, given the subject matter, instead ended up as a high point in the career of both men. Depp's Brillo pad coif and chalky complexion are comfortably at home in the monochromatic gothic milieu of Burton's cinematic world, all the better to contrast with the explosive bursts of gore when the nasty business of murder rears its bloody head. Burton's casting choices have always been uniquely right—think Michael Keaton in *Batman*, Winona Ryder in *Edward Scissorhands* and Martin Landau in *Ed Wood*. For *Todd*, we have Helena Bonham Carter as Mrs. Lovett, Alan Rickman as the evil Judge Turpin and even *Borat* himself, Sacha Baron Cohen, as rival barber, Signor Pirelli, all of whom must also sing. And while Josh Groban won't be losing any sleep, the *Todd* cast rise up gamely to the occasion and acquit themselves nicely. While some have called this Burton's finest film, it is really just the continuation of his journey as one of cinema's true provocateurs.

CLASSIC CORNER

BONNIE & CLYDE—Like a cannonball shot across the bow of conventional cinema, this 1967 masterpiece shook up audiences and critics, alike, and announced to the world that movies were going to be different from now on. Written by then fledgling scribes Robert Benton and David Newman and directed by Arthur Penn, the movie was produced by a cocky heartthrob actor named Warren Beatty who saw the potential in this story about a pair of young bank robbers who cut a swath across the mid-west in depression-era America. The movie seesaws wildly between the comedic and the horrific, with hardly a chance to catch your breath, as the scenes tumble pell-mell over you on this very cinematic roller coaster ride. The casting is also first rate, with Faye Dunaway as Bonnie Parker (in one of her first big roles) perfectly in synch with Beatty's Clyde Barrow. Gene Hackman as Clyde's hayseed brother, Buck, nearly steals the movie, while gnome-faced Michael J. Pollard adds considerable comic relief as the bumpkin-like henchman, C. W. Moss. Estelle Parsons, as Buck's long-suffering wife, Blanche, won a much-deserved Oscar, and Denver Pyle creates a suitably steely adversary with his portrayal of Texas Ranger, Frank Hamer. Rounding out the superb cast is Gene Wilder, in his first movie role, as reluctant hostage Eugene Grizzard, in a brief comic interlude. Why it took so long to come out with a two-disc special edition of this benchmark film is anyone's guess, but thank god they finally got around to it. The remastered DVD brilliantly highlights Burnett Gaffey's Oscar-winning cinematography, while the aural remix allows you to fully appreciate the dense sound design along with Flatt and Scruggs' iconic banjo-picking score. For those who thought the 1967 summer of love was all hippies, flowers and rock and roll, the truth is a couple of twenty-something hicks from 1930s Texas made the biggest splash that year with their machine guns, funny looking jalopies and a soundtrack of old-timey music. Who'd a thunk it?

THERE WILL BE CLASSICS: Reassessing Paul Thomas Anderson's *Blood* Saga

(May 2008)

Sometimes you see a movie and you just know you are in the presence of greatness. Such is the case with *There Will Be Blood*. From its fifteen-minute mute opening to its operatic Grand Guignol conclusion, at every step you are in the hands of a master filmmaker. It was certainly the only movie to give *No Country For Old Men* a serious run for its money this awards season. But the strangeness of *Blood*'s metaphoric conceit and its insistence on creating a new paradigm in storytelling, one where every shot and line of dialogue carried a symbolic weight that many film patrons found too burdensome to bear, meant that, like 2006's *The Fountain*, it fractured its audience into two distinct camps, those that loved it and those that hated it. Any time a filmmaker dares to push the envelope of "form," whether it's King Vidor with his silent classic, *The Crowd*, Walt Disney's *Fantasia*, Orson Welles with *Citizen Kane* or Paul Thomas Anderson with *Blood*, it is bound to meet some resistance from the masses. Critical success, commercial failure. There have been exceptions—*2001: A Space Odyssey, Pulp Fiction, Memento*—but generally speaking, originality is not rewarded in its own time. Thanks to home video we all have the chance to reassess those unusual films that did less than boffo box office on their initial release. *Blood* was by no means a commercial failure, but it never did the kind of business it should have. And despite a few negative barbs, it got a fairly positive response from the public, especially for Daniel Day-Lewis's stunning performance as oil baron Daniel Plainview. I do not begrudge *No Country* for its success; it is a great film and it was the Coen Brothers' time. But *Blood* will come into its own someday and years from now we may all look back on this time and say, "Why didn't we appreciate its greatness, then?" The answer we come up with will say as much about us as about the film.

NEW IN THEATRES

THE CHRONICLES OF NARNIA: PRINCE CASPIAN—With *Indiana Jones 4* and *Iron Man* duking it out this month, does anyone even care about what else is out there? Well, in fact, there is the second cinematic chapter in the *Narnia* saga, from the series of children's books by C.S. Lewis. In this story the Pevensie siblings, Peter, Susan, Edmund and Lucy, who were introduced in *The Lion, the Witch and the Wardrobe*, are back to help Prince Caspian fight the repressive Telmarine King and save the land of Narnia once again. While the first Narnia film failed to be the next *Harry Potter* or *Lord of the Rings*, it did respectable business and was true enough to the source material to please fans of the books. Original director Andrew Adamson steps up to the plate with his precocious young cast to have a second go at Lewis's remarkable fable. Everything being equal, if you liked the first film you're sure to enjoy this one as well.

NEW ON DVD
THE DIVING BELL AND THE BUTTERFLY—While *There Will Be Blood* and *No Country For Old Men* were the Oscar favorites this year, for some film enthusiasts, this was the best movie of 2007. Painter turned filmmaker Julian Schnabel expertly told the true story of French Elle magazine editor Jean-Dominique Bauby who suffered a crippling stroke at age 43, leaving him with the ability to blink only one eye. How Bauby overcame his fate is what makes this tale of the human spirit so uplifting. In a year that had more than its share of dark, edgy fare, this was a tragic story that dared to soar into the light.

CLASSIC CORNER
ACE IN THE HOLE—They don't come much more cynical than this 1951 indictment of the media directed by Billy Wilder and starring Kirk Douglas as a hard ruthless reporter who will stop at nothing to get a good story. For those who thought that trashy media coverage was something new, you're in for a rude awakening. When down-on-his-luck reporter Douglas learns about a trapped man in a mine cave in, he finds a way to orchestrate the event to slow down the rescue plan, knowing that it'll make for a better story. I can best sum up the cold black heart of this astonishing film by quoting leading lady Jan Sterling when she sees Douglas's true nature for the first time; "I met a lot of hard-boiled eggs in my life, but you, you're twenty minutes."

THE BIG CHEESE
GREY GARDENS—A crumbling manor house in East Hampton, New York, and the eccentric mother/daughter bluebloods who inhabit it, are the quirky subjects of one of the strangest documentaries you will ever see. Shot in 1975 by the Maysles brothers (best known for their 1970 Rolling Stones concert flick, *Gimme Shelter*), 80-year old Edith Beale and her 58 year old daughter, Little Edie Beale (aunt and cousin to Jackie Kennedy Onassis), provide the entertainment as we watch them bicker, sing, dance and try to stave off boredom in their dilapidated 28-room East Hampton home which they share with numerous cats and at least a couple of wild raccoons. Edie mostly laments the loss of the life she could've had (she modeled briefly) were it not for her invalid mother whom she must care for. Old Edith, though unable to walk much, is still a force to be reckoned with and is constantly chipping away at Edie's self- esteem as only a mother could. While they obviously love one another, being a witness to their

quarrelling is like watching a train wreck, or more precisely, given their upper crust upbringing of finishing schools and cotillions, like watching the sinking of the Titanic. As in most of their work, the Maysles dispense with narration and just allow the subjects to tell their own story to the camera. As a result, much goes unexplained, such as Edie's penchant for head scarves (you never see her without one) which raises the notion that she may have lost most of her hair. What most clearly comes through is Edie's sense of loyalty to her family. When asked why she agreed to return home to care for her mother all those years ago she says simply that it never would have occurred to her to do anything else; that it was what was expected of her. In that cogent statement, Edie completely redeems herself to the viewer. What had appeared to be cheap liver pate on stale crackers is miraculously transformed into the finest of meals. Dig in with gusto.

LET THE SUMMER CINEMA BEGIN
(June 2008)

Another steamroller, pile driver summer movie season is upon us with a hundred-plus films in the offing. Most of us will never have the time or money to see even half of what's out there, but here's a list of some of the more promising titles for June. The animated *Kung Fu Panda* starts off the month with voices by Jack Black, Dustin Hoffman and Angelina Jolie. *You Don't Mess With The Zohan* brings Adam Sandler back for his usual shtick. M. Night Shyamalan returns after his *Lady in the Water* fiasco with *The Happening* starring Mark Wahlberg and Zooey Deschanel in an ecological thriller. *The Incredible Hulk* gets a reboot with Edward Norton Liv Tyler and Tim Roth. *Get Smart* gets updated for the 21st century with Steve Carell, Anne Hathaway and Alan Arkin. *The Love Guru* brings the return of Mike Myers spoofing the New Age with Jessica Alba and Verne Troyer. On a more serious note is the documentary *Trumbo*, about blacklisted screenwriter Dalton Trumbo, directed by his son Christopher. Finally, there's the big budget action film, *Wanted*, starring James McAvoy, Morgan Freeman and the ever lovely Angelina Jolie. So jump into these June entries with both feet and remember there's still July and August to contend with.

NEW IN THEATRES

WALL-E—The great animation studio, Pixar, has never been one to sit on its laurels. After a phenomenal string of eight-for-eight successes, beginning with *Toy Story* in 1995 right through to *Ratatouille* in 2007, they continue to push the animation envelope. Here, in a far off future, we find our eponymous robot cleaning up the residue trash of the earthlings who have moved off-world hundreds of years ago. WALL-E (for Waste Allocation Load Lifter-Earth class) works alone except for a friendly companion cockroach until one day when a sleek robot named EVE arrives to check on his status. WALL-E is smitten and therein lies the Pixar tale. Director Andrew Stanton, who previously helmed Pixar's highest grosser, *Finding Nemo*, is well at home pulling on your heartstrings. But as in all the other Pixar films, he knows how to keep the emotionalism from turning into saccharin sentimentality. Eschewing conventional dialogue for the most part, Stanton has his love sick robotic characters "speak" almost entirely in beeps and whistles, as did robot droid R2D2 in *Star Wars*. Will it work or will it fail? I'm betting Pixar will go nine-for nine. And if it doesn't, I'll have the satisfaction of knowing that the best animation studio ever is still pushing the envelope.

NEW ON DVD

FUNNY GAMES—Sometimes a movie can be unpleasant and fascinating at the same time. Following its all too brief theatrical run, Michael Haneke's shot-for-shot remake of his own Austrian version a decade ago, this glossy English language simulacrum stars Naomi Watts and Tim Roth as a well to do couple who are invaded by a pair of young, preppie-ish thugs eager to engage in sadistic mayhem, a la *Clockwork Orange*. Haneke, who also did the terrific *Cache*, employs a stately, Kubrickian pace which further alludes to *Clockwork* as a leitmotif. And like Kubrick, Haneke is not afraid to push the violence. What raises this film above the standard, lowbrow shocker is that the director confronts the audience's participation in observing the grotesqueries by having the chief thug address the camera directly on several occasions about what is going on. It's both chilling and a slap in the face to be reminded that the artist and the audience are equally responsible for a work's impact on society.

CLASSIC CORNER

THE THIEF OF BAGDAD—One of the best fantasy movies ever is this 1940 extravaganza from producer Alexander Korda, directed by Ludwig Berger, Tim Whelan and Michael Powell. This colossal entertainment is brimming with near-East atmosphere (lots of turbans and baggy pants) in its telling of the little thief (Sabu) who saves a kingdom. Boasting extravagant production values and eye-popping art direction, the movie contains many memorable set pieces including the superb Rex Ingram as the gigantic, long-nailed genie; Sabu stealing the Eye of the Idol from what looks to be a hundred-foot tall statue; and of course the inevitable flying carpet ride. As in *The Wizard of Oz* the previous year, *Thief* is a movie for all ages; a film that will appeal to adults as much as it does to children. A new 2-disc set from Criterion finally gives this classic film its due. Watch it and be mesmerized all over again.

THE BIG CHEESE

SYMBIOPSYCHOTAXIPLASM: TAKE ONE—Conceptual in the extreme, this 1968 fiction/documentary hybrid by William Greaves is ostensively about the making of a movie drama. In reality, Greaves turns this concept inside out as he not only films the actors but films the making of the movie and films the making of the making of the movie. In addition, the crew decides to film a series of rap sessions where the members discuss what they think Greaves is up to, given the free form style in which the movie is shot. Sometimes these various elements are shown in a split screen or even tri-screen format to illustrate the levels of artifice at work. Greaves, a noted documentary filmmaker, thought it would be fun to use cinema as a way to explore the medium, itself. Here, he deliberately rejects the conventional parameters of the three-act structure, story arc or even the notion of entertainment (which had served our culture for over a thousand years) in favor of exploding the idea of what these conventions mean. While it is a curious conceit in which many others partook, the movement ultimately foundered since it produced far more baloney than insight. Still, Greaves' film holds much value in showing the mindset of that generation of filmmakers who tried to grapple with the then burgeoning phenomenon of the mass media invading our culture.

SUMMER CINEMA: PART 2
(July 2008)

In the June Irregular I listed a number of films being released that month which looked to be potential winners. As it turned out, some were and some weren't. Despite that mixed bag result the rest of the summer beckons, so here are my picks for what looks to be worth catching for the rest of the season.

JULY
Will Smith leads off the July 4th holiday as he's done for the past decade, this time with *Handcock* about a very flawed superhero. Mexican director Guillermo del Toro returns to his superhero canon after the success of *Pan's Labyrinth* with *Hellboy II* which brings back Ron Perlman and Selma Blair. Following the superhero trend comes *The Dark Knight*, the highly anticipated Batman sequel by Christopher Nolan starring Christian Bale, Michael Caine, Aaron Eckhart and (most interesting for many) the late Heath Ledger as The Joker. Lighter fare comes in the form of *Mama Mia*, from the ABBA-inspired Broadway musical and starring Meryl Streep, Amanda Seyfried, Pierce Brosnan, Colin Firth and Julie Waters. The final week offers up three very different choices which include the return of *The X-Files,* directed by series creator Chris Carter, starring David Duchovny and Gillian Anderson. Next is *American Teen*, a documentary by Nanette Burstein about four Indiana teenagers with heavy problems. Lastly, there is the film remake of the 1980s TV miniseries *Brideshead Revisited*, which was based on the classic Evelyn Waugh novel and stars Emma Thompson and Matthew Goode.

AUGUST
The last summer month is always the trickiest, and this year is no different. First out of the gate is *The Rocker* a metal band comedy starring *The Office*'s Rainn Wilson and directed by *The Full Monty*'s Peter Cattaneo. *The Mummy* is back with Brendan Fraser and newbies to the franchise Maria Bello and Jet Li. *Pineapple Express* is a stoner comedy starring James Franco and Seth Rogen. *Sisterhood of the Traveling Pants* comes back for a second installment with Blake Livey, Alexis Bledel, Amber Tamblyn and *Ugly Betty*'s America Ferrera. Big laughs are promised in *Tropic Thunder* about a group of actors in a Vietnam War movie starring Ben Stiller (who also directs), Jack Black, Robert Downey, Jr. (as a white actor in blackface!), Nick Nolte, Steve Coogan, Matthew McConaughey and a cameo by Stiller's buddy, Tom Cruise. Harrison Ford hangs up his Indiana Jones fedora to star in *Crossing Over*, a straight-up drama with Sean Penn, Ray Liotta and Ashley Judd. *The Accidental Husband* stars Uma Thurman and Jeffrey

Dean Morgan in a screwball comedy romance directed by Griffin Dunne. Finally, at summer's end is Woody Allen's latest (this time in Spain), *Vicky Cristina Barcelona* starring Penelope Cruz, Javier Bardem and Woody regular, Scarlett Johansson.

CLASSIC CORNER

EIGHT MEN OUT—Summer and baseball go hand in glove, so what better time to commemorate one of the all-time great baseball flicks, especially now that it's available in a new special edition DVD. Made in 1988 by director John Sayles, it took the maverick writer/director/actor eleven years to see this project about the notorious "Black Sox" scandal of 1919 reach fruition. The powerhouse cast of then mostly young unknowns included Charlie Sheen (fresh from *Platoon* and *Wall Street*), D.B. Sweeney, Michael Rooker, John Cusack, David Strathairn, and seasoned character actors John Mahoney, Studs Terkel, John Anderson, Clifton James, Michael Lerner and Christopher Lloyd. Sayles, himself, plays sportswriter Ring Lardner, to whom he bears an uncanny resemblance. Despite its low budget status, Sayles and his production crew beautifully evoke the era and never cause you to feel you're being cheated out of the epic scope of the story, especially during the ballgame sequences which are terrific. The previous DVD release was a sad, bare bones edition, not worthy of the film. The new DVD release includes a thoughtful commentary track with Sayles, along with a two-part retrospective documentary and a "Story Behind the Movie" featurette. While still a sport's film, *Eight Men Out* is also a trenchant and compelling historical look at early 20th century America when the public truly lost its innocence and which the powers-that-be knew that it never really existed.

THE BIG CHEESE

EARTH VS. THE FLYING SAUCERS—The "flying saucer" hysteria which swept the world in the 1950s, perhaps found its fullest cinematic expression in this dandy little 1956 tidbit by producer Charles M. Schneer and stop-motion animation maestro, Ray Harryhausen. It is to his artistic credit that the legendary animator was able to impart character into the nearly featureless saucers almost entirely through their movement. Though the plot is paper thin, the interplay between actors Hugh Marlowe and Joan Taylor has a snappy, grown-up feel to it. While the story arc follows a typical pattern of alien attacks and American military response, the Washington, D.C. denouement provides a fitting climax where we see the saucers crash into as many iconic buildings and monuments as the budget would allow. A new 2-disc special edition DVD of this classic picture includes interviews and commentary by Ray Harryhausen (still alive and kicking in his 80s), along with several retrospective featurettes about the film and those who worked on it. As an extra bonus, the DVD offers the viewer the option of watching the movie in its original black & white or a new colorized version. Harryhausen, himself, approved of the process (done by Legend Films who've "painted" everything from *Reefer Madness* to Shirley Temple's films), which is far superior to the previous efforts at colorization. Two other Harryhausen films, *It Came From Beneath the Sea* (1955) and *20 Million Miles to Earth* (1957), have also been released in special edition color-option DVDs which Mr. Harryhausen states would have been shot in color if they'd had the budget for it back then. In an era where most effects work wears a soulless corporate veneer, it's nice to go back to a time when good old hands-on craftsmanship was the order of the day, even if it was in the service of a cheesy little flying saucer flick.

SAVORING SUMMER, ANTICIPATING AUTUMN

(September 2008)

The 2008 summer movie season is one that will be remembered. In addition to seeing the return of *Indiana Jones*, movie goers were also treated to such satisfying entertainment as *Iron Man, WALL-E, The Dark Knight, Mama Mia, Pineapple Express* and *Tropic Thunder*, to name only a few. There were a few losers, of course, but all in all, it was a good season. And now it's the fall, when serious movies make their appearance at the local multiplex and not just at the art house cinema. While the fluff of summer was an enjoyable distraction and even included some high quality fare, it's time to prepare for the big guns that will lead the way through Christmas and into the Oscar season. There will be more junk as well, but the best of the year is on its way.

NEW IN THEATRES

BURN AFTER READING—Now that the Coen brothers have an Oscar-winning picture to their credit in *No Country For Old Men*, not to mention the Best Director prize as well, the world is eagerly awaiting their newest release. This time out the brothers serve up a dark comedy (what else?) about two Washington, D.C. gym employees (Brad Pitt and Frances McDormand) who find the unpublished memoir of an ex-C.I.A. official. Hilarity, of a sort, ensues. The supporting cast includes John Malkovich, Tilda Swinton and, in his third go-round with the Coens, George Clooney. Those who have followed the twenty-plus year career of these unique filmmaker siblings know that they never do what you'd expect and they never repeat themselves. Sometimes that means they stumble (*The Ladykillers* and *Intolerable Cruelty* were lesser efforts), but they never fall. Their films always improve on repeat viewings and that says something about their talent. Plus, with a best picture Oscar now on their resume, the Coen brothers are a part of cinema's elite, something their fans have known all along. Where they go from here is strictly up to them.

NEW ON DVD

SPEED RACER—Based on the Japanese cartoon TV series from the 1960s, this big budget, live action remake by the Wachowski brothers (*The Matrix* trilogy) was one of the most anticipated movies of 2008. Unfortunately, it laid a colossal egg as it crashed and burned upon its release in May. Despite the best efforts of its cast (Emile Hirsch, Christina Ricci, *Lost*'s Matthew Fox, John Goodman, Susan Sarandon) not to mention the eye-popping, candy-colored neon palette, the Wachowski brothers just seem to be spinning their wheels. While the visuals careened into overdrive, the story (not that we're expecting *Hamlet*, mind you) remained in neutral. The brothers haven't had a really good film since the original *Matrix* back in 1999. Go, Speed Racer, Go became No, Speed Racer, No! For those who missed this misfire in the theatre (and saved a bundle of cash), you can now check it out yourself for the mere price of a rental fee in the comfort and privacy of your own home. You might even want to see the old cartoon, again, just to remind yourself of the cheesy thrill it once gave you.

CLASSIC CORNER

THE ADVENTURES OF BARON MUNCHAUSEN—This 1989 film was director Terry Gilliam's big budget follow up to *Brazil*, a project that was mired in considerable controversy. However, *Brazil*'s travails were nothing compared to the out-of-control circus that befell the making of *Munchausen*. Based on Rudolph Erich Raspe's tales about the noted 18th century confabulator (i.e. liar), who boasted of fighting off Turkish armies single-handedly and even making a trip to the moon, this whimsical fantasy seemed to be a perfect match for Gilliam's unfettered imagination. Starring John Neville in the title role along with Uma Thurman, Jonathan Pryce, Eric Idle, Oliver Reed, Sarah Polley and an unbilled, insanely funny extended cameo by Robin Williams, the movie is bursting at the seams with imagination and fantasy that is reminiscent of such earlier cinematic excursions into magical realms as *The Wizard of Oz* and *The Thief of Bagdad*. Despite the chaos of its making, the final product works brilliantly as a reminder to all of us of the need for fanciful storytelling in our culture, as well as just how thin the line can be between the real and the unreal in our lives. To commemorate its upcoming 20th anniversary, a new 2-disc DVD edition was recently released laden with extras. An hour-long retrospective with reminiscences from most of the principals, along with an entertaining commentary track by Gilliam and his long-time writing partner Charles McKeown, offer insight into the madness which defined this very unique production. The mercurial Gilliam has had his ups and downs since this production (after the success of *12 Monkeys* in 1995 his films, while all innovative and unique, have either tanked at the box office or come undone during their making), but his talent and vision as a filmmaker remain unimpeachable. *Munchausen* was certainly his most "out-of-control" film production, yet it (along with *Brazil*) shows him as an artist at the height of his powers.

THE BIG CHEESE

PEYTON PLACE—It is hard to believe that this 1957 film, and the book it was based on, could ever have been considered scandalous. The tale of a small 1940s

New England town with a closet full of tawdry secrets (adultery, rape, incest, murder, suicide, abortion, nude swimming!) written by Massachusetts housewife, Grace Metalious, became a huge bestseller and revealed the salacious underbelly of 1950s prim facade. The film version, directed by Mark Robson and starring Lana Turner, Lee Philips, Hope Lange, Arthur Kennedy, Lloyd Nolan Terry Moore, Russ Tamblyn, Lorne Greene and newcomer Diane Varsi, was a smash hit as well, garnering nine Academy Award nominations but no wins. Still, the film was a major triumph in presenting frank, grown-up situations in a mature manner. It also helped bolster the careers of established stars (Lana Turner's only Oscar nom) and up-and-comers (Russ Tamblyn, Hope Lange, and a pre-*Bonanza* Lorne Greene) alike. An inferior sequel and nighttime TV series followed, the latter starring the then fresh faces of Mia Farrow and Ryan O'Neal. The DVD contains wistful commentary from co-stars Russ Tamblyn and Terry Moore (who was twenty-eight when she played the high school vamp). There is also an AMC retrospective featurette that provides historic insight into the book and film. Perhaps most chilling is the real life tragedy for Lana Turner which echoed the story's melodramatic courtroom scene. Only days after the Academy Awards, Turner's mobbed-up boy toy, Johnny Stompanato, was stabbed to death by Turner's fourteen-year old daughter in self-defense. The trial transcripts could have come right out of the film. Sadly, fame was a burden for author, Metalious, who only seven years after the film's release, died of alcoholism. But her legacy of *Peyton Place* remains, the fictional town's name having become a synonym for unsavory, gossipy enclaves the world over.

SCOPING OUT THE FALL
MOVIE SEASON
(October 2008)

The hors d'oeuvres of the summer movie season are behind us and now it's time to dig in to the main course. Even with the news that the latest *Harry Potter* has been pushed back to next summer, the autumn movie schedule is shaping up to be another winner with many notable titles in the offing. Already in September we've had the Coen brothers' *Burn After Reading*; writer/director Ed Zwick's *Defiance* with Daniel Craig; Ed Harris starring in and directing *Appaloosa*; the powerhouse pairing of DeNiro and Pacino in *Righteous Kill*; and on the distaff side, Meg Ryan, Annette Bening and Eva Mendes in a remake of George Cukor's classic, *The Women*, to name just a few. October brings us Anne Hathaway in Jonathan Demme's *Rachel Getting Married*; Dakota Fanning and Queen Latifah in *The Secret Life of Bees*; Angelina Jolie and John Malkovich in Clint Eastwood's *Changeling*; Oliver Stone's presidential bio, *W.* with Josh Brolin in the title role, and perhaps most intriguing of all, screenwriter extraordinaire, Charlie Kaufman (*Sunshine of the Spotless Mind, Adaptation*), in his directorial debut, *Synecdoche, New York* with Philip Seymour Hoffman and Catherine Keener. While this already seems like a pretty full meal, November and December promise even more courses, but for now, these early fall delicacies should suffice in satisfying our appetite for good movies, at least until month's end when we'll be ready for seconds.

NEW IN THEATRES
BODY OF LIES—It's been more than a dozen years since Russell Crowe and Leonardo DiCaprio first acted together in the Sharon Stone homage to Sergio Leone-style westerns in *The Quick and the Dead* (directed by then up-and-comer Sam Raimi). Now they're reunited under the baton of master filmmaker Ridley Scott for this tale of shenanigans in the CIA during the war on terror. This marks Crowe's fourth collaboration with Scott (*Gladiator, A Good Year, American Gangster*), so you know they like working together. DiCaprio, on the other hand, is a first-timer in "Ridleyville," though he's had his own thing going lately with Martin Scorsese (*Gangs of New York, The Aviator, The Departed*). Obviously he wants to work with as many A-list directors as he can—later this year finds him in Sam Mendes' (*American Beauty*) *Revolutionary Road* with his *Titanic* co-star, Kate Winslet. So, the match-up with ace actor Crowe in the service of a smart political thriller directed by one of the best visual stylists working in the business looks to be a winning choice for him and filmgoers alike.

NEW ON DVD

IRON MAN—A surprise hit early in the summer movie season, this comic book adaptation, directed by Jon Favreau (*Elf, Zathura*) and starring Robert Downey, Jr. and Gwyneth Paltrow, helped lead the way for *Hancock*, not to mention *The Dark Knight*. Weapons magnate, Tony Stark (Downey, in a cool, retro goatee), creates the Iron Man suit to escape his Afghan captors (who think he's making them the cluster bomb they've demanded), and in turn, uses the suit (in an upgraded version) to fight against war and the weapons he once made. Of course, with his newly-found conscience come some new enemies, including his bearded, bald-headed corporate partner, played in a scarily understated turn by Jeff Bridges. Though the action sequences with Stark flying about in his mechanized suit of armor are nifty and believable, director Favreau makes sure to flesh out the relationship between Downey and Paltrow, who plays assistant and love interest Pepper Potts (a comic book name, for sure). Lately it seems as if the action hero genre has grown up a bit (*Superman Returns*, Christopher Nolan's *Batman* franchise), so it's nice to see this latest cinematic player successfully continue the trend. I'm sure the makers of the next year's *Watchmen* are equally glad.

CLASSIC CORNER

THE HAUNTING—In this age of over-the-top horror films, with their attendant gore and outrageous scenarios, it may be hard for some to appreciate the restrained artistry of a psychological thriller which relies on mood, atmosphere and finely drawn characters instead of special effects. Imagine a ghost story where there are no ghosts to be seen, only the cacophony of noise echoing throughout an old house wherein a group of occupants are spending the night. Made in 1963 by Robert Wise, and based on Shirley Jackson's novel, "The Haunting of Hill House," the stellar cast includes Julie Harris, Claire Bloom, Richard Johnson, Russ Tamblyn and Lois Maxwell. Director Wise (who's done everything from *The Sound of Music* to *The Andromeda Strain*), extracted wonderfully compelling performances from his actors, especially the female leads, without ever resorting to arch self-consciousness or hammy histrionics. Instead he makes excellent use of unusual camera angles and wide lenses to affect an almost Kafka-esque air of helpless dread. The DVD boasts an insightful commentary by Wise, screenwriter Nelson Giddy and actors Harris, Bloom, Johnson and Tamblyn. The inferior 1999 remake, directed by Jan De Bont (*Speed, Twister)* and starring Liam Neeson and Catherine Zeta Jones, which featured phenomenal sets but little in the way of compelling storytelling, should be avoided at all costs. Make your Halloween movie party a memorable one by

- 255 -

skipping the *Saws* and *Hostels* and going directly for some classy and refined viewing. You might just surprise yourself.

DVD ALERT

DARK CITY DIRECTOR'S CUT—It isn't often that a filmmaker is allowed to go back and restore a movie to his original cinematic vision, especially if the film in question did only middling business during its theatrical run. Fortunately, Alex Proyas was given the chance to retool his 1998 cult classic back to the way it was intended. The result is a marked, though subtle, improvement on the theatrical cut that, until now, was all we had. The director has a short, but memorable oeuvre (*The Crow, I Robot*) which has earned him a devoted following. *Dark City* is his best and most original work, melding imagery from forties film noir, cyber-punk comics and 1920s German Expressionist films into a satisfying whole. The cast is equally eclectic with Rufus Sewell, an ingénue-ish Jennifer Connelly, Kiefer Sutherland and William Hurt playing archetypal characters who inhabit a world shrouded in eternal night that can't possibly exist. The original DVD contained several extras, including two commentary tracks (one with the director and crew, the other with film critic Roger Ebert). The new DVD has three new commentaries (Proyas, the writers, and Ebert, who truly is a serious fan). There is also an extensive retrospective featurette which examines the film's history and legacy as a major work of cinematic art. Seeing this new edition reminds us that *Dark City* is a great movie, not just a good one.

"BLU" CHRISTMAS?

(November 2008)

For those of us with large DVD collections, the time is fast approaching, maybe even by this Christmas, to embrace the Blu-Ray DVD format. The superior sound and picture quality, plus the larger information storage capacity, means that Blu-Ray offers to enrich the movie watching experience, especially for the discriminating cineaste. With so many new titles being released this year, it might be a good time to put Blu-Ray editions on your Christmas list, even if you don't yet own a Blu-Ray player. I'm waiting for the player prices to drop a bit more, but the discs are already reasonably priced (considering the extras they offer) to warrant a purchase option now. This makes even more sense if you purchase an upgraded version that you already own on DVD. And having a couple BR discs on hand may just be the incentive you'll need to break down and buy that new player the next time they go on sale.

NEW IN THEATRES

THE ROAD—Aussie director John Hillcoat (*The Proposition*) takes the reins on the film version of Cormac McCarthy's post-apocalyptic novel (which had garnered both a Pulitzer Prize and a slot in Oprah's Book Club). The plot revolves around a father and son (Viggo Mortensen and Kodi Smit-McPhee) as they make their way across a decimated America after an unspecified catastrophe. To help leaven the bleakness, the lovely and talented Charlize Theron is along for the ride. While the grim nature of the story could be a real downer, last year's Oscar winner, *No Country For Old Men*, proved that a dark story, if told correctly, can still rake in audiences and awards. Expect this one to be on everyone's short list of 2008's best.

NEW ON DVD

WALL-E—The animation powerhouse, Pixar, continues its string of successes, both financial and artistic, with this sweet fable about a futuristic, garbage-strewn, uninhabited Earth, and a pair of robots who fall in love. While there is some clever social commentary about our consumer society, the movie is never heavy-handed in this regard, preferring instead to deliver its eco-message through subtext and visuals. And speaking of visuals, the production design is extraordinary, from the mechanics of the robots and other technology to the image of the abandoned Earth cities made up of skyscraper-sized piles of compacted trash. Everything is so completely well thought out that, if it weren't for the overly plump, deliberately cartoonish-looking humans, you'd swear you were actually watching a real-life documentary about our world. As for the limited use of dialogue, especially in the first half, Pixar proves once again that they are masters of innovative storytelling as well as animation. In a return to form for the studio, the DVD extras include an audio commentary track, a feature that has been missing from the last two Pixar DVD releases.

CLASSIC CORNER

HOW THE WEST WAS WON—Cinerama was the IMAX of its day. Invented by Fred Waller and used to bolster the slump in movie attendance due to the emergence of television in the post-war 1950s, Cinerama first released a series of scenic travelogues including *This is Cinerama, Seven Wonders of the World* and *South Sea Adventures*. The process involved using three interlinked 35mm cameras shooting three separate images which would later be shown using three synchronized projectors onto a deeply-curved screen to create a single panoramic image that would engulf the audience. By 1960 it was decided to try more traditional storytelling and in 1961 *HTWWW* , based on a series of articles for *Life* magazine, went before the cameras with three directors (Henry Hathaway, John Ford and George Marshall). Released in 1962 with an all-star cast including Henry Fonda, Gregory Peck, Jimmy Stewart, Debbie Reynolds, George Peppard and John Wayne, the five-part story (narrated by Spencer Tracy) told the multi-generational saga of a pioneering family's struggle to survive the treacherous dangers of the untamed west. Highlights featured a buffalo stampede, a shootout atop a runaway train and a scene shot inside a covered wagon as it rolls over and over down a cliff with the occupants tumbling about. All in all, it is first rate entertainment of the highest order. A new "Ultimate Collector's Edition" DVD set includes a digitally remastered picture which removes the annoying "joins" between the three images, commentary, featurettes, plus a 20 page press book reproduction, a 36 page Cinerama souvenir booklet and 20 rare photo cards, all of which bring back the nostalgia and excitement of old school, big time movie promotion.

CHRISTMAS CLASSIC

HOLIDAY INN—This classic Bing Crosby/Fred Astaire/Marjorie Reynolds 1942 vehicle, about a love triangle and an inn only open on the holidays, finally gets the special edition DVD treatment. Despite a slender plot, the movie is enormously entertaining thanks to a boatload of holiday tunes from Irving Berlin, including his Oscar winner, "White Christmas." Don't get suckered in by the 1954 partial remake, *White Christmas* (with Danny Kaye and Rosemary Clooney along with Bing), which isn't nearly as good as *Inn*. The special edition comes with commentary and featurettes along with a CD of songs from the soundtrack that is sure to please every fan of this joyous little confection. If you're looking for a great DVD holiday gift, either for yourself or a friend, remember, *Inn* is in.

YEAR END ROUNDUP
(December 2008)

Some might say that as we look back on 2008, cinematically it has been a lesser year. That is the hue and cry that seems to be raised every year when an assessment is made prior to the really big guns being released. One forgets that in many cases the Oscar-worthy films don't arrive until the Christmas holiday is over (after a perfunctory limited release to qualify for 2008). So, while we've already had such serious first rate contenders as *The Dark Knight; WALL*E; The Changeling; Rachel Gets Married; W; Milk* and *Synecdoche, New York*, still waiting in the wings are *Revolutionary Road* re-teaming *Titanic* couple Kate Winslet and Leonardo DiCaprio; *Marley & Me*, based on John Grogan's bestseller; *Doubt* starring Oscar powerhouse Meryl Streep; *Valkyrie* with Tom Cruise as a Nazi; *The Wrestler* a Venice film festival winner starring Mickey Rourke in what many are calling the comeback story of the decade; Edward Zwick's war drama *Defiance* with Daniel Craig; *Gran Torino*, a study of racism directed by and starring Clint Eastwood and *The Curious Case of Benjamin Button*, a reverse-aging drama based on an F. Scott Fitzgerald story starring Brad Pitt and directed by David (*Zodiac*) Fincher. And, as always, there will be a few interesting films that no one saw coming which will surprise us all. I guarantee that this time next year we'll be wondering why the films of 2009 aren't as good as those from 2008. And we'll be just as wrong then, too.

NEW IN THEATRES

FROST/NIXON—One of the highlights of the post-Nixon era was when our fallen ex-president (he resigned from office rather than face impeachment hearings over the Watergate scandal) sat down in 1977 for a one-on-one interview with TV personality, David Frost. Frank Langella (who first came to fame back in the 1970s in the stage and screen versions of *Dracula*) manages to embody Nixon without ever resorting to mimicry, while Michael Sheen (best known for his remarkable portrayal of Tony Blair in *The Queen*) does an equally masterful job as Frost. The script (by Peter Morgan, adapted from his own stage play) pits the two characters against each other in a cinema verite filming style that suggests a prize fight confrontation. Director Ron Howard, who came of age during the Nixon administration, handles the material with a knowing sensibility. While the script takes some fictional liberties for the sake of drama, the essentials of the truth remain intact. Now that we have a new Democratic president replacing what many feel was a corrupt and incompetent Republican regime, there is no better time than now to revisit the sins of the Nixon White House years.

NEW ON DVD

MAMMA MIA—It's hard to kick a film that wears its cheese so lovingly on its sleeve, which is one way of saying that the screen version of the ABBA-inspired stage musical isn't high art but it is more entertaining than it should be. Chief amongst its assets are those infectious ABBA tunes with their hook-laden, disco-pop frivolities that never-the-less seem to have a deeper meaning beneath their swirling, upbeat arrangements. The girl-friendly story of a daughter (Amanda Seyfried) who invites her mother's three old flames (Pierce Brosnan, Colin Firth and Stellan Skarsgard) to her upcoming wedding, hoping to find out which one is dear old dad, provides the necessary tension to keep you interested, but it's a fragile framework to be sure. The pleasure of this film resides in the music and the go-for-broke attitude of the cast who appear to be having the time of their lives and act as if they have nothing to lose by hamming it up to the hilt. At times it all seems a bit rough around the edges, but with Meryl Streep joyfully slumming it as "mamma," and Julie Walters and Christine Baranski along for support, you are likely to forgive any shortcomings as you get caught up in the manic energy everyone generates. There is a reason the members of ABBA are gajillionaires; they made some of the most giddy/friendly pop tunes in history, guilty pleasure or not.

CHRISTMAS CLASSIC

A CHRISTMAS STORY—A classic that gets better with each passing year, this edgy, yet warm look at a family in 1940s America, directed by Bob (*Porky's*) Clarke, is based on humorist Jean Shepherd's autobiographical book, "In God We Trust, All Others Pay Cash." The story revolves around little Ralphie (a terrific Peter Billingsley) who, more than anything else, wants a Red Ryder B-B gun for Christmas. Narrated by Shepherd in the gauzy haze of a first- person reminiscence, the film clearly evokes a simpler time when the worst one could imagine in owning an air rifle was the possibility of shooting your eye out if you weren't careful. However, the movie is anything but sentimental as the tone suggests the slyness of a child who must cope with all manner of inanities from schoolyard bullies to parental idiosyncrasies. The top notch cast includes veterans Darren McGavin and Melinda Dillon who perfectly inhabit their roles as Ralphie's parents. Ironically, the film, which did only middling business upon its 1984 release, has gone on to achieve full cult status and launched an industry of tie-in merchandise, including the infamous leg lamp. A new "Ultimate Collector's Edition" DVD has just been released in a commemorative tin case which contains an extras-loaded two-disc set and an apron in case you plan to cook your own holiday turkey.

THE BIG CHEESE

TROLL/TROLL 2—What can you say about a film in which Sonny Bono morphs into a landscape? That's just one of the many puzzles you'll face when you watch this 1986 low budget stinker. A quirky couple (Michael Moriarty and Shelley Hack, obviously in need of a paycheck), move into a new apartment complex with their young son and daughter (*NeverEnding Story*'s Noah Hathaway and cute-as-a-button newcomer Jenny Beck). After the girl wanders into the basement she meets a sinister looking troll who takes her place. His plan is to turn each apartment into a troll world inhabited by slimy troll puppets. (Oooh-kay.) *WKRP*'s Gary Sandy, a pre-*Seinfeld* Julia Louis-Dreyfus, the aforementioned Mr. Bono and *Lost in Space*'s June Lockhart, all hamming it up heartily, play the apartment residents. The film makes very little sense and was obviously an excuse for director John Buechler (a special effects man) to have at it with cheesy effects. Less understandable is how he lured his cast to partake in this nonsense. Hack, at least, would fare better the following year in *The Stepfather*, a nifty shocker starring *Lost*'s Terry O'Quinn. As bad as *Troll* is, however, it's practically *Citizen Kane* compared to the 1991 sequel, which aside from the title has no relation to (and even less of a budget than) the original. Nothing I can say will prepare you for the rank amateur nature of this lamest of sequels, from the high school drama class bad acting of its no name cast, who are forced to spout some real howlers, to the very pedestrian lighting and editing style of the filmmakers (and I use the term loosely) themselves. The film has inexplicably gained a dubious cult following on the Internet, somewhat akin to those other grade Z productions, *Plan 9 From Outer Space* and *Manos: The Hands of Fate*.

FEEDING THE AWARDS SEASON BEAST
(February 2009)

With the Golden Globes behind us and the Oscars dead ahead, now is a good time to assess which films from 2008 stand above the rest. Both *Slumdog Millionaire* and *The Wrestler* have proven to be surprise hits with critics and moviegoers, alike. *Doubt* and *Frost/Nixon* have shown that stage plays can be transformed into compelling movies, while *Revolutionary Road* and *The Curious Case of Benjamin Button* remind us that literary adaptations can also be successfully mounted. *The Dark Knight* and *WALL*E* each took a second-class genre (comic books and animation) and delivered first-class entertainment which were both financially successful and artistically respectable. The range of subject matter for the best picks of 2008 has been truly eclectic, from female-themed stories, *Rachel Getting Married; The Reader; Happy-Go-Lucky,* to gay rights, *Milk,* documentaries, *Man on Wire; Waltz With Bashir; The Class,* and even comedy, *Tropic Thunder* and *Burn After Reading*. Finally, there were some low-key winners—*The Visitor; Synecdoche, NY; Tell No One*—that might have escaped your notice. In most cases, however, an Oscar or Golden Globe win is merely a transient victory, providing an economic windfall to a studio's bottom line. The real test of validation on this (or any) year's crop of cinematic self-congratulation is whether or not we'll still be talking about them ten years down the line.

NEW IN THEATRES

THE PERVERT'S GUIDE TO CINEMA—Don't let the provocative title scare you off; this clever little documentary by Sophie Fiennes (sister of actors Ralph and Joseph) invitingly explores the Freudian underpinnings of a number of classic films by Chaplin, the Marx Brothers, Hitchcock and David Lynch, to name only a few. Our guide through cinema's id is Slovenian philosopher, Slavoj Zizek, who presents his psychoanalytic argument on films ranging from *The Wizard of Oz* to *The Birds*; and from Coppola's *The Conversation* to Lynch's *Lost Highway,* occasionally at the actual locations where they were shot. This "you are there" aspect adds enormously to the film's entertainment value, giving one the impression of the best college course field trip ever. Currently in limited release in New York, there's no way of knowing when or if this tantalizing flick will make its way here. If you do get to see it, one thing's for sure—you'll never look at your favorite classic movies in the same way.

NEW ON DVD

VICKY CRISTINA BARCELONA—Writer/Director Woody Allen continues his love affair with European locations (his last three films were set in England and Ireland) with this tale of amorous love in the titular Spanish city. Two young Americans, Vicky and Cristina (Rebecca Hall and Scarlett Johansson), become romantically involved with Juan, a seductive artist (Javier Bardem) and his sexy, hot-blooded ex (Penelope Cruz). While the libertine qualities of the story may seem a bit much to the more bourgeois of us, the writing is still witty and the performances (especially Bardem and Cruz) are great. Besides that, there's also all that great Spanish scenery to drink in. It doesn't hurt, either, that the film took a Golden Globe for best comedy.

BRIDESHEAD REVISITED—It took a lot of gumption to do this theatrical remake of the beloved 1982 TV version of Evelyn Waugh's classic novel, but the filmmakers acquit themselves nicely. Starring Haley Atwell, Matthew Goode, Ben Whishaw and Emma Thompson, the story of two young men from different social classes and the complex relationship they share with each other and the one man's sister makes for riveting entertainment. Though not nearly as long as the 11-hour TV miniseries, this theatrical version stands on its own as a more compact retelling of Waugh's tale. As in the earlier version, Castle Howard is again called into service to play the eponymous estate. The DVD also has a serviceable commentary track for those who appreciate such things.

CLASSIC CORNER

L.A. CONFIDENTIAL—A true classic of modern cinema that had the unfortunate luck, Oscar-wise, to come out in the same year as *Titanic*. The film version of James Ellroy's fifties-era crime novel did take home Oscars however for adapted screenplay and supporting actress (Kim Basinger), and garnered numerous other accolades and awards. The movie boasted a terrific cast of then up-and-coming Aussie actors Russell Crowe and Guy Pearce (doing flawless American accents), Kevin Spacey (fresh off his Oscar win in *The Usual Suspects*), plus Basinger and Danny DeVito adding star power to the mix. The real beauty of the film is how director Curtis Hanson was able to evoke the film noir era without ever pandering to the stereotypical mustiness of nostalgia. By not putting the period in parentheses, the movie remains contemporary and timeless. A new, two-disc special edition DVD offers a much appreciated upgrade to the previous release, including new featurettes about the film, and an enjoyable commentary track with cast and crew (excepting Hanson, curiously), revealing their pride in working on this project. An added plus is a TV pilot for a proposed series, starring Kiefer Sutherland, which never took off.

THE BIG CHEESE

TRISTRAM SHANDY: A COCK & BULL STORY—Actor/comedian Steve Coogan and director Michael Winterbottom, who previously collaborated on *24 Hour Party People*, decide to have a go at Laurence Stern's "unfilmable" post-modern 18th century novel. Comment on the period's mores is derived by having the film be about filming the story, jumping back and forth between dramatized scenes from the book and fictionalized contemporary scenes of the filmmakers as they shoot the movie within the movie. The result is sort of like *The French Lieutenant's Woman* meets *Barry Lyndon*, but with as much emphasis on celebrity as on literature. Co-stars include Rob Brydon, Jeremy Northam, Kelly MacDonald and Gillian Anderson. The savvy cineaste will delight in the score which is appropriated from other period films like *The Draughtsman's Contract*, *Amarcord* and *Barry Lyndon*. Closing credit watchers are treated to a conversation between Coogan and Brydon (as their actor counterparts) who engage in a hilarious "Dueling Pacino's" bit that will have you on the floor. Equally entertaining is the commentary track with these two men who obviously had a lot of fun making the movie.

THE STANLEY KUBRICK LEGACY
(March 2009)

Hard to believe, but this month marks the 10th anniversary of Stanley Kubrick's untimely death. The famed film director, who created such innovative works as *Dr. Strangelove, 2001: A Space Odyssey* and *A Clockwork Orange*, died at 70 of an apparent heart attack in March 1999 after completing what would be his final feature, the Tom Cruise/Nicole Kidman erotic thriller, *Eyes Wide Shut*. Known for his perfectionist bent and long, secretive film shoots, Kubrick has left a legacy of unique movies the like of which will never be seen again. Luckily for the world of cinema there are a number of filmmakers who have, to various degrees, followed in the great director's footsteps. Visual stylists like Ridley Scott, the Coen brothers and Terry Gilliam; techno wizards like James Cameron, David Fincher and Peter Jackson; and intellectual dramatists like Paul Thomas Anderson, Christopher Nolan and Darren Aronofsky are just some of the better-known talents poised to assume Kubrick's awesome mantle. In the decade since he passed, Kubrick's reputation has continued to grow as critics and scholars, alike, pore over his baker's dozen oeuvre for a deepening insight into his quirky genius. His personal cinematic style has become akin to that of Hitchcock and Welles, characteristically recognizable and equally idiosyncratic to even the casual filmgoer. And like those iconic filmmakers, Kubrick's place in the pantheon of cinema greats is secure. One can only hope that the ensuing decade sees that legacy thrive.

NEW IN THEATRES
WATCHMEN—Thanks to recent successes in the comic book movie genre like *Iron Man* and *The Dark Knight*, Zack (*300*) Snyder's adaptation of Alan Moore's ambitious 1986 graphic novel (considered by many to be the pinnacle of long-form comic books), is now being awaited with intense anticipation, especially by hardcore comic fans. A dense and layered examination of the superhero ethos, where moral dilemmas abound and characters wrestle not only with their own consciences, but with their overlapping relationships to each other, as well. The murder of a superhero (in the story's 1980s alternate universe where Nixon is still president!) is the catalyst for intrigue and distrust among the other costumed crusaders as we learn the backstory of their glorious past and eventual fall from grace. Solid character actors Billy Crudup (*Big Fish*), Patrick Wilson (*Hard Candy*), Matthew Goode (*Match Point*) and Jackie Earle Haley (*Little Children*) help lend gravitas to what is otherwise a bunch of borderline head cases wearing crazy outfits. A slew of other filmmakers have tried to get this project off the ground over the years, Terry Gilliam, Paul Greengrass and Darren Aronofsky

among them, but it is Snyder's version that has won the day. If it is half as good as the comic, prepare to be amazed.

NEW ON DVD

RACHEL GETTING MARRIED—Actress Anne Hathaway secured a best acting nomination for her raw, honest portrayal of a black sheep sibling who attends her sister's wedding. Director Jonathan Demme, who has turned in some Oscar-calibre work of his own (*Silence of the Lambs, Philadelphia*) shows that he's still got the goods, even if this movie did get passed over in the best picture department. (As I write this the Oscars have not yet been given out, but Kate Winslet is expected to take home the prize for *The Reader*.) Regardless of who wins, Hathaway is proving to be a force to be reckoned with, thanks to her strong work in *The Devil Wears Prada* and *Brokeback Mountain*. Along with this latest, it's almost enough to make you forgive her for this year's *Bride Wars*.

CLASSIC CORNER

MISHIMA: A LIFE IN FOUR CHAPTERS—The life of noted Japanese author Yukio Mishima who, at the height of his fame, committed ritual suicide in 1970, is the grist for this extraordinary 1985 film. Director Paul Schrader (*American Gigolo, Cat People*) employs a formalized structure, which rivals anything Kubrick or Hitchcock ever did, by breaking up the narrative into four acts (beauty; art; action; harmony of pen and sword), each of which uses three separate filming styles. Mishima's last day is chronicled in a hand-held documentary format while episodes from his childhood and early adult life are shown in crisp black and white. Finally, three of his novels are adapted as dramatizations on highly-stylized theatrical sets rendered in rich, saturated color schemes. The blending of these elements, tied together with Philip Glass' amazing score, effortlessly captures the essence of the creative drive and how it is bound up in an artist's own nature. A new two-disc DVD from Criterion includes a digitally-remastered director's cut with new commentary by Schrader, featurettes about the film and an hour-long BBC documentary on Mishima, made in 1985, with rare archival interviews with the author.

THE BIG CHEESE

BE KIND REWIND—French filmmaker Michel Gondry has a talent for zeroing in on the emotional heart of whatever subject he chooses to film, be it the unconscious world of our dreams in *The Science of Sleep,* the vast, ever-changing landscape of memory in *Eternal Sunshine of the Spotless Mind*, or here where he explores our love affair with movies and how they can inform our modern folklore as a form of expression. When a small, rundown, storefront business is threatened with demolition to make way for an upscale, modern establishment, efforts by the young clerk (Mos Def) and his ne'er do well buddy (Jack Black) lead to the accidental erasing of the store's VHS rental tapes. They attempt to cover up the catastrophe by making their own 20-minute versions of several of the movies (*Ghostbusters, RoboCop, Rush Hour 2*) and create instant classics for the neighborhood. In metaphoric terms, the remaking of these films (in an obsolete format, no less) becomes the retelling of our collective myths which are handed down through the generations. The notion of looking back, which is inherent in the title, finds full flower when the neighborhood bands together to make a no-frills documentary based on an apocryphal event connected to the store's location. The skills learned in making the cheesy little movies end up being enormously useful in the making of this new "myth." Gondry and company employ some very clever techniques to pull off their zero budget knock-offs which include some hilarious recreations of famous, iconic moments from such films as *King Kong, 2001,* and *Men in Black.* This isn't just cheese, it's cheese whiz!

UNTITLED

(April 2009)

If April showers bring May flowers, they also bring the first real films of the year prior to the onslaught of the summer movie season. While February and March saw the release of the hugely imaginative stop-motion animated *Coraline* and the highly-anticipated *Watchmen*, respectively, April has its share of "must-see" releases including *17 Again* starring Zac Efron and Matthew Perry in the latest version of the "adult turning into a child" story; the numerology thriller, *Knowing* with Nicolas Cage and directed by Alex (*Dark City*) Proyas; the Jason Statham action flick *Crank High Voltage* and the live action version of the manga favorite, *Dragonball: Evolution* with Chow Yun-Fat. None of this stuff is particularly highbrow, mind you, but that is generally the case for the first three-fourths of the year. Until the fall gets here in six months, 90 percent of the movies that are given a wide release are going to be at this level. But that doesn't mean you can't have a good time anyway.

NEW IN THEATRES

STATE OF PLAY—A shaggy-haired Russell Crowe plays a tough-guy crime reporter investigating an assassination attempt in this edgy drama (based on the British series) directed by Kevin Macdonald. Rachel McAdams, Helen Mirren and Ben Affleck provide solid support as they square off opposite the awesome Aussie. As he proved in his harrowing mountain climbing documentary feature, *Touching the Void* (2003), the Scottish Macdonald is a passionate, innovative filmmaker who brings quite a bit to the table. Given the calibre of the cast, expectations are running high for this film to deliver the goods.

NEW ON DVD

SYNECDOCHE, NEW YORK—This one's a real head-scratcher, written and directed by Charlie Kaufman, who has previously teased our subconscious with scripts for *Being John Malkovich, Eternal Sunshine of the Spotless Mind* and *Adaptation*. The title, pronounced "sin-neck-doe-key" (a deliberate riff on the town of Schenectady where the main character lives), is a figure of speech in which a part of something stands in for the whole, as in "all *hands* on deck" where the hands represent the entire person. Here, the story concerns Caden Cotard (the brilliant Philip Seymour Hoffman), a theater director who stages a decades-in-progress play of his life, hiring hundreds of actors and building an ever-expanding full-scale replica of New York City in a humungous hangar that just happens to be smack dab in the Big Apple, itself. As his life and art seemingly merge, the play, which never gets beyond its endless series of rehearsals, becomes a metaphoric representation of his life, just as the stage set is the synecdoche of the city. And through the process of telling Cotard's story the film examines the nature of mortality and the desire we all harbor for our lives to have meaning. As in Kaufman's previous work, a strong thread of absurdist intent is woven into the fabric of the story, and here, perhaps, maybe even becomes the fabric. The supporting cast includes Catherine Keener, Samantha Morton and Tom Noonan, all of who turn in stellar performances. The impenetrable nature of the script may be off-putting for some, but for those willing to wrap their heads around it, the rewards can be plentiful. Either way, you are not likely to see a stranger film this side of David Lynch.

CLASSIC CORNER

FUNNY FACE—This classic Gershwin musical about a fashion photographer (Fred Astaire) who turns a fresh, young salesgirl (Audrey Hepburn) into a chic, high fashion model, has lost none of its charm since it was first released in 1957. Written by Leonard Gershe and based on anecdotes from Vogue editor, Diana Vreeland about famed photographer Richard Avedon and his wife, Doe, who had been a model, it seemed to be perfect material for a winning musical. Unfortunately, it languished for years until director Stanley Donen and producer Roger Edens got hold of it. The Cinderella tale was then beautifully realized by Donen, who used a striking color palette to create a highly stylized look and, along with the memorable songs, lush cinematography and winning performances, combined to make for one unforgettable "*Face*."

THE BIG CHEESE

11:14—This first feature film from young director Greg Marcks proves to be a highly confident exercise in stylish hokum. A series of disconnected events involving a corpse among a disparate collection of low-class denizens are shown as they intersect and overlap at the titular late-night hour. However, there is a deeper subtext at work here which is not that obvious upon a first viewing. Beneath its white trash veneer the story, such as it is, carries an existential motif about the innate randomness of fate and the connection between seemingly disconnected parties. Despite its miniscule budget a surprisingly robust ensemble cast was put together, including Hilary Swank, Patrick Swayze, Henry Thomas, Colin Hanks, Barbara Hershey and Rachel Leigh Cook. Writer/director Marcks cites the Coen brothers as a prime inspiration for the film's quirky style (notably *Blood Simple*), but the structural hand and pulpy residue of Quentin Tarantino is also present, as well as a nod to Jim Jarmusch's *Mystery Train*, whether intentional or not. As in those directors' films, the characters are often difficult to relate to, due to their crass and/or inept nature. To his credit, Marcks admits in the entertaining commentary track that the antics of one such group—the boneheaded, teen jerkwads in the van—are largely autobiographical. By no means a great film, but certainly entertaining, and one that hints at potentially better fare down the line.

THE BLOCKBUSTER PARADOX
(May 2009)

With the Oscar season behind us and the summer blockbuster season poised before us, we are faced with the inevitable schism between art and commerce wherein it seems that the dumbest films invariably make the most money. While this situation is not confined to the summer months alone (just look at what the top grossing films are for any week), it just seems more noticeable at this time. It is truly a sad state of events when a film as completely empty and stupid as *Transformers* makes more money than all the Oscar nominated best picture films combined. There was a time when audiences made hits out of films with substance like *Lawrence of Arabia, The Godfather* and, yes, even *Titanic*. It still happens, but far too much schlock is making far too much money for us to be anything but ashamed. Entertainment should not be a mindless pursuit. Having your mind stimulated should not be looked upon as a hindrance to enjoyment. Think about that before you plunk down your money to see *Transformers 2*. We can do better than that.

NEW IN THEATRES

STAR TREK—It was forty years ago that the original *Star Trek* TV series was cancelled (due to low ratings) but instead of disappearing into the night, it went on to become a cult phenomenon when it took off like a starship in warp drive through syndication. Since then, the *Star Trek* franchise has spawned ten theatrical movies and numerous TV series spin-offs which have run the gamut from occasionally great to mostly mediocre. Now, thanks to J.J. Abrams' new reboot, it's time for *Star Trek* to be great again. The creator of such hit TV shows as *Alias* and *Lost* turns his attention to the saga of Kirk, Spock and the starship Enterprise in what looks to be the sci-fi event of the year. Opting for an origin story in which we learn how the characters from the original show came together, we follow James T. Kirk (Chris Pine) and Mr. Spock (Zachary Quinto from *Heroes*) through their days at Starfleet Academy, picking up Dr. McCoy (Karl Urban), Scotty (Simon Pegg) and Uhura, Sulu and Chekov along the way. Meanwhile, Eric (*Munich*) Bana weighs in as a nasty Romulan villain to help complicate matters. While Abrams has supposedly tinkered with the series' backstory, somewhat (the series and movies had inconsistencies anyway), he believes the fans will not be unduly upset. For what it's worth, the original Mr. Spock, Leonard Nimoy, who has an extended cameo, has given the new film his blessing. A second film is already in the planning stages which would seem to indicate that, as Mr. Spock's aphorism states, this franchise will live long and prosper.

NEW ON DVD

*THE READER—In a year of top flight Oscar-nominated movies, this was the one that gave *Slumdog Millionaire* the biggest run for its money. It didn't win best picture, but it did give Kate Winslet her first win as best actress, beating out Meryl Streep from *Doubt*, among others. The story about a woman who has an affair with a young man (David Cross) during the Nazi era, only to be tried as a war criminal a decade later, was directed by Stephen Daldry and adapted by David Hare, the team who brought us *The Hours* in 2002. Like that earlier film, there is a shifting between timeframes, where the adult version of the young lover (Ralph Fiennes), now a lawyer, attempts to intervene on behalf of Winslet. While the steamy sex scenes lend the film its notoriety, it is the handling of the collective nature of Germany's guilt about the Holocaust which provides the audience with something even more provocative to contemplate.

CLASSIC CORNER

*THE GRAPES OF WRATH—Based on the classic John Steinbeck novel of the same name (published in 1939 and celebrating its 70th anniversary) about Depression-era tenant farmers traveling to California in search of work, this 1940 film, directed by John Ford and starring Henry Fonda, seems more relevant than ever given our country's current economic plight. The book created a huge uproar when it was released, with its raw (for the time) language and depiction of moneyed interests squeezing the disenfranchised, and was actively banned in several states. However, the story of the Joad family's journey along Route 66— "The Mother Road"—in search of a better life, caught on with the public in a big way. Even so, it was brave for a studio like 20th Century Fox to take on such controversial material at that time and do it without significantly watering down its message; ironic, too, given that the funding came from the very banking industry that was portrayed so harshly in the story. One of the standout pleasures in watching this film comes from the awesome black & white cinematography (unaccountably not nominated for an Oscar) of Gregg Toland which depicts everything from hot, dusty desert days to cool night interiors where faces swathed in shadow peak out of the darkness, lit by a single candle. Toland would shoot *Citizen Kane* with Orson Welles the following year, outdoing his work here and at least garnering a nomination for his effort. Also of note is John Carradine as a Christ-like former preacher named Casy (his initials are J.C.) who is a friend of the Joads. The DVD extras include a lively commentary with scholars Joseph McBride and Susan Shillinglaw in which, at one point, they engage in a lengthy dispute over director Ford's complex political leanings, plus a documentary on producer Zanuck; president Roosevelt's comments at the 1941 Academy Awards where *Grapes* took home Oscars for best actress (Jane Darwell as Ma Joad) and best director (John Ford); three Movietone News dustbowl drought reports from 1934, and more.

THE BIG CHEESE

THE STARLOST—This Canadian sci-fi series from 1973 about a giant space ark made up of domed worlds where the inhabitants are unaware they are on a spaceship, now looks hopelessly dated. Made on the cheap, it was shot on video with bland lighting in front of blue-screened backdrops, along with a few uninspired sets made of vac-u-formed plastic. Created by legendary sci-fi author and industry gadfly, Harlan Ellison (who was so embarrassed he used his alias, "Cordwainer Bird") and Douglas Trumbull (the special effects whiz behind *2001* and *Silent Running*), it's hard to believe such talent was so badly squandered. The show starred Keir Dullea who, despite the '70s hair and mustache, still retains his signature blandness which had made him so perfect as Dave Bowman in *2001*. Co-starring with Dullea are Gay Rowan and Robin Ward as his equally bland shipmates who are trying to prevent the ark from meeting a fiery fate with an approaching star. Week after week the trio goes from one dome to another (there are over 100, all interconnected, which make up the ark), meeting isolated, clueless cultures and having "adventures," though I use that term loosely, given the turgid pacing and shoddy direction. At this time, *Star Trek* reruns still dominated the sci-fi airwaves, though shows as diverse as *Search, Night Gallery* and *Kolchak* proved intelligent fantasy TV was still possible. Clearly *The Starlost* series wanted to continue this trend, but from the outset, despite its high-minded intent, it was hampered by poor production values and a misguided notion about what constituted dramatic entertainment. Ironically, a few years later the sci-fi market would explode with the unexpected success of *Star Wars*, which completely changed the game. As such, *The Starlost* occupies a unique place in the sci-fi hierarchy of the time, falling between the highbrow intellectualism of *2001* and the populist hegemony of *Star Wars* a decade later. At a time when we were still going to the moon, sci-fi was about more than just making a buck, even if the effort was done badly.

ROARING INTO SUMMER
(June 2009)

This year the summer movie season has opened with a bang as several high-profile films have rolled out in the first wave of May. *Wolverine, Angels & Demons, Star Trek, Terminator Salvation* and *Night at the Museum* are just some of the big guns that have already fired the first volley. June promises to continue this trend with Will Ferrell in the *Land of the Lost* reboot; Sam Rockwell and Kevin Spacey in the *Twilight Zone*-ish *Moon*; *Whatever Works*, starring Larry David and directed by Woody Allen; Denzel Washington, John Travolta and James Gandolfini in Tony Scott's remake of 1974's *The Taking of Pelham 123*; John Krazinski and Maya Rudolph in Sam Mendes *Away We Go*; Michelle Pfeiffer and Kathy Bates in Stephen Frears' period drama, *Cheri*; Eddie Murphy and Thomas Haden Church in *Imagine That* and Cameron Diaz in *My Sister's Keeper* just to name a few that look to be the most interesting. At a time when the economy is so tight, it may be asking a lot of people to see more than a couple films a year, much less in any given month. However, if you have the means, this is shaping up to be a very good time to visit your local multiplex.

NEW IN THEATRES
UP—Pixar is at it again! Not content with nine blockbusters in a row, they're trying for a perfect ten with this latest, a tale of an old codger (Ed Asner) who ties a really big bunch of balloons to his house so he can sail away to South America. Directed by Pete Docter (*Monsters, Inc.*) the story appears to have all the heart and whimsy that the Pixar studios are noted for. Maybe someday this animation powerhouse will produce a clunker, but for now, they seem to have a lock on making masterpieces. So, just how big of a hit will this latest Pixar film be? Well, that depends on your definition of how high is *Up*!

NEW ON DVD
THE CURIOUS CASE OF BENJAMIN BUTTON—Though the premise of this ambitious film by David Fincher is patently ridiculous—a character ages backwards, being born as an old man and growing younger in the ensuing years—you buy into its conceit as a fable which explores the nature of existence and how that informs the main character's relationships with others. Adapted by Eric Roth (who did the same for 1994's *Forrest Gump*), the ghost of that earlier movie hangs over this one for better and for worse. Like Forrest, Benjamin functions mostly as a metaphoric stand-in for a collective belief, though here it seems to be less about American perseverance and more about the universal existential conundrum of life and aging. Water imagery plays a role as a

harbinger of both life and death, from the threat of hurricane Katrina, which runs through the contemporary framing story, to Ben's life at sea during the war, and especially to baby Ben's near drowning fate at the film's beginning. The movie is at its most *Gump*ish in its narration where Brad Pitt (doing a southern drawl) spouts nuggets of wisdom through homespun homilies that he gleaned from his adopted mama, such as "You never know what life's gonna bring" (which is clearly a cousin to Forrest's "box of chocolates" line). Roth also thought it necessary to resurrect his "I have to go pee" phrase, this time putting it into the mouth of the lovely Cate Blanchett. Well, the guy did win an Oscar for *Gump* (where he used that line again during his acceptance speech), so who am I to nitpick? But I think it's time he found some new material. On the plus side, the movie is visually stunning and won Oscars for its make-up and digital effects which are absolutely flawless. Whether or not *Benjamin* works for you, however, will depend on just how well Fincher pushes your buttons.

CLASSIC CORNER

CLEOPATRA—Nearly three decades before Elizabeth Taylor snaked her way into Richard Burton's heart in the 1963 overstuffed debacle that nearly bankrupted 20th Century Fox, legendary director Cecil B. DeMille worked his own magic on this lavishly produced epic released in 1934. Starring Claudette Colbert in the title role, with great supporting performances by Warren William, Henry Wilcoxen and Gertrude Michael, the film still holds up to a surprising degree. The black & white cinematography by Victor Milner won a much deserved Oscar, the only win of its five nominations. Its first time appearance on DVD marks the film's 75th anniversary and includes audio commentary and other extras that are fit for a Queen. It's also a revealing peak at an old time Hollywood epic by a master filmmaker in the early days of sound motion pictures.

THE BIG CHEESE

LAND OF THE LOST—This month sees the release of a big budget comedy remake of the 1970s series, so now's a good time to revisit the original which is available on DVD. The saga of the Marshall family—father Rick (Spencer Milligan), and his kids, Will and Holly (Wesley Eure and Kathy Coleman)—who plummet over some falls in their inflatable raft and end up in a strange world of cheesy stop-motion dinosaurs, low-rent ape men and lizard-like villains called "Sleestaks," is remembered fondly by those who grew up in that era. Created by Sid and Marty Krofft, who ruled Saturday mornings with such shows as *Lidsville* and *H.R. Pufnstuf*, *Land* had well-crafted, moral-laced stories beneath its low budget trappings. *Star Trek* scribe, David Gerrold ("The Trouble with Tribbles") was the story editor, here, and he brought a level of seriousness to the scripts that offset the campy, bargain basement aspects of the show. The entire series (43 episodes) is now available in a special limited edition DVD set, housed in a retro metal lunchbox, and includes interviews and commentary from the Kroffts, Gerrold and the cast that will transport you back to your childhood past, quicker than a trip over the falls.

NO-SWEAT SUMMER MOVIES
(July 2009)

The best thing about summer movies is that, for the most part, they're just for fun. That doesn't necessarily mean dumb, as *Star Trek, Up* and *The Taking of Pelham 1 2 3* have already proved. Unfortunately, finding the good stuff isn't always easy, and even the most well-informed of us have been burned by the come-on of a slick trailer. However, a little common sense should suffice in helping you make your choices. Since most people only know the films of a handful of directors, such as Steven Spielberg, Tim Burton, Peter Jackson and maybe Ridley Scott, it's a toss-up whether or not the lesser known names are any good. Thanks to the Internet, it's now easy to find out what other films a director, writer or even a producer has done before. Scan the credits of those upcoming films you're thinking of seeing and then Google the names to see what they've done. Knowledge is power, and with this info in hand you can increase your chances of enjoying a no-sweat summer at the movies.

JULY

The heart of the summer brings out the films with the biggest bang. Of the twenty or so movies slated for release this month, which include such heavy hitters as *Harry Potter, Ice Age3, Bruno* (with Sacha Baron Cohen) and *G-Force*, there are three films that look to be especially interesting. On July 1st, Johnny Depp and Christian Bale shoot up the screen in Michael Mann's John Dillinger actioner, *Public Enemies*. On the 17th, in a bit of counter programming, comes *(500) Days of Summer*, a romantic comedy starring Joseph Gordon-Levitt and Zooey Deschanel which promises to be both smart and stylish. Finally, on the 24th there's another romantic comedy, *The Ugly Truth*, with Katherine Heigl and *300*'s Gerard Butler, about a female producer who tangles with a loutish shock jock. Not unusual in this type of genre, anger gives way to passion.

AUGUST

Generally speaking, August has traditionally been the dumping ground for bad summer films with no hope of success. That point of view is changing as studios realize they can position movies with a stronger narrative drive that might play well into the early fall. With a score of releases highlighted by Meryl Streep in *Julie & Julia*, Brad Pitt in Quentin Tarantino's gloriously misspelled war flick, *Inglourious Basterds* and Dennis Quaid in *G.I. Joe*, you might also want to check out a few other lower profile choices. On the 7th, Paul Giamatti stars in *Cold Souls*, a surreal tale in the *Being John Malkovich* mold about an actor who has his soul extracted and put into cold storage. Director Ang Lee brings us a blast from the past on the 14th with *Taking Woodstock*, about America's last days of hippie innocence. On the same date comes *District 9*, a sci-fi thriller about extraterrestrials in 1980s Johannesburg, produced by *Lord of the Rings* maestro, Peter Jackson. Not a bad slate and certainly enough to hold us until the fall.

CLASSIC CORNER

MY DINNER WITH ANDRE—Written by and starring playwright/actor Wallace Shawn and theatre director Andre Gregory, this quirky classic is literally two hours of conversation (during a restaurant dinner) between the principals as they ruminate on their lives and their philosophical beliefs. At turns serious and funny, and even absurdist, it is certainly one of the most daring and unique films of its time. Like any good dinner party, however, your level of enjoyment may depend upon the company you share it with. For some, the movie may wear out its welcome before the end; for others, it is a feast to be savored. As for myself, I'm still waiting for Shawn and Gregory to extend the invitation again, since I'm more than ready for seconds.

BURIED TREASURE

SUNDAY IN THE PARK WITH GEORGE—The Pulitzer Prize-winning 1985 musical play written and directed by James Lapine with music and lyrics by Stephen Sondheim about the life of artist Georges Seurat and the creation of his painting, *La Grande Jatte*, is dazzlingly captured in this videotaped stage production starring Mandy Patinkin and Bernadette Peters; (both would work again with Lapine in the 1991 film, *Impromptu*). Through the use of an imaginative set design which employs flying flats, front and backlit scrims and an eclectic cast of characters (some real, some painted, a few of whom occasionally rise up from beneath the floor of the stage), Sondheim and Lapine brilliantly evoke the notion of artistic creation and its connection to the real world. The two-act structure covers the making of the painting and then jumps ahead one hundred years to a modern day fundraising exhibition of the work, using the same cast in new roles. It's a delight, too, to see such now-familiar faces as Charles Kimbrough (*Murphy Brown*) and Brent Spiner (*Star Trek: The Next Generation*) in supporting parts. Costuming mimics the clothing seen in the painting and is even used to comic effect, as when Seurat's mistress Dot's pregnancy is revealed by having her bustle rotate 180 degrees to her front. An included commentary track with Sondheim, Lapine, Patinkin and Peters is richly informative and entertaining as they reminisce about the production all those years ago. It is obvious that the play was a watershed moment for all of them. For those who are interested, check out the book, "Seurat and the Making of *La Grande Jatte*", from the Art Institute of Chicago which documents the creation of this pointillistic masterpiece.

THE BIG CHEESE

RIFFTRAX—The wisecracking guys from *Mystery Science Theater 3000* are at it again. Once their show was cancelled, after a nice ten year run, it appeared to be the end of a hilarious era of riffing on bad movies. But it seems you can't keep a good concept down. Writer/performers Mike Nelson, Kevin Murphy and Bill Corbett have put together a DVD series of some of the cheesiest films out there (none of which were done during their *MST-3K* days) and have given them just what they deserve. Released under the name *Rifftrax,* the titles are all top of the line, bottom of the barrel classics and include *Reefer Madness, Plan 9 From Outer Space, House on Haunted Hill, Carnival of Souls* and even the somewhat respected *Night of the Living Dead.* At ten bucks apiece, they're a bargain you won't want to pass up. For the "Misties" out there, this is like a gift from the gods. And for those who have never experienced the joy of an *MST-3K* riff session, I have only one thing to say to you: "Join us!"

BLU-RAY WAY
(September 2009)

Blu-ray is here to stay... for now, anyway. The latest DVD format has finally settled in as the next step in the home video market. As more and more people buy high-definition TVs, the increased clarity in both picture and sound of Blu-ray has allowed it to gain a tangible foothold in the industry. Even without an HD-TV, the value of BR discs is evident, due to their higher level of storage capacity which translates into better picture quality. For film buffs who are also audiophiles, it means you can also have both dts sound *and* audio commentary tracks. And studios have seriously got on board in releasing just about every new film in BR, while also stepping up on the number of classics and reissues in this new format. Some recent releases like *Unforgiven, An American in Paris* and several of the Pixar films (*A Bug's Life, Cars, Ratatouille*) have received glowing reviews, while other high profile titles (*Gladiator, Braveheart, Lord of the Rings*) are on the way. Some are predicting that this will be the last manufactured retail format before hi-def downloading and storage to a hard drive becomes the norm. For us old-timers, there is still something to be said for the notion of having a made product you can hold in your hands (like a book, say) that may hopefully keep the packaged DVD around for a while longer. But once that era is over, we may find ourselves looking back with a bit of nostalgia for the time when we were still living here in Blu-ray Way.

NEW IN THEATRES
9—An audacious animated film produced by Tim Burton and Russian filmmaker, Timur Bekmambetov (*Wanted, Night Watch*) and directed by Shane Acker, based on his Oscar-nominated short. Together they bring an atmosphere of moody, East European Gothic morbidity to this post-apocalyptic tale of ragdoll-like characters (one of whom is named "9"), dressed in burlap and sporting goggle eyewear. The film is also blessed with a voice cast to die for, including Elijah Wood, John C. Reilly, Jennifer Connelly, Crispin Glover, Martin Landau and Christopher Plummer. Whew! Fittingly, the movie's release date is 9/9/09. Not to be confused with the musical *Nine* set for release this November.

NEW ON DVD
SUNSHINE CLEANERS—The producers of *Little Miss Sunshine* evidently know a good concept when they find one. Take one quirky family, a lovable tyke and a warmhearted, yet wacky grandfather (preferably played by Alan Arkin), stir well and don't forget to put the word "sunshine" in the title. Whether by choice or

coincidence, this film does bear enough similarities to its *Little Miss* predecessor to make you wonder, but that's mostly for the better. Amy Adams (*Doubt; Julie & Julia*) plays Rose, a single mom who, along with her younger sister Nora (Emily Blunt from *The Devil Wears Prada*), operates a crime-scene clean-up business. While lacking the breezy momentum of the earlier film, the female characters, here, are especially well-drawn, thanks to Megan Holley's screenplay and Christine Jeffs' insightful direction. On the male side, Steve Zahn (*Joy Ride*) contributes his usual panache, along with Arkin, making the story both entertaining and engaging. While not quite up to the level of *Little Miss*, this *Sunshine* is still worth your time of day.

CLASSIC CORNER

REPULSION—This Roman Polanski-directed thriller (his first in English) from 1965 starred French actress Catherine Deneuve as a psychologically unbalanced, sexually repressed young woman whose grip on reality disintegrates. Working as a manicurist in a London beauty salon, her wallflower persona does little to placate the owner who gently chides her for her contradictory nature ("still biting your nails, eh?"), or to reassure her older sister with whom she lives. When sis goes off on vacation with her beau, Deneuve's character, left alone, finds that her idiosyncratic behavior soon gives way to full-blown psychosis with murderous results. The movie is moody, powerful and creepy, all in equal measure, and Deneuve, at the time, was arguably the most beautiful and desirable woman on the planet (despite her nail biting!), making her descent into madness all the more unexpected. The black & white cinematography by Gilbert Taylor (*Dr. Strangelove, A Hard Day's Night*) adds immeasurably to the movie's overall atmosphere of dread and despair. A new Criterion edition DVD includes a luminously remastered picture and a dishy commentary with Polanski and Deneuve who relate their experiences in making this masterpiece.

DVD-TV

BATTLESTAR GALACTICA THE COMPLETE SERIES—The idea of remaking a cheesy *Star Wars* knock-off show from the 1970s seemed like a joke just waiting for a punch line, but this rebooted series turned out to be not just great sci-fi, but great TV as well. Anchored by well-known names, Edward James Olmos (*Blade Runner; Stand and Deliver*) and Mary McDonnell (*Dances With Wolves; Sneakers*), the remainder of the cast was a mix of knew faces and seasoned character actors, all of whom helped lend credibility to the series. Even Richard Hatch from the original series (he played Apollo) appeared in a continuing role to lend legitimacy to the show. With grown-up storylines laced with contemporary political references, *BG* was more about social commentary than offering fan geeks collectable action figures. Now that the series is over, the entire program has been released in a limited edition mega box set covering all four seasons. That's 74 episodes on 25 discs clocking in at over 67 hours. On top of that are never-before-seen footage, featurettes, interviews and a lot more. There's even a collectable Cylon robot action figure for the fan geeks. Well, this is sci-fi after all.

THE HORROR, THE HORROR. MOVIES FOR A HALLOWEEN NIGHT
(October 2009)

When did Halloween come to be exclusively about serial killers, dismemberment and grotesquery? Especially in movies, we seem to have become a culture of slasher- driven, "torture-porn" cinema in which we worship at the altar of Freddie, Jason and Jigsaw, to name just a few of our gods of menace. While I'm not a prude (I loved *Alien, The Exorcist, An American Werewolf in London, Seven* and the first *Hellraiser*), the point is there's more to providing entertaining scares than just mindless butchery. Whether you lean toward art house fare (*The Wicker Man, Cat People, The Others*) timeless classics (*Invasion of the Body Snatchers, Psycho, Rosemary's Baby)* or modern works (*The Hitcher, Silence of the Lambs, Shallow Grave*), there is plenty of scary material out there that won't insult your intelligence.

NEW IN THEATRES
THE ROAD—Originally scheduled for release a full year ago, this post-apocalyptic tale of a man and his young son, based on the novel by Cormac McCarthy and starring Viggo Mortensen and Charlize Theron is finally hitting theatres. The reason given for the delay was the extensive digital work needed to bring about the realistic devastation through which the characters make their way. While the subject matter is grim, the book itself was a substantial hit and even garnered the all-powerful Oprah recommendation, so it has the potential for widespread appeal, not to mention significant Oscar buzz. Given that it has been a somewhat thin year for serious fare, so far, especially with Scorsese's *Shutter Island* being moved to next year, *The Road* may just be at the head of the pack come awards season.

NEW ON DVD
DRAG ME TO HELL—Just in time for Halloween is this insanely fun and nightmarish horror film from Sam Raimi. Taking a break from his big ticket *Spiderman* franchise, Raimi returns to his low budget *Evil Dead* roots (but in PG-13 mode) to show he can still deliver the goods on the cheap. Alison Lohman (*Big Fish*) plays a bank exec who incurs the wrath of a gypsy's curse when she refuses to renew the old hag's mortgage. She then spends the remainder of the film being assaulted in various and sundry ways that are vintage Raimi. For those who like their fright flick jolts with a generous dollop of humor, this is the horror show for you.

CLASSIC CORNER

THE WIZARD OF OZ—If ever there was an iconic American movie this is it. The tale of young farm girl Dorothy Gale and her adventures in the magical Land of Oz has thrilled countless generations since the publication of L. Frank Baum's book in 1900. To commemorate the 70th anniversary of the classic 1939 film which starred Judy Garland, Ray Bolger, Jack Haley and Bert Lahr, an all-new DVD box set has been released (in both regular and, for the first time, Blu-ray) that shows off the glossy Technicolor palette as never before. There are also loads of extras, from commentary and featurettes to earlier film versions that will satisfy your *Oz* urges from here to over the rainbow faster than you can say, "I'll get you, my pretty, and your little dog, too!" Take a trip down the yellow brick road with this ultimate DVD set and you'll find that those bricks aren't just yellow, they're pure gold.

HALLOWEEN TREAT

STRANGERS ON A TRAIN—There was a time when people went to see a thriller to be entertained and to have "a bit of a fright," as opposed to the current trend of splatter fest snuff porn that passes for having a good time at the movies. Director Alfred Hitchcock was the master at making lurid tales about twisted characters palatable to the mass audience. With *Strangers*, one of his best, Hitch made a truly scary movie that won't gross you out with blood and gore. Two men meet accidentally while taking a train; one, Guy (Farley Granger), is a famous tennis pro and the other, Bruno (Robert Walker), is a pampered, psychopathic momma's boy. They engage in small talk where each reveals they have someone in their life who is causing them problems. Bruno then speculates about how to commit the perfect murder by having two strangers, who have no connection to the victims, swap murders so they will not be suspected. Guy, of course, thinks Bruno is speaking hypothetically and agrees it is a good idea, if only to placate the man. Thus is set in motion a murderous plan that will tie these two strangers together.

Released in 1951, *Strangers* heralded a string of top notch thrillers by Hitchcock (*I Confess, Dial M For Murder, Rear Window, The Man Who Knew Too Much, Vertigo*) that would culminate at the end of that decade with *North By Northwest* and *Psycho*. Like all of his films, *Strangers* is well-crafted and polished to a high sheen, with several stylish and memorable Hitchcockian set-pieces that have become classics of cinema. There is the introduction of the two men where we see only their shoes as they unknowingly move toward their fated meeting with one another; the tennis match where the crowd is seen as a sea of gyrating heads shuttling back and forth except for Bruno who remains steadfast in his gaze; the amusement park murder shown as a warped reflection in an eyeglass lens and the out-of-control merry-go-round climax that still pacts a wallop. If you want to do something a little different this Halloween, buy or rent this exquisite gem of a movie (in glorious black & white, no less), snuggle up in front of the TV with a special loved one and see how an old-school fright-meister shows you how it's done. Sometimes less is more.

A MEMORABLE MOVIE CHRISTMAS
(November 2009)

While it appears as if the economic recovery is underway, albeit slowly, it has been a hard year for most of us. With the holiday movie season upon us, a trip to the multiplex is not necessarily in the cards for many who are on a budget. So while there are several good cinematic choices available this month—Wes Anderson's *Fantastic Mr. Fox*, in cheesy stop-motion animation, Disney's old school cartoon animated *The Princess and the Frog* and Rob Marshall's film version of the Broadway musical *Nine*, starring Daniel Day-Lewis, Penelope Cruz, Marion Collard, Judi Dench and Nicole Kidman, all look like winners—more than a few of us may have to settle for a trip to Blockbuster Video or await a delivery from Netflix. That's okay since the holidays should be about sharing time with family and friends. But if you do decide to treat yourself to a night out at the movies, make it an event you'll want to remember.

NEW IN THEATRES

A CHRISTMAS CAROL—A few years ago director Robert Zemeckis revolutionized the film industry with his motion capture animated version of *The Polar Express*. He continued to refine that technique with *Beowulf* in 2007. Now, he has used the lessons learned in those previous efforts to bring new life to one of the most oft-filmed and enduring stories of the Victorian era—Charles Dickens' tale of the miserly Ebenezer Scrooge and his fateful transformation of heart after interacting with a number of spirits on Christmas Eve. As in those previous efforts, there is a lot of kinetic action (Scrooge flying over Victorian London) and an incredible use of illustrative lighting to evoke a wide range of atmospheric mood from the dreadful to the joyous. Jim Carrey provides the vocal and movement performance for Scrooge as well as a number of other characters (just as Tom Hanks did for *Polar Express*), allowing him to flex his considerable range in a way not usually available to him in a single role. The technology for this type of CGI animation, which strives for a more painterly ambience, rather than strict photo-realism, has become very sophisticated in rendering even the most subtle nuances of skin tone and surface texture, which allows Zemeckis and his artistic team the means to capture the characters and backgrounds in a most evocative manner. Just check out the little hairs on Scrooge's nose! While it's hard to imagine any version of Dickens' timeless tale ever usurping the 1951 Alistair Sim classic, from the look of the preview, at least, it appears as if this *Christmas Carol* has the potential to become a modern holiday tradition.

NEW ON DVD

UP—It's hard to believe, but the talented people at Pixar Studios just keep outdoing themselves with each new film they release. Simply put, they are the Meryl Streep of animation. The quality of the design and imagery they produce is matched brilliantly by the depth of the characters they create to inhabit these worlds. That depth increased by one dimension with the introduction of 3-D technology to the Pixar canon. Their first foray into this new realm is thankfully free from the "poke you in the face" chicanery that lesser films feel the need to indulge in to keep their audience interested. Instead, Pixar chose to tell a phenomenally good story (imagine that!) about a crotchety old balloon peddler who ties a million or so of his helium-filled stock to fly off to South America to fulfill a lifelong dream. As in every Pixar film, there is much more going on than that brief description allows. *Up* has the sweeping historical insight of *Citizen Kane* and the thrilling, seat-of-your-pants adventure of *Indiana Jones*, along with their trademark emotional heart that has been a staple of this studio from day one. For those who feel movies have lost a sense of innocent wonder, all I have to say to you is pick any Pixar movie and you will be rewarded beyond your expectations.

CLASSIC CORNER

LAST YEAR AT MARIENBAD—Worshipped and reviled in equal measure, this angst-ridden piece of French surrealist existentialism is most certainly an acquired taste. However, it is also one of the moodiest and most dreamlike cinematic experiences you are likely to have this side of *Eraserhead*. The story involves a group of people at a fancy hotel chateau in Germany where one mysterious fellow (Georgio Albertazzi) approaches a French beauty (Delphine Seyrig) claiming they'd had an affair the previous year "...at Frederiksbad or perhaps at Marienbad," though the woman vehemently denies it. While this 1961 head-scratcher (written by Alain Robbe-Grillet and directed by Alain Resnais) won the grand prize at the Venice Film Festival, it also drew the ire of many film critics who felt the film's icy examination of malaise and ennui was just a bunch of hooey. The rich black & white cinematography by Sacha Vierny and creepy organ music score by Francis Seyrig add considerably to the enjoyment of this complex, ambiguous and, at times, infuriatingly obtuse motion picture. If nothing else, the film is an exploration of cinematic storytelling in which time and memory, fact and fiction, past and present are juxtaposed in a continuous Moebius-strip loop that appears to have no beginning or end. The unnamed characters (all acting in a trance-like fashion) may be in heaven, hell or somewhere else entirely. At its simplest level, the film reflected a spiritual decline that was then prevalent in modern society and which the burgeoning Art House cinema in particular understood all too well. If this sort of thing is your cup of intellectual tea, then you'll be well served. Otherwise, you'll probably just be bored to tears.

THE BIG CHEESE

GREY GARDENS—This is the HBO dramatic film, based on the Maysles brothers' 1976 documentary of the same name, about Edith and Edie Beales (aka big Edie & little Edie), blue-blooded mother and daughter who are related to Jackie Kennedy Onassis and lived in a moldering mansion in East Hampton N.Y. The film covers their heydays from the 1930s on up (in flashback) while showing their struggle to cope with life in the 1970s amid their dwindling fortunes. At the time of the documentary, the women (79 and 57) lived without heat, running water or electricity while co-habiting with numerous cats and a couple of raccoons. The Edies are brilliantly portrayed by Jessica Lange and Drew

Barrymore, each in extensive make-up to depict both the elder and youthful versions of their characters, while Jeanne Tripplehorn does a knockout turn as the iconic Jackie O, complete down to her trademark big sunglasses. While the documentary has a devout cult following, the HBO film is far more inviting in that it puts these eccentric characters into perspective so that you can better appreciate the arc of their lives.

MOVIE MAGIC UNDER THE TREE
(December 2009)

A little more than a generation ago the concept of owning movies (then on VHS) was still a bit of a novelty, and the notion of such extras as making-of featurettes and commentary tracks were rare, even in the niche laserdisc market. Since then, our culture has grown to become a media-centric entity where movie ownership is a given and even the humblest household has scores if not hundreds of home video titles in its collection. With the economy still in a somewhat low gear, many of us are counting every penny in maintaining our budget. Going out to the movies has become, for many of us, a rare treat, though there are several that look to be enjoyable big screen events this month including James Cameron's *Avatar*; Terry Gilliam's *The Imaginarium of Dr. Parnassus*, which has the late Heath Ledger's final screen performance; *Nine*, the musical starring Daniel Day-Lewis, Nicole Kidman and Penelope Cruz; and *Sherlock Holmes* with Robert Downey Jr., Jude Law and Rachel McAdams. Those on a tighter budget will have to rely on DVDs to get their movie fix. A few titles slated for home release between now and the end of January include *Julie & Julia* with Meryl Streep and Amy Adams; the 5th season of *Lost;* Johnny Depp in *Public Enemies;* Ang Lee's *Taking Woodstock;* the South African alien parable, *District 9* and the intense war drama *The Hurt Locker*. With most new releases on sale for under $20.00 and older titles available for even less, there's no reason to deny yourself or your loved ones the gift of movie magic this holiday season.

NEW IN THEATRES
UP IN THE AIR—George Clooney stars in this delectable romantic comedy by director Jason Reitman (*Thank You For Smoking, Juno*) about a corporate downsizer who makes nice with fellow air traveler, Vera Farmiga (*Orphan*). While Mr. Clooney loves to play against his movie star charisma with loopy characterizations in off-kilter fare (*Burn After Reading, The Men Who Stare at Goats*), his real strength has always been when he embraces that charm along with an equally attractive co-star, as he did in *Out of Sight* a decade ago. You can see for yourself that he's still got what it takes with this latest offering. Given Reitman's track record, this is one flight you won't want to miss.

NEW ON DVD
INGLOURIOUS BASTERDS—After the apparent misstep of his "Grindhouse" collaboration with Robert Rodriguez, the uniquely idiosyncratic Quentin Tarantino came back with a vengeance earlier this year with his Jewish revenge fantasy world war II epic starring Brad Pitt, Diane Kruger, Melanie Laurent and former Easton resident Omar Doom. However, the standout performance goes to Austrian-born Christoph Waltz as the evil "Jew Hunter" Nazi, Hans Landa. Tarantino revels in his own film savvy geekdom by sprinkling in numerous film history references and having a critical sequence take place in an old, lavish cinema. As a Cannes brat, he even has a character spout, "We're French. We respect directors in our country." In Tarantino's case, it is respect well earned.

Unfortunately, the film geek extras are a bit light. However, though there is no commentary (c'mon Quentin), there is a round table discussion about the movie with Tarantino, Brad Pitt and film critic Elvis Mitchell.

MOON—Coming in January is this fascinating, offbeat tale, written and directed by Duncan Jones (son of rocker David Bowie) and starring Sam Rockwell (*Confessions of a Dangerous Mind; Frost/Nixon*) and Kevin Spacey, about a lone astronaut stationed at a lunar base with a talking computer called GERTY as his only companion. The look and tone of the film have been compared favorably to that of Kubrick's *2001*, so for that reason alone it is a must-see. Sci-fi at the movies tends toward the juvenile for the most part, though there have been some striking exceptions (*2001, Contact, Solaris* and *Watchmen* all come to mind), so it's heartening to see another such example, here. Add in great performances by the two leads, along with an intriguing story and there's still hope for this genre. The DVD includes a making-of featurette and commentary with the director, producer, cinematographer and concept/production designers. The one thing you can be sure of is that this is no *Transformers*.

BLU-RAY WAY
HOWARDS END—The filmmaking team of producer Ismail Merchant and director James Ivory (neither of whom is British, by the way), was at the top of their game with this splendid adaptation of E.M. Forster's novel about class disparity in Edwardian England. Starring Anthony Hopkins (fresh off his Oscar win for Hannibal Lecter in *The Silence of the Lambs*), Emma Thompson, Helena Bonham Carter, Vanessa Redgrave and Samuel West as poor clerk Mr. Bast, whose livelihood and fate are thrown into disarray when his lower class path crosses that of upper crust society, the film won Oscars for best actress (Thompson) screenplay and art direction. Thompson and Hopkins would team up again for Merchant/Ivory the following year to do the equally fine *Remains of the Day*. This new Criterion edition includes several new documentary featurettes, along with a vintage 1992 one, an essay by film critic Kenneth Turan and a wistful look back at the late Ismail Merchant by Ivory.

HOLIDAY TREAT
A CHRISTMAS TALE—Directed by Arnaud Desplechin and starring the luminous Catherine Deneuve, about a woman who hosts a holiday family gathering because she needs a bone marrow transplant from a blood relative. If this sounds like Hallmark territory, fear not, but be prepared to have your preconceptions challenged about what a holiday movie should be. The movie has numerous volatile scenes between the various characters, something familiar to most of us when family members come together. The acting is impeccable and Desplechin's direction is subtle, yet nuanced, digging beneath the usual histrionics associated with such fare. The director previously worked with Deneuve in 2004 in *Kings and Queens*. If you're looking for a different kind of holiday treat this year, this heady French drama may be just the ticket.

IS THERE AN OSCAR IN THE HOUSE?
(February 2010)

As everyone has heard by now, the Motion Picture Academy has decided to open up the Best Picture category to ten films, rather than the usual five slots. This is not unprecedented, given that the Academy once had a more expansive slate of nominees during its early years. The reasoning behind this decision now is due to the perceived notion that elitist art house titles nudge out populist fare (as if that's a bad thing!). By doubling the choices the feeling is that the nominations will reflect a more eclectic selection of popular films that will translate into more viewers tuning in on Oscar night. The last time they had good ratings was in 1998 when *Titanic* swept the awards. By the time you read this the nominees will already have been chosen. Will doubling the choices diminish the cache of the award by allowing inferior works to stand alongside the best? Or will this permit some less prominent small gems a chance to find their way into the marketplace? It remains to be seen. More immediately, though, will this new ploy remedy Oscar's sagging ratings? For that, we only have to wait until March 7th to find out.

NEW IN THEATRES

DEAR JOHN—Just in time for Valentine's Day comes this romantic drama based on the novel by Nicholas (*The Notebook*) Sparks. Allentown's own Amanda Seyfried stars as Savannah, a young co-ed who meets and falls in love with stalwart soldier boy John (Channing Tatum). Their relationship is going along fine until September 11th causes him to re-enlist to help fight the war on terror. Their separation and the anxiety over wartime peril provide the grist for this particular mill. Seasoned actors Henry Thomas and Richard (*The Visitor*) Jenkins add some necessary gravitas in supporting roles. While there have been other 9/11 movies, this may be the first time the event is being used as the backdrop for a love story. Director Lasse Hallstrom (*The Cider House Rules; The Hoax*) has always had a knack for making films with interpersonal storylines, so this should be right up his alley. I'm sure the producers are all hoping lightning will strike twice and they'll have another *Notebook* to market.

NEW ON DVD

A SERIOUS MAN—Whatever goodwill the Coen brothers had with the general public after the release of their Oscar winning *No Country For Old Men* and to a lesser extent their comedic gem *Burn After Reading,* has since evaporated as they pursue their very idiosyncratic muse. Their latest offering is a quirky meditation on Jewish life which draws upon the brothers' own upbringing in 1960s middle America. A Midwestern college professor named Larry Gopnik (Michael Stuhlbarg) seeks advice from a trio of rabbis to help cope with his disintegrating life. It seems his wife has left him, his kids are out of control and his feckless, unemployed brother Arthur (Richard Kind) is camped out on the living room couch. The DVD is light on extras, as is usual with the Coen brothers, with only three short featurettes and no commentary. It's ironic that some of the best directors out there do little or nothing to promote the scholarly interest in their work. For the Coens' latest film, given its cultural and religious underpinnings, this is especially perplexing. Seriously!

BLU-RAY WAY

THE LADYKILLERS—This classic 1955 British comedy from the famed Ealing Studios, starring Alec Guinness, Herbert Lom and Peter Sellers, was directed by Alexander Mackendrick who made a name for himself with Guinness in 1951's *The Man in the White Suit* and would later make the acidic American drama *Sweet Smell of Success* with Burt Lancaster and Tony Curtis. A pack of dim bulb crooks (led by Guinness) tries unsuccessfully to "off" the kindly old landlady who stands in the way of their big time burglary scheme. If this sounds vaguely familiar it's because the Coen brothers helmed a modern remake with Tom Hanks in 2004. However, while that one has its own peculiar charm, the original is definitely the one to see. Those who only know Guinness from David Lean epics or the *Star Wars* films will be pleasantly surprised to see just how funny this "serious" actor can be. A new Blu-ray edition comes out this month packed with extras including audio commentary with film historian Philip Kemp, an introduction by filmmaker Terry Gilliam and the documentary, *Forever Ealing*, about the legendary British studio.

THE BIG CHEESE

BUCK ROGERS: 70th ANNIVERSARY—First released as a 12-chapter weekly serial in movie theatres back in 1939, this early sci-fi series directed by Ford Beebe and Saul A. Goodkind, chronicled the adventures of the intrepid comic book space hero Buck Rogers as he battled against the evil forces of the tyrannical Killer Kane. Starring Larry "Buster" Crabbe as Buck (Crabbe had also starred in the similar 1936 serial *Flash Gordon*), Constance Moore as Wilma Deering and Jackie Moran as Buck's jovial sidekick Buddy Wade, this "on the cheap" production (sets, props, acting and special effects were all rudimentary, at best) still managed to be thrilling and fun to watch. Viewed today the Art Deco production design, though obviously dated, remains spacey and futuristic, and the cliffhanger endings are mostly effective. While there weren't any romantic sparks generated between the two lead characters, attractive as they were, there was plenty of the other kind coming out of the spaceship models as they sputtered and dangled on their clearly visible wire rigs. In spite of all that, there's still a great deal of enjoyment to be had in revisiting this simpler era's take on the evils of fascism made when the world faced the truly evil reign of Hitler's Nazi regime.

TEN LITTLE OSCAR NOMS
(March 2010)

What is one to make of the ten nominations for Best Picture in this year's Academy Awards? The idea was to open up the top category to a larger number of titles so as to include some smaller films (*An Education*) as well as big budget entertaining ones (*Star Trek*) which otherwise wouldn't have a chance of being recognized. To a certain extent it worked, though it was Pixar's *Up* rather than *Star Trek* that benefited. However, if you take the five directorial nominations and line them up with the ten for Best Picture, it becomes obvious that the remaining ones are simply also-ran Prom attendees without a date, and have little chance of generating serious consideration. For most handicappers the choice this year comes down to either *Avatar* or *Hurt Locker*, though I wouldn't rule out *Up in the Air* or *Inglourious Basterds* by any means. In the case of *Precious*, it is just happy to be included at the Prom. Some feel *Avatar* could suffer from a Cameron backlash (it's the only nominated movie to not get a writing nod) and that *Locker* is simply too bleak for a Best Picture win though everyone seems to feel director Kathryn Bigelow is a cinch for her slot. Whatever the case, it appears as if this year's Oscar show will be a real horse race with plenty of nail-biting tension. Though I'm writing this before the telecast on March 7th, many of you won't read this until it's all over. One thing is certain though, it appears as if the Oscars are back.

NEW IN THEATRES
ALICE IN WONDERLAND—It is hard to think of a better stylistic fit than the gothic eccentricities of director Tim Burton and the florid, trippy writings of the Reverend Charles Dodgson (aka: Lewis Carroll). Rather than doing another standard film adaptation of the Carroll classic, Burton has elected to do a sequel story so that his Alice (played by 19-year old Mia Wasikowska) can be older and also to beef up the Mad Hatter role (essayed exquisitely by Johnny Depp). Taking advantage of digital manipulation technology, Burton has warped and twisted his live action cast (which include Helena Bonham Carter as the Red Queen and Matt Lucas as both Tweedle Dum and Dee) making them appear as if they had been photographed through a funhouse mirror. Other big names who lend their support) some as full-on CGI characters) are Crispin Glover (Knave of Hearts), Anne Hathaway (White Queen) Christopher Lee (Jabberwock), Michael Sheen (White Rabbit) and Alan Rickman (Caterpillar). Whether this new version will have the good Reverend spinning in his grave or smiling a Cheshire-like grin of approval from the great beyond is anyone's guess.

NEW ON DVD
PRECIOUS—This year's "little film that could" boasts fine acting and directing in a searing tale of an overweight, illiterate teen (Gabourey Sidibe) who is pregnant with her second child (by her father!) and gets little comfort from her mother (Mo'Nique). A glimmer of hope appears when the girl is invited to enroll in an alternative school where her life can head in a new direction. The movie's

stature as an Oscar nominee will certainly give it a high profile in the home video marketplace, especially if it wins in any of its six categories. Its strongest chance for Oscar gold is Mo'Nique's brave supporting actress performance. Director Lee Daniels is a real up and comer, who previously produced, directed and appeared in the 2005 assassin thriller, *Shadowboxer*, which starred Cuba Gooding, Jr. and Helen Mirren. With *Precious*, he has entered the ranks of the big time. The DVD comes with audio commentary by Daniels, making of featurettes, a conversation between author Sapphire and Daniels, Gabourey Sidibe's screen test and more.

BLU-RAY WAY

TOY STORY 1 & 2—"To infinity and beyond!" More than a simple catchphrase, those words have come to define Pixar studio's success since their first feature was released fifteen years ago. The "ten-hit wonder" studio is poised to make it eleven this May with the third installment of the *Toy Story* franchise (in 3-D no less), so what better time than now to release the first two (also in 3-D of course!) on the Blu-ray format? Pixar's love affair with Blu-ray has paid off handsomely for consumers as, one by one, the studio has offered up its digital work in stunningly superior transfers that are a true testament to the scope of their talent. For those who can't wait for the inevitable three-pack this Christmas, *TS 1 & 2* are now available loaded with the extras that Pixar typically lavishes on their Blu-ray releases. Add to that the visual and audio splendor inherent in this format and you have an upgrade you can't afford to be without.

CLASSIC CORNER

DREAMCHILD—For those who can't get enough Wonderland in their diet, there is this darkly beautiful gem, directed by Gavin Millar in 1985, about the Reverend Charles Dodgson (a brilliant Ian Holm) and his intensely devoted relationship to Alice Liddell, the young girl who was the inspiration for the "Alice in Wonderland" stories. In 1932 the 80-year old Alice (Coral Browne) travels by ocean liner to New York to attend a special 100th anniversary celebration of Dodgson's birth. Upon her arrival in the Big Apple, the old woman finds herself the center of attention by reporters who want to know why Dodgson wrote the book for her. The past relationship between the author and child that led to the creation of the tale is revealed in what appear to be memory-laden flashbacks. More disturbing are the nightmarish dream sequences in which the Wonderland characters (created by Jim Henson's Creature Shop) become the unconscious Freudian embodiment of Dodgson's desires and the grown-up Alice's own fears. These scenes, presented in the pre-CGI era of live effects, give the film a singularly stirring quality that compliments the heady script written by Dennis Potter. A full generation before *Persepolis, Coraline* and *Where The Wild Things Are* redefined what constituted a children's film, Millar and Potter went down the rabbit hole first and came out the other side with this haunting work of cinematic art.

APRIL SHOWERS BRING DVD FLOWERS
(April 2010)

Once the Oscars are over, a curious thing occurs—a lot of really good movies suddenly appear on DVD. All those year-end flicks vying for Oscar gold now must move on to the home video market. Whether it's a crowd pleaser like *Sherlock Holmes,* the horror thriller *The Collector,* art house crossovers like *The Young Victoria* and Peter Jackson's *The Lovely Bones* or a bona fide blockbuster like *Avatar*, there is something for everyone. And that's just the beginning; more great films are headed to home video over the next few months. April showers bring May flowers, but they also bring good movies.

NEW IN THEATRES

DATE NIGHT—A case of mistaken identity turns a New York City married couple's night on the town into a rollicking adventure. On the surface, this *After Hours* wannabe doesn't seem like much, but when the couple in question is played by Tina Fey and Steve Carell, well, that's a comedy team worth anyone's time. The supporting cast isn't too shabby either with Mila Kunis, Mark Wahlberg, James Franco, Mark Ruffalo and Ray Liotta all pitching in to help. The director, Shawn Levy, is best known for his *Night at the Museum* films, while writer Josh Klausner cut his teeth crewing on the Farrelly Brothers comedies before writing and directing his first feature, *The 4th Floor* a decade ago. Since then he's made a living writing for the *Shrek* franchise. All the ingredients for a first rate comedy appear to be in place, here, so it really depends on just how good a script Mr. Klausner was able to concoct. Both Fey and Carell have been pretty savvy with the material they've chosen in the past, which means this is a date that's probably worth keeping.

NEW ON DVD

THE IMAGINARIUM OF DOCTOR PARNASSUS—Say what you will about iconoclastic filmmaker Terry Gilliam (*Brazil; 12 Monkeys*), the former Monty Python member has created a catalog of films which are singularly unique in their vision. This latest is no different, and even borrows liberally from the visual excesses of his own 1989 epic, *The Adventures of Baron Munchausen.* At heart, a fable of good vs. evil (with Tom Waits as the Devil against Christopher Plummer's eponymous doctor), the film is clearly a throwback to mythic storytelling. There is something of the old hippie in Gilliam as he tilts at our culture's windmills again and again in his work. Not surprising, then, that he hopes to reboot his *Don Quixote* project which fell apart a number of years ago. Of course, *Imaginarium* had its own production fiasco when co-star Heath Ledger dropped dead prior to completing his character's performance. Gilliam managed to pull off a heroic feat of legerdemain when he tapped Johnny Depp, Jude Law and Colin Farrell to take over the part, while still using the Ledger footage, a move that ended up being oddly appropriate and appeared to be integral to the original intent of the film. The DVD extras include an excellent commentary track with Gilliam and several behind-the-scenes featurettes. Imagination is in short supply with most movies these days. Gilliam's film is just the sort of "Imaginarium" moviegoers need.

BLU-RAY WAY

APOLLO 13—Houston may have had a problem, but director Ron Howard and star Tom Hanks apparently did not, when they made this pitch-perfect 1995 drama about the very real 1970 moon flight of Apollo 13 that nearly ended in disaster. For those who were alive during that time, the attention to period detail in the film is staggeringly accurate, from the clothes and hair-dos to the cars and NASA hardware which, while on display, never takes center stage away from the story, itself. The supporting cast is as good as it gets, with Kathleen Quinlan, Gary Sinise, Kevin Bacon, Bill Paxton and especially Ed Harris all turning in top notch performances. This was also the first film to use real zero gravity for some of the weightless scenes within the Apollo space capsule. This was accomplished by building the set inside a cargo plane and have it fly in a series of up and down parabolas (like a roller coaster) to simulate the effect. This bit of information and plenty more are available on the new 15th Anniversary Blu-ray edition, which carries over all of the extras from the previous DVD along with several new features. These include the U-Control on-screen pop-ups "The Apollo Era" and "Tech-splanations." For my money, though, the best extra remains the commentary track from the original DVD release with former astronaut Jim Lovell and his wife Marilyn (played in the movie by Hanks and Quinlan) who, in a truly post-modern conceit, reminisce about this very harrowing event in their lives while they watch the filmic retelling.

THE BIG CHEESE

CLASH OF THE TITANS—In the wake of the phenomenal success of *Star Wars* in 1977, stop-motion animator Ray Harryhausen, who had created a string of imaginative, low-cost adventure and sci-fi flicks with producer Charles H. Schneer in the 1950s and 1960s (*Earth vs. the Flying Saucers; Jason and the Argonauts*), found his fortunes change for the better. He and Schneer were able to get a substantial budget for their Ancient Greek action saga and to hire A-list actors like Lawrence Olivier, Maggie Smith and ... Harry Hamlin?! That's right, the future *L.A. Law* star first romped it up as Perseus, the mortal son of Zeus, in this sincere, but slightly clunky 1981 effort. Unfortunately, what had been innovative and clever back in the 1950s seemed positively quaint compared with the standards set by George Lucas two decades later. Desmond Davis' mediocre direction didn't help either. It would only be after Lucas and Spielberg had codified their successes into the mainstream of Hollywood over the ensuing years that pioneers such as Harryhausen would achieve respect and wider recognition for what they'd accomplished. So, what is the saving grace behind this failed attempt to bring the stop-motion maestro's vision into the big leagues? Surprisingly, it's the old-school animation effects. The dual-edged sword of modern-day CGI trickery is that while everything is now possible, very little of it actually has the stamp of authenticity. Harryhausen brought a sense of craftsmanship to the very real models and puppets he worked with, so that despite the limitations of the technology, he made you believe. That is the X-factor which is missing from many of today's special effects extravaganzas. The technology that brings it to us is so cold and heartless that we are no longer invested in believing what we're seeing. While the new *Clash* (out in theatres this month) may have its own virtues, I'd be willing to bet it will be minus a soul. As director Terry Gilliam (see New on DVD) once said about Harryhausen's work, when you saw it, you knew that it had been created by "someone with fingers," meaning that the human dimension was apparent. Sadly, that is mostly gone now, but the legacy of Ray Harryhausen (still alive and kicking in his eighties) is that even in a flawed effort such as this, there is still a touch of magic to be savored.

GOODBYE OSCAR, HELLO SUMMER
(May 2010)

Now that the Oscars are but a dim memory, the time has come to embrace the approaching summer movie season. May has traditionally been the precursor quake which heralds the following tsunami of June/July/August. This year is no different with two dozen films slated for May alone. The big "tent pole" flicks are very much out there this month, most notably in the videogame-inspired *Prince of Persia* with Jake Gyllenhaal and Ben Kingsley, as well as sequels to *Iron Man, Sex and the City* and *Shrek*. However, there is also some very good counter programming that is geared to appeal to the more discriminating cineastes out there, everything from documentaries *Casino Jack and the United States of Money* (about the fall of lobbyist Jack Abramoff) and *Babies* (chronicling the first year in the lives of four tykes from around the world), to dramas like *Letters to Juliet* (starring our own local sensation Amanda Seyfried) and *Mother and Child* (an absorbing meditation on motherhood starring Naomi Watts, Annett Bening and the always interesting Samuel L. Jackson). So, let the summer movies begin.

NEW IN THEATRES
ROBIN HOOD—The combination of a virile Russell Crowe and seasoned director Ridley Scott, both in top form and full action mode, is a guaranteed recipe for a hit of *Gladiator*-style proportions. Add a diverse supporting cast that includes Max von Sydow, Cate Blanchett, Matthew Macfadyen, Danny Huston, William Hurt and *The Full Monty*'s Mark Addy and you have what appears to be one of the most anticipated films of the summer. Though this is first and foremost an action flick, Scott and screenwriters Ethan Reiff and Cyrus Voris have also endeavored to mine a deeper vein than any previous adaptation of the legendary swashbuckler. That said, fear not, there are arrows aplenty flying through the air to slake the thirst of even the most intensely rabid action fan. You know that Scott and Crowe wouldn't have it any other way.

NEW ON DVD
INVICTUS—Clint Eastwood is proving to have one of the more interesting second acts in his long and illustrious career. The actor best known for his Dirty Harry persona in the 1970s and '80s has forged a name for himself now as a sensitive and artistically astute director with works as varied as *Bridges of Madison County* and *Letters from Iwo Jima* (not to mention his Oscar nom for *Mystic River* and win for *Million Dollar Baby*). His latest, the inspiring true story of how Nelson Mandela (Morgan Freeman) joined forces with the captain of South Africa's rugby team, Francois Pienaar (Matt Damon), to help unite their

country, was inexplicably overlooked at the Oscars this past year. Based on the book, "Playing the Enemy: Nelson Mandela and the Game that Made a Nation," the film shows how the newly elected President Mandela tried to bring his people together (in the aftermath of apartheid) through the universal language of sport. While the DVD is light on extras, there is a nice bit of footage documenting a meeting between Nelson Mandela and actor Morgan Freeman.

BLU-RAY WAY

M—Fritz Lang's 1931 German Expressionist masterpiece about a child murderer (Peter Lorre in his film debut) brought to justice by the Berlin criminal underworld is still a remarkably potent piece of filmmaking. Visually dazzling, with moody black and white cinematography by Fritz Arno Wagner and Gustav Rathje, this early "talkie" proves just how sophisticated the cinema arts were back then. This Criterion Blu-ray edition DVD includes a wealth of extras such as audio commentary with German film scholars, a long-lost English-language version of the film, a documentary featurette on the making and subsequent restoration of the movie, a conversation with director Lang and much more. Lang (who died in 1976) had a long, successful career in film, both in Germany and later in Hollywood, which included such gems as *Metropolis, Crimes of Dr. Mabuse, Fury, Western Union, Rancho Notorious, The Big Heat* and *While the City Sleeps*. He was one of the founding pioneers of German Expressionist cinema and this film came at the crossroads between the silent and sound eras. For many film buffs, the movie's title stands not just for "murderer," (the letter "M" is scrawled on the back of Lorre's coat to identify him), but also for "masterpiece" as well. This is a must-have DVD for the serious cinephile.

THE BIG CHEESE

ROBIN HOOD: MEN IN TIGHTS—With the release of the Russell Crowe blockbuster, what better time to bring out Mel Brooks' (mildly) amusing 1993 send up of Robin and his merry men. Starring Cary Elwes as Robin of Loxley, along with Tracey Ullman as the sorceress Latrine, Richard Lewis as Prince John, Dom DeLuise as mob boss Don Giovanni (!) and Mel Brooks himself as Rabbi Tuckman, a none too subtle variation on Friar Tuck, the film takes a number of juvenile potshots at everything from chastity belts to Kevin Costner's lack of an English accent in his own 1991 *Robin Hood: Prince of Thieves* film. Roger Rees (as the Sheriff of "Rottingham") and Dom DeLuise provide the best laughs in a film that, at best is hit or miss. Unfortunately, the 1990s saw a serious decline in director Brooks' talent, with such mediocre comedies as *Life Stinks* and *Dracula: Dead and Loving It* being a far cry from his heyday of 1968's *The Producers* and 1974's double play of *Blazing Saddles* and *Young Frankenstein*. It's fittingly ironic, then, that he finally reinvigorated his career (along with his bank account) by returning to his roots and transforming his first film into the Broadway hit, *The Producers*, which then spawned a big budget filmic remake in 2005.

THE SUMMER MOVIE SEASON HEATS UP
(June 2010)

What will the summer movie season of 2010 have in store for us? As usual, there will be a mix of sequels, remakes and a few originals, some good, some bad, and many simply mediocre. So, of the 20-plus titles set for release this month, what are the ones worth seeing? For the kids, there's *The Karate Kid* remake with Jaden Smith (son of Will Smith & Jada Pinkett-Smith) and Pixar's third installment in their *Toy Story* franchise, perhaps the only sure bet this summer. For the overwrought teen market comes the third chapter in the *Twilight* series, *Eclipse*, another critic proof hit. Fans of TV's *The A-Team* will be treated to a big screen version, starring Bradley Cooper, Liam Neeson and Jessica Biel, based on the classic show, while those in search of a good, entertaining documentary can sate their appetite with *Joan Rivers: A Piece of Work*, which follows a year in the life of the brash comedy icon. Comic book aficionados will relish *Jonah Hex*, starring Josh Brolin, Megan Fox and John Malkovich, about a hideously scarred wild west bounty hunter on the trail of a crazed terrorist (a role tailor-made for Malkovich). Finally, there's Tom Cruise, Cameron Diaz, Peter Sarsgaard and Paul Dano in *Knight and Day*, directed by James Mangold about a secret agent protecting a scientist (Dano) who's invented an unlimited power supply. Of course, that's just an excuse for some rousing action and a bit of romance with Cruise's *Vanilla Sky* co-star Diaz. As you can see, there are lots of movie choices this month, and hopefully a few of them will turn out to actually be worth your time and money. Good luck.

NEW IN THEATRES

SPLICE—A solid cast headlined by Adrien Brody and Sarah Polley helps breathe life into this horrific tale about two scientists who create a new organism through some experimental gene splicing. The creature itself, a sort of female human/chimera hybrid called "Dren" (that's "nerd" spelled backwards, by the way) quickly morphs from deformed baby to winged monster, a move necessitated in this sort of film to advance the pace of the plot. Director Vincenzo Natali and producer Guillermo Del Toro offer up a nice mixture of thrills, scares, dark humor and a few unforeseen twists, all of which more than a passing nod to Del Toro's own horror fantasy, *Pan's Labyrinth* from a few years before. With so many bad horror films floating around these days, it's refreshing to see a filmmaker actually put some effort into being original and truly frightening.

SHUTTER ISLAND—There's just something about Leonardo DiCaprio's look that works well in period films. Whether he is essaying a poor, but idealistic Edwardian-era artist in *Titanic,* or billionaire playboy Howard Hughes in *The Aviator*, or simply a 1950s married suburbanite in *Revolutionary Road*, he sells the period with his face and mannerisms. For this mystery thriller set in the 1950s and directed by the inimitable Martin Scorsese, Leo plays U. S. Marshall Teddy Daniels who is investigating the disappearance of a patient at Boston's Ashecliffe Hospital on Shutter Island. His search leads him to suspect foul play by the hospital's medical staff, though proving it becomes somewhat difficult as his own grip on sanity appears to be slipping. While the film got mixed reviews, the movie is quite effective and Scorsese seems to relish the gloomy, snake pit potential of the story. Ably assisting Leo in his slide into insanity is a supporting cast that includes Mark Ruffalo, Ben Kingsley, Emily Mortimer, Michelle Williams and the always reliable Elias Koteas.

BLU-RAY WAY
MYSTERY TRAIN—Indie director Jim Jarmusch's quirky, 1989 existential triptych about foreigners adrift in the land of Elvis during a single night in Memphis plays like a funhouse fever dream musical benediction. The trio of overlapping stories concerns a pair of Elvis-worshipping Japanese teen lovers, a young, hapless Italian widow and a sleazy Brit, all of whom spend some time in a deliciously shabby hotel (run by Screamin' Jay Hawkins, no less) where their lives intersect in a most interesting way. While most of the cast are unknowns, at least to American audiences, there are a few ringers on tap like Steve Buscemi, Joe Strummer and the voice of Tom Waits as the ever present radio DJ that hangs over the film like a gravelly angel. Jarmusch's minimalist style is very much in evidence, as is his penchant for how we view the passage of time. This new Criterion Blu-ray DVD comes with a number of fine extras that include two video Q&As with the director, an original documentary on the Memphis locations and the musical and social history they embody, on set and behind the scenes photos, a booklet featuring essays by writers Peter Guralnick and Dennis Lim, and even a collectible poster. For fans of this very unique slice of American pop culture, this set delivers the goods. As the king himself would say, "Thank you. Thank you very much."

THE BIG CHEESE
THE WOLF MAN—As horror film myths go, the wolf man/werewolf canon has rarely been able to rise above its mostly ludicrous origins. From 1935's *Werewolf of London* to 1941's *The Wolf Man* with Lon Chaney Jr. to the shapeshifting flicks (*Howling, American Werewolf in London, Wolfen*) in the

early 1980s to the 1994 arthouse attempt Wolf with Jack Nicholson, no one has really been able to legitimize this particular monster. Well now director Joe Johnston (*The Rocketeer, October Sky*) and actor Benecio Del Toro (*The Usual Suspects, Traffic*) give it the old college try with mixed results. The A-list cast (Del Toro, Emily Blunt, Gemma Whelan and Anthony Hopkins) do what they can, and director Johnston (who got his start as a special effects man) has a real flair for the genre, but the whole shebang just doesn't (dare I say it?) have any teeth. A few good extras help make this a worthwhile DVD, such as behind the scenes transformation secrets, making of featurettes and on the Blu-ray disc historical data on werewolf legend and lore plus two alternate endings.

PANNING FOR SUMMER GOLD
(July/August 2010)

While some critics feel that the first half of the summer movie season has been a bit lackluster, with the notable exception of Pixar's *Toy Story 3* (which fortunately was not the *Godfather 3* of animated films), there is still some hope that the remainder of the season can be salvaged. To that end, fifty movies will be vying for your attention in July and August, and while none are likely to be the mother lode that TS 3 has proven to be, a few just might be sleepers that will yield a substantial bag of nuggets.

JULY

The month gets off to a great start with *The Last Airbender* (based on Nickelodeon's animated *Avatar* show) which finds director M. Night Shyamalan trying yet again to recapture the magic he once wielded in *The Sixth Sense*. *The Kids Are Alright* concerns a lesbian couple (Julianne Moore, Annette Bening) whose 18-year old daughter tracks down her anonymous sperm donor dad (Mark Ruffalo). *Despicable Me,* a splendidly loony 3-D animated comedy from the producer of *Ice Age* is filled with villains (voiced by Steve Carell, Will Arnett and Julie Andrews!) who all appear to be, well, despicable. *Great Directors*, as you might guess, is a documentary about great filmmakers. *The Sorcerer's Apprentice* reunites *National Treasure* star Nicholas Cage with director Jon Turtletaub for a CGI heavy adventurous retelling of the classic tale, most familiar to us from the Mickey Mouse segment of Disney's *Fantasia. Dinner For Schmucks* pits Steve Carell against Paul Rudd in an unapologetic lowbrow comedy from director Jay Roach. On a more serious note, *Life During Wartime* examines the romantic politics of three sisters (Allison Janney, Shirley Henderson and Ally Sheedy) in a story decidedly not for kids. *Salt* depicts the smoldering Angelina Jolie (co-starring with Live Schreiber) as a kick-ass agent in a role that was originally planned for a male. On the other hand, *The Adjustment Bureau* stars Matt Damon as a politician in a star-crossed relationship with a ballet dancer played by Emily Blunt. Finally, rounding out the month, there's *Get Low*, a quirky 1930s drama starring the powerhouse duo of Robert Duvall and Bill Murray

AUGUST

The true story of a Chinese ballet dancer's defection is the basis for *Mao's Last Dancer,* the latest from director Bruce (*Driving Miss Daisy*) Beresford. Another true-life story informs *Middlemen* with Luke Wilson, Giovanni Rabisi and James Caan about a Texas business man who tapped into the online porn industry in the early 1990s. Less serious-minded is *The Other Guys,* a cop buddy comedy starring Will Ferrell and Mark Wahlberg. Documentary lovers will find *The Wildest Dream,* (about those intrepid souls who choose to brave Mount Everest) both satisfying and disturbing. Julia Roberts and Javier Bardem bring serious star power to *Eat Pray Love,* based on Elizabeth Gilbert's bestselling memoir about a divorcee's globe-hopping efforts to put her life back together. The graphic-novel origins of *Scott Pilgrim vs. the World* find an ideal interpreter in director Edgar Wright (best known for the Simon Pegg comedies *Shaun of the Dead* and *Hot Fuzz*). Here, he teams up with Michael Cera and Mary Elizabeth Winstead in this off-kilter romantic comedy. Emma Thompson returns in *Nanny McPhee 2* as the very unorthodox au pair. We close out the summer with Drew Barrymore in *Going the Distance,* a raunchy romance comedy about a journalism grad student who struggles to keep her bi-coastal love life on track. The movie co-stars Christina Applegate, Ron Livingston and Drew's real life love interest, Justin Long.

NEW IN THEATRES

INCEPTION—Writer and director Christopher Nolan is one of the brainiest directors working in Hollywood today. All of his films (*Memento, Insomnia, Batman Begins, The Prestige* and *The Dark Knight*) contain a hot, molten core of intellectual magma beneath their cool surface crust of mainstream entertainment, just waiting to erupt. For his latest, starring Leonardo DiCaprio, Ellen Page, Joseph Gordon Levitt, Marion Cotillard, Ken Watanabe, Cillian Murphy, Tom Berenger and Michael Caine, the stakes are high in a world where one's own dreams are a commodity to be bought or stolen. This globe hopping adventure thriller has a stellar cast and great locations, though none more intriguing than the landscape of the unconscious mind that the characters find themselves in. The trippy visuals alone make this a must see experience, but as in all of Nolan's work, there will be substance beneath the flash.

NEW ON DVD

BROOKLYN'S FINEST—A bleak vision of burned out and corrupt police officers is at the center of this intense drama which stars Richard Gere, Don Cheadle, Ethan Hawke and Wesley Snipes. Director Antoine Fuqua has covered similar territory in 2001's *Training Day* (which also starred Ethan Hawke), but here he goes much deeper into the heart of darkness of law enforcement corruption. However, the film presents these failings in a much more complex manner than simply being about clear cut good and evil. To that end, the DVD extras include featurettes on what the world of being a big city cop is like, along with pieces on the writer and director, plus an informative commentary by Fuqua.

THE LEOPARD—This magnificent retelling of Italy's unification is one of the best films ever about the passing of an era. In Sicily during the 1800s, the aristocracy found itself being marginalized by the new democratic revolution. Though the reigning Prince tries to hold onto the past, he eventually must come to terms with the modern world. This 1963 French/Italian co-production, directed by Luchino Visconti and starring Burt Lancaster, Alain Delon and Claudia Cardinale, is rich in historical detail, all lushly photographed by the masterful cinematographer Giuseppe Rotunno. The hour-long banquet scene which concludes the film is one of the all-time great set-pieces in movie history. This cinematic masterpiece finally makes it to Blu-ray with a wealth of extras fit for a Monarch. In addition to a commentary by film scholar Peter Cowie, there is a terrific retrospective documentary, *A Dying Breed: The Making of The Leopard*, featuring interviews with Claudia Cardinale, screenwriter Suso Ceccho D'Amico, Rotunno, filmmaker Sidney Pollack and many others. There are also video interviews with producer Goffredo Lombardo and Professor Millicent Marcus who talks about the history behind the film. The total DVD package, which includes a booklet as well, is a must-have for any true aficionado's collection.

THE BIG CHEESE

JASON AND THE ARGONAUTS—In recent years, there has been a resurgence in the popularity of old-school effects pioneer Ray Harryhausen's work. The man responsible for wowing wide-eyed kids with his stop-motion animation wizardry in everything from 1949's gorilla-at-large *Mighty Joe Young* to the monster-laden *Sinbad* flicks in the 1960s and '70s formally ended his career in 1981 with *Clash of the Titans*. Thanks to this year's remake of Ray's swan song, as well as recent extras-filled DVDs of many of his films, Mr. Harryhausen is squarely in the public eye again. It doesn't hurt that among those championing his name are such heavyweight icons as George Lucas and Steven Spielberg who were mere lads when Ray was in his prime. This most recent special edition DVD title in the Harryhausen canon is among his very best. The 1963 adventure about Jason's search for the Golden Fleece boasts some of the maestro's most amazing animated marvels, including a jaw-dropping sword fight finale between Jason and his two companions against seven (count 'em, seven!) blade-wielding skeletons. Despite the low-tech approach, this sequence still packs quite a punch. Though the film was directed by Don Chaffey (who previously helmed Disney's live action *The Three Lives of Thomasina* (and would later direct a fur-clad Raquel Welch in *One Million Years B.C.*), it is Ray who gives *Jason* its lustre. The extras on this new DVD include a look back at Harryhausen's legacy and an interview with the 80-something year-old man himself by another smitten fan who grew up to be a big time director, John Landis.

FALLING FOR THE FALL
MOVIE SEASON
(September 2010)

Having made it through another summer of mostly forgettable films (with the notable exceptions of *Toy Story 3, Inception* and not much else), it's time to take a look at what the fall has to offer. Right at the top of the month is the George Clooney thriller *The American* in which the normally genial star sheds his dapper persona to play a brooding killer. Next up, director Robert Rodriguez expands on his *Grindhouse* joke trailer *Machete* with Danny Trejo as the revenge seeking ex-federale. Jeff Fahey, Jessica Alba, Robert DeNiro and Lindsay Lohan co-star. Ben Affleck and Jon Hamm face off against one another in *The Town* about a bank robbing gang in Boston, directed by Affleck. Woody Allen is back with the London-based *You Will Meet a Tall, Dark Stranger*, starring Antonio Banderas, Josh Brolin, Naomi Watts and Anthony Hopkins. *Never Let Me Go*, based on Kazuo Ishiguro's offbeat 2005 novel about British boarding-school students stars Carey Mulligan, Keira Knightley and, directed by Mark (*One Hour Photo*) Romanek, promises to be a real treat for mystery lovers. Finally at month's end, hunky heartthrob Ryan Reynolds finds himself confined to a coffin with only a cell phone and a lighter in the aptly named *Buried*. There are a few other potentially good films set for release this month, but the ones I listed will at least get you started.

NEW IN THEATRES
WALL STREET: MONEY NEVER SLEEPS—Gordon Gecko is back! The fictional Wall Street maverick (whose mantra "Greed is good," fairly defined the Yuppie 1980s) has returned, older, grayer, but still every bit the force of nature he was then. Ten years into the 21st Century, the world has changed in ways we could never have imagined when director Oliver Stone gave us his 1987 take on American financial institutions. In the wake of the Enron debacle, corporate bonuses, international terrorism, the recent bank meltdowns and other institutional chicanery, the time seems more than ripe for a re-evaluation of all things fiscal. Michael Douglas reprises his most iconic character while Charlie Sheen is a now middle-aged Bud (the same age as Gecko was in the first film), and Shia LaBeouf takes on the role of the "new kid" on Wall Street's block.

NEW ON DVD
LETTERS TO JULIET—A 50-year old letter and the search for a lost love are the catalysts in this sweetly romantic tale set in modern-day Verona, Italy (famed

stomping grounds for Shakespeare's tragic star-crossed lovers). Aspiring writer Sophie (Lehigh Valley's Amanda Seyfried) finds the lost missive, tracks down the mysterious author named Claire (Vanessa Redgrave) and the two set off on a road trip, along with Claire's handsome grandson (Gael Garcia Bernal) to locate the letter's intended recipient. Unabashedly romantic without ever being cloying, director Gary Winick makes good use of his sun-drenched Italian locations as well as Ms. Seyfried's own considerable charms.

BLU-RAY WAY

THE TWILIGHT ZONE—A few years back the entire original *Twilight Zone* series (created and hosted by the inimitable Rod Serling) was released on DVD in what was called "the Definitive Edition." All five seasons were lovingly restored, remastered and loaded with extras that included audio commentaries and interviews with many of the actors, writers and directors who worked on this classic show from 1959 to 1965. Now, "submitted for your approval," (as Rod used to intone in his opening introductions), this superb edition is being released on Blu-Ray (in seasonal box sets) for the first time. All the extras from the earlier version are being carried over along with the promise of superior picture and sound. Anyone familiar with the show knows that it had some of the best black & white cinematography on TV at the time, with elegant use of deep shadows, expressionistic set design and dramatic close-ups. The brilliant half-hour scripts were penned by such legendary writers as William Matheson, Charles Beaumont and, most notably, Rod Serling himself, who was responsible for over two dozen in the first season and set the tone for the entire series. Very few shows from the early sixties have stood the test of time as well as *TZ*, with its solemn and poetic introductions by Serling, stylized direction and instantly recognizable theme music. Before *Lost, The X-Files, Twin Peaks, Star Trek* or even *The Outer Limits, The Twilight Zone* blazed the way for imaginative, speculative television and has yet to be topped. For the Blu-Ray connoisseur, this is a must have set. You'll definitely approve.

BLU CHEESE

FORBIDDEN PLANET—Years before Leslie Nielsen became the punchline and go-to guy for a string of movie parodies from the 1980s on, he had a legitimate career as a handsome leading man. One of his more exotic films of that time was this 1956 big budget, A-list sci-fi adventure, which was actually based on Shakespeare's "The Tempest." Nielsen commands a crew of space rangers (clearly modeled on military protocol) in their interstellar saucer when they intercept a signal from a long lost mission on a faraway planet. Once landed, the stalwart astronauts find an aging scientist named Dr. Morbius (Walter Pidgeon), his grown daughter (a super sexy Anne Francis) and his robot servant, "Robbie."

The rest of the mission crew are long dead and Morbius himself is reluctant to leave. It turns out the planet has some pretty big secrets tied to a race of super intelligent beings called the Krell who once inhabited the world and then mysteriously disappeared. The Blu-Ray edition of this sci-fi classic is a welcome treat , coming a couple years after the 50th anniversary DVD release. Like that earlier version, this one has many cool extras including interviews and featurettes on the film, its groundbreaking effects and its very radical electronic "score" which is still provocative. Everyone involved in the making of this film has very fond memories and are clearly very proud to have been a part of it. While some of the attitudes seem a bit dated, the movie as a whole holds up surprisingly well. Even in the world of cheese, there are some that age just fine.

THE COOL FALL MOVIE SEASON GETS HOT

(October 2010)

Continuing the trend from last month, the fall movie season has a number of interesting films being showcased in October. At the top of the list is David Fincher's Facebook movie, *The Social Network*, as well as Clint Eastwood's multi-layered *Hereafter* with Matt Damon. Bruce Willis, Morgan Freeman, Helen Mirren and John Malkovich team up in *Red*, based on the CIA-themed graphic novel, while Hilary Swank and Sam Rockwell play siblings in *Conviction*, the true life story about a man wrongfully convicted of murder. Rounding things out are *Paranormal Activity 2* and *The Company Men*, with Ben Affleck, Chris Cooper and Tommy Lee Jones, in a timely tale about corporate downsizing. These are only a few of the promising titles that await us this month.

NEW IN THEATRES

NOWHERE BOY—The early 1950s pre-Beatle days of John Lennon (played here by *Kick Ass* star Aaron Johnson) are chronicled in the feature film debut of artist-turned-director Sam Taylor Wood, who concentrates on the young Brit's complex relationships with his aunt Mimi (Kristin Scott Thomas) and estranged mother Julia (Anne-Marie Duff). While the birth of Lennon's first band, The Quarrymen, figures in the story (along with his legendary meeting with a teen-age Paul McCartney), the real focus of the movie is in the strained family relationship that led the moody art student and would-be rock musician to become one of the truly iconic pop figures of the twentieth century.

NEW ON DVD

THE GATES—In February of 2005 when the husband and wife team of Christo and Jeanne-Claude unveiled their latest project, The Gates, in New York's Central Park, it was the culmination of a 25-year long quest by the pair of artists who had made a name for themselves over the years with their on-of-a-kind installations. Their works include the wrapping of the Reichstag in Berlin and the Pont-Neuf bridge in Paris, the 24-mile (39 km)-long artwork called *Running Fence* in Sonoma and Marin counties in California, and the Surrounded Islands in Biscayne Bay in Miami Florida. For The Gates, Christo envisioned 7,500 arches (gates), curtained with orange cloth that waved and billowed and decked miles of walkways in Central Park. This documentary by Antonia Ferrera, Albert Maysles, David Maysles and Matthew Prinzing chronicles the years-long endeavor by the artists to win approval from various mayors and commissions who all turned down the project. Ultimately the pair found a champion in Mayor Bloomberg who gave it the okay, perhaps as a way to help heal the city that was still reeling from the events of 9/11. Whatever the reason, when The Gates unfurled (for only 16 days, since part of Christo's intent is that all his large-scale works are impermanent), the 23-mile long installation was an immediate hit with nearly all New Yorkers, though, as in all of Christo's projects, there were a few grousers who didn't appreciate the work's visual splendor. But for everyone else, the vibrant ribbon of orange snaking its way through the late winter bleakness of the city, it was a metaphorical testament that New York City (and the artistic, creative lifeblood of humanity, itself) was alive and well after the devastating attack of September 11th. As a side note, Nurture New York's Nature (NNYN), an organization started by Theodore Kheel, famed New York labor lawyer who represented Christo (and business partner with Easton resident Peter Koehler), is the proud recipient of an exclusive, world-wide, royalty free license from the artists, Christo and Jeanne-Claude, to produce events and programs commemorating their work of art, *The Gates, Central Park, New York City 1979 - 2005.* In that connection, the artists have generously donated signed *Gates* and other art prints from their 40 year career to support NNYN's programs. The net proceeds from sales are used to help protect and restore the City's natural environment and to create public awareness of the importance of those undertakings to the health and well-being of the City's inhabitants. The fulfillment center for these prints is housed in Easton at the Nurture Nature Center building, owned by Nurture Nature Foundation.

CLASSIC CORNER

*PSYCHO—Few films in the history of cinema have had the seismic impact of Alfred Hitchcock's 1960 masterpiece of horror. Some younger people today may wonder what all the fuss is about over this little black & white flick in which there isn't much blood (at least by today's standards) and the scares come few and far between. But for those who grew up in that era, Hitch's low-budget thriller signaled a new paradigm in filmmaking and exhibition. Janet Leigh plays a 30ish office worker who, in an act of irrational desperation, steals $40,000 from a rich client to make a new life with her debt-ridden boyfriend (John Gavin) who lives in another town. On the way, she stops at an isolated motel and there meets the young owner, Norman Bates (Anthony Perkins), who, it turns out has been living too long under the influence of his domineering old mother. To say any more would be unfair to those who haven't seen it and unnecessary for anyone else. The plot twists, story structure, visual set pieces, stellar acting from the phenomenal cast and the innovative, all-strings score by Bernard Hermann with its shrieking violins all come together under Hitchcock's brilliant direction to create a film viewing experience that still packs a punch some fifty years later. To commemorate this half-century anniversary, a Blu-ray DVD is being released that carries over all the extras from the standard version 2-disc special edition of a couple years ago and includes audio commentary with Hitchcock author Stephen Rebello, two documentaries ("The Making of *Psycho*" and "Hitchcock's Legacy"), the Hitchcock/Truffaut interviews, behind the scenes production photos, posters, ads. lobby cards and much more. Ironically the film was not looked upon kindly by many of the critics during its initial release, though audiences embraced it immediately and made it Hitchcock's biggest hit ever. But before the year was over, *Psycho* was being hailed as a masterpiece. They can make horror films that are scarier, more intense and certainly more gruesome, but fifty years on, no one has made one better. *Psycho* is for the ages.

BLU-RAY WAY

THE THIN RED LINE—Visionary director Terrence Malick has had one of the quirkier careers in Hollywood. After making a name for himself in the 1970s with two of the most stylistically unique films of the time, *Badlands* (1973) and *Days of Heaven* (1978), the reclusive filmmaker pulled a Rip Van Winkle, only to return twenty years later in 1998 with this poetic adaptation of the James Jones World War II novel about the battle at Guadalcanal. A deeply philosophic film about the nature of war, it had the bad misfortune of coming out several months after Spielberg's more visceral and emotionally direct *Saving Private Ryan*. Both films have their strengths, but for my money Malick's take is the more satisfying, with a first rate cast of Adrien Brody, Jim Caviezel, Ben Chaplin, John Cuzack, Woody Harrelson, Elias Koteas, Nick Nolte, Sean Penn and cameos by George Clooney and John Travolta. This new Blu-ray release boasts some stellar extras including audio commentary (though not with the reclusive director), cast and crew interviews, as well as an interview with the author's daughter, plus much more. This stunning work of art that was sadly overlooked on its initial release finally gets its due in this special edition DVD.

THE MOST WONDERFUL (MOVIE) TIME OF THE YEAR
(November 2010)

As the year winds down toward the holiday season, some pretty big cinematic guns make their way to the local multiplexes. Multiple choices are offered in every genre for your viewing pleasure. If you fancy a comedy there is *Morning Glory* starring Harrison Ford, Diane Keaton and Rachel McAdams about the goings on at a morning TV show, and *Due Date* with Robert Downey Jr. and *The Hangover*'s bearded breakout star Zach Galifianakis on a wild road trip. Animation buffs can choose between *Tangled*, Disney's retelling of Rapunzel, and *Megamind,* the alien supervillain comedy with voices by Will Ferrell, Tina Fey and Brad Pitt. Heavy drama can be found in Danny Boyle's *127 Hours* about mountain climber Aron Ralston, played by James Franco, who was forced to cut off his own arm when it became caught in a boulder back in 2003, and *The King's Speech*, with Colin Firth and Geoffrey Rush, about King George VI's assuming the throne in pre WWII England. For the action thriller junkie there is Russell Crowe and Liam Neeson in *The Next Three Days* about a daring prison escape, and Denzel Washington in Tony Scott's *Unstoppable*, a race-against-time runaway train nail-biter that's actually based on a true story. There are plenty more, but this should get you started.

NEW IN THEATRES
FAIR GAME—Directed by Doug Liman (*The Bourne Identity*) and starring Naomi Watts and Sean Penn, this is the dramatic true story about the outing of CIA agent Valerie Wilson, whose status became compromised after her husband, Ambassador Joseph Wilson, wrote op-ed columns that accused the Bush Administration of manipulating intelligence about weapons of mass destruction to justify the invasion of Iraq. Regardless of one's political views, this was a heinous act of retribution that seriously endangered our National security as well as the life of a Federal agent. As a film story, it stands as one of the more powerful entries in the late fall release schedule and will, no doubt, be a contender come Oscar time next year.

NEW ON DVD
A CHRISTMAS CAROL—After a number of less-than-stellar films, comedic whirlwind Jim Carrey struck gold playing alpha miser Ebenezer Scrooge in Robert Zemeckis' latest foray into the animated motion capture field with this frenetic, eye-popping version of Dickens' Christmas classic. Carrey was also

tapped to essay several other roles (including the ghosts of Christmas past, present and future) making him the first actor to do so in a major movie version of this timeless tale. The extras include featurettes on how the film was made, deleted scenes plus, on the Blu-ray edition, the Bonusview feature Behind the Carol- the full motion capture experience, a digital advent calendar and the 3D exclusive "Scrooge's Wild Ride." The special edition 4-disc set includes 3-D Blu-ray, regular Blu-ray, standard DVD and a digital copy, so you can experience this holiday extravaganza in multiple ways.

CLASSIC CORNER

THE ICE STORM—Ang Lee's directing career is one of the most eclectic around. From his early Taiwanese films like *Eat, Drink, Man, Woman* to his doing Jane Austen's *Sense and Sensibility* in 1995 and the controversial "gay cowboy" film *Brokeback Mountain* in 2005, he's shown himself to being in tune with stories from every culture. One of his very best was this 1997 take on the Watergate-era drama, based on the novel by Rick Moody, about American suburbia during a freak New England ice storm in the winter of 1973. Working with an amazing cast—Kevin Kline, Sigourney Weaver, Joan Allen, Tobey Maguire, Christina Ricci and Elijah Wood—the film captures the tone of ennui that pervaded the period when America seemed to truly lose its innocence in the wake of Vietnam and the Watergate scandal. While the film was both powerful and sensitive, it had the bad luck to be released the same year as *Titanic* and *L.A. Confidential*, and so was lost in their higher profile glare, being completely ignored by the Oscars without a single nomination. Initially released in a bare bones DVD back in 2001, it finally gets the full-on Criterion treatment in this lavish 2-disc special edition. In addition to a lively and informative commentary with Lee and his longtime writer/producer James Schamus, the second disc is a treasure trove of interviews, documentaries and deleted scenes that all pay tribute to the lasting legacy of this truly classic film that has definitely stood the test of time. As a period piece snapshot of American culture, it's ironic that it took this soft spoken Taiwanese filmmaker to see our world so clearly.

BLU-RAY WAY

PATHS OF GLORY—This is the film that is considered by many to be the one that placed director Stanley Kubrick into the league of serious filmmakers (his previous efforts Killer's Kiss and The Killing were stylish, if simplistic, noir programmers). Based on Humphrey Cobb's novel of the same name (which in turn was based on true events), the film tells the story of a botched military assault by French troops on a German stronghold. To cover his blunder, the French General in charge (despicably played by George Macready) orders the execution of three innocent soldiers for cowardice. Kirk Douglas (who also served as producer) plays the idealistic Colonel Dax who led the doomed assault and defends the men in what is obviously a very rigged trial. As the three convicted soldiers, Ralph Meeker, Joseph Turkel and Timothy Carrey all deliver nuanced performances that really make you feel for the predicament of the men. Kubrick's virtuosity with the camera is simply astonishing, from the endless tracking shots through the elaborate maze of trenches, to the assault itself (which is as good as anything in *Saving Private Ryan*), to the fluid dolly shots in the Chateau headquarters where the Generals plot and scheme for political advantage while their men huddle in muddy trenches at the front. Until recently, most Kubrick DVD releases were light on extras, no doubt due to the reclusive director's penchant for secrecy. However, since his death in 1999, his family (who control the Estate), have become more open about sharing production information with the public through books, interviews, documentaries and commentary tracks for the most recent DVD editions. As the first release of a Kubrick film on DVD for Criterion, the prestigious company has pulled out all the stops. In addition to a commentary by critic Gary Giddins, there is a 1979 interview with star Kirk Douglas, new video interviews with Kubrick's longtime executive producer (and brother-in-law) Jan Harlan, *Paths of Glory* producer James B. Harris, and Kubrick's wife Christiane who played the German girl seen at the end of the film who is forced to sing for the occupying French soldiers. There is also an excerpt from a French television program about real-life World War I executions similar to the events dramatized in the film. Hopefully this is only the first of many Criterion editions of Kubrick's work.

A CHRISTMAS FAR MORE GLORIOUS THAN GRAND

(December 2010)

As usual, the big cinematic guns are out at year's end, vying for your attention and the contents of your wallet. Artist turned filmmaker Julian Schnabel does his take on Rula Jebreal's novel, *Miral*, about a Palestinian orphan, while another chapter in *The Chronicles of Narnia* series, *The Voyage of the Dawn Treader* comes our way. Shakespeare's *The Tempest* with Helen Mirren is given a reboot by Julie Taymor, and Mark Wahlberg plays a boxer making a comeback in *The Fighter*. Reese Witherspoon returns in James L. Brooks' *How Do You Know* and Disney has revved up the light cycles once again for *Tron: Legacy*, the long-awaited sequel to the 1982 cult classic. Comedy comes courtesy of Jack Black in *Gulliver's Travels*, a 3-D update of Swift's satiric novel while Sofia Coppola directs Stephen Dorff and Elle Fanning in the father/daughter drama, *Somewhere*. Finally, on Christmas Day, the Coen Brothers unveil their remake of the 1969 classic *True Grit* with Jeff Bridges in the John Wayne role. This is a truly bountiful holiday movie season with something for everyone.

NEW IN THEATRES

BLACK SWAN—If there is a thread that runs through all of director Darren Aronofsky's work it is the notion of a character who is consumed by their passions. Whether it's a mathematical equation in *Pi*, drug addiction in *Requiem for a Dream*, a timeless love affair spread over a thousand years in *The Fountain* or finding a measure of self-worth in the theater of the absurd milieu of professional wrestling in *The Wrestler*, this theme can be found in all of these films. Now Aronofsky examines this idea again in the high pressure world of professional ballet as a New York City Dance company prepares to put on a production of Swan Lake. Natalie Portman and Mila Kunis play rival ballerinas in a tale of twisted loyalties and dark explorations of the soul that has become the signature fingerprint of this filmmaker's oeuvre. Lending fine supporting performances are Winona Ryder, Barbara Hershey and Vincent Cassel. Aronofsky regulars, cinematographer Matthew Libatique and composer Clint Mansell are also on board for the ride.

NEW ON DVD

WAKING SLEEPING BEAUTY—Walt Disney Studios has always been a name associated with top of the line entertainment. For forty years, from the creation of Mickey Mouse in 1928 through to the release of *The Jungle Book* in

1967, the presence of Uncle Walt as overseer and "keeper of the flame" made sure his name continued to burn bright. However, with Walt's passing in 1966 there ensued a fallow period for nearly twenty years as polarization between new employees and seasoned veterans led to infighting and a lack of focus or vision on the part of those who were running the company. It wasn't until the mid-1980s that the studio found its footing to herald an animation renaissance of staggering proportion—*The Little Mermaid, Beauty & the Beast, Aladdin, The Lion King*— that continues to reverberate to this day through Disney's live action features and its association with Pixar animation. This documentary, by Disney insiders Don Hahn and Peter Schneider, tells the not-always-pretty story of how the mouse house regained its stature during the dark days of its discontent. Included are candid insights by many top names in the film industry—Don Bluth (Anastasia), Tim Burton (The Nightmare Before Christmas) and John Lasseter (Pixar)—who all served a frustrating apprenticeship at Disney before embarking on their own success. In the case of Lasseter, he eventually returned to the fold and, under a more benevolent regime, is now in charge of the animation division. Through these interviews, along with home movies, internal memos and unseen footage, you get a real insider's look at how tense this period was before its eventual rebirth. But like all Disney stories, this one has a happy ending, which is clearly evident by the continued output of great (and innovative) entertainment still being produced. As this film genuinely shows, the story is far from over.

CLASSIC CORNER

TRUE GRIT—While waiting for the Coen Brothers remake, now is a good time to revisit the original 1969 John Wayne version. Filmed by veteran western director Henry Hathaway, the cast also includes Robert Duvall, Glen Campbell, Jeff Corey, Dennis Hopper and 21-year old Kim Darby as the headstrong young teen Mattie Ross. The story of a young girl who hires a drunken, overweight Marshall to help track down her father's killer was a huge hit and a comeback role for Wayne when it was released in the late sixties hippie era. All these years later, it still holds up and makes for an entertaining good time. Shot on location in the picturesque mountain regions of Colorado (instead of Arkansas as stated) the film is glorious to look at thanks to the fine cinematography of Lucien Ballard who worked with such idiosyncratic directors as Stanley Kubrick and Sam Peckinpah. The DVD includes making of featurettes and informative commentary by old west scholars Jeb Rosebrook, Bob Boze Bell and J. Stuart Rosebrook. All these extras are also on Blu-ray release which comes out on the 14th.

BLU-RAY WAY

FANTASIA/FANTASIA 2000 BOX SET—Despite all the technical advances that have been made in the field of animation in the last 20 years, the artistic high-water mark remains the 1940 concert feature called *Fantasia* that was dreamed up by Walt Disney in collaboration with noted conductor Leopold Stokowski. The result was a feature-length film that took animation to new heights with its fusing of cutting edge imagery with classical music. Though clearly an artistic success, it was a financial failure at the time and did not recoup its costs until thirty years later when it was reissued in 1969 where its strikingly experimental tone found an appreciative audience in the hippie generation. Sixty years after its release it spawned a reverently inspired sequel, *Fantasia 2000*. Now, a decade later, the two come together in a long awaited Blu-ray set that promises to give new life to this aging masterpiece with improved picture and sound to rival the latest CGI attraction. In addition to many of the extras that were on the original DVD release in 2000, the Blu-ray edition boasts some wonderful additions including the debut of the Disney and Salvador Dali short *Destino*, along with an accompanying documentary about the unlikely pairing of these two very different artists. For anyone who believes that animation can be an art form as vibrant and deep as any other, Walt Disney's *Fantasia* and its loving sequel are all the proof you'll need.

CHRISTMAS TREAT

MR. MAGOO'S CHRISTMAS CAROL—The term "classic" gets bandied about a lot these days, but one of the true works to actually deserve this moniker is this delightful, animated television Christmas special (the first ever!) that appeared in homes like a welcomed guest back in the winter of 1962. A faithful retelling of the Dickens classic, with the myopic Mr. Magoo as Ebenezer Scrooge, the hour-long holiday cartoon become a perennial favorite for many years thereafter. Of course since nothing lasts forever, it eventually fell from the media radar and more or less disappeared from the cultural zeitgeist. However, after languishing in video limbo in a number of bare bones VHS and DVD editions, this endearingly entertaining musical is back with a vengeance (and on Blu-ray, to boot), thanks in large part to the dedicated efforts of Darrell Van Citters, former Disney animator and author of "*Mr. Magoo's Christmas Carol*: The Making of the First Animated Christmas Special," which can be purchased online at the author's website, mrmagooschristmascarol.blogspot.com. Like a Christmas morning brimming with presents under the tree, the features-packed DVD includes a commentary track with Van Citters and surviving cast and crew, a production art montage set to the long lost musical overture by composer Walter Scharf, a rare song demo recording performed by songwriters Jule Styne and Bob Merrill, storyboard sequences synched to the existing soundtrack and compared against the final picture, a 16-page pamphlet of text and images excerpted from Van Citters' book that provides a broad overview of the film's genesis and production, and more. For many people, Christmas just wouldn't be Christmas without Mr. Magoo's enchanting portrayal of Scrooge's heartfelt transformation from uber-miser to saintly savior during one special Christmas Eve. With this new, special edition DVD you'll be able to savor the abundant wonders of this very special holiday classic even more. Just don't forget the razzleberry dressing!

BONUS CHAPTER: Unpublished Review
Drinking Deep from *"The Fountain"*

With five films in a dozen years under his belt, director Darren Aronofsky has finally arrived. After scoring big with the critics and public with the micro-budgeted *Pi* in 1998 and the indie art house hit *Requiem for a Dream* in 2000, Aronofsky continued on his idiosyncratic way with the trippy time warp exploration of eternal life, *The Fountain* in 2006, which, despite its lofty goals (and star power from Hugh Jackman and Rachel Weisz), failed to connect and was considered a major flop. He eventually returned to the good graces of the public with his next two features, *The Wrestler* in 2008, which also revitalized Mickey Rourke's career and in 2010, *Black Swan*, a psychosexual thriller about professional ballet that has earned the director his best reviews yet. If nothing else, Mr. Aronofsky has certainly been eclectic in his choice of subjects. Instead of focusing on his quartet of successes, however, I am more interested in examining his central film which I consider to be anything but a failure.

I come to praise *The Fountain*, not to bury it. Rather than mourn the box office death of 2006's most misunderstood film, I, instead, wish to resurrect it by applauding its uncompromising vision. While most movies cater slavishly to the film-going public's need for instant gratification by explaining every aspect of the plot and tying up the ending with a tidy bow of convention, writer/director Darren Aronofsky's esoteric and imperfect masterpiece will have none of this. By turns dazzling, ambiguous, exultant, trying and, yes, even maddeningly obtuse, it aspires to be a work of art which posits many more questions about its meaning and structure than it ever cares to answer.

Even though the failure of *The Fountain* at the box office bodes ill for innovative and thoughtful filmmaking, the unprecedented polarizing love-it-or-hate-it views from the public and critics, alike, mean it will not go quietly into the night. Thankfully, its release on DVD has provided the film a second life, and the world another chance to reassess this bonafide classic.

In Mr. Aronofsky's previous films, *Pi* (1998) and *Requiem for a Dream* (2000), he dealt primarily with the subjective nature of experience, be it a mad math genius who suffers from chronic migraines, or the social addictions in our culture which run the gamut from food to television to drugs. For *The Fountain*, he explores the notion of eternal life in a similarly subjective manner, refracted here through the prism of a millennium-long odyssey with characters that might or might not be the same people

The movie is divided into three interwoven narratives that are structured as a sort of broken glass triptych, where parts from each are reflected back onto the others. In the first, we find a 16th century conquistador named Tomas Creo (a bearded, shaggy-haired Hugh Jackman) who is dispatched to "New Spain"—aka Central America—by Queen Isabel (a radiant Rachel Weisz) to search for the mythical tree of life which offers the potential for immortality. Not surprisingly, the Inquisition, which thrives on keeping the populace in line through torture and the fear of damnation in the afterlife, is out to bring down the Queen and considers her holy quest to be an act of heresy.

In the second story strand, set in our contemporary world, a brilliant research scientist named Tommy Creo (again Jackman, sans beard and with slightly shorter hair), working with plant extracts taken from a Central American tree cutting, is obsessed with finding a cancer cure and is racing against time to beat the disease that has afflicted his wife, Izzi (Weisz with a short, post-chemo, 'do). She has taken to studying astronomy, specifically gazing at a dying star nebula in the constellation Orion that she says the ancient Mayans called "Xibalba," which was the sacred underworld for their dead. "How amazing," she muses, "that the Mayans chose a dying star to represent their underworld." With her own mortality looming, it's not surprising that she has fixated on this bit of arcane history. Her interest has also led her to write a book-length manuscript about the Spanish quest for the tree of life, as embodied in the story of Isabel and Tomas, which she has titled "The Fountain."

The final strand in the story is set in some unstated, but obviously far off future (it is only through Aronofsky's penchant for symmetry that we may intuit it could be the 26th century). Here, a lone, bald-pated astronaut named Tom Creo (Jackman, of course), floats serenely in a giant soap-bubble spaceship as it makes its way toward that distant nebula which so intrigued Isabel/Izzi in the previous segments. Tom's only companion in the crystalline orb is a huge, withered tree which may be the progeny of that millennia-ago tree cutting by Tomas or, perhaps, it's some future incarnation of Weisz's character; (the hairs on the tree's bark respond to Tom's touch much as the hairs on the back of Izzi's neck reciprocated the attention and proximity of her husband, Tommy). The cue-balled, monkish-looking Tom occasionally is shown cutting off tiny pieces of bark which he then consumes with all the ritual and solemnity of one who is taking the Host. He also sees visions of Izzi and Isabel that suggests an intimate familiarity with them.

There is a denouement, of sorts, in which the three storylines coalesce and you get a sense of closure about what has been going on, but it's hardly conventional. Much as Kubrick did in the end of *2001: A Space Odyssey*, Aronofsky seems to realize that even when the filmmaker knows what each specific shot is supposed to mean, it plays out much better if you don't tip your hand to the audience too much. Which isn't to say that he is entirely successful in maintaining the integrity of his cryptic house of cards; for many, the finale is as much of a head-scratcher as the rest of the film.

So, then, what are we to make of all this? Is Aronofsky trying to tell us something about the eternal spirit of love through these centuries-apart couples? Or has he concocted an elaborate shell game wherein the ball is really only beneath the contemporary story, and the past and future episodes are merely empty phantoms of the imagination, being, respectively, Izzi's actual, romance-tinged historical novel and Tommy's possibly fanciful retreat from reality, after Izzi's death, into a sci-fi universe where he can be all things (warrior, savior, scientist and lover) to his eternal companion?

The simple answer, I believe, is that it's both and neither; that the movie's very ambiguity lays the groundwork for interpretations that are as individual as the viewers who see it. In a lesser work, this formulaic assumption might seem to be a dodge against the filmmaker's inability to tell a coherent story. But Aronofsky has already proven his mettle, and like Kubrick, Bunuel, Tarkovsky, Lynch and even Tarantino, he has earned the right to build his exotic sandcastles on this protected beach, away from the crashing waves of cynicism that too often erode the public's acceptance of such cinematic experimentation.

The truth of Aronofsky's art, and thus of our ability to appreciate what he has accomplished, can be discerned in the stylistic flourishes he employs—the reflected candles in the Queen's castle which emulate the starry heavens; the Moorish architectural elements from the past which find their way into the present settings; and the previously-mentioned living hairs on the tree that echo those on Izzi's neck. It is through this layering, the echoes upon echoes which binds the storylines together, that we are able to experience the ephemeral nature of memory, of longing, of loss, desire and sacrifice, all in the name of love. And while the cryptic finale does little to fully explain what has come before it (a commentary track on the DVD would've been most welcomed, here), the pleasure of this film does not reside solely in simple analysis (e.g. what are we to make of the reductive nature of the characters' names and hair length?). Unlike astronaut Tom, we should not harness our needs to a specific destination, but instead, must find our satisfaction in the taking of the journey, itself, be it two hours in watching his film or across a thousand years of historical speculation. Thankfully, in the case of *The Fountain*, Mr. Aronofsky allows us to take both paths simultaneously.

The End